This story is a compilation of essays and newspaper articles which I wrote at the end of my active years in politics. Although it does not follow a tight story line, it is my hope that the reader will glean from it the excitement and intrigue of the period under review, especially that of the leadership struggle within the ruling Labour government of 1979 to 1982.

"Heaven knows we need never be ashamed of our tears, for they are rain upon the blinding dust of earth, overlaying our hard hearts."

Charles Dickens: Great Expectations (Vol.1)

For Rachael and Arthur Josie

My parents who did everything they could to ensure their children did not suffer the disadvantages of ignorance and illiteracy that was the common lot of so many in the St. Lucia of the nineteen thirties when they were growing up.

ACKNOWLEDGEMENTS

Since the events leading to, and including what was popularly called 'The Leadership Struggle' within the government of Saint Lucia (1979-1982) I have been encouraged to give an insider's detail for posterity. When it became known that I was attempting such an exercise, friends and former political allies often stopped me to enquire about progress. The exercise of recording these exciting political events in the history of our small country proved more complicated than I had at first anticipated. Initially, I tackled it by publishing weekly excerpts in the local Mirror newspaper. I soon discovered, however, that I often repeated important titbits, thereby making the need for closer more professional editing necessary.

As the work progressed I came across persons who would not read the weekly accounts in the Mirror newspaper and who preferred to await the complete story in a book. Such persons I also discovered were as interested in the details of the leadership struggle, years after the fact, believing there may be new information from an insider's perspective, as well as new lessons that may be learnt.

In this my first effort at recording in a book the events which led to the demise of what many at the time considered the most popular government of Saint Lucia since adult suffrage, I have had help from several sources.

Guy Ellis of the Saint Lucia Mirror newspaper provided early critical advice and editing and was a source of constant encouragement. Guy is an Editor and writer for over forty years. He also wrote the foreword to this book.

The management and staff of the Saint Lucia National Archives were always ready with back issues of newspapers, government releases and whatever other information I may have needed as research material. Melissa Celestin-James was particularly helpful, there.

The Voice Publishing Company and its Editor, Victor Marquis, as well as Rick Wayne of the Star Publishing Company helped in sourcing relevant pictures. Indeed, Rick Wayne went as far as transferring images from his precious pictures archive onto CD's, thereby making copying and placing of his and other photos easier and more manageable.

Lyndell Gustave of the Parliament office in Castries facilitated my research by providing back issues of Hansard, the verbatim recordings of the procedures of parliament and a quiet place to sit, read and write.

Edmund Regis of the National Printing Corporation (the Government of Saint Lucia) allowed me extensive research into back copies of the official Government Gazette.

My friend Digby Ambris, a former Manager of Barclays Bank International was a tower of strength throughout. Digby offered several useful tips and advice. Towards the end he even offered marketing suggestions pointing me to specific names and addresses of book sellers in the Caribbean, with whom he was familiar.

Kenneth (Ken) Springer edited the first hard copy manuscript before it was reprinted a second time – minus certain errors. Rupert Branford, (Branny) a longstanding friend, sports writer (and editor) helped with further editing and refinement. In addition, I also received editing help from Patricia James to whom I was introduced in my search for more diverse editing assistance.

Lennox Honeychurch, along with my friend and colleague Vanoulst Jon. Charles, both of Dominica, were helpful with information on the role of Prime Minister Eugenia Charles in the demise of the Grenada revolution. I was particularly struck by the depth of information both men possessed on Dominica's (and the Caribbean's) 'Iron Lady', the first Prime Minister of her gender in the region. They were both friends of the former Prime Minister.

Philip David and Ferron Lowe, of Grenada, guided me to relevant websites and gave first hand information on the events in Grenada during the period of the Grenada 'Revo'. These two also helped in my personal recollections of the events and political personalities in Grenada, at the time in question. The death in 1983 of Prime Minister Maurice Bishop along with his ministerial colleagues and several other Grenadian citizens, was a sad blow to Grenada and the wider Caribbean.

Several other persons from Grenada also offered eye witness information; many recalling the visit Prime Minister Louisy, his Foreign Minister George Odlum and I paid to Grenada during the short rule of the People's Revolutionary Government (PRG) and specifically the massive rally we attended and addressed at Queens' Park Oval, St. George's.

Garvin Louis, Rondell Springer and Olson Pindar, competent young men in many aspects of word processing helped put the entire project together. Their task was to ensure that pictures, quotations and chapters were put in their proper places and the pages accurately numbered. They followed my instructions to the letter and I thank them all for this. Anicia Eugene, formerly of the Voice Publishing Company as well as Isabelle Sankar (originally from Trinidad) also assisted with valuable tips on publishing, including paper quality, suitable book dimensions as well as type faces and sizes and quality of binding and layout for the finished product.

I have done my best to bear true witness to all the facts as they were and as I have remembered them. Any mistakes or questionable judgement calls are my own. I therefore accept full responsibility for any errors or omissions.

Peter Josie

A pen portrait by George Odlum;

(From the St.Lucia Labour Party (SLP) 1974 elections manifesto)

Anyone who sees the tall, handsome, bearded face of Peter Josie must find him striking to say the least. The earnestness behind his eyes gives him a brooding, haunting look. His opponents are slightly uneasy about this half-menacing look, but those who know him realize that it is the hard gem-like flame of his sincerity and humanity burning its way through that pensive look. Yet, it is amazing how that set face can burst into creased jollity, laughter and almost puckish lightheartedness.

Born in the outskirts of Vieux-Fort and educated at the Vieux-Fort R.C. School and St. Mary's College, Castries, Josie is essentially a country lad. Milking cows and handling manure is his métier. So he waded through cricket, football and cadets at St. Mary's and quite predictably shot off to the East Caribbean Farm Institute in Trinidad, where he obtained a diploma in Tropical Agriculture. Then followed a short spell in Agriculture extension before he proceeded to the University of the West Indies, to study for a degree in Agronomy.

It was no doubt the concourse of ideas among young West Indians at the University which kindled a deep consciousness in the young agriculturist. He saw the historic vision of the same agriculture which was used to enslave a whole people being an effective instrument for liberating them. It is this vision which is the key to Josie's personality. He has a scientific, almost clinical approach to any task he undertakes. On his return to St. Lucia he was a rather dedicated Agricultural Instructor with the Department of Agriculture, soon promoted to Senior Agricultural Assistant and by January of 1971 he was appointed to the post of Agronomist and Officer-in-Charge of the Banana Rehabilitation Scheme.

By this time, Peter Josie had completely won the hearts of farmers throughout the length and breadth of the island for his painstaking devotion to Agriculture and for the casual easy manner in which he rapped to the farmers. The intimate relationship with farmers was almost identical to the rapport he built up among members of the Casuals Club in Marchand of which he was a founding member.

But it was certainly not all light and sweetness with a man of Peter Josie's conviction and dedication. His casual smile can cradle into an ominous frown. He does not suffer fools gladly; and so when the official Government policy on Agriculture became insincere rhetoric and Tourism became the economic pace-setter, Peter Josie resigned his job and took to the more contentious and variable world of politics.

The St. Lucia Labour Party has endorsed Peter Josie's candidature for the East Castries seat which embraces all of Marchand where he has lived for more than twenty years. His wife Carol is from the well-known Labour family – the Mauricette's of Marchand – and his children Beverley, Petra and Lance are all well known in the Marchand area.

Peter Josie's youth, dynamism and deep conviction about the role of Agriculture in the evolution of Third World countries should prove an asset to any government in St. Lucia today.

Foreword

One of the complaints that has often been made about the constantly evolving Saint Lucia is that not enough of its history is being recorded. However, in recent times, various writers have been racing against time — some catching up with time as well — to fill that void and chronicle for posterity some of the most exciting moments in St Lucian history, especially in the post-independence era.

Peter Josie is one of those who has caught up with time in this pursuit. Like a journalist providing actuality in news reporting, Peter is not writing from published reports of others or from hearsay. He is writing as a participant, a major player in the events which unfolded during his comparatively short sojourn in the politics of his homeland.

One cannot have followed Peter's three decades of political activism without recognizing and admiring the relentless and passionate manner in which he performed, through highs and lows, never sacrificing the ideals and principles that helped define his mission. Ironically, there were more "lows" than he would have liked with most of his time spent in constant struggle for the perpetuation of these ideals. But Peter was also for 18 years, a member of the Parliament of St Lucia, held Ministerial positions in three Cabinets and was leader of the St Lucia Labour Party, at the time of possibly its lowest ebb in the island's politics, when no one else wanted the job. His involvement with other political organizations on the island during his journey has helped round up his own education and given him the legitimacy to speak with authority on the issues discussed in his book.

In 1979, the SLP, with Josie in tow, won an important general election, ousting the incumbent United Workers Party, under the indefatigable John Compton from power. It was an election that ought to have ushered in a new dispensation in the island's politics, but in the end brought it only grief with a power struggle among the new "progressives" of the party against the old guard "conservatives" that ended in disaster half way through the SLP's five year term. Even in this dark hour, Peter's talents and ability came to the fore and few can forget his glowingly successful hosting in 1980 of the first ever general assembly of the Organization of American States (OAS) to be held in Saint Lucia. Taking place at the time it did, in the year after the Grenada Revolution and with the Caribbean region firmly embroiled in super power "Cold War", it was indeed a remarkable achievement.

The rise of the political "left" in the Caribbean is given considerable attention in this book and with good reason. To this day, Peter is convinced that the vast majority of the people of the Caribbean were uninformed about the extent to which the major powers, in Washington, London and elsewhere went, to stem the march of the emerging left in the Caribbean in the wake of the Grenada Revolution, and keep the status quo in control in these islands.

Many are of the view that Peter Josie stayed too long in the shadow of his political twin and close friend, George Odlum. Yet, the records will show that when circumstances demanded standing up for his own principles, Peter was never found wanting, a sign, if one was ever needed, that he was always his own man, pursuing his own agenda and with the conviction and determination that became hallmarks of his own political life. Through it all, his ultimate aim was always about empowering his fellowman.

Peter Josie's contribution to the documenting of the historical political highlights of Saint Lucia, must prove of immense value to present and future generations seeking to acquire a deeper understanding of the various issues that made their country tick. Coming from one who was involved, a major player in his own right is the icing on the cake.

GUY ELLIS
Journalist, St. Lucia

Preface:

*History makes one aware that there is no finality
in human affairs; there is not a static perfection and
an unimprovable wisdom to be achieved.........*

Bertrand Russell:
Portraits from Memory.

I first entertained the idea of writing this book after the passing of George Odlum in September 2003. He was one of the leading figures in the political life of Saint Lucia between 1974 and 2003. The idea had its genesis in a series of articles which were published in the weekly Mirror newspaper on the island, after his passing. I was encouraged by some persons to tell more and to compile the whole story of the events of that period into a book. I concurred and by so doing extended my researches in order to verify certain facts and to make this account as accurate and as truthful as possible. I continued my contributions in weekly articles to the Mirror in pursuit of this book's agenda. I have tried to impart the results of my experience (with George Odlum and his politics) candidly. If the narrative seems flat and uninspiring at times, it may be on account of the sameness of the unpalatable news the island endured each day, during the leadership struggle in the St. Lucia Labour Party Government between 1979 and 1982. Then, it appeared George Odlum was at the very summit of his political career. I have dealt at some length with the leadership struggle, and I think it may prove the most talked and written about event on the island. I have tried to do this without bitterness or animosity. There were times however, when I felt cheated of the full contribution I had set myself to accomplish for the people of my island. I therefore hope that any perceived disappointment on my part has not unduly soured the neutral tone I aimed to pursue in this narrative. I also pray that the passage of time has created a sufficient distance and perspective to allow those who were negatively impacted by the role which I (and others) played in it to forgive, when they could with justice, resent.

For Saint Lucia - as indeed for the wider Caribbean - the seventies can be said to have had its genesis in the events which swept the entire region in the preceding decade. The Black Power phenomenon of the sixties was rekindled in the United States by another son of the Caribbean - Stokely Carmichael - whose parents had earlier migrated to that country from their native Trinidad, when the lad was only two. He was to later re-create Garvey's struggles of the thirties and forties for the sixties and seventies of our times.

The new consciousness accompanied by a search for cultural roots swept into the Caribbean at the same time the region was seeking political independence from Europe. It was therefore a period of popular debate and high academic exchanges; even of great upheavals. The attempted military coup in Trinidad in 1970 may well have had its origins in the 'Black Power' debates of the sixties, which fuelled discontent within the army and the disgruntled poor.

The decade of the sixties in turn was born out of the global reach of the Second World War and the desire of the then colonized world to chart a new path to peace, prosperity and political independence, away from the examples of bloody conquests and wars set by Europe.

Having received a decent foundation in education at the Vieux-Fort Roman Catholic Boys School, the natural progression, in those days, if one were to continue one's studies, was to St. Mary's College (S. M .C .) in Castries, the only secondary school for boys on the island at the time. My early years at both primary and secondary school were uneventful. My dad worked all of his active life in the service of the State as a fire fighter, and my mother kept the house and made sure that all was in order during the long hours my dad worked. My father encouraged me to read and to do so as often as I could. 'Read everything' he said 'and hold on to what is true'.

The successful overthrow of the dictator Fulgencio Batista by Fidel Castro in Cuba during my later years at St. Mary's College may have marked my first conscious search for information beyond that which would allow me to pass the requisite school exams. I recall a lively discussion at the College between my colleagues and friends after Fidel Castro had overthrown president Batista.

From that moment I made a point to continue listening to the BBC World News, as it was from that source I had first learnt of the success of Castro's Cuba revolution. Soon thereafter the events which were to lead to political independence in Nigeria, Kenya and Tanzania (all African countries) were analyzed and explained on the BBC world news. By that time, I also searched out the 'Commonwealth' magazine which covered stories of African states seeking independence as well as other stories from the rest of the 'British' Commonwealth.

By the time the West Indies' Federation was shattered in 1962 and Jamaica - and later Trinidad and Tobago proceeded separately to political independence, I was fully immersed in the politics of the region. Indeed I count myself fortunate to have witnessed the final lowering of the Union

Jack (of Britain) and the hoisting of the Red, Black and White banner of Trinidad and Tobago, on 31st August 1962. I was also fully aware of the other events which were to lead other former British colonies in the Caribbean into independence. In the case of Trinidad and Tobago, I made a point of reading as much as I could about the country and its first Prime Minister - Dr. Eric Williams. It did not escape my attention that we were both born around the same date in September; he was of course of a much earlier vintage.

At the time of my growing interest in Caribbean politics, I had not yet formulated any plans for my own future involvement in the art and science of politics and government. I was at the time quietly observing and filing at the back of my mind the political debates which had impacted (and excited) the people of the Caribbean – Saint Lucia included. From the Cuban revolution to the search for independence in the Lesser Antilles and on the continent of Africa, every political event was important to conscious people of colour. Later, I set out to immerse myself in the public life of my own little island in the Caribbean basin - Saint Lucia. This book is also the story of how I got into politics and the main characters who occupied center stage at the time. As the story unfolds, the names of the persons who helped shape the politics of the day are revealed. Indeed, this effort is as much about the central players such as Allan Louisy, John Compton, George Odlum and Winston Cenac, as it is also about the more peripheral ones such as Michael Pilgrim, Jon Odlum, Frances Michel, Kenneth Foster, Evans Calderon, Remy Lesmond and others. Each of the four main characters may well be deserving of a chapter in a book on Caribbean history, on their own record. Some persons may even argue that Compton belongs to that select group of Caribbean leaders deserving of further analysis and a more comprehensive work (book) devoted to his life's struggles and to his social and economic achievements, for his adopted homeland of Saint Lucia.

I have not attempted to describe the physical characteristics of any of the individuals whom I have written about here as I did not think appearance and physical qualities were important to the various roles they played in politics. Besides, given the circumstances which existed on the island at the time and taking into account the ideological 'cold' war between the United States of America and the Soviet Union (Russia) no one can say for certain that the leadership struggle described in this book would have been any different, had another group of politicians been in office.

To compound Saint Lucia's problems at the time, Maurice Bishop, a long-standing friend of the progressive left in the Caribbean, had seized power from Eric Matthew Gairy, Prime Minister of Grenada. By so doing

Bishop and his comrades had raised all manner of red distress flags in the region, as well as in London, Washington and Paris. He also put the rest of the conservative world on full alert to the political awakening of the East Caribbean.

The book makes no claim to any sort of intellectualism. It does not pretend to offer a standard of high sophisticated narrative as that of the learned literary artiste. It may, with charity however, be said to concern itself with the way external geopolitics impacted the Caribbean before the 1960's and since. These forces are believed to have led to the demise of Maurice Bishop, George Odlum and other left-leaning, progressive politicians in the region - and possibly elsewhere. It is my hope that, as one reads this book, one will also get the sense of the forces which were arrayed behind the scenes to ensure that the status quo was preserved, and that in order to do so Prime Minister Compton was to be returned to office in Saint Lucia followed by a litany of other conservative voices (of political leaders) in the Caribbean.

Also of note is the fact that, at the resignation of Allan Louisy as Prime Minister of Saint Lucia I had at first been the clear favourite among the elected Labour Party parliamentarians - minus the Odlum brothers and Pilgrim - to replace him as Prime Minister. All that I needed for a clear majority among all the elected Members of Parliament was the vote of Remy Lesmond, which he had earlier promised me. But later, during an internal meeting of the elected Labour parliamentarians (and Cabinet) at the Prime Minister's official residence at Vigie, Remy Lesmond left the meeting room to make a telephone call, in an office two doors away. On his return to the meeting room, the entire process of selecting someone to replace Louisy as Prime Minister was restarted, upon his request, and after a long discussion Winston Cenac emerged as Prime Minister, to replace Allan Louisy, and with Remy Lesmond's vote going to Cenac. No one knows for certain to whom Lesmond had spoken when he made that telephone call, although subsequent events seem to suggest it may have been to either George Odlum or to a well known businessman from the south of the island, both of whom perhaps had personal reasons why I should not then be selected Prime Minister of Saint Lucia.

I claim two special privileges for writing as I have done here, except that I was present and often at the centre of the events which are described in this book. I repeat that I was an active participant as well as a close observer in most, if not all of the events which I have described in this book. Second, everything that has been written is the truth and the facts are verifiable. The occasions during which I was the only eye witness are rare. I also wrote this because I am aware that others may attempt to recreate history and events surrounding the leadership struggle, in order to please themselves and those whom they serve. In addition, there is sufficient evidence all around to prove that people will distort facts for no other reason than to satisfy their own egos. Hopefully, in sifting through this book, one will be able to discern, even in its occasionally disjointed state, what are the facts and what are opinions. For the most part, I have also written for my own enjoyment. I have persevered in the hope that it will become a lasting memento to all who will read and learn from it, and for those who were participants. It is also my wish that past mistakes of political judgement will not be repeated here or elsewhere in the Caribbean. There is no need to reinvent the wheel. This has been a labour of love lasting close to five years and I have enjoyed most, if not all of it.

There are many details which have been deliberately omitted because to have added them, would have made this work too long.

After reading this account of politics in a small island State, there will be many questions which will come to mind. For example, could Maurice Bishop have become Prime Minister of Grenada through the ballot box in elections called by Prime Minister Gairy? Had Maurice Bishop become Prime Minister through the ballot, would he have built an international airport, where the dashing and flamboyant Gairy before him had failed? Would Cuba have come to Bishop's assistance in Grenada's airport construction project, had Bishop achieved political power through fair and democratic elections, instead of the way he did? Would America have decided to invade Grenada, had Maurice Bishop not been brutally murdered by his former friends and political allies? Perhaps more to the point: would the leadership struggle in Saint Lucia have assumed the significance it did, had Maurice Bishop and his New Jewel Movement not seized power in Grenada, as and when they did? Finally, would George Odlum or Peter Josie have achieved such name recognition individually, or would their political partnership create waves which each could not have done on his own?

I chose the title 'SHATTERED DREAMS' from a list sent to me by persons whose views I canvassed. To my mind, that title captures more aptly the sad - and shattered - ending to the fairly solid political bond which had been built up between George Odlum and me over many years, and the potential for meaningful change in our island's affairs which that bond had at first represented. The Odlum /Josie nexus (or political relationship, if you prefer) had caught the fancy of the Saint Lucia electorate more than any other, before or since. 'Shattered Dreams' captures the utter dismay which the political struggles of the day had left the people of the island in their wake. Many were to go to their graves bearing the heart wrenching and bitter disappointment of these struggles, following the election of 1979.

One will observe that the story oscillates back and forth rather than pursuing in a one continuous linear direction, as perhaps a day to day historical account might have done. That, dear reader, is to be expected as so much of what happened from one moment to the next was so bound-up with events which had preceded it. For example, the rehabilitation of agriculture after the passage of hurricane Allen in 1980 had to be described in terms of the broad agriculture policy which had been adopted in 1979, while at the same time taking account of the plans that were in progress in order to achieve the same. Again, if the leadership struggle were to make sense, or be properly understood, one had perforce to revisit the meeting of certain Caribbean political activists in Saint Lucia, (Rat Island) in the early seventies, and even the emergence of Maurice Bishop as Prime Minister of Grenada. Such retracing of ground previously trodden as one went ahead, will hopefully give the reader a fuller appreciation of the true dimension of the Louisy/Odlum confusing 'dance of death' between 1979 and 1981.

I claim no special blessings or privileges to have been the one whose duty it has been to write the record of that most turbulent and exciting period in the political annals of Saint Lucia. However, I thank God and all the heartfelt prayers my mother and father offered in my name long before I knew myself. I feel a deep sense of gratitude for their efforts in making certain they worked hard to see that I attended school. This is the reason I have dedicated this book to their memories so many years after their passing. I feel very indebted to them. In addition, I readily admit to any biases in emphasis which may intrude in this narrative, and I wish to repeat here that everything I have written in this book is as factual and truthful as I remembered it. Happy journey.

Contents

My Early Years:
School, Soldiers, Empire Day

Train up a child in the way he should go;
and when he is old, he will not depart from it.
                                        - Old Testament, Proverbs, 22 : 6.

Other than that reported incident of the shooting of the young man and his dog at the entrance of the U.S army base at Vieux-Fort, there are few others which stood out for me except the long and sometimes boring school days that were relieved by organized cricket and football matches against other schools, in the south of the island. Each child was allowed to try his hand at these games and the teacher determined who was good enough to make the school team. Girls did not, at that time, participate in cricket or football. The reason one suspects may have been tied to the particular view of certain male-dominated religion and cultural mores, which held sway in my youth.

Before I was registered at the Vieux-Fort R.C (Roman Catholic) Boys School I began to wish, and perhaps even to pray, that I would be spared the thick cowhide that the School Master at the time, one Mr. Henry, alias "Kokeen" was reputed to gleefully apply with a heavy and precise hand on the backs of boys who were either late for the school bell or who were slow in grasping his learnt English Grammar. To hear some older students tell it, that school's 'dictator' would not spare to use his heavy leather belt on any cause, worthy of his attention. He had an especial punishment for lateness and truancy. Those mischievous types who were unlucky to be sent to him by a class teacher or whom he may have himself caught staring out blankly through an open window (thereby assuming that that particular victim was inattentive) received the full fury of Kokeen's misguided leather disciplining. Such was the fear created in the hearts of the poor young charges attending his school or who were earmarked to attend it the following year; one wondered in later years how it was possible to learn anything in such an environment. Young wide-eyed innocents who were bound for that particular school and to Kokeen's brand of no-nonsense forced-feeding from his cured cowhide, somehow survived with their dignity in tact. Young boys who were preparing to follow in the footsteps of older brothers or cousins were known to spend a large part of the summer holidays devising various schemes by which to avoid both school and headmaster, when that time came.

In those days parents did not complain about the excessive use of force in schools because it was believed that such enforced discipline was not only about ensuring a child a proper education, but also providing him with guidance and discipline for life. It was as though every parent back then had read and agreed with the Book of Proverbs admonition 22 : 6 - in the Old Testament - which advised Christians to train up a child in the way he should go; so that when he gets old it would be quite impossible for that child to depart from such training. Kokeen was the full embodiment of such biblical edict.

To the relief of everyone who had experienced his wrath, that particular disciplinarian soon came to the end of his productive teaching life and the authorities (some older students swore it was God) replaced him as Headmaster with an Angel from Choiseul named Gilbert Stanislaus. I think I am correct in saying that our group, entering the Vieux-Fort Boys Primary School that year (1950) was among the first set of students to have experienced the era of 'modern' approaches to education wherein brute force and harsh punishment were dispensed with as a tool to learning and strict discipline. Stanislaus was therefore different in every way from the man he had replaced. On reflection, the British Authorities at the time must have decided to give the natives a break from enforced corporal punishment at such a place of learning as a school should be.

Stanislaus and his teachers were a joy to be with each school day.

I enjoyed every minute of that particular school era and the only incident which stood out for me at the time was hurting myself badly one afternoon after school, attempting to catch a cricket ball across a large and deep drain near the schoolmaster's house. I was then rushed to the Vieux-Fort hospital, where the nurses suggested stitching the wound. On hearing this I fled to the safety of my home and would not return to the hospital even after they had retrieved me from beneath my mother's bed. They first had to promise in the presence of my mother that they would neither stitch nor sew that wound and that only medication and the appropriate bandage would be applied. And so it was.

I had an easy time at school. I liked all those who worked and taught there. My fondest memories are of teachers, Girard Thomas and Thomas Johannes. I feel confident in saying that I was inspired by both those teachers and although I may not have become all that they felt that I could have been, I have had the honour and pleasure to thank these gentlemen for their care and kindness, after I left that school. Teacher Thomas has passed on. Before he did I had the pleasure of being his house guest in the town of Vieux-Fort after he had completed several years of work and study in England.

At that time I was made to skip 'standards' two and four as the classes were then called. Upon entering the school at the same time as Stanislaus, I attended only standards one, three and five. Afterwards it was the Common Entrance test for a place in the only secondary school for boys, St. Mary's College, in Castries, which my dad insisted that I had to attend. It was teacher Johannes who finally sealed the concepts of proportions and percentages in my youthful imagination. He held an orange to the front of the class one morning and proceeded to cut it open; first in two equal portions, then each half into quarters and so on, whilst taking pains to bring the whole thing cautiously together again so as to confirm to all present that, all proportions (and fractions) have their origins in a whole which constitutes one hundred percent of the thing.

If teacher Johannes could be said to have instilled an appreciation for math in his young charges, it was Stanislaus, our Headmaster, who taught us to analyze and parse English sentences both simple and compound. 'Stan', as the more senior students had affectionately renamed him, may even have introduced us to the concept of logical thinking with the 'then' in math representing the distributive middle in logical thinking. The 'if', 'then', 'therefore', mathematical form helped us understand its application to math as well as to logical reasoning. From this basic concept the sky should have been the limit. The reason it was not so is another story entirely. I soon came to appreciate that the key ingredient at every stage of development is self confidence. And I believe nothing nourishes that virtue more than love and discipline at home and at school; with the resulting mastery of the simple chores which one is given. We therefore learnt early the meaning of duty at home; obedience at school; social responsibility to community (by not littering and disposing of empty containers in which mosquitoes could breed) and even obligations to 'Queen and Country'.

Apart from the perfunctory school lessons and games which I soon learnt to cope with, I was always happiest when touring another town or village to engage another school at the game of cricket. The annual celebrations of Empire Day were also a source of great joy to me in those early school days. I have said elsewhere that many truant boys (and girls) at the time, made it a point of attending school around the celebrations of Empire Day. Of course everyone knew these children had shown up merely for the treats which each school offered the attendees on that important holiday. Every child sang 'God Save the Queen' at the time. Many of my generation were too young to have had to sing 'God save the King' in honour of King George the Sixth who passed away before we were old enough to ask God to save him.

I have also stated that the American soldiers stationed at the base at Vieux-Fort treated the school children of the town to a fair helping of delicious ice cream, each Empire Day. We learnt later that other schools around the island were not as fortunate as we were since their Empire Day treat was paid for by the British government who were very tight fisted and masters at cutting every budget presented to them.

Yet another memory that stands out are the constant warnings that young children between ages five and seven, often received from parents and teachers alike, which was not to touch or pick up those six or seven inch slender plastic 'balloons' (prophylactics) which were strewn all over the alleys and byways of Vieux-Fort back then. But some children either did not hear or did not listen. It was therefore not unusual to see one of those things in a little boy's mouth blown full stretch like a toy balloon at Christmas. We soon learnt that such litter was the result of the prostitution which flourished nicely at the time in the town, evidence of the many young men (soldiers) who were stationed there. I was assured by those who should know that many ladies of the night came from far and wide to seek the 'Yankee Dollar' at Vieux-Fort. The mistaken 'balloons' of these innocent town urchins were the results of frantic nightly activities by female visitors and residents alike. The used 'rubbers' were proof that off duty American soldiers had facilitated the nightly search for work and had most likely paid the going rate for such services. To the club owners and in rum shops where juke box music blared all night, the ladies who transacted business in the world's oldest profession were a welcome boost to business, especially when accompanied by an army uniform. On weekends, juke boxes which seemed to be located at every street corner of the town were paid to spin the latest songs from the USA. Often the locals would join the soldiers on the floor in shaking to the beat of jazz, mambo, or to cha-cha-cha as they danced the night away. Vieux-Fort was the "swingiest" town this side of paradise as the apparently free flowing US dollar made the place a hive of activities by day as well as by night.

This and much more was part of my early history. Feeding pigs, rearing cattle and caring for sheep, goats and chicken were also part of that upbringing. I never complained about chores unless they began to impinge on my play time with my friends. But my mother, who was not a sports minded person, seemed then to understand a boy's need for sports and games and she always organized the chores in a way that allowed me free time when my friends whistled that it was time for the open field. Of course I was not aware that I was privileged and that to be in a position to have so many animals to feed and water was never seen by me as a blessing. Although it never seemed as a curse either, I never associated these poor creatures with personal wealth until I was about age ten, by which time I had owned three sheep, two goats, three pigs, a cow, about six layers and two roosters. I actually enjoyed feeding and caring for my animals. I never thought they would one day be part of my history and what I loved the best while growing up as a child in Vieux-Fort. These animals were a part of my early recollections and they probably shaped the person that I am, more than I will ever know.

None of this seemed to have unduly interrupted the early education of the youth of Vieux-Fort, as back then even the poorest parents seemed able to provide their children with the basic requirements for school. By the time I got ready for the common entrance and St. Mary's College there were already loud whispers about the possible closure of the American base at Vieux-Fort. At the time I did not quite get what all the fuss was about. And so after solid doses of Stanislaus, teacher Girard and teacher Johannes, it was on to St. Mary's College where very few boys from my town ever ventured in those dark, backward colonial days. As I have said, I had no choice in the matter and I could not condescend to fail and not move on because I had by then accepted my duties and responsibilities (obligations even) to keep my school colours flying high; not to mention fulfilling the long held dreams of my father. It was therefore with this solid foundation that I finally said goodbye to my friends at Vieux-Fort and relocated to Castries as it was deemed too burdensome to make a three hour return trip to and from Castries each school day.

Vieux-Fort ..... Early Recollections

For that is what history is about. It's about human society,
its story and how it has come to be what it is.......
A. L. Rouse: The use of History

I cannot tell for certain when and what may first have fired my imagination for an active role in politics. There may have been more than one reason I was attracted to a life of politics. But try as I may and no matter how many times I have searched my mind, it keeps throwing up and repeating one incident which happened at Vieux-Fort when I was just past the toddler stage of my innocent youth. That incident was the shooting death of a young man from Vieux-Fort by an American soldier who was on duty guarding the main entrance to the United States Air base, at Beane Field. The Americans had gotten there by means of a Land/ Lease agreement between the United States and England as part of both countries' war efforts. In that agreement Prime Minister Winston Churchill of England agreed to make available suitable land from certain selected colonies in the Caribbean which were to be used for the building of U.S. Air Base. In return, the United States was to provide the British Government with an agreed number of warships (fifty in total) and other paraphernalia for the use of British troops in the defense of the 'motherland' and her territories against the might of Hitler's all conquering German war machine.

The Americans therefore built one Air Base at Vieux-Fort, in the south of St. Lucia which they named Beane Field after one of their noted Army Generals. They also built a submarine base at Rodney Bay in the north of the island and they did not distinguish it by any particular name. These two were among several such bases built in the Caribbean by the Americans at that time. The others were at Chaguaramas Bay and Wallerfield in Trinidad, and on Antigua in the Leeward Islands. Each of the mentioned countries has put these deactivated bases to some economic use. Sixty years on they continue to serve a positive purpose for peace and economic development of the islands. They therefore form a part of the continuing human story of the Caribbean region.

But it is to Vieux-Fort and the Airbase we must return, perchance to discover that seed which was so deeply planted in the heart and mind of an innocent little boy who was then too small to fully appreciate all the deeper implications of the war or how and why there were soldiers based in his little home town. For me that is what history is about; it is about human society - ours at Vieux-Fort and St. Lucia - and how we came to be what we are today.

I remember the incident as if it had happened only yesterday. Perhaps the reason for this is years after, almost everyone in the town who was old enough kept talking about it. In this regard my parents and grandparents were no different. So this recurring telling of this particular incident left a deep impression on my mind and may very well have contributed to the attitudes I later assumed on global political matters.

The incident involved a young man and his dog. That young man was employed at the American Base at the time. It is reported that he was making his way to work when it was discovered that his dog had followed him to the official entrance to the base which was always guarded by armed military personnel. On presenting his pass to the soldiers at the gate the young man was asked to keep the dog from entering the base. The report gets fuzzy from here. Reports could only have been garnered from the few locals who were also making their way to work at that base that day. There is therefore no concrete record from any of them on how and why the young man was shot by a US soldier as he entered the base. It appeared that the dog got loose and ran into the base crossing the 'No Entry' sign at the entrance. On seeing this, the young man ran after it trying to retrieve his dog. That young man was then shot dead at point blank range; so was his dog! Talk about being shot and dying like a dog. That day Vieux-Fort experienced the full brunt of public protest from citizens who may have had enough of the rough treatment at the hands of the Americans stationed there.

That death touched the entire town. It even seemed to have affected the surrounding neighbourhood. I recall my mother having two very difficult tasks on her hands at the time and perhaps for sometime thereafter. The first was making certain that I was always within her sight and her reach as she made the short trip from her house at New Dock Road (formerly Anstraphal Lane) to the Vieux-Fort Hospital to where the body of the victim had by then been moved, before its quick transfer to the American Army Hospital at Augier. The second and perhaps the more difficult of her two jobs, was keeping my father calm and less agitated. It appeared that the whole of Vieux-Fort was at boiling point. The more vibrant male citizens, including my dad, were determined to group themselves together for some action against the Americans who were protecting their own. It also seemed certain that the young man who had been shot was a regular fellow and it was even rumoured that the soldier who shot him wanted the victim's girlfriend for himself.

I cannot attest to any of those stories but a play written by Saint Lucian Stanley French – called 'Ballad of a Man and His Dog' which I saw many years later at the Castries Town Hall did not appear from my recollection to have delved into any possible relationship between the shooter and the victim. French was at the time of the incident a young man in the town with Vieux-Fort connections. He wrote the play years later while studying Engineering in England and the details of that shooting incident may also have been lost to him. It is my understanding that shortly after the shooting; doctors at the U.S. Army Hospital at Augier in the north west of the town had resuscitated the victim sufficiently to hear from him what had led to the shooting. Information reaching Vieux-Fort was that the soldier who did the shooting was whisked out of the island and flown back to the safety of the United States, and no one ever heard from him or from the authorities ever again. It is doubtful whether any compensation was ever paid to anyone in Vieux-Fort as a result of that young man's death. For my part it was the first time that I had seen such hostility in so many eyes including that of my own father. It was even rumoured that the deceased was related to my dad. But I don't think that was true because after much time had passed and things had cooled down, there was no reference to the incident as far as I remember.

That incident was also the first of its kind to have brought so many people out on the streets of Vieux-Fort. Emotions were running very high that day and many were weeping openly whilst others were loud in protest. Everyone, it seemed had something to say about the shooting death. Even my mother shared her feelings with her sisters and her friends; they were not nice feelings. Perhaps it is the reason that that has stayed on my mind for so long. It might also be the reason I feel the way I do whenever I hear of the treatment of the natives wherever foreign bases are built, especially as I know now that these only exist for the furtherance of the occupier's interests. In fact, given all the evidence which I have gleaned between then and now, there is no other conclusion to which a rational person can arrive. Military bases exist only at the pleasure of the strong, for the benefit of the strong and all power comes from the barrel of a gun. No matter what anyone says to the contrary, that is the only correct conclusion which can be arrived at from the shooting death at Vieux-Fort in 1945 or 1946.

In those days Vieux-Fort was a sleepy little town of less than four thousand mostly poor souls, and the construction of the American Air base there had brought much needed jobs for many including our neighbours from other Caribbean islands, notably, Barbados. To this day one can identify the children and grandchildren who settled in St. Lucia as a result of the base construction in Vieux-Fort. They all have their own stories about their arrival in St. Lucia and their jobs in Vieux-Fort with the Americans. But for this one little boy who was thrown innocently into a violent cauldron of protest that day at Vieux-Fort, the seeds of politics may have been sown in his soul. Unfortunately, it was not in the interest of the colonial power who had brokered the land for warships deal with the United States to train colonials for anything other than to further the process of colonialism and exploitation. Luckily, political activism does not require the benediction of any particular group or race. It is a calling that will burn most vigorously in the breast of people who yearn for freedom and for a fair share of the natural resources of their country in particular and of Mother Earth, in general.

After the excitement of those early years I was relocated to Castries where I was supposed to make my father proud by carrying the dreams of an entire generation and more, on my slender shoulders. I did not feel pressured in any way to attend St. Mary's College, and my father may even have said to me it did not matter to him personally if I did not pass the requisite entrance exams. Yet I was to discover days later that he had also caused my name to be entered for the island-wide police scholarship entrance examination. He later informed me that I had not done badly but that the only available award that year had gone to one Robert Philip of La Clery. From the effort at these police tests he was certain I would be among the fifty or so boys who would attend the College that year. So my life was being monitored and programmed for me, and all I did was what I was told. At that time, I was left with no option but to please the only bread winner in the family - my dad.

I was not certain whose burdens I was carrying at the time, but it certainly did not seem as my own. Only later did I discover that part of my dad's burden was what was imposed on him by colonialism, racism and a deliberate backwardness and a deliberate witholding of education.

Proceeding Onwards

Across the fields of yesterday He sometimes comes to me,
a little lad just back from play - the lad
I used to be - T. S. Jones, Jr., Sometimes.

In January 1954, I entered St. Mary's College without much fanfare. I travelled that morning from Vieux-Fort on one of those locally built wooden framed buses along with the four or five other boys – the total contingent from Vieux-Fort that year. Next to me was seated Michael Hippolyte, whose family hailed from Vieux-Fort and who was returning to Castries – and College – after having spent the Christmas, and end of school year holidays in the south. He introduced himself and soon afterwards informed me that he was the captain of Abercrombie House at the College and that he would like to select me as a member of that house later that day when school had formally convened. Of course the way he explained it, I was left with little choice in the matter of my school house, as was the case with so many other youngsters entering the college for the first time.

I duly made it into Abercrombie House and five years later, without asking for the honour, I was voted as House Captain. I also recalled the challenges which Latin and French posed because I had still not acquired the habit of learning to retain what were essentially two new languages at once. By the time I came to appreciate the usefulness of Latin to a fuller comprehension of the root and foundation of many English words in common usage, I had too much catching up to do, and to service my other several subjects, at the same time. But I fought on bravely and soon it was 1955 and I found myself in form two.

So I endured a second year at St. Mary's; challenged now, in addition to Latin and French, by Mr. George Odlum - yes the same Odlum of whom so much is written in this book - and his English Literature classes. In addition there was the farmer and craftsman Brother Albert who continued to torment with his rapid mental mathematics and of course his enticement to work off any detention, on 'his' land preparation projects on the hill side which surrounded the school and which he seemed determined to convert to arable pasture for his cows. Frankly, most kids preferred the Albert option of afternoon manual labour to the alternative of having to turn up on Saturday mornings at the College and to sit quietly in a class room with other boys doing home work. Detention seemed then a sort of scheme to trap the more robust and vigorous breed of boys and to render them effeminate - or perhaps, less masculine may be a better, and more charitable way to put it.

I had often fallen into that detention trap and had always exercised the afternoon work option on the farm. Such an option left my Saturdays free for matinee at Clarke's cinema and also for house chores. Saturday morning was the only time Clarke's cinema replayed cowboy (also called western) movies which many College boys yearned to see but could not find the time to do so during the week. So yes, although no one particularly enjoyed Brother Albert's methods of manual labour, some boys found it preferable to the Saturday morning vigil at the school. Besides, once a boy worked out his detention in an afternoon of manual labour, no parent or guardian ever found out what 'mischief' his or her boy was up to during school hours. Back then, I saw detention as a nuisance and a waste of time because I believed that all we were engaged in doing was being 'boys' and behaving with the youthful exuberance that our growing font of hormones dictated that we should.

To be otherwise was tantamount to secreting a higher level of oestrogen and displaying early girlish tendencies which was a definite 'no-no' in those macho colonial days of the fifties. Even with such a new awareness of self, my early childhood in Vieux-Fort kept coming back to me across the open fields of La Tourney, Derriere Morne and Coco Dan; perhaps in the same way as T. S. Jones' - 'Sometimes'. 'Time and tide waits for no man' was one of many such sayings students were supposed to inculcate back then and to endeavour to apply these morals to their lives. Before I knew it a second year at the College and the closed-up environment of Castries had come and gone and it was time to move on up.

Then, it was on to form three and Mr. Edsel (Cy) Edmunds who taught Biology, one of my favourite subjects. That, along with the other science subjects as well as History and Geography were to remain the loves of my life even as I performed better than average in Mathematics, and the two still compulsory subjects English Literature and English Language.

Dr. Edmunds or 'Cy' as he was later known, actually took pains to 'teach' the subject he was assigned. Biology came alive during his forty or so minutes assignment of each class. To be certain, there were students who must have missed the whole point of his classes, but as a rule one felt a certain level of comfort not only in the subject he taught, but in his very demeanour and general pleasant attitude towards the boys with whom he interacted. We certainly did not sleep during his classes. He kept the attention span alive and exciting by use of frequent tests which one was always pleased to face. Early in the academic year (which in those days started in January) one of his 'biology' questions was 'who was the author of your Biology book'? And even that, some students did not get. I wonder if these now grown "hard back" men finally got the point of author recognition in the printed world.

Edmunds had earlier distinguished himself as an opening batsman for St. Mary's College in the bi-annual inter- secondary school tournament that was played among the Windward Islands of Dominica, St. Lucia, St. Vincent and Grenada. The 1954 tournament was played in St. Lucia and Edsel Edmunds and Stanley French were to distinguish themselves representing the College in cricket. Desmond 'Sage' Sealy was another. Also in that Inter-Secondary Schools Tournament, Ken Morgan won the Victor ludorum. He finished first in the 440 yards, 880 yards, mile and pole vault. Augustus "Pan" Andrew also excelled in cricket, capturing six wickets for 58 runs in a match. He also played football for his school then later represented Saint Lucia at both cricket and football.

The year soon ended and as usual we were to lose another bunch of local 'masters' (teachers) who had by then accumulated sufficient funds to study at Universities overseas. One or two had either become the recipients of the bi-annual island scholarship or of their parents' borrowings to allow them to pursue advanced education. By then I was sufficiently in the know to discover that Edmunds had proceeded to Puerto Rico to study agricultural sciences. This subject even then, had appealed to me as a career path that I too might wish to follow. The difference was – and a very significant difference it turned out to be - that when my turn came to leave St. Lucia for overseas studies I chose Trinidad because of the renowned Imperial College of Tropical Agriculture (ICTA) which the British Government had established there. Besides I did not at the time fancy the challenge which I imagined the Spanish language spoken in Puerto Rico, would have posed. On reflection, the Puerto Rico experience would have opened up for me the possibility of a new language – Spanish – and perhaps the United States tertiary education system – still, I had no regrets choosing Trinidad. Edmunds had proceeded to Cornell University after Mayaguez in Puerto Rico. Later his Spanish was to serve him well as St. Lucia's Ambassador to the OAS in Washington. Would I have become a different person if I had chosen the Puerto Rican option? Different certainly, but would I have served my country better, as a result? That is not easy to tell. Had I chosen Puerto Rico I would not have come under the influence of the great Doctor Eric Williams (PhD, Economics, Philosophy, History, and Oxford Univ. Eng.), Prime Minister of Trinidad and Tobago and father of that country's political independence. Apart from that little incident at the American base at Vieux-Fort, it may well have been Doctor Eric Williams, who had helped to stoke that early political fire, in me. So blame him and other Caribbean leaders of his generation, if I have followed them into daring to try and control the commanding heights of our national economy and patrimony.

Edmunds had hardly finished making an impression on my then very fertile mind, when up came Brother Ignatius Flahive with his stern demeanour and his even sterner marking pen. In his notoriously famous English Language classes, Brother Ignatius – 'Iggy' - was a class act. A perfect introvert if ever I saw one; one who was chosen to act as headmaster of the College upon the departure of Brother Canice Collins, who had served in that capacity for a number of years before his departure from Saint Lucia, and an early death. Upon entering the College it was my recollection that every quiz and every term test question was marked with ten points being the maximum each question could carry. Brother Ignatius was the only person who marked his English language questions, whether home work or other wise, out of six. Yes, six points were the maximum for each question in Brother Ignatius' English Language world. What was to me even more telling was that it was possible for a student to get a mark as low as minus four for an English essay which 'Iggy' (as he was affectionately known by all and sundry) thought a boy had completely botched. In fact, I can recall students who are now successful businessmen in St. Lucia and who I feel certain would hate to be reminded of the times when they received from Brother Ignatius a zero or worse, a minus mark for their precious little worthless essays.

What such a poor performance meant at the time, was that such a student may have been challenged to excel in his next English assignment as he would then be starting a new week of classes 'owing' Brother Ignatius marks. Such a student therefore had to do more than just pass. He had to excel, and to be absolutely brilliant in the next assignment, in order to save face. Brother Ignatius was therefore always an enigma and a huge challenge. He was the first and only person I know who, in Form Three, asked his students to read out of an English essay or composition text book and to correct the language of that text. Correct the language! Up to that time one never associated the printed word, especially in books as needing correction. I learnt not only that text books could be corrected but one did not have to agree with the contents or ideas expressed therein. In all my years at school including University, that was my most important lesson.

I think I owe it to Brother Ignatius for opening my eyes in my early teenage days to not accepting as gospel everything one read in school text books or indeed even in the Christian Bible. Perhaps Iggy never meant to imply that the boys in his charge should ever question the Holy Book. But on the other hand he did not specify any exception to the critical eye he tried to inculcate in us. Even today, so many years later, I confess that I hardly read a book without finding something that could have been said differently or which was completely free of the printer's devil. In all of this I had not yet been introduced to the interpretation of the history of the Caribbean peoples as the proponents were to later read and interpret it for persons such as I, who certainly had not grown up either learning to pour scorn on the zombies of my ancestors, for I had also been taught to love all family both the living and the dead. I was led to believe that my African side (paternal) had worked himself to the point where he owned a small sugar estate and sugar mill in the valley between Belle Vue (Vieux-Fort North and Desruisseaux) called Fond Josie. On my maternal side I learnt early that had the British Government not compulsorily acquired my grandparents' property and handed it over to America as part of the land for warships swap, I may well have been financially well off, perhaps even wealthy today. Had this wholesale seizing of private lands not taken place, I may well have also been lost to politics in the pursuit of commercial agriculture and business.

Much later but, still at St. Mary's College, I discovered whilst reflecting on Brother Ignatius' methods that he in fact marked out of ten, except that his lowest mark was minus four and his highest was plus six. The minuses were to prove, if one were sufficiently perceptive, that even the best of us can fall so completely out of favour that, we must first return to ground zero, before beginning to move ahead again. Getting up on one's feet after a major disaster is similar to starting all over again, from ground zero. Such reflections have helped me pick up myself more often than I care to recount and have therefore proven a useful lesson in my life. Perhaps the number zero is more useful and carries more significance than many care to credit it with.

Cambridge Certificate and Beyond

And the youth of a colonized country, may well grow up
to pour scorn upon the zombies of his ancestors......
Frantz Fanon: The Wretched of the Earth.

When news reached us here in St. Lucia that George Odlum had won some kind of Bursary or Scholarship to Oxford University the whole of the student body of St. Mary's College and the small band of the Castries 'Intellectual' Community were elated. It seemed everyone knew the history of the great English institutions of Oxford and Cambridge. It was Philosophy, Politics and Economics (the greats) to which Odlum was directed by his Professors at Bristol University who no doubt were impressed with his debating skills. The young Odlum and his ability for expressing what was best of the English Literary tradition, certainly made a good impression. Perhaps one can now understand more clearly why so many from Castries, years later, were to see George Odlum as an Educator, rather than as a politician and still later, after his involvement in politics, as a Minister of Education of the government rather than a Prime Minister.

In the meantime, I had endured another year of growing consciousness and friendships in and around Castries (as opposed to St. Mary's College) even as I continued to visit Vieux-Fort and family there. My visits to the south of the island during the school summer vacations were mainly to Vieux-Fort. I was also encouraged to visit my mother's relatives at the little village of Laborie and my father's at Grace and in the rural communities of Banse/La Grace, in Vieux-Fort north.

During my year in Form Four I was to experience several interesting encounters with the teaching personalities of the day. Brothers De. Lellis, Ignatius, and Marcus come to mind as well as Mr. Hilary Roach from Barbados. I recall one had to prepare the following year for what was in those days the most important examination to many boys and girls on the island. These young persons were the very lucky ones who had made it to the only two secondary schools on the island. After Form Four came Cambridge examinations which would finally determine who fell through the cracks in the society, and who would likely survive and make a better life for themselves. At least that was the common wisdom at the time, not only in Saint Lucia, but in the entire Caribbean. For that examination English Language and Mathematics were compulsory subjects. To these, each student was expected to add another four to six subjects of his choice. I chose Chemistry, Biology, History, Geography and Scripture, in addition to the compulsory ones. Scripture, because I was by then fully attracted to the life story of Paul the Apostle, (formerly Saul) and especially the recorded method of his conversion to the early teachings of Jesus Christ. His former life as Saul, and later his Damascus moment, and his conversion to Paul, have always fascinated and intrigued me. I used my love for geography to help me memorize his missionary journeys in the Middle East and Rome. His journeys were therefore a source of much interest to me at an early age. They dovetailed nicely into my love for maps and places of historical interest. Also, at the time, the journeys of Paul were sure questions in any exams related to the Acts of the Apostles. I therefore determined I could easily ace scripture rather than chance French or any of the other subjects on offer. In addition I also found the awkwardness of early English embedded in the Literature (English) at the time too challenging to memorize. The English plays which I read quite often blurred into each other; perhaps because I tried too hard memorizing too many at a time.

I passed that particular exam but the most memorable thing about it was Lennard 'Dada' Riviere, (deceased) who hailed from the town of Soufriere and who later became a Member of Parliament and Attorney General of St. Lucia. He finished in half the allotted time and at the end of it all received a distinction for his effort. No one could quite believe the record time in which he had finished that particular Cambridge Scripture examination. As adults we always joked about Saul (Paul) and whether his conversion really happened the way we were told.

By the end of the fifth year the teachers and Brothers all had a fairly good idea of those who would pass for the ordinary level Cambridge certificate. Those who passed would then either leave school to enter the world of work and others would continue for another two years in order to sit the Advanced level certificate and hopefully thereafter find a place in a recognized University. During that time the teachers helped students to determine the subjects which they were likely to pass or to excel in. They also advised against those subjects they thought were not likely to bring merit to the student or honour to the school. The more passes the students attained, the better the school looked - and felt.

It was now time to ponder: What was I to do after the Senior Cambridge exams? I had by then set my sights on a professional career in Agriculture, which meant that I had to accumulate some Advanced level subjects and also some much needed cash which, to this day is the single most important impediment to the educational advancement of young West Indians. Significant budget outlays remain a central plank within the education portfolio in the island's social development, although many still argue for more money to be spent on education.

I had to quietly retreat from sixth form as by then fatherhood was staring me in the face, a fact that I was ill prepared for, but which I determined would not get in the way of what I wanted to do with my life. So I took a job at the Inland Revenue department for the princely sum of seventy two dollars and few cents per month. However, before I had fully settled there an opening for an agriculture science course in Trinidad came along, for which I duly applied. Mr. Charles Cadet, later Ambassador to London, was then Superintendent of Agriculture and I may have impressed him sufficiently to get that opportunity to study the subject I had set my mind on. I was also to receive at the same time a lateral transfer from the Audit department to the Ministry of Agriculture, for which I had also applied. Whilst in Trinidad, I continued to receive a monthly allowance, again thanks to Cadet. I spent twenty-two months in Trinidad and there achieved beyond Cadet's expectation. I also distinguished myself in cricket and soccer and at one time the Trinidad national selectors for the Colt's cricket team came seeking me out for a place in that country's trial team. After being informed of my Saint Lucian birth certificate I was politely excused, and that was that.

I have often wondered what might have happened had I decided then to accept the invitation to try for the Trinidad second division cricket team, which entailed giving up my Saint Lucia birthright as so many West Indian were doing at the time in favour of other countries, including Canada, America and England. Perhaps I should have forgotten about the land of my birth, at least for a while. I was then in the sunrise of my twentieth year and have since that time foolishly blamed that fact, for the turns my life took thereafter. I returned to St. Lucia in 1963 and served in the Ministry of Agriculture, Extension division for eighteen months before setting off again for Trinidad, and UWI, St. Augustine campus, in pursuit of further training in Agricultural Sciences.

The Enigmatic, Self-Effacing Brother De. Lellis

He held in his hand a golden staff, twined about with the
sacred wreaths of Apollo Shootafar and made his petition
to the Achaean people in general......

Homer: The Iliad

Of the Presentation Brothers who taught at Saint Mary's in my time, the one who was most difficult to put a finger on was brother DeLellis a.k.a. Ti-Pap. He was (and is) an enigmatic and self-effacing man; small in stature at the time (hence, Ti-Pap or Little father, literally and culturally; but, note also that Roman Catholics refer to their priests as 'father'). Ti-Pap bore a serious demeanour and even among his colleagues from Ireland he seemed always distant and detached. I remember him as dapper, always neat in attire and appearance, in his white priestly-like garments squeaky clean and lily white, exposing to my youthful mind a conscious quality of self, otherwise hidden in his casual unassuming bearing. His neatness was not a quality one could have ever associated with the Brother Albert or, even the tall and ungainly brother Mac. Cartan, the one whom I recall, collected the school fees and who was rarely seen without his little suitcase of cash. He was also in charge of the bookshop and stores. I often wondered whether any school boy was ever so possessed by the thought to commit the unpardonable mischief of depriving Brother Macartan of his little 'grip' of money. That would have been fun especially if the same case was to turn up later, empty, except for a note within saying that Macartan had been given a blue note to his parents and stood to be expelled from the College if he did not return the Brothers' property promptly.

Brother De. Lellis taught mathematics (Algebra, Arithmetic and

Geometry) and was probably an intellectual among light weights, hence his apparent lonely distancing from the madding crowd. On the other hand, perhaps he was from a special part of Ireland where the root of Roman Catholicism had not been fully established and where British politics did their usual trick of divide and rule. Perhaps it was just his family's trait – and persona - to be humble and not be seen or heard. What may have contributed to my assessment of the man at the time was the fact that I could not recall ever meeting or seeing him on the field of play, as I had Brother Anthony (Ti-Plon) or Brother Marcus. His seeming lack of sports and games may therefore have helped to distinguish the man rather than to have demeaned him.

Besides, he may have belonged to some innocuous house whose colour was either red or purple or even yellow. Yet at times as he stood at the front of his math classes contemplating the morning faces of his young charges, it was possible to imagine him as some ancient mythological Greek figure enjoying the adulation and reverence of the little people who paid homage to them.

I often wondered too whether his role was that of an Ambassador or a spy who saw everything, asked the right questions, distilled the correct responses and therefore understood everything about the country, its boys, and their parents with whom he interfaced regularly. As I write, Brother De.Lellis is still a part of the St. Lucian landscape; still teaching and still saving young boys and young men from themselves and from the ever present forces of darkness which continuously strut their stuff in the ever changing world. He once suggested that I leave school and start a family. That was in Form Four where I have already disclosed that the vanity of which poor Lucifer was accused, had visited my excited sinful soul, conditioned by the flood of progesterone which raged through my young body, making it difficult to concentrate on the things that both parents and teachers instructed us to believe was best for us. Brother De. Lellis had given the entire class certain geometry problems to solve at home as was the custom. The early portion of the next math class was devoted to discussing home work and solving any difficulties on the class black board.

Brother De.Lellis apparently became stuck on a particular geometry problem that morning while attempting the solution on the black board. Seeing this, I and my hormones offered to help. He accepted. After I had finished solving the problem in front of the whole class, I came to hand over the chalk to Bro. De.Lellis, but my hormones tossed the white four inch slender marking instrument towards him. By then I was a mere four feet away from him. He caught the chalk without difficulty, but that was not the end of the matter. The boldness of that insubordinate infraction was not lost on either brother De.Lellis or on the rest of the class. The entire class was then as quiet as the Choc cemetery on a Christmas night. De.Lellis reacted to that little bit of showmanship by saying loud enough for all to hear that if I was so bright why didn't I leave school and go start a family. I did just that. I may even have started before the time which Brother De.Lellis had suggested. But I should not have taken his words seriously as with that little display that morning I could have found myself in much deeper trouble. The fact that I spent so many years of happily married life owes more to the choices I made, with the little information then available to me than to anything Ti Pap said or did at any time during my stay at St. Mary's College.

I have subsequently met Brother De.Lellis on several occasions since saying good bye to St. Mary's but too often we were both about our separate businesses. Unlike some 'old' boys whom I know, I have never had the pleasure of a long frank talk with Ti-Pap or to engage him in any useful reminiscences especially with the feeling among the Brothers at the time of how the British (and French) had helped divide their country along religious lines. This may be a good time to correct that lapse.

Over the past half century or so Brother De.Lellis must have taught more citizens of St. Lucia than any other teacher I know. I confess that I have never taken an interest in St. Lucia's national awards to the point of ever nominating anyone for recognition. I am not certain how one came to be named and how one qualified - outside of what a small body of people described – to be honoured by the State. I have also long been convinced that the highest honour this nation could confer should be reserved for its teachers. If such a teacher were then to gravitate to the highest political office this nation has to offer, then certainly the highest honour should also follow him or her there. But I repeat that Brother De.Lellis deserves the very highest honour this island has to offer and I feel quite certain there are thousands, both male and female, who agree with this idea. We should therefore begin to organize to get it done. If I had remained sufficiently long in government that would have been one of the many tributes I would have ensured was paid to one who has contributed so much to our small nation. And there you see another reason why politics is so important to me and to those who understand the uses of political power.

Since putting these thoughts to print I have learnt of very cordial and friendly visits between Brother De Lellis and some former students of the college, who all have passed their fiftieth year. It was their way, I was told, of thanking the goodly gentleman for his guidance and advice during their more formative years at St. Mary's. By the turn of the twentieth century Brother De Lellis had spent at least fifty years teaching several generations of boys on the island. During my time   I was then too young and inexperienced to discover whether such dedication was a trait of the Irish people or whether it came from the learned discipline of the British. To his many former students, who later became his admirers, Brother De Lellis loomed as tall and as large a God of Greek mythology - an Apollo - that held in his hands the tender goblet which contained the precious gemstones of this country's future. Many of us were not aware at the time of the impact which he had made on our lives.

Even before form four, news was filtering to St. Mary's College (and Saint Lucia) that George Odlum was distinguishing himself between the uprights not only for his Bristol University soccer team, but also for other semi-professional football teams in England. George was rechristened the 'Flying Darkie' by his English and Welsh peers and football enthusiasts alike for his continued agility and spectacular prowess keeping goal for his various football teams. The next I was to hear of him was his migration from Bristol to Oxford University to which he received a scholarship. There he took a dose of the 'greats' - Philosophy, Politics, Economics, (PPE).

Leaving Home a Second Time

But the things I did not notice and took for granted were more enduring: The British reticence, the British self-discipline....
C. L. R. James: Beyond a Boundary.

When the opportunity presented itself for further studies abroad in my chosen field, I welcomed it with both hands. Agriculture, it seemed had chosen me unto itself from childhood, because of the environment into which I was born, rather than me choosing it. So I was very happy for another opportunity to further my studies in that field. I duly left for Trinidad and the St. Augustine Campus of the University of the West Indies, rather than to Puerto Rico which was at that time a popular choice for St. Lucians studying agriculture. At that time, St. Lucians also travelled to Puerto Rico to study other subjects such as Housing Design and Construction, Woodwork, Carpentry and Community Organization and Administration.

The B. Sc degree course in Agriculture at St. Augustine campus, UWI, presented a challenge in those days. It was however made more tolerable by some of the more interesting (and outstanding) personalities I was privileged to have met, or with whom I worked during my stay at St. Augustine.

Frank Worrell, (later Sir. Frank) the famous West Indian cricketer and the first person of African roots to captain the West Indies cricket team, was then Dean of Student Affairs on campus. Worrell lived a stone's throw from Milner Hall - one of the two halls of residence during my time there. Cricket was still Frank's passion and he organized many weekend cricket matches on campus among the student body - both resident and non-resident - and also between a campus team (on which he also played) and other teams from various parts of Trinidad.

During one such friendly match I recall taking a catch off Worrell's bowling while fielding at square leg mid way to the boundary. It was a firmly pulled shot, and the ball was coming at me pretty quickly. Thankfully, my eye to hand co-ordination was still intact and although I was partially blinded by the sun at the moment the ball sailed towards me, I was able to hold on for what turned out to be a fairly straight forward catch about head high. That happened to have been the ball before the last of Frank's over. When the over ended and the field was rearranging itself for the start of the new over, the captain (Worrell) called out in my direction: 'Rah, your bowl'. I looked around to see who 'Rah' was as I knew for certain the skipper knew my name and that of every other member of his Campus team. I soon discovered who 'Rah' was, when Frank added in his best Barbadian dialect 'you caught that ball looking into the sun which reminded one of Ra, the sun god.' That name did not get campus - wide recognition but for a while stayed among its cricketers and discreetly shared between Worrell and me.

There was one other outstanding St. Lucian sportsman on the St. Augustine campus cricket team at the time, in the person of Bornwell St. Rose, who hailed from Hospital Road in Castries and from a line of illustrious brothers (and sisters) many of whom also distinguished themselves in athletics, cricket and football, both at St. Mary's and elsewhere. Bornwell had completed a Bachelors degree in Canada and was at the time, conducting research at U.W.I. St. Augustine, and leading to a Master's degree in Soil Science. Upon returning to St. Lucia, after the completion of his 'Masters,' Bornwell met an untimely death while a patient at Victoria hospital. That great sportsman succumbed to Leukemia a blood condition from which it was reported Sir. Frank Worrell had also met an untimely end.

During that cricket season at St. Augustine, one still heard stories about David Holford. He was a former student on campus from the island of Barbados. He had at the time the dubious honour of breaking a glass in an upper floor window in the administrative building, which was some fifty feet from the eastern boundary of the pitch. Holford was cousin to the great Sir. Garfield Sobers and he distinguished himself (with Sobers batting at the other end) in the memorable Test match at Lord's in 1966 against England, when the pair put on 274 runs for the sixth wicket to save the West Indies from defeat. It was Holford's only test century of his career; and what a time to make it! Whilst on campus, Worrell also organized Sunday morning football competitions in which it seemed every male student participated. Gender inequality in sports was unfortunately fully alive at the time and that kept the University women's team to netball and athletics back then.

Worrell also ensured that U.W.I. lecturers and senior research fellows of the University participated fully in these Sunday morning soccer matches. After a game with his team, he would invite the players from both sides to his house for beverages. It was at such gatherings that one was afforded an opportunity for a one on one exchange with the great man. I recalled many questions being asked about his cricketing experience and overseas tours with the test team. His house guests never tired of asking questions about other test players or of that famous tied test match versus Australia in 1961.

I was frankly intrigued when he once revealed that of all his overseas cricket tours playing for the West Indies, he enjoyed India the most. I think he pointed to the generosity and graciousness of the Indian cricket administrators and the general love which India had for the game of cricket.

During that first year at St. Augustine, I roomed at Canada Hall which had only recently been opened. That hall of residence was a gift from the Government and people of Canada. It was opened by the late John Diefenbaker, Prime Minister of Canada, around the beginning of the 1963 academic year. Canada is regarded by many Caribbean people as a genuine friend. They seem always willing to help the Caribbean in their quest for social and economic advancement without the attached strings and kickbacks which others so often demand. Perhaps the most memorable and widely appreciated gifts from Canada to the Caribbean were the two cargo and passenger ships called the Federal Maple and the Federal Palm. These two vessels did more for Caribbean integration and unity, in my view, than anything else, then or since. One feels that there are still many UWI graduates in every Caribbean country who may never have visited another Caribbean island were it not for those Federal boats. And there are many in both the public and private sectors throughout the Caribbean who would do almost anything for the reintroduction of two or more similar vessels to serve the people of the region. It is a strongly held view by many Caribbean personalities, that better shipping schedules within the region would boost trade and facilitate easier movement of people, and thereby lead to more robust economic growth, regionally.

Unfortunately, Frank Worrell did not stay very long at St. Augustine. Before he left, however, I applied for and got a transfer from Canada Hall to the West block at Milner Hall. Unfortunately, West block had already begun to develop the reputation of boisterous and lively living and was further maligned (for whatever reason) as the block which never slept. The latter, had more to do with the exuberance – 'partying' is a poor substitute - of its young occupants (all male) than anything resembling the beating of academic books. But it also produced its fair share of decent Engineers and at the same time protected the reputation of its young Einsteins very well indeed.

I felt privileged to have been allowed to sit in some of the classes of Professor Lloyd Best in West Indian history and the use of English course which he shared with Professor James Millet at the time. Later Lloyd Best became even better known in his native Trinidad when he launched his Tapia House movement, a sort of political grass roots discussion group which added to the national (and Caribbean-wide) debate for identity and economic power.

Professor Duncan who hailed from the island of St. Vincent was a Botanist who knew and enjoyed his work. It appeared to me that this gentleman was a born teacher and educator. He seemed more interested in the welfare and development of his students than any person I had come across in those days. Later, Professor Haynes, from Barbados, a plant physiology specialist and Professor Ahmad, (a Soil Scientist) originally from Guyana, were to prove equal to Professor Duncan in the care and attention which they paid to developing those whom they were assigned to instruct and educate.

Midway into that academic year, the University campus at St. Augustine was abuzz with activity, as preparations began for the visit of two famous world personalities- the indefatigable Her Majesty Queen Elizabeth the Second, and later His Imperial Majesty, King of Kings, Lion of the tribe of Judah, President Haile Selassie of Ethiopia in North Africa. The visit by the latter dignitary was highlighted by the fact that by that time, the sub-culture of Rastafarianism in Jamaica had spread to Trinidad and the South Caribbean.

Visits by Queen and Emperor

Then it will be our duty to select, if we can, natures which are
fitted for the task of guarding the city?

Plato: Republic

During my last year at Canada Hall and before transferring to Milner, a competition was held among its residents (all male) for a suitable crest to represent that hall. At that time Canada Hall was made up of students from the Caribbean. I was thrilled to have won that particular competition, which earned me a place of merit on the students' annual Honour roll, placing me among others who had distinguished themselves in some way while resident in Canada Hall. I felt especially happy when St. Lucian students, returning home from summer workshops at St. Augustine, in the late sixties and early seventies, told me how proud it made them feel to see one of their own on that honour roll. That, I think was my first blow for St. Lucia and it felt good - really, really good at the time.

I left Canada Hall the following year and transferred to Milner Hall, West Block, to be precise. I represented Milner Hall in the first ever football match between the two halls of residence on campus in 1965. That match ended in a one nil victory for Milner Hall. And guess who scored the only goal of the match? And it was a beauty if I may say so myself. The result of that match caused much distress to my former Canada Hall colleagues, many days following the event. Those Canada Hall students who were fresh from K.C. (Kingston College, Jamaica) were a particularly unhappy bunch. These young Jamaicans thought that they were the little Brazilians of Caribbean soccer. Who fooled them, I still have not discovered. That goal was scored from just outside the penalty area and it entered the uprights near the top left hand corner, making it very difficult for any custodian to save. It left my friend Clem Wakefield, a competent Jamaican goalkeeper, staring at me with a look of incredulity which I had not seen before on that pleasant African face. The weekend following that match, I attended a party at Canada Hall which at one point became so heated with debate over football that I decided to leave, even though I felt no particular pressure to do so. But I detected that my presence was too much for some of my 'friends' to bear, so I made it easy on those who were from K.C. and J.A and supporting Canada Hall. That Canada Hall football team was made up of young stallions mostly from top secondary schools in Kingston, Jamaica who were obviously coached in the finer arts of the game. On the other hand the Milner Hall team was a mix of Trinidadians, Barbadians, Windward Islanders, including of course yours truly. That day I think we might have brought tears to the eyes of the Canada Hall fans. My claim to whatever football skills I had acquired then was due largely to my exposure in St. Lucia to the many talented footballers who regularly visited the island from our next door neighbour - Martinique. I also learnt much from the coaches who visited St. Lucia from time to time including those from Martinique who came often for short stints. Some visiting Martinique players had played professionally in France and Europe. Their football prowess was always something to be admired. It was therefore inevitable for one who loved the game to develop a keener appreciation for the finer art of the sport by simply observing how the professionals did it. And that was my secret weapon which my Jamaican friends never discovered.

During the mid sixties the University of the West Indies was developing and expanding quite quickly in anticipation of the explosion in student registration, which would soon materialize in the post independence era. The attainment of full University status followed soon after political independence for Jamaica and Trinidad and Tobago. Perhaps in recognition of their new status, both Trinidad and Jamaica were visited by two Heads of State within months of the other. First was Her Majesty Queen Elizabeth the Second of Britain and then it was the turn of Emperor Haile Selassie of Ethiopia. Both distinguished visitors also visited the new University campuses in Jamaica and Trinidad. Visits by members of the Royal Family to the Caribbean were not new and so the Queen's visit did not have the same impact as that of the Ethiopian Emperor at the time.

The Caribbean peoples at that time seemed to be finally rising again from their drunken stupor of excessive religion and other colonial indoctrination. Such excesses coupled with the long hurt of the Rastafarian brethren and their long lost tribes of Ethiopia, now resident in Jamaica, may have heightened the excitement by the mere mention of the name Selassie. This grew into frenzy when the Emperor's visit to the region was first announced. For the Rastafarian brethren no less a personage as that of Jah, (Jehovah himself), was to visit. It was for many a miracle which they never expected in their lifetime. In Jamaica it was reported they fell on their knees on the streets of Kingston wailing and giving praise to the Most High for this mighty blessing. The campuses of our newly independent University were not quite as demonstrative but the adulation the Emperor received there was a close cousin to that which he received in Kingston. After all Selassie was the Conquering Lion of the tribe of Judah, King of Kings, Lord of Lords, His Majesty, God, Jah and Jehovah all wrapped in the little thin faced man with graying hair and vacant distant look in his deeply set brown eyes. On witnessing these events, my skeptical questioning mind, stubbornly unbelieving at times, was not overly impressed and certainly not overwhelmed by these visits. But I kept my feelings to myself. There was to be sure great rejoicing and ceremony at the arrival of His Excellency, the most eminent Emperor Selassie, in Trinidad and Tobago. The reason one supposes such visits are important is that they demonstrate to the populace and to the world at large that these countries – and their leaders – were now serious actors on the world stage and were therefore to be taken seriously, by all and sundry. Specifically the visit of Emperor Selassie was to demonstrate that the Caribbean had cast aside the shackles of the past and was now ready to embrace Africa and all things African. At that time too, no African leader captured the imagination of the Caribbean (and the world) as did Selassie.

If anything of significance was said there on that particular visit, I confess that I completely missed it. What I recall is that Selassie was decked out in his khaki army uniform with suitably attached pins and ribbons indicating rank and seniority. His face was thin and bearded and carried the distinct mark of genetic influences from the Arabs who had earlier occupied (and still do) much of north and east Africa. One detected beneath it all a certain gentleness of character accompanying a calm assertive demeanour even as that bearded face remained dead-pan and unsmiling. Some non-Rastafarian reporters from the Caribbean had even suggested that there was a hint of haunting saintliness about the Emperor. On seeing him I attributed all the elevated spiritual connections that were heaped on him to the tiredness of a man who, by then, was well past the prime of his life.

If he had indeed descended from Jesus Christ and the kingly line of the biblical King David, he did not say. Nor I suspect was he ever asked a direct question about his lineage. So he left the Caribbean and I as well as many others in the region, still have no idea whether the Emperor is, or was, related to the great Jah-ho-vah.

The Emperor came and left. One felt certain that at the end of his State visits to Jamaica and Trinidad and Barbados the usual communiqués promising to work together for world peace and to co-operate in the common causes were signed by the Prime Ministers of Jamaica, Trinidad and Tobago and the Emperor of Ethiopia.

Within months of the Emperor's visit, Her Majesty Queen Elizabeth the Second and Prince Philip paid us a visit at the St. Augustine campus of the U.W.I. That visit was probably to say a final farewell to the newly independent university. A new Royal Charter had earlier affirmed what was already on everyone's lips: that the University College had become a full fledged, independent, degree-granting University. The University of the West Indies - UWI - was officially launched.

But as was so typical of the British colonial system, it kept one of their own in charge for a little bit longer, to ensure that the natives got a firm handle on things. To that end, Princess Alice, the Countess of Athlone became the new University's first Chancellor and the Caribbean's own Sir Arthur Lewis its first vice Chancellor. Princess Alice soon retreated into the background making way for Sir Arthur Lewis who later also became St. Lucia's and the Caribbean's first Nobel Laureate.

Her Majesty, the Queen of England, was well received by many students, University professors, employees and parents, guardians and friends who took time to gather near the staging point, the weather beaten steps at the east entrance of the Administrative building. That building was put there to serve the purposes of Imperial England one hundred years or so ago. What struck me with both the Queen's visit and that of the Emperor, was that normally busy people who would not be distracted for one moment from the task at hand, were willing to change their schedules, drop everything, just for a glance at these distinguished visitors. I can't recall ever being moved by such visits and having had ample time to reflect on them I am fairly certain the only two persons I would have wished to meet would have been Adolph Hitler and Mahatma Gandhi. The first to discover from the horse's mouth what grave sin the Jewish people had committed against him, and why he was so violently opposed to them. The second, perchance to discover the true source of Gandhi's stated doctrine of 'non-violence' in political protests'. Perhaps after further consideration I would probably add Marcus Garvey to these two.

The time soon came to say goodbye to Trinidad and to return to my native country. By then I had considered Trinidad a second home and I had cultivated many long-lasting and beautiful friendships. I was therefore sad to leave, but I felt then, that Saint Lucia needed my talents more than Trinidad did at the time. So with the fractured interest of the rise and fall of the game of life, I packed and shipped my books home by boat, and soon followed them on the Caribbean's favourite airline. By then I knew that life seemed an unending series of events as the game of cricket certainly has proven to be, during my active participation in it.

Goodbye Trinidad, Hello St. Lucia

Within the fluctuating interest of the rise or fall of the game as
a whole, there is this unending series of events.....
                              C.L.R. James: Beyond the Boundary.

Before my final return to the island, St. Lucia had progressed (in 1967) to become an independent state, in association with Britain. The phrase Associated Statehood, was a fancy constitutional provision of partial political independence (only the Brits could have created such an oxymoron) in which Britain was to continue to see after the island's Foreign Affairs and Defence, leaving the local government to take care of the other responsibilities as Health, Education, Law and Order, Agriculture, and so on. By November of 1966, Barbados had proceeded to political independence, and the Barbadians on campus put on an Independence fete in which many students and well wishers participated. Interestingly, my life path continued to cross with those of a few of the outstanding Caribbean students on campus, at that time. They are fraternal brethren who do not allow petty political or religious differences to intrude at any time during the twenty-four cycle of any given day. They too are aware of the advantages of education by which means alone, we believe, we are rendered fit members of regularly organized society.

I was elected president of the Harland Society –an organization for agriculture students (at the time) – and working with David de La Rosa, General Manager of Pan American airlines in Port-of-Spain, we organized a trip for the society to Brazil. The Pan Am General Manager offered me a free ticket if I were to induce a touring party of thirty or more persons to make that trip. I met the challenge, but regrettably I had to decline De La Rosa's offer because of the urgency - which I later discovered was hugely over stated – of returning home to resume my role in the Ministry of Agriculture. My regret became even more profound after I discovered the wicked and tormented individual who then acted as head of the department. I feel certain that the trip to Brazil would have added to my experiences, and that furthermore I would have been presented an opportunity to say thanks and farewell to the final year class which had elected me to lead them and the Harland Society.

On resuming work at the Department of Agriculture in St. Lucia, it soon became clear to me that Tourism and Agriculture would not at the time co-exist easily, within the same portfolio. I soldiered on even though that man at the helm of the department was a boastful, egotistical and insufferable chief, whose main preoccupation seemed to do whatever the politicians of the day asked in order to guarantee his stay in St. Lucia. Sometimes I think St. Lucia can be such a beautiful place; if only the majority of St. Lucians were smart enough to recognize that and to treat their countrymen with a little more love and respect. Before long the Chief Agriculture Officer (C.A.O.) one Dr. Blair, was getting under my skin. At every turn he seemed to be ready to pick a fight with me. And I was not ready for a fight. To fight then would probably have meant having to leave St. Lucia a third time and to accept other job offers overseas. I was at one time tempted to do so, and I almost did, but in the end I decided that I ought not to give way to a foreigner.

I subsequently discovered that the C.A.O. had information about my previous involvement in campus politics, at St. Augustine. That man probably knew then - what everyone later discovered - that my name was among those on a list of about sixteen past students whom the Trinidad government agents on campus may have deemed as ring leaders at the time. Trouble makers may be too strong a phrase. My personal involvement was a simple matter. I served as a member of the entertainment sub-committee of the Students Guild, as the governing body for students affairs was called at the time, and its president was Geddes Granger (later Makandal Daaga). The Students Council, under the former Geddes Granger, had organized some public protests on campus and in Port-of-Spain in support of Guyanese born History lecturer Dr. Walter Rodney who was debarred from entering Jamaica after an overseas trip. That protest march was my first overt political act and I was conscious that pictures were being taken which may have fingered me as one of the enthusiastic students on that march. Even with the lapse of so much time, I can readily say that I was not a 'leader' in any of those marches. But I was very vocal against the banning of Walter Rodney from Jamaica and I kept thinking that had that island not been independent the British colonial rulers would probably not have acted in the way the Jamaican authorities at the time did. In one of the demonstrations on Port-of-Spain, I recall citizens of Trinidad joining in the march and strengthening the protest. There was also an address made at Woodford Square in Port-of-Spain at the end of which a petition was delivered to the Prime Minister's office seeking assistance to get the Jamaica Government to rethink the ban against Rodney. That petition was delivered by a delegation of students led by President Granger.

After I left St. Augustine, Trinidad, I lost touch with the persons who were making waves on campus during my stay there. However, I continued to follow the progress of protests in Trinidad, especially those in which Granger and other names I recognized at the time were involved.

Following my own engagement with the St. Lucia Forum, I became very pre-occupied with furthering the uplifting of the political awareness of the people of Saint Lucia, and therefore lost my personal contacts in Trinidad. I was aware that the struggle had intensified in that island and that both Dave d' Arbeau and Geddes Granger had assumed new names. It was with much pleasure that I was able to make contact with Khafra Kabon in the late nineties after many years of absence. I was pleased to see that he was as deeply involved in the cause of the Caribbean and African Diaspora as before. I have not had the pleasure of meeting Makandal Daaga but I have followed his progress and I was very pleased when the auditorium at the St. Augustine campus was named after him. It also warmed my heart when I learnt that he was named Cultural Ambassador Extraordinaire for Caricom, by Prime Minister Persad-Bissesser of Trinidad and Tobago in 2010. Khafra Kabon in the meantime continues to work with the poor and dispossessed brethren of Trinidad and the wider Caribbean. He was an active and conscious young brother when I was on campus and our names and that of Daaga were on the list of those banned from entering St. Vincent by Son Mitchell in 1970/71. We became acquainted and I recall attending a meeting at Khafra's home in Port-of-Spain two blocks away from St. Mary's College (CIC). Of course both these names were on the list of banned persons from St. Vincent. By the turn of the twentieth century both these brothers were well known citizens of Trinidad and Tobago. The banning from St. Vincent by its enthusiastic Prime Minister Mitchell probably only served to highlight the Caribbean leaders who were emerging from the St. Augustine campus and who would be in the news long after that Prime Minister had quit politics. What I found most amazing at the time was that Blair was by far the blackest person I had ever been introduced to or worked with in my life, but he was against the Black Power movement and even the name offended him. He was born in St. Vincent and later migrated to Trinidad and became a national of that country after independence. He studied Agriculture at The Imperial College of Tropical Agriculture (ICTA) in Trinidad and later took a PhD in Plant Pathology at Cornell University. Whilst working for the Colonial office in Trinidad he was transferred to Saint Lucia to act as Chief Agriculture Officer in the service of the British Crown. Before returning to Trinidad he got married into a well known Saint Lucian family. He was again transferred from Trinidad to Saint Lucia in the late sixties on loan from the Trinidad government, ostensibly to help hasten the pace of agriculture diversification and development.

To frustrate Blair's moves I decided on a strategy of counter attack. I therefore invited a few other Saint Lucian graduates to my house at Black Mallet gap, (off the Marchand main road) for a chat and to launch what I thought would become a quasi- political group of black empowerment advocates. That was duly organized and at that first meeting the group of five decided to invite certain local persons to prepare position papers on relevant aspects of the political, economic and social interests for study within the group. George Odlum was at the time Secretary General to the West Indies Associated States Council of Ministers with head offices in Castries, St. Lucia. He was one of those invited to share his ideas (on paper) on the evolving politics of the region. On receipt of our invitation Odlum pounced on it like a lion that had not eaten for many days. Rather than accede to our request, he invited us instead to his home ostensibly to talk a little more on our interests. He also took the liberty to invite some others who were friends of his from the St. Lucia Arts Guild of the fifties and early sixties. At first I did not like the atmosphere of the meeting. I felt then that this wider party represented the same mind-set which I saw as the problem which we were attempting to solve.

Notwithstanding my own apprehensions at the time, Odlum turned out to be a very gracious host. He even invited us to stay for a game of scrabble after the discussions had ended. He volunteered that, he too, had thought of forming such a group and so he was very happy to accept our invitation, to that first meeting. At a subsequent meeting at his home when we were brain storming for a suitable name, he suggested we call the new group, 'The St. Lucia Forum' after the early Roman Forum of Emperors and other high public officials.

It was not the name I had in mind but it appeared that those present were happy with the less pointed and more conciliatory 'FORUM' than the militant black liberation movement that I had envisioned - and suggested. We continued to meet amongst ourselves to exchange ideas and get to know each other better. Those of more academic bent prepared position papers on various topics, such as public health, trade unionism in the Caribbean, governance, Caribbean politics amongst others, which were then discussed. These discussions were not unlike tutorials with a professor charged with honing a young mind to its chosen purpose.

We persevered with the internal meetings of the group and although not yet formally launched we continued to gather momentum. At that time I often thought we were akin to the underground movement that helped black people escape the southern USA into Canada, and freedom. Increasingly, the presence of the group became a matter of common knowledge. The curious wished to see who were those involved in such a bold initiative. Many were certain that the FORUM was a new political party. That thought might have helped to heighten interest in our work. But I did not like it. I did not think that party politics would help the cause which the group intended to espouse. Besides, I had always held strongly to the view that it would take a united people - not one divided by partisan politics - to achieve the goals of true nationhood and lasting self worth. I still believe wholeheartedly that psychological damage and self hatred inflicted by slavery must first be addressed before a united and prosperous nation can be built from the abuses and excesses of the past.

Those early Forum days (the Forum legacy if you prefer) are remembered for the manner they brought George Odlum and myself together and the long and often difficult road we travelled as kindred spirits in the vineyard of local politics. We had set out to make people discover themselves and to learn that, in the fluctuating interest of the game of cricket (and life) there was as a whole an unending series of events, as C. L. R. James had observed, in 'Beyond the Boundary'. There are few things more rewarding than that of asking a broken and dispirited people to stand up, take up their beds and walk - and to see them do it. That is the most empowering feeling I know. To see people grow from little or no self-confidence and later walk like they owned the whole world. Such is the miracle of transformative thinking which I believe every true leader desires to instill in his/her followers. In my early difficulties within the Ministry of Agriculture in Saint Lucia I came close to packing up and leaving the island, on several occasions. I survived thanks to two senior civil servants who stood by me at the time (when I was not aware of their support). Much later when the Chief Agriculture Officer had left I discovered that Charles Cadet and Dr. Greaham Louisy had stuck with me when I most needed such intervention at the administrative level in government. After I had finally settled without having to constantly look over my shoulders, I soon became involved in public discussions which would then mark me for the rest of my life. It is not for me to judge whether that was good or bad. All I can say for sure is that it was a time which bore great promise for the island, and I felt happy to be part of helping to shape that future.

Before then, I had been through hurricane Edith, and had dealt with many farmers individually, and I knew first hand the difficulty of educating them to acquire a new and greater respect for themselves. It was the type of work which took centuries to achieve, but we did not have the luxury of time. I believed then that only change on the dramatic size and scale of the French and American revolutions would usher in the type of deep and profound developments that were needed in Saint Lucia. No half measures would do. Yet, it was plain for all to see that the cold ideological war at the time would not permit room for another successful Cuban revolution within the American sphere of influence.

Besides, how does one take a people from almost total darkness and ignorance and teach them how to find beautiful meanings in a life of poverty, ignorance and backwardness? Education was the obvious long term solution. But how does one feed and clothe the poor whilst educating them? Besides, what language does one use in such education, especially adult literacy? It was in answer to this specific question that the St. Lucia Forum rediscovered the language of the people - Creole - and sanctified it with a new grace and gave it back to them. We believed at the time that, it was only through language and culture that people could claim their patrimony, their human dignity and their rights. In addition, he that is once admitted to the right of reason is made a freeman to the whole estate according to Ralph Waldo Emerson, the well known American poet and writer.

Unfortunately, in the same way that hard drugs made their way into the marijuana distribution network on the island and destroyed so many young lives, there has been an equal infiltration into the Creole language. Rather than the original emphasis of empowering the Creole-speaking peoples, there are those who see an opportunity for themselves. The vision of empowerment and raising a people to take charge of their lives seems a thing of the past. The purpose of these confidence building measures seemed to have been lost on those who have hijacked Creole as a money making device.

A Search for Excellence

He that is once admitted to the right of reason is made
a freeman to the whole estate.....
                    Ralph Waldo Emerson:
              The Essential Writings of R.W. Emerson.

After Trinidad and St. Augustine I returned to St Lucia somewhat unhappy and a little disappointed. Unhappy, because I had sacrificed a free trip to Brazil with the Harland Society on campus, of which I was chairman; and disappointed, because there was not a more challenging job for me in the Ministry of Agriculture, St. Lucia. My first assignment was to landscape and at the same time to direct the supervisor of the prisoners who worked on the grounds – it was actually called a garden - at the official residence of the Premier of the island. I made up my mind there and then that the decision to post me in such a job was not a wise one and I wasted no time telling this to the Director of Agriculture Blair from Trinidad. I of course earned the man's immediate displeasure and he never let me forget it. I was surprised by the turn of events as I felt certain that I was very polite in my address to that gentleman. In addition, I had told him the truth about my limited knowledge of ornamental plants at the time.

I soon discovered that Blair, who was born in St. Vincent, seemed unable to endear himself to his colleagues in Trinidad. It may therefore have been for this reason he used his marriage to an upright and well connected family in Saint Lucia, to make available his talents to the island, by secondment from his post in Trinidad. I discovered many years later that acting Permanent Secretary Dr. Greaham Louisy and Charles Cadet, Advisor on Trade, may have had a hand in my assignment to a new position in which I felt more challenged and therefore more useful.

I was transferred to investigate and report on the cultural methods employed by banana farmers on the island and what might be done to improve such practices and hopefully help increase production and productivity of the country's farmers. It was during that study I realized how deficient in every aspect of banana cultivation the majority of farmers on the island were at the time. Also, there seemed a reluctance on the part of almost everyone I met either in a public or a private work related business, to speak their minds openly, frankly and truthfully.

Such studied silence (or a rather calculated determination) to conceal one's true feelings, did not sit well with me. I had returned to the island after being fully involved in many of the social upheavals which were challenging the old colonial prejudices in Trinidad and Tobago, where freedom of speech had taken deeper roots than in St. Lucia.

Upon my return to St. Lucia I found an island where people only seemed to speak in whispers behind closed shutters, except they were drunk and had few cares in the world. It was frustrating to one who by that time was always in the midst of some discussion or who had available to him daily news papers unlike the one weekly paper one came back home to. When one adds on top of this my early difficulties in the Department of Agriculture, I may well have contemplated an early escape from the island had it not been for Louisy and Cadet.

Even before I learnt of their involvement in my differences with Blair over the job I was handed, I had an appreciation of both Greaham Louisy and Charles Cadet. The former was the only Veterinarian on the island for many years and so it was impossible for a farmer who grew animals for a living – such as my grand parents had done - not to have known Louisy. I have also said to all who cared to listen that, Charles Cadet was the person responsible for giving me my first break to study agriculture. He was at the time Superintendent of Agriculture and I, a young greenhorn who had been employed at the Audit department, had asked to be transferred to the Department of Agriculture where I wished to pursue a career. Even at this early stage I paid close attention to the work of the early pioneers in Saint Lucia, especially in the field of Agriculture.

These early pioneers in the Ministry of Agriculture of whom I had heard so much when I was a child growing up at Vieux – Fort may also have been partly responsible for the path of agriculture I followed after school. It was common knowledge back then that these men were in a continuous search for excellence. Many of these pioneers in agriculture on the island hailed from other Caribbean territories such as Jamaica, Dominica and St. Vincent. But it was the Anguilla born Swithen Schouten who was reputed to have made the biggest impact and left the longest lasting legacy on the island's agriculture. He was not the first or only person from that tiny island, situated within the Leeward group of islands, who had travelled south to Saint Lucia to make a new life for themselves. Schouten came to St. Lucia as a young graduate from Cornell University, in New York, USA. He first studied at the Imperial College of Tropical Agriculture, (ICTA) in Trinidad, before moving to Cornell. He was a workaholic who seemed born with the gift of vision and true pitch. He seemed also at the time to epitomise the high work ethic of those on whom religion had imposed a strict and rigorous discipline. Yet he was not a practising Methodist as so many in his family were reputed to be. He could therefore be described as one who did not hold the slightest wink, to any sort of religious conviction. Schouten was head of the Department of Agriculture in Saint Lucia in the late fifties and early sixties. By consensus amongst his peers, as well as by general acclamation, he was also a man of great physical stamina and mental strength. He has been described by those who knew him well as a kind hearted soul who had a keen appreciation for the privations of the labouring class, many of whom toiled for pennies an hour, in the hot Saint Lucia sun. At that time the work of these early pioneers in the field of agriculture may have seemed menial and lacking in mental preparation. However, nothing was further from the truth. On closer examination it would soon be discovered that due attention was devoted to planning and preparation for the orderly development of agriculture on the island. Such information was not widely known and later when the banana industry began to dominate agriculture - in the late fifties – agriculture planning appeared to have lost much of its focus and in its place came a mad and vulgar rush to bananize the entire island. Soon thereafter, the island became distracted from its former well balanced agriculture development programme and in its place came a monopoly of banana production. At the time of this writing some forty plus years later, no one that I know has attempted to compute the true balance sheet of the effects of the bananization of the island by politicians seeking change, without thinking long term or planning strategically as far as agricultural diversification is concerned. It is therefore not surprising that the long-held fallacy that agriculture was about hard manual labour in the hot tropical sun has not been completely erased or dispelled, at this time. Notwithstanding any of this, the work and achievement of the early pioneers in the field of agriculture in Saint Lucia cannot be denied. Neither can it be denied that back in the day there was a concerted search for new varieties of crops to be cultivated, new ways of reaching for higher yields per unit area of land for both crops and animals. It was under Schouten's watch that farm machinery was first introduced into the island and feeder roads were constructed at a brisk pace.

The construction of feeder roads to serve the newly emerging cultivated lands and the introduction of fertilizers for bananas and other crops were all begun under the leadership of Swithen Schouten who was then ably assisted by his young Research Assistant, Saint Lucia born Charles Cadet, who had graduated from Mc. Gill University in Canada with a Master's Degree after having first attended Halifax Technical Institute. He was selected by Schouten to replace the indefatigable James Mitchell who hailed from St. Vincent and the Grenadines and who had strong family ties in Saint Lucia. After vacating his post of Agriculture Research Officer in Saint Lucia, Mitchell returned to his native land where he was then employed in a similar capacity. He later became that country's second Prime Minister. Still later, and towards the end of his political career he was knighted by Her Majesty, Queen Elizabeth the Second of England, and is now more properly called, Sir James.

During this early period one felt a strong urge and desire on the part of leading technocrats of the Caribbean towards a continuous search for knowledge and excellence in the application of such information. Indeed, as Ralph Waldo Emerson had earlier observed, it could justifiably be claimed that these early pioneers made themselves freemen to the whole estate by their ability to reason, to plan and to execute with urgency and purpose that plan for agriculture development for the island. Each of these early trail blazers therefore became a household name in Saint Lucia. It would surprise no one if a suitable tribute were to be published some future day, on the work and achievement of these early pioneers in the field of agriculture. Indeed, it may well prove useful to broaden such a study to include those in other fields of endeavour such as teaching, policing, land surveying among others who came from other Caribbean lands and who served St. Lucia and served it so faithfully, so well and for so long. It was in the receding shadows of these early pioneers and the local senior agriculture officers that they had trained, that I returned to the island to join the Ministry of Agriculture, as a relative unknown. To add to my misery and to exacerbate my disadvantages, I was first stationed in the unfamiliar north of the island, Babonneau to be precise, to minister to the needs of those who called themselves farmers, back then. Even at my relatively early stage of work in the field of agriculture in Saint Lucia, I quickly became aware of the tremendous effort it would entail to get both peasants and small farmers to acquire a new and more progressive mindset – a new thinking, as it were – towards the wise use of the land, for earning a decent living. At the time, it was a boastful claim of certain politicians that they were the persons who had liberated the many landless labourers from the harsh sugar estates and made them into small farmers and banana producers. Perhaps the politicians forgot to add, they did not educate the 'farmers' that they had created.

These former labourers had therefore entered into banana agriculture with the same mindset and dependency syndrome of those labourers who had previously weeded and harvested the sugar cane. Sadly, the more important work of teaching those former labourers to think was never tried or even attempted, by their political friends. It was not surprising therefore to discover that whenever change became necessary in the banana industry, no matter how desirable such change, it was always extremely difficult to implement because it was always stoutly resisted by those who either refused to think, or were incapable of so doing. It was not without significance that change within the industry always seemed to have been initiated from outside – by the buyer, the selling agent, or the marketer. It could be seen then that with the introduction of bananas and the great rush to harvest the new 'green gold' all objective scientific thinking had been thrown out the window. Even with the establishment of Winban Research Centre at Roseau Valley in Saint Lucia, little concrete results were achieved due to the refusal of many 'farmers' to be schooled by anyone in the correct methods of designing contour drains and the spacing and fertilizing of their banana crop. It was therefore clear from the very outset that the same plantation mind set had followed certain persons from the sugarcane fields, into what was clearly a more lucrative and regular form of agriculture – the cultivation of bananas. The former labourers on the sugar estates had become 'independent' farmers but they had brought with them the same attitudes they had acquired as labourers whose value to production was never manifested by the plantation owners in any way, shape or form. The attitude against such abuse was so endemic that it undoubtedly followed the poor fellows even when they no longer worked for the sugar estates but for themselves.

It meant therefore, that neither their thinking, nor their attitude towards work as bona fide 'independent' farmers had changed. The effort to get banana farmers who were earning a regular income from their crop to think of a broad base agriculture diversification programme was frustrated at every turn. To add to this unfortunate situation, there were many perfectly intelligent persons both in the field of agriculture and at the community leadership level who simply refused to consider the possibility that the removal of preferential treatment in the UK market for the island's bananas would lead to the demise of that important source of revenue. Such thinking also reflected a lack of political will by those who were better placed to cause a switch in farmer behaviour. It was also a reflection of the hold which the banana industry had on the psyche of the entire rural community

– indeed on that of an entire country. To prove this one often came across perfectly intelligent and rational persons on the island who would assure one unthinkingly it seemed, that the island could not do without bananas. With that, one should not be surprised to discover that the leading lights of the day, including politicians, were saying the exact same thing about sugarcane and the sugar industry on the island in the nineteen fifties. Sugar cane cultivation was at one time, like the rest of the Caribbean, this island's largest industry. When it finally perished in the mid-fifties due to inefficiency and increasing competition from other sources neither a hint of sorry nor a ready tear drop was discerned amongst those who had laboured there all their lives. And no one died with king sugar when it finally passed away! By the end of the twentieth century agriculture had become very serious business which was being driven inexorably towards a global economic order. This new order in turn was being dictated to more and more each passing day, by productivity and efficiency at every stage from production to supply, including transportation. Rising costs of inputs such as fertilizers and pest control chemicals and labour were also playing a major role in ensuring that only the fittest and best producers survived in this increasingly dog-eat-dog, globalized economic environment.

There was much to be learnt from my work in the rehabilitation of the banana industry after hurricane Edith, in 1963. I saw the very low level of farmer education which existed at the time, and the large gap in knowledge between the average Agriculture Field Officer and the more promising farmers. A concerted long-term effort in farmer education was an absolute necessity, if the island was to become self-sufficient in food production, some day. In addition, it would need a new and broader education of all the people if they were to see food security and efficiency in food production in a more holistic and nationalistic way.

Since my first appointment with the Ministry of Agriculture, there has been a quiet, measured and continuing search for excellence on the island. It is as if those in charge are afraid to open the flood gates too wide lest they be swept away by the tide of change. This policy of building a better, more educated people has expressed itself through the construction of more (and larger) primary and secondary schools. There are many more University scholarships on offer today and bank loans are available for those who wish to pursue tertiary education. Today, many deserving students leave the island for further study abroad. There has also been the introduction of Agriculture on the teaching syllabus at the Sir Arthur Lewis Community College, on the island. The College has its own farm which it uses for practical teaching and demonstrations in agriculture techniques.

To the more perceptive observer, however, all this must seem like groping in the dark, by one who is visually challenged. To begin with, no food production targets sufficient to feed the island's population or for even replacing a portion of its food import bill are published for public consumption and support. No one knows for certain what the food import bill for the rapidly expanding tourism sector looks like. In this situation how can there be a realistic attempt to tackle the food and nutrition needs of the visitor if such basic information is not available to the planners and the farmers of the country alike? There may well be several useful plans for reducing the food import bill. However, their successful implementation would require for all such plans to be constantly before the public's eyes for discussion and debate. Besides, follow-up work of updating and refining such plans ought to be on a bi-yearly basis, at least. This is what a search for excellence ought to be about. It is the continuous striving to be better. It is a never ending search for a better way of producing food (and everything else) more efficiently. It involves constant review in order to determine how far one has travelled and estimate how much more there is to be done. It is a never ending battle to stop the laws of inertia and laziness from getting the better of a people and a nation.

No inventory has ever been taken, as far as I am aware, of the food needs of the island for say, one month. No one in the private or public sector has ever suggested what the island's response would be, if no ships came to the island with food for a month or so. Perhaps the reason no one wants to address that question is that such thinking involves hard work which may not be glamorous and high paying. Yet it may be the most important long term task to be undertaken for the island's economic growth and survival. The reluctance to do so may well have a religious foundation, since much of formal education had been historically controlled by the church. Even in the age of science and technology, and the search for excellence in many other parts of the world, the Caribbean still lags far behind the more technologically advanced countries. In the past we learnt by cramming and retention not by reasoning, questioning and doing. Thankfully, this too is changing.

A sad development which some observers, including some senior civil servants of the day, believe has taken root in Saint Lucia since the nineteen eighties, is that many persons who earned a first University degree then, pursued the master's programme or higher, not in a continuing search for excellence, but rather as a means of leap-frogging to a another higher salary scale. Little or no contribution is made by these types unless of course they happen to be in the teaching profession. There too it may be seen that the search for excellence becomes very circumscribed. Too often University graduates see their qualification as a personal cost item and see no reason why they should share their knowledge with others except for a fee. Indeed some explain their determination not to contemplate such pursuit of excellence for its own sake, and the sharing of new ideas for improvement of their country as too demanding and with too few rewards. Can we then ask whether the country would have been better off without such selfishness?

This is a question which will loom larger with time. It underlies what many see as the continuing dearth of sensible debate and discussion by the island's brightest and more capable sons and daughters, on matters of national importance. There are, to be certain, much more complex reasons so many refuse to think beyond their personal needs for food, clothing and sex. What seems a little frightening to those who take the time to reflect on such attitudes, is the fact that a people who fail to exercise long term strategic thinking are doomed to dwell forever as hewers of wood and drawers of water. And who is to help develop such thinking, the former colonial powers or those of our own who are now equipped with the knowledge to keep their people from perpetual ignorance and poverty? Thankfully, there is emerging a small group of prospects mainly from the private sector, who are prepared to think strategically and to go wherever the thought process and new development opportunities may lead. This is an encouraging sign which is to be applauded and encouraged.

Soon the more competent, fearless and bold persons within the public sector will have to begin convening for the purpose of thinking strategically and beyond the requirements of their regular jobs. In this endeavour these public officers will need the courage and strength to venture beyond party politics and personal peeves, and beyond their comfort zones. This is not easy in a small society, where feelings are so easily bruised and personal space so often disrespected. All citizens ought to be encouraged to think long term and far outside narrow party politics, if they are to prepare themselves to face the increasingly globalised world. Hopefully, these are the ones who will find beautiful meanings in the things their private and joint initiatives will help to create on this island, and indeed in the Caribbean.

Hurricane Edith, 'Banana Politics'

*Those who find beautiful meanings in beautiful things
are the cultivated. For these there is hope.....*
Oscar Wilde: The Picture of Dorian Gray

During my short stint as an Extension Officer with the Ministry of Agriculture, I was posted in the northern part of the island (The Northern Division, by the Department of Agriculture dictum) under the supervision of Mr. Victor Stewart, the District Agricultural officer responsible for the northern region - which comprised the entire area from Barre-de-L'isle to Cap Estate at the island's northern tip. There were three other officers besides myself who helped Stewart cater for the needs of the farmers. Bernard Thomas, Carl Arlain and Lennox James and I made up the entire northern team at the time. Back then the offices of the Ministry were situated on St. Louis Street opposite the Castries Town Hall and officers were required to report there each Saturday morning by nine for meetings with their respective District Heads and other Extension colleagues. The hours were long and the work was challenging. At that time too it is believed that by the introduction of bananas, the St. Lucia agriculture and economic landscape was slowly being transformed. Some have argued that it was at the cost of a more sustainable and well planned agriculture, and others have counted only the weekly income from bananas and how this changed the lives of so many Saint Lucians. In fact it has been said that the island changed from one of peasants riding their mules and asses to one of a growing farming class driving their own vans and pickup trucks.

During the dreaded Hurricane season of 1963, the island was visited by at least one named major storm. Edith was a terror! She caused extensive damage to the developing banana industry. Immediately after the winds and rain had subsided extension officers took to the fields to assess the damages in their respective areas. They helped farmers fill the necessary damage assessment forms and reported their findings to the regular Saturday morning meetings, which were also used to exchange notes and ideas on how one should overcome reported difficulties in the fields, and to prepare a suitable itinerary for the coming week. These gatherings often included meetings with the staff of the entire Northern Division under the chairmanship of Victor Stewart. This senior officer was a capable and caring boss who was one of several Jamaican nationals who came to Saint Lucia in the early forties and who later distinguished themselves in the field of agriculture extension work. These trained agriculturists from Jamaica appeared to have been carefully hand picked by the British Government and they were to set an example of hard work for locals to copy. The others in that group were Harry Atkinson, Stanley Mullings, Ronald 'Speedy' Miller, Sammy Gage all from Jamaica, Horace 'Cocoa' Williams of St. Vincent and Algernon Pemberton from Dominica. 'Speedy' Miller returned to the St. Lucia, which he loves so dearly and now resides at Reduit Park surrounded by his wife, the former Patricia Drysdale and two pairs of 'children' from that love-struck relationship. At time of writing they were all in good health. 'Cocoa' Williams was of the same ilk as those above but he was from the sister Windward Island of St. Vincent. As his sobriquet implies he was the point man for the restoration and establishment of Theobroma Cacao (Cocoa) throughout the island. Another 'importee' who distinguished himself in the Ministry of Agriculture in the forties was Algernon Pemberton, 'Pemby', as we called him, who spent many years working in the field of agriculture in Saint Lucia.

Hurricane Edith came to visit us as these storms are known to do during the rainy season. Even with accurate hurricane predictions, crop farmers are often helpless against these furious winds that can top 100 miles per hour near the centre, (the eye of the storm) and the burden of repairing the damage done to agriculture and farmers' properties was indeed a daunting task. Still under British rule in 1963, and remembering that the banana industry was introduced and encouraged by British government policy, aid funds were obtained from the Colonial Office, in order to restore the industry and put farmers back to work. I was to visit all wind damaged farms and help farmers fill out damage-assessment-forms which I then had to take to office the following Saturday morning for totalling, in order to determine the value of support required in my area.

In filling out those forms I had one experience which has stayed with me to this day. That particular farmer (male, about forty-five) could neither read nor write. So I helped him fill his application form. After that I encouraged him to mark an 'X' where his signature should have been, on that form. I first explained I could not lawfully sign his name, for him. He then reluctantly took the ball point pen and proceeded to make a perfect backward sloping line within the space provided on the form which said: for 'Farmers' Signature'. However, the next line to complete the 'X' was a different matter altogether. That line was to prove a problem beyond any such thing I had previously seen. That farmer started the second line as he did the first but then he could not stop his hand within the space provided and wherein lay his first mark. I therefore calmly asked him to stop when he had marked past his allotted space but he did not stop. At that point a dialogue broke out between the two of us. He asked when to stop and I repeated "Now! Now! Now" even as he continued his gentle and purposeful decline unto the end of that page. How could that hand which had made such a perfect start have gone so completely berserk reaching and over-penning the bottom of the page and going completely off it? That man was inches away from me and I asked in a very calm voice why he didn't stop when I asked him to. He fought back tears and confided that he could not. Luckily, it was about 5.30 p.m. and I was thinking of calling it a day as that farmer was the last remaining applicant. Afterwards I invited him for a drink since we were doing this application exercise in the open and within 100 feet or so from a country rum shop. In those days these shops sold every possible concoction of bush mixes in over proof white rum which was supposed to be good for everything from rheumatism to the common cold. Unfortunately, it did not claim to add to one's intelligence or ability to read and write. I have often wondered about that particular farmer and what he truly felt that afternoon.

It has always amazed me that persons who could exhibit such dexterity with the use of a sharp cutlass and when walking to and from work cradle it in the crook of their arm as if it were the most delicate thing, could at the same time feel so completely intimidated by a harmless pen, weighing only a few grams, in those same hands. There is a certain blank, dead-pan face that stares at a pen in hand as if it were a witness to something alien and untrustworthy. I wonder what such persons would answer those who manned the pearly gates of heaven, when they are asked by what or whose authority had he allowed himself to be deprived of the skills of writing and a basic education.

Hurricane Edith had also brought winds of change to the political landscape in St. Lucia. The young stallions of the St. Lucia Labour Party, who had returned from studies in the United Kingdom and elsewhere, soon tired of the slow, bungling and inebriated products of the Trades Union movement which had thrust them into party politics – through no fault of theirs - after the granting of adult suffrage in 1950. The banana industry was set to be the new economic saviour of St. Lucia and sugar cane cultivation had slowly but surely given way to it. Those who were employed for three or four months of the year in the sugar industry now found gainful employment in the banana fields where there were weekly shipments of fruit and fortnightly pay throughout the calendar year. Mr. John Compton, who was then Minister for Trade, Industry and Agriculture in the Colonial Office - supervised government of George Charles' Labour Party, called the senior personnel of agriculture together and expressed his wish for St. Lucia to begin cultivating bananas for export, and that the driving force should be the department of agriculture as it was then called.

At that time the island of Dominica (another in the Windward group of islands) was already producing bananas for export and it was decided that Messrs. Sammy Gage and 'Speedy' Miller should go to Dominica to select and purchase the necessary planting material for propagation and distribution in St. Lucia. They duly left St. Lucia sometime in the mid-fifties on the sailing vessel 'Missy Wallace' which was owned and operated by Mailings Compton, uncle of John Compton. This vessel was built in St. Lucia by that boat building shipwright and craftsman - Mailings, who hailed from Canouan in the Grenadines. That journey was undertaken by the two chosen Jamaican-born agriculturists with the understanding that it would be a two day affair. It turned out that the ship's engine broke down soon after pulling out of Castries harbour and it took fully five days to Dominica and back. 'Speedy' and Gage brought back some twenty thousand Robusta plants from Dominica which were propagated at Union, (Castries) Errard, (Dennery) Beausejour, (Vieux-Fort) and Bath, (Soufriere). The successful introduction of banana cultivation to St. Lucia was undoubtedly a policy decision prompted by the British Authorities who held sway at the time. Its implementation by the energetic Minister in the George Charles government, John Compton, could not have succeeded as it did without the work of Swithen Schouten and several others. Other agriculture officers such as Cuthbert Henry, Lennox James, Horace Giraudy and Cadet Henry played a large part in establishing the banana industry of Saint Lucia.

Charles Cadet was also an early pioneer. He was one of the early Research Officers responsible for the establishment of the crucial banana industry (Green Gold, in its heyday) on the island. Granted that, at time of this writing, many persons living in Saint Lucia – foreigners as well as native-born – and to whom the name Charles Cadet may be familiar, would more readily associate him with the arts, and specifically his highly acclaimed singing ability. Such an association is understandable as Charles, as he is known by his friends, has thrilled audiences far and wide with his widely acclaimed music – a gift he was aware of from early childhood. By brilliant use of that melodious voice he has rendered many local and folk songs internationally acceptable and placed the island on a higher plain of musicality and international recognition. Included in his repertoire are several brilliant renditions of songs written for the listening pleasure of persons with a religious bent and an inclination towards an appreciation of a truly unique cultural form. His early pioneering work however, was in the profession of his choice – Agriculture. He was appointed by Superintendent of Agriculture, Swithen Schouten, to replace Research Officer Mitchell, when the latter left to take up a similar appointment in his native St. Vincent.

That period was a great learning experience for me and to have served with some of these men in the fields in those days, was a pleasure. The real Saint Lucia was exposed in all its glorious nakedness for all who cared to see. It has always puzzled me how so few men and women at the time raised their voices to protest the abject poverty one came across in those days. One of the few persons who did and referred to the level of poverty and the many children who died at infancy due to water borne diseases was John Compton. Perhaps because he too was born elsewhere, he could see beyond the ignorance and blind religion which taught the poor to focus on the after-life, rather than teach them to extricate themselves from the quagmire of poverty, ignorance and disease.

What could explain the reasons men had imposed such conditions on their brethren and fellow men? Better still what reason prevented those to whom the wrong was done from rebelling and casting aside their chains in anger? Are men driven to commit injuries through fear or through hate? If fear, then what was there to fear by those who kept these poor natives in such abject state of want? If through hate, why was there a need for those who were in control – including the church which supported them – to hate these poor, illiterate and largely harmless natives so deeply and completely? Such questions were still occupying my mind when I made the decision that the vast majority of persons on this island, including farmers, needed to wake up from their induced slumber and begin to transform their lives and create the changes which would bring them respect and prosperity.

In times past, the opportunities to advance themselves through education were severely limited and many have argued that this was deliberately made that way by those who governed. A view has been expressed that the people ought to be educated to find beautiful meanings in beautiful things, because for such people hope dwells eternal.

With such hope the citizens of Saint Lucia may develop the confidence to enquire whether men commit injuries through fear or hate, or whether there is a deeper, more sinister reason.

The Forum Revisited

For men commit injuries either through fear or through hate.....
Niccolo Machiavelli: The Prince

After the very successful launching of the St. Lucia Forum in 1970, the group decided to keep similar public meetings and groundings in all the major towns and villages on the island. This was a very demanding task indeed. It was made more so by the fact that we did not pace ourselves properly, neither did we make the most judicious use of our meagre financial resources. One example of the latter that comes readily to mind was the constant and accumulating cost of petrol, the most important commodity on the list of expenditure for such an ambitious island-wide undertaking, even in the early seventies. At that time petroleum and its by-products had not yet hit the centre of world trade and its politics. Its pricing mechanism had not yet threatened to turn those not blessed with that resource back to the horse and buggy days. The purchasing of that precious commodity was, for many in the Caribbean, a very expensive nightmare. It was far more expensive than food. Sometimes, the latter was offered at minimal cost to us by sympathizers. At the time the people in the rural communities believed they were forgotten after elections were over.

I often offered advice to the farmers on crop diversification, planting cycles and the best combination of crops to plant on their land to optimize farm production and maximize their income from the land. This I did on my free time in the name of the Forum, hoping to enlighten farmers and help boost the island's agricultural development. Interest in the group soon began to grow islandwide. This gave us reason for hope. Our growing mutual respect for each other was slow and steady and the more we visited and spoke to persons in the rural communities the less hassle we felt from the known political operatives who lived in those communities.

The lack of proper rationing of our energies did not leave the more active members of the group sufficient recovery time, before the next outing. It should be remembered that however enthusiastic and young as we all were at that time, we were all still actively engaged in our various regular vocations for providing our young families with the basic necessities for growth and survival. Besides, we also believed wholeheartedly that if we were to be effective in what we had set out to do, our first converts and most loyal supporters had to be our spouses, children and our extended families. In this we experienced various levels of success. And although it was only mildly admitted by some, this lack of support at home one suspected was a major reason certain otherwise useful members, dropped out of the group.

The regular visits to the out districts therefore became a constant challenge, not to say tiring, even bothersome, and took much courage to keep up with in the face of dwindling public speakers. Certain leading members had by that time decided on a safer and less confrontational and challenging path to their personal family lives. These drop outs we sincerely regretted, because it set back our work and we felt it would affect the long term political, social and economic development of St. Lucia. We felt that the broad education offered by the Forum held the key to involving the electorate more meaningfully in their community's development. To the few members of the Forum who were left behind to spread the good news of the group's call to a closer examination of ourselves, the task became increasingly more difficult. It required a mission of faith and a greater spiritual fortitude (and calling) to carry on. The job was increasingly looking like an impossible mission. On the many very late nights driving back to Castries and home, questions about the usefulness of the exercise we had just completed inevitably crossed my mind.

One wondered at times to what true purpose was the exercise to serve the people of St. Lucia. One wondered quietly to oneself the real reason that God may have chosen as he did for the mission at hand. How could one help to open the eyes of the people of St. Lucia, to the real power that lay within them had they been able to live and act in unity? Was it wrong for the poor to want to remove their oppressors from their backs by whatever means necessary? It was Franz Fanon, that great Martiniquan psychiatrist who first posited the view that there can be no real cleansing of a country, in which there is excessive exploitation and abuse, until that country is cleansed by the letting of blood. Fanon's theory seemed to make sense at that time especially to those Caribbean brothers and sisters who may have experienced racial discrimination and prejudices first hand. But how was one to explain this idea to a society which had been numbed against the historical abuses it had suffered. A more troubling question for many conscious young graduates of the day was whether organized religion had been part of the plot to keep the natives from any earthly rewards while their labour was exploited for the benefit of others? Should liberation only come after a bloody cleansing as theorized or could it eventuate by a process of slow, consistent and peaceful increments of progress? In short, what was the quickest and surest path to economic control and development? Would any other bloody revolution in the Caribbean have any upside to it after what Castro had accomplished in Cuba to the chagrin of the United States of America? What was the quickest way to rid St. Lucia of its self-loathing and mendicant attitude and bring it to the light of freedom, prosperity and charity?

During those late nights of self examination and introspection, while driving back home from a Forum assignment, one was constantly bombarded with such difficult questions. The answers seemed inextricably bound to religion and the way it had betrayed, destroyed and mesmerized the minds of those whose bodies had been enslaved by the help of that same source. These and other questions would not leave my mind no matter how hard I tried to replace them with other more pleasant and simple ones. They kept popping up in my head even when I had arrived home and afterwards tried to submit to sleep. It was not unusual to question the very existence of God and the inexplicable unfortunate hands (by every measure of man's teachings) he had dealt the African race. It was not difficult, at moments like these, just before being overtaken by sleep to imagine that perhaps the poor should take matters into their own hands, forget about all politics and politicians and just make religion and religious leaders total rulers of the place. But one knew that this was a cop out. Were these the idle thoughts of one who knew first hand some of the vagabonds and religious leaders that had used the name of God for their own financial gain? Did God have the power to intercede on behalf of the poor and exploited if those in charge did not want him to? Is it possible to have complete faith in a supreme goodness without at the same time asking why so much evil?

I often wondered how many members of the Forum harboured such troubling thoughts. True enough, we had made snide passing references to the 'images and idols' we saw in certain places of worship. But these were no different to those which other Christian faiths had made - and even quoted scripture in making their point - about the worshiping of idols in certain churches. However, neither the topics of God nor of religion ever came up for discussion at any indoor meeting of the Forum at which I was present. Perhaps at the time everyone present also struggled with the same questions and was too timid to say so. Frankly, we should have discussed the idea of God and religion more openly as we did other issues. We were all aware of the deep psychological hold which it had on the mind of the average citizen. We saw religion as an almost abusive enterprise of indoctrinating young minds with narrow religious perspectives before they were fully capable of making reasoned sense of religion. But this was St. Lucia in the early seventies where backwardness and ignorance still reigned supreme.

By late 1972, a mere two years after the grand public launching of the St. Lucia Forum, the group was all but finished. At that time the early and agreed declared purposes of the group were constantly being refined and reworked for the reason that only George Odlum, Michael Pilgrim, Frances Michel and I were left to carry the movement forward. True, others offered support in the background but we needed speakers up front, and on the platform. It is my deeply held conviction that the constant absence from family and friends - whose support was absolutely essential to continued political sacrifice – took a toll on the life of the political activists.

Too often one finds oneself in the midst of families and friends who are insensitive to any and all political ideas. They see no reason why any sensible and nice person should enter the political arena. I have met with many of my countrymen both here and in the wider Caribbean who are terrified by the word 'politics'. Why that should be so, I should attempt to speculate later. For now, it is sufficient to record my personal observation that the pressures of an active political life take a toll on the family unit which is unsurpassed by anything I know, save perhaps a medical crisis with high financial costs. Therefore, deciding to go public with a political view which challenges the very system of belief of the society, seems a sure road to failure. But once in each lifetime such a sacrifice as few men or women will ever know demands attention and commands the wandering soul forward. That is why I suppose there are so few politicians in the world who are in this class of leadership. The gravity of the challenge often places the visionary and thoughtful politician truly in a class by himself. I feel blessed to have been in a unique position to understand the challenges such people face. When they may appear to be brusque and impatient and even short tempered, it is because of the greed of trusted friends who attempt to exploit their goodwill and generosity. In addition, the growth of the electronic media has worked to ensure that the politician is always under scrutiny and he is sometimes followed around more than he likes. Besides, he perceives that the reason some reporters observe him so closely is that they seem to be in love with their own voices and would often distort the news in order to preen their egos. This happened regardless of the events which were impacting the country. Too often one got the impression that only those who were able to pay got the spin they wished for from the media.

One lesson which the Forum taught before I became more active in politics is that political representation is a very costly affair and persons who are poor in pocket ought not to enter elective politics. Besides, there is no financial gain in politics unless of course one is intentionally corrupt and unscrupulous. Political representation was believed to be completely outside the realm of personal financial gain, during the early days of adult suffrage. The mark of a truly great man and politician is that he came when called upon to serve, and then when his work was done he left public life no richer or better off than when he first agreed to serve his people. It is difficult, if not impossible, from all that I have learnt and seen, to leave active politics with anything but one's dignity and self respect. In fact, if one were to make a quick survey of St. Lucia and the rest of the Caribbean, it would be seen that the leaders who left the more lasting legacies to their country's development were themselves as ordinary and without property and wealth as when they first said yes to representing and working for their constituents. To say that such men (and women) died in a state of near poverty would probably be putting it too harshly. It is gradually becoming acceptable wisdom that it is far better for a politician to leave a legacy of a good solid name and a worthy reputation to his children, than to leave loads of stolen public money in overseas banks - or hidden anywhere else. Dishonesty in office is more likely to haunt a politician and shame a family name. Sadly, these truths only hold in societies where the electorate has developed a sense of self and moral uprightness.

Apart from the certainty of poverty, one more sting still remains for the political visionary who is morally upright and who refuses to compromise the oath of his office. It is the sting of disrespect for the ideas which he once sacrificed. The idiotic and senseless trashing of those ideas by those who have lost hope and respect is often a slippery road backwards to misery. This exposure of the lack of mental rigour is a sure sign of regression, however one chooses to call it. To take time to think and reflect is a responsibility that no true person of honour could willingly leave to another. To a young inexperienced distance runner, therefore, the unkindest political cut of all is the deliberate shutting down of one's inquisitive faculties. And if one were to take a little time to reflect, one would also see that the giving freely of one's time is a truly great gift that people everywhere can offer for the greater good of society. Giving voluntarily of one's time to help others is perhaps the most crucial element of true greatness. Thinking about this even now - and in the midst of global warming, famine and hunger, racial conflicts, tensions, crime, disease and war - those who are making the greatest mark to help resolve these situations are either volunteering their time freely, or are otherwise working longer hours than their salaries or conditions of work demand.

Time is precious and it is quite often the only commitment required of those who wish to bring positive change. Indeed, time is all that many people have to offer. A perceptive leader therefore takes this one step further and encourages those whom he leads (including students) to take time to think about the social and economic conditions of their country, its place in the world and what they may do to improve it. Individuals and groups such as the needy demand even more attention (and time) today than they did at an earlier period when the rest of the world had less to offer. In the heyday of the St. Lucia Forum, it was popular to read how newly independent nations especially in Africa were tackling the huge backlog of poverty and underdevelopment that the former colonialist had left behind. I credit the St. Lucia Forum's activities among the grassroots St. Lucia for opening up my awareness of the fact that there is absolutely no substitute for the personal care and attention in bringing relief to those who need it the most. The need for one's personal time and attention is by far in greater demand where the people are poor and lacking information and the level of official care, either rudimentary or non-existent.

While on the question of care, it bears noting here that much of the assistance which the Forum was able to organize for the poorest in the communities which we visited was greatly assisted by the goodwill of others especially the bakeries and grocery shops in or near such communities. The owners of these businesses know themselves and they may feel embarrassed if their generosity became public knowledge. There soon came a time when the community work of the St. Lucia Forum began to annoy the authorities in power. From that moment they began plotting and devising schemes to destroy the group. It appeared that the tipping point came when the group volunteered to work freely on certain public roads, filling potholes which were either deliberately neglected or completely missed by those charged with fixing them. We were informed by our sources that our messing around and game playing at road repairs had not sat well with certain Ministers of the government. In fact our scheme had sent a Minister or two into a fit of uncontrollable rage, not to mention panic and anxiety. The official response was first, to quickly fix those same pot-holed roads. Afterwards the jobs of the few remaining members of the group came under attack. The authorities claimed that what the group was setting out to do in its road repair job was to embarrass the government. The government Ministers for their part remained stoic, stern-faced and distrustful, cynical even. It was alleged that a line had finally been breached by the group which now demanded a stern and effective response. The Forum for their part swore that the whole idea of the road works was to demonstrate its passion and commitment to the country and merely wished to match its words with deeds.

That such commitment included the giving freely of our time to teach, educate and open the nation's eyes to new possibilities about its collective power, meant nothing to the authorities. The rest of the nation merely stood aside and listened and watched as would patrons at public theatre. The sprinkling of former war veterans who had served in the Second World War and who often had a word of encouragement, were now shell shocked at the government's attitude and they immediately withdrew to the background.

The Forum's attempt at mobilizing and empowering local communities to help themselves and not depend on government handouts soon came to a screeching halt. One weekend we organized the pot holing project at upper Water Works road and that had inadvertently invited big trouble for the group. But rather than be driven underground the Forum decided instead to challenge the government's excesses by joining a political party and contesting general elections. By mid-year 1973 we were members of the St. Lucia Labour Party, SLP. Our growing support base in Castries and in the urban communities had given us reason to believe that we had taken the correct decision at the time.

The obvious conclusion from our road project as far as politicians from both sides were concerned was that, if the citizens were able to help themselves, then they did not need politicians as they had been led to believe. And this I subsequently discovered first hand is anathema to every insecure and insincere political instinct. To this day, a few kind souls still believe that the Forum's message is relevant to the island's continuing social and economic progress. This especially as it continues to promote tourism as its new gospel of hope and economic liberation. If that industry is to be successful, the people of St. Lucia need to be nice and friendly at all times, to everyone, including the visitor. To sustain this attitude, requires pride in self and country. For example in the growing tourism industry it is imperative that each citizen - and not only industry workers - fully appreciate the difference between service and subservience. The latter may first have to be exorcised from the subconscious before the former can be allowed to establish and become a measure of discipline, sophistication and personal growth. That is one more reason for continuing education of adult workers outside the school syllabus, especially with the growth of tourism in the national economy.

Interestingly, the voluntary road 'pot-holing' effort of the Forum was one which the Forum believed that the then leader of St. Lucia understood very well indeed. It was well known that Compton's early claim to fame was his pioneering efforts at self-help in order to bring potable, (pipe-borne water), to the people of Micoud, which constituency he represented in the Parliament of St. Lucia. It is fair to say that those early self-help projects which he copied from the cultural folkways of the island, the 'coup-de-main', served him well throughout his fifty or so years in politics. It may even be said that his participation in self-help projects sealed him as a true friend and leader, especially to those whose children had previously perished from the water borne diseases of dysentery, typhoid and Bilharzia in those days.

Another activity undertaken by the Forum was the organization of a friendly cricket match at Victoria Park, (later renamed Mindoo Philip Park). This was organized in such a way that ladies batted right handed and the men left. That too turned out very successfully. The passage of time has now dimmed the cricketing outcome of the event, but the real outcome was to cement in everyone's mind that this was a new group of people who were giving a new name and a smiling face to community involvement. Nothing the politicians did could dampen the camaraderie and celebratory atmosphere which prevailed at the public functions of the group. However, it also became increasingly clear that we were not attracting new workers into that particular vineyard and that the time was fast approaching to 'call that George' - to pack our bags and move on, so to speak.

As an afterthought, it may be worthy of note that no member of the St. Lucia Forum who participated in these sporting events or who followed the fortunes of women in sports in St. Lucia would be surprised that the first St. Lucian to play a 'cricket test match' for the West Indies, was a woman. From the earlier cricket event the St. Lucia Forum gained a few more admirers which may have invited additional jealousies. The end result was a tightening of screws to ensure the final demise of the group. Those who were left persevered until the bitter end when fate and political reality finally took their toll. By then it seemed that the obvious political place for those who wished to pursue an even more public political agenda was the St. Lucia Labour Party, from where we hoped to continue the Forum's message to the grass roots.

The only reason we chose to join the St. Lucia Labour Party when we did was that the pressure to abandon the Forum had come from the government of the day. The other reason was that the majority of the poor and marginalized back then seemed to have gathered beneath the blood red workers international banner, of the Labour Party and all that it implied for revolution and change. On reflection, I think the most important thing which the St. Lucia Forum did for the people of Saint Lucia was to arouse their curiosity and consciousness in things local and African, and at the same time to re-ignite their cultural identity which had been slowly and deliberately eroded over many generations. It would not be an exaggeration to say that the Forum also stirred cultural activities on the island, especially by making Creole more acceptable to those who had at first either denied it existed or did not wish to identify with its use. It is also important to emphasize that the Forum never promoted Kweyol as an alternative to English. Instead, it believed both languages (and others too) could be developed and used as necessary. English, to our minds would remain the official language of the island. The group also advocated research into the orthography of Creole words with such research undertaken jointly with other Creole-speaking countries.

It was noticeable that persons who were at first hesitant to speak Creole in public were suddenly free to use it when and where they pleased, especially at 'Jounen Creole (Creole Day) in the month of October. The down side to this was those who had at first put forward these ideas on the use of culture and language to liberate their people had these ideas stolen from them in broad daylight, by some of the same forces that had always kept our people in darkness. People used the growing popularity of the use of the language to promote all sorts of peripheral money-making schemes, but the blue-print for using the language for full and complete emancipation was thrown away by those who were not privy to how the ideas had first evolved. It is still a widely held view on the island that Creole interferes with the way St. Lucians learn and speak English. Many of course disagree, pointing to the many persons who are fluent in both Creole and English. The secret may be the homes in which children first learn to speak. Those who grew up hearing correct English spoken and later learn to speak Kweyol, having been raised in homes in which English was dominant, usually end up speaking both languages to acceptable standards. It does not work out the same way when the early language is Creole. Translating Creole into English as one speaks does not cut it.

Unfortunately such empowerment can take an ugly turn, especially in its early stages as the dispossessed youth of the St. Lucia come to understand the disparity in wealth and see it as an English-speaking versus a Creole-speaking conflict and national problem. Sadly, the political leaders who are emerging in St. Lucia speak English which is lathered with a healthy dose of 'Creole' sometimes inviting ridicule. The national agenda for economic development ought therefore to be crystal clear in its policy on the language. Should the people be invited to consider themselves officially bi-lingual as the people of Canada for example, or should some other formula be agreed to?

The St. Lucia Forum was not formed with the idea of solving every social, political and economic problem which existed on the island at the time. But it sincerely believed that only a mature, self-confident and self-reliant people free of the psychological shackles which the institutions of slavery and religious dogma had imposed on them would be able to claim a seat at the table of international brotherhood as an equal and independent member. Since the demise of the St. Lucia Forum no other group has emerged to take its place. And having observed the island's development as a disinterested spectator might do, it is clear to me that if there is to be a holistic and integrated approach to development, there must emerge a national agenda which every political group and government must pursue, with minor differences- wherever these are deemed expedient - in the methods of implementation.

If the country's development were to proceed as a continuous series of miss-steps every five years or so when a new government is elected to office, then clearly the local bourgeoisie will not have prepared enough fences to keep off those who have fallen through the cracks of their skewed economic development models.

S.L.A.M....A Minor Distraction

*The Western bourgeoisie has prepared enough fences and
railings to have no real fear of the competition of those
whom he exploits and holds in contempt
....Frantz Fanon: The wretched of the Earth.*

Prior to joining the St. Lucia Labour Party it had become clear to George
Odlum and I that it was pointless to continue with the St. Lucia Forum. To
survive, that project needed many more workers than just the two of us,
as the main characters. There were too few workers in the local vineyard
who were prepared to come forward and openly identify themselves with
the Forum's important task of public education. To establish a more solid
foundation based on teaching the people to recognize their own power and
worth and to convince them of their potential for excellence and continued
progress was the core policy of the St. Lucia Forum. But by the middle of
1973 that dream lay shattered in ruins. There were several options open
to us, but we chose the road of joining and trying to transform the St.
Lucia Labour Party into the new politics of people empowerment. The
new politics needed a new language which was then Greek and Latin,
combined, to old Labour. Those who agreed with us were in the minority
in the Labour Party at the time. But we accepted the difficulties we faced
with the shrug of the shoulders and moved on.

The challenge, however, remained the continuous struggle to build a
more solid political organization with people who did not understand the
economic, political and social structure that that would entail. But was
our Western trained Caribbean bourgeoisie ready for such a task? The
dream of the early pioneers and working class of the party was by the mid-
sixties overtaken (and derailed) by an assortment of middle class aspirants
who were licking their lips at the prospect of political power and fame.

The former Forum members remained suspicious of some of the leading characters on the executive of the party, but we also remained convinced that this was a long distance race in which we needed to participate. We also knew that that Labour bunch at the time was unable to bring about the social, political and economic liberation which the country sorely needed. But before all of this there was the flirtation and a minor distraction called SLAM - the St. Lucia Labour Action Movement.

At first it was hard letting go of the St. Lucia Forum. We had developed a cadre of like-minded individuals who, on sitting with politicians for the first time in negotiations to form SLAM, were very uncomfortable, to put it mildly. There did not seem then a shared vision of and for the country. For starters those who were 'tainted' by party politics seemed reluctant to speak their minds freely and honestly. Although I was also committed to party politics I held back from membership of SLAM due to my job with the government. After I had discussed my plans with my family and close friends and had received their support, I decided it would be wiser to join the more established St. Lucia Labour Party, (minus SLAM and Odlum) if it came down to that. I soon tendered my resignation from the Ministry of Agriculture and thereafter was free to enter national politics. It was a tremendous sacrifice on my family's part and henceforth we would survive on the income of Carol, my dear wife at the time, until I was able to get my proposed landscaping business off the ground. I was encouraged by some Forum sympathizers who were convinced that my future lay within the Labour Party. One such person was of course my father-in-law, Whitney Mauricette and the other his good friend, George Murray. So although the Forum dream had been shattered, that nightmare did not follow me out of bed or out of the department of agriculture.

As the time drew nearer to a fuller participation in the public life of my island I calculated that there were at least three constituencies which I could win if I worked really hard. They were Vieux-Fort north, Vieux-Fort south and Castries east. By that time I thought that I carried sufficient name recognition and that my work in the Ministry of Agriculture was also well known by many persons. I therefore no longer had to sell myself as a complete novice to the electorate in the new game which I was soon to embark upon. There were to be certain dissenting voices, which saw both myself and SLAM as threats. These persons were from both the United Workers Party (UWP) and the SLP. I did not take any of that seriously even though I was aware that not everyone who listened to the Forum when it was in full bloom was an unswerving supporter of mine or of the group. I was also aware that the electorate comprised the same persons one passed on the roads each blessed day, and with whom one came into contact quite often as is to be expected in a small space, such as St. Lucia.

I had also set my mind to do whatever it took to establish the name Peter Josie indelibly on the political landscape of the island and perhaps even on the wider Caribbean. I aimed to do so in such a way that, long after my political sojourn had run its course, it would leave behind a long and clear echo reverberating with some substance and meaning.

In our discussions before the formation of SLAM, George Odlum and I agreed we needed a strategy to enter party politics. We determined to enter as Generals and Commanders and not as ordinary foot soldiers. We thought ourselves better in many respects than others from either of the two political parties on the island. Our only prayer was that such confidence was not mistaken for arrogance or vanity or something even worse. Knowing how fickle, Christian and hypocritical the society was at the time, we were always wary of that old colonial induced mindset, which was worse with religious indoctrination. We were aware that the contest was for the minds of the people. Sadly, we encountered certain thinking at the top of these organizations which was frankly no better than that of those whom they led.

Persons who had been rejected by the leaders of the SLP and UWP came together to form SLAM, with the remnants of the Forum thrown in for good measure. Those who had at first seemed reluctant to hold frank discussions were now eager to move forward. They seemed to have suddenly acquired a new spirit after it was hinted that veteran politician and former leader of the Labour Party, George Charles, would be approached with a view to lead the new party. Unfortunately, that new party - the St. Lucia Labour Action Movement - (SLAM) appeared doomed from the start. The main reason was that the person whose coat tails the opportunists wished to cling to in their search for political power, was reluctant to play ball. George Charles was floated as leader in order to try to unite the entire labour force in the country. I was also aware that there were other persons working towards the same purpose. I had by that time been introduced to certain key personalities in the St. Lucia Labour Party by my father–in–law Whitney Mauricette who along with George Murray was working quietly behind the scenes to bring SLAM and SLP together. They were also speaking to George Charles and his faction of supporters from the original Labour Party. For good measure and perhaps to have a bigger say in the discussions which were aimed at uniting labour as a single political force, SLAM suggested making a formal approach to George Charles, and invite him in as leader of the new party. But the SLAM horse was dead before the riders got onto its back at the starting gate. Those who thought they would use the George Charles card to negotiate a larger say in a united labour movement were to be disappointed.

Odlum and his SLAM mates may not have known at the time that Mr. George Charles, the former Chief Minister of the island had quietly become friendly to Premier Compton, who was alleged to show much kindness to the former Labour parliamentarian. Because of this, certain persons close to SLAM whispered in Castries that Charles would not turn up on the SLAM platform that evening. Premier Compton had reached Charles before anyone else had done and persuaded him to refrain from attending the public meeting.

I had also learnt from certain SLP elders that the bad blood which existed at the time between new leader Ken Foster and ousted leader Charles was used by the other political party to woo Charles and to treat him with more respect and dignity than did his former central executive. So I knew there would be no appearance by Charles, no matter what promises he may have made to the persons calling themselves S.L.A.M. Compton, it soon emerged, had advised Charles, to tell S.L.A.M...SCRAM! - Which he did. I was never a member of that group although I attended certain indoor meetings at the invitation of George Odlum. My role was to give Odlum my personal reading of the body language of those who had gathered at his Marisule house for the first of several indoor meetings of the new group.

At these meetings I tried to introduce the concept of an awakening consciousness of our African roots and heritage as part of the group's campaign strategy, but everyone went cold whenever such concepts were mooted. Any introduction of history was anathema to that new political party. So how in God's green earth, I asked myself, were these men preparing themselves to govern St. Lucia if, heaven forbid, they were ever to be entrusted with the government of the island? On what ideological foundation or body of ideas would they develop the country?

At that time, to refer to any of those potential candidates for national elections as African, would have been a great insult to them. Yet they were neither Indian, nor Chinese or Caucasian. Instead they called themselves St. Lucians and West Indians - a classic cop-out. It was elementary to point out to those who would listen that persons of Chinese origin were called Chinese, regardless of their place of birth; that Caucasian, whether from England or France or elsewhere were always seen as white no matter how they defined their particular nationality. Also, the Indian always identified with Mother India, yet for some reason people of colour had difficulty being Africans. Some Black Power advocates claimed the opium of religion and the psychological damage of slavery for that reluctance to identify with Africa. Many insightful scholars have also claimed that without the teaching of docility and acceptance and the reward which awaited after death, the institution of slavery would not have lasted for as long as it did.

It had been my strongly held view that those who were paid agents of the State and or of the local private sector had only one purpose in mind at the time of SLAM and the Forum - which was to obstruct the Odlum and Josie political struggle, as best they could. It did not matter who suffered or what price the island paid. Cold war propaganda was used to good effect, against the group. Perhaps this is a statement about the backwardness and fear engaging the minds of the citizenry at the time more than anything else. One recalls that Communism was also the bogey man that was used to break up the West Indies Federation in 1958 by politicians using fear and guile to divide the peoples of the Caribbean. Bustamante had told his Jamaica Labour Party followers that if they owned two cows the government of Norman Manley's Peoples National Party, (PNP) would take one of them and give it to the poorer islands of the south Caribbean. He could not have said the same for Trinidad because that island was blessed with petroleum and natural gas, and was therefore more economically viable than Jamaica itself.

Sadly, none of the new S.L.A.M. men were prepared to publicly restate some of the principles which were formerly espoused by the St. Lucia Forum. That of liberty, economic empowerment, pride in self and country and the right to think freely and independently without the humbug of religious demons directing one's path to happiness. Also of importance was the right to compete for the scarce resources of the world, the right to political independence, the end to discrimination based on race or gender, and the right to education and work. All these arguments were set aside by our detractors, who were determined to show that the new unknown whom we constituted, was contrary to the laws of God and nature.

Certain elements in S.L.A.M. whose parasitic instinct seemed always geared to latch on to others of talent in order to further their own personal agendas, were put off badly by that announcement from Charles. They suggested the cancellation of the public meeting but George Odlum, to his credit, would have none of this. He in fact proceeded at the meeting to put a nice spin on the night's proceedings by heaping praises on the absent Charles. Odlum praised the old warrior, and traced his record of public service to the people of St. Lucia. Odlum may not have been at his best that evening, but he must have warmed the hearts of 'old' Labour who may have seen new hope in the rumours that were flying all over the island, then. His speech must have said to the old guard that there was still hope for the man they once called 'Le petit Napoleon noir' - the little black Napoleon. Odlum himself must have made some new admirers that evening for sounding like one who had not completely given up on George Charles, and may have even wished to resurrect him that night.

That evening I elected to attend the first public political meeting of S.L.A.M. as an interested spectator and to cheer for Brother George and Servillus Jeffrey. Odlum and I had our suspicions about some of the novices who were to appear on the SLAM platform that evening. Unfortunately our suspicions proved spot on when those who spoke that night gave such a poor account of themselves. No one in particular stood out. The meeting was perhaps a peg above warmed over Labour Party stuff of an earlier period before John Compton and his pals left the party. I kept thinking that what S.L.A.M. platform lacked was the energy and zeal of a fire brand of which there were many in the Caribbean at the time. I counted myself lucky I was not among those on the platform that night. Such an appearance would have seemed as a fall from grace and into mediocrity from which I had sworn to distance myself. Besides, my avowed determination to have the people examine the reason each politician agreed to become involved in party politics may not have gone down well with certain persons speaking at that first SLAM meeting.

Every speaker that night went through the motion of speaking words without conviction. Their body language said to me that they would rather be elsewhere. I thought there and then, that even a secondary school debating team could have performed better than some of those men who had gathered on lower Micoud Street near Columbus square that night. If people who offer themselves for public office could not speak with any conviction, and did not seem to fully grasp the subject of their speech, then how were they expected to win the upcoming general election - or any election for that matter? The answer may be that there are certain 'politicians' who expect to be carried into parliament by the popularity of their political leader, and hide their incompetence and lack of a national image behind the coat tails of such leaders.

Someone in the audience disturbed my reverie when she reminded those addressing the meeting, in an ear splitting shout not far from where I stood, that elections were only a few short months around the corner. Perhaps she had been reading my mind. That same woman let out a softer but unkind observation that those on stage could not inspire her mute son far less the minds of the more active voters who were in search of new inspiration (and political candidates) for which to vote. The St. Lucia electorate, who, by that time had the benefit of listening to giants such as Hunter Francois, Henry Giraudy, Maurice Mason, St. Clair Daniel and George Charles among others, was loath to settle for less.

Earlier, I indicated that there was one person other than George Odlum on that S.L.A.M. platform that night, to whom I was interested in listening. He was Servillus Jeffrey who hailed from Vieux-Fort, as I had. Early in my public life I had considered myself somewhat out of the pale of the

Castries brethren who shared public political platforms with me. I think my newness and the fact that no one from Vieux-Fort had ever made such a song and dance on a political platform in Castries, (with the exception of Henry Giraudy), forced my listeners to study me a little more closely. So I thought that with the political debate which I helped to fire-up in St. Lucia at the time of the St.Lucia Forum, it would have been nice to have another person from Vieux-Fort, make a name for himself too. Besides, ignorance and hypocrisy were still very much alive and well all over Castries and it would take a bold outsider from Vieux-Fort to put things right. Or so I thought at the time. I had also considered the fact that Jeffrey, coming from the same experience of the presence of the American base down south, had to have given some thought to the extreme poverty that still haunted the people there, so many years after the departure of the Americans and their war paraphernalia, from Vieux-Fort. On such a night it would have been useful to remind the people of Castries, of the events at Vieux-Fort during the Second World War and how attitudes there were still militating against a holistic approach to development in the South. Jeffrey's public account of events at Vieux-Fort, I thought, was bound to hit some raw nerves in Castries since there were many in that place who were as destitute as their broken brethren, down south. Above all, I thought that his should become a valued addition to the voices of progress which were emerging throughout the Caribbean at that time. To say that Jeffrey played safe and defensively that night would be to borrow a cricketing jargon in order to save face.

Thankfully, I was able to see right through all the mischief and wicked misinformation that were directed at both Odlum and myself, around that time. We were painted as the 'bête noir' of local politics, when every one with half a brain knew differently. There was no logical analysis of anything we said or did at the time. The idea was to focus on what we wore and the image we presented in the public domain. No one suffering from borderline kwashiorkor (mal-nutrition) for want of a job or whose children missed school and were themselves too poorly educated - even after they attended classes - was ever asked whether the mode of dress of either Odlum or Josie was suitable or practical for the time and the place. No labourer or worker who was unhappy with his wages and conditions of pay was ever asked whether the vision described by Josie or Odlum either in Creole and English, gave them hope of a better future. No, those questions were never asked, because those who were spending their waking hours reconfiguring the future on behalf of 'democracy' and their personal bank accounts, knew the answers to all these questions. Frankly, we felt then that perhaps our opponents were too ashamed or frightened to face themselves in the mirror. Many simply refused to confront their own poverty of mind and spirit. To face a constituency which was similarly exploited was therefore tantamount to returning to the past of which these would-be leaders were so ashamed - and afraid.

So although much appears to have been written describing the insignificant stuff that was shaping the lives of the new St. Lucia and Caribbean peoples in the early seventies, very little in-depth analysis was ever offered. No one took the responsibility to invite the populace out of the darkness of its past and into the bright light of freedom, the rule of equitable laws and impartial justice for the haves as well as those who languished in poverty. Continuous references to Fidel Castro who had taken Cuba by bloody revolution from the hands of the dictator Fulgencio Batista - a facilitator of American prostitution of Cuban women - were meant to distract and frighten people from the true message of both George Odlum and myself. These attempts were pathetic, to say the least. They were also disingenuous. Part of the dastardly act of reporting and slanting every news item at the time was to keep the dying spectre of colonialism and its local surrogates in office. To change that situation was a tall order and so we knew that our jobs were not going to be easy.

To add to the local political drama, the entire Caribbean was on the boil back then. It appeared that there was a political virus which was affecting one island after the other. There was the incident with Patrick John of Dominica – former Premier - and the threatened overthrow of the government there. Then there was Tim Hector in Antigua and his Black Liberation struggles. And there was Maurice Bishop of Grenada and his New Jewel Movement that had at first been battered into submission by Gairy's Mongoose Gang, an imitation of the dreaded Tonton Macoute of Haiti. Then in Trinidad the army and its cohorts from the ghettos attempted to overthrow the government of Eric Williams in 1970. And of course there were others in St. Vincent, St. Kitts, Barbados and Jamaica demanding an end to exploitation and discrimination and better economic conditions, including better working conditions for wage workers.

It was not surprising therefore that in such an atmosphere, there were persons whose entire day seemed dedicated to placing obstacles in the path of the new thinking on 'their' island. In fact it should surprise no one that certain individuals with nothing to lose or gain were as determined to make themselves a nuisance at that time, wherever any sensible conversation held sway. Not surprisingly, at every street corner there were always a few vagabonds whose only purpose appeared to have been to stop the march of change and progress. In the early seventies on St. Lucia, Peter Josie and George Odlum were 'the change' long before others gave that phrase its added popularity.

I was determined to invite the people of St. Lucia to look with fresh eyes at Haiti and Cuba. These two countries had long decided to take their destinies into their own hands. And that has not been easy for either country. Why? Because the conservative world ganged up against both Haiti and Cuba and were determined to make them both pay for the audacity of presuming that people of colour and of 'third' world origin were capable of managing their own affairs. The U.S. blockade of trade with Cuba and the constant intervention of the army (with outside help) in Haiti did not help matters either. The frequent reminders by the Western media that Haiti was the poorest country in the Western hemisphere, without adequate explanation of how this came to be, are part of the continuing political propaganda. I repeat Cuba and Haiti may be economically challenged even in the twenty-first century, but it was always the view of Odlum and myself that these are the only two truly 'independent' countries in the entire Caribbean.

We were therefore determined to claim political freedom for St. Lucia regardless of where that freedom train took us. I was quite certain that the St. Lucia Labour Action Movement was not going to be the vehicle to take us there. Even an innocuous slogan such as: 'it is better to die standing up, rather than live on your knees' was frowned upon by the neophytes in S.L.A.M.

How then could one imagine that this group would ever agree to my constant harangue which was frequently issued to my listeners that: "those who wished for omelettes must first be prepared to break eggs". Of course such a loaded statement was expanded and explained and whipped to death far beyond anything that I had intentionally ascribed to it. Those words were meant to suggest that only by our hard work, improved education and continuous struggles would we achieve progress and prosperity. No one will do it for us. Those who wished to keep the people in darkness and delay the inevitable would eventually fail.

All of this and more was the new politics. Such straight talking had not previously been heard on the island. And my dead-pan physiognomy seemed to confirm that every word that I uttered was to be taken seriously. Up till then, the island had experienced only 20 years or about six general elections under the new system of adult suffrage - the popular vote. In 1951 the British had condescended to grant the right to vote to every adult 21 years of age and older. Hitherto, the vote was confined to those who were in possession of a profession or who had property of a certain value, and healthy bank accounts. It did not matter how one got one's money. The coming of adult suffrage gave every person of the qualifying age of 21 and over, the right to cast a ballot for the candidate of his or her choice, at elections.

The efforts of former political activists especially those who, like George F. L. Charles of the St. Lucia Labour Party, had been raised from the ranks of the Trade Union movement into party politics, were to peacefully pressure Britain to grant constitutional reform to these islands. It meant that constitutional advancement was determined by Britain and only in her good time as she felt the natives were ready for such change. The primacy of the role played by Britain and the how and whence the sources of such a role was derived was never questioned by any local politician in Saint Lucia or in the wider Caribbean.

The St. Lucia Forum (and Odlum and myself in particular) was to change all that, by attacking the power relations between the colonized and the colonizer. Specifically, we tried very hard to hammer an indelible new stamp on the subservient and undemocratic politics practiced in the island at the time - as indeed it was in the rest of the English speaking Caribbean. We were to insist that one ought to be fully in charge of one's destiny, and to do that we demanded political independence. We had taken that stand long before any of the Windward or Leeward Islands had done so. Of course our calls fell on deaf ears. How ironic that nine years later, in 1979, we were accused of not wanting Independence for St. Lucia!

We believed it is the duty of every true patriot to first determine which way the future lay and then to plan and achieve set political, social and economic goals for his country and people. To arrive on the political stage without such plans firmly embedded into one's psyche is, to my mind, tantamount to a guarantee that one would inevitably leave that stage a disappointed, unhappy and unsuccessful politician. We had always advocated these basic ground rules and the possession of a political game plan as a 'sine qua non' for every entrant into politics. In particular, I often did so with more passion and feeling than many would have risked at the time. Notwithstanding what some may have put down to recklessness I was considered a marked man from the very beginning of my public political journey. I was not aware then, that whenever anyone showed such a marked propensity for political change one was always very carefully scrutinized and studied by persons within and without, seemingly with little interest in the island. Those who refused to toe the line were always put under the most strict (and cruel) examination and sometimes became the subjects of suspicion and loathing.

In those days I was fully convinced that at an earlier period of world history, a Jewish patriot lived and was put to death on a cross, by the betrayal of persons who supported the Roman occupiers of their land. The young Jew, (Jesus), and his followers, had risen in protest. Without this rebellion and the events which followed, the world would have been a very different place, I think. Therefore the rebellious nature of the foundation of Christianity still fascinates me, and so it should, those who profess Christianity. I have also noticed that blind faith in certain people with whom I am familiar is merely a struggle to find that mustard seed within their own breast. One also discovered very early that how one succeeds in public life, depends in large measure on one's appreciation of the blind religiosity of a large percentage of the population, to whom one is appealing for support.

All of these questions and experiences alone with hard work and determination were to be taken towards the next step of the struggle, meaning life in the fast lane of party politics. By that time it had become clear to close observers within the Labour Party that Mr. George Charles would not reconcile his differences with Kenneth Foster, the new political leader. I felt then, that Charles had reached the end of his political journey and that Foster was then the emerging force in local politics. But my friend and political brother George (Odlum) was reluctant to join the Labour Party with Foster at its head. Around that time Ken Foster had met with me and suggested that I become General Secretary of the party. He also suggested that such a move would strengthen my political standing island wide and prepare me for greater things later. For a moment, I toyed with the idea of accepting Foster's offer, but I was also reluctant to do so without the other Forum members coming on board.

Frankly, I liked the idea of island wide party recognition, but I was not able to sell it to the others with whom I had by that time formed a strong and fairly convincing political partnership. That partnership I suspect was nearing the end of its useful political life, as it was obvious to me that the SLAM group should henceforth function simply as individuals within a new political organization.

Kenneth Foster was at the time both the de jure and de facto leader of the Labour Party, but moves were already afoot to sideline him by the formation of an election campaign committee to be headed by someone new to the party. Although Mr. Foster's support within the divided party was taking a hit, many were of the view that the party would bounce back if the leader would resign and allow another to lead. The general feeling was that the Labour Party had the potential for growth and that if it was properly mobilized, could go places.

I made up my mind that I would negotiate my way into the SLP, even with Foster as its leader. The general election of 1974 was closing in on us and we could not afford to sit it out. It was far easier, I thought, to use that shell of a political party, reenergize it, and from there work for better days. To my surprise George Odlum who had always advocated the idea of collective leadership – of which many were suspicious - was against the idea of Foster remaining as political leader of the Labour Party. I figured that all this negative talk about Odlum and I would be dumped after we had successfully become a part of a recognized and restructured Labour Party, and I shared that opinion with George. Of course he did not agree with my point of view.

But Odlum did not offer me any reasonable explanation for his reluctance to join the St. Lucia Labour Party with Kenneth Foster as its leader. But then in a small island with a small population, one hears things; gossip travels very fast. Such gossip is often embellished by the rumour mills to render them more authentic and 'juicy'. The 'stories' which were circulating at the time are too delicate to reveal in public. They are believed to be related to a brilliant female lawyer who practised in the chambers of Foster and Company. That person also happened to be George's spouse at the time. So to save face I graciously turned down Foster's offer to be Secretary of the St. Lucia Labour Party and also decided - for Odlum's sake – to wait and join the SLP together with him and other former members of the St. Lucia Forum. I was not informed whether either of these two gentlemen ever settled their differences and at the same time exercised the core teachings of Jesus to forgive each other's sins. Had that been done early, the fortunes of the next Labour Party Government may have turned out differently.

George Odlum and I were in constant dialogue at that time and I communicated whatever vibes I picked up at the first - and last - public meeting of S.L.A.M. to him. I was convinced that the public meeting of SLAM was being treated by many who had gathered there that night as free public theatre for the idle and the curious.

The middle class may have come to assess for themselves whether their loyalties should remain with Compton or whether there was anything exciting in this new SLAM group which would commend itself to them. To be certain, there were those who also came purely to oil their gossip mill. Their purpose was to witness the night's proceedings and then immediately thereafter proceed to put their own spin on what they had seen and heard so as to suit their inward hunger for attention, and mischief.

The consensus was that the first (and last) public meeting of the St. Lucia Labour Action Movement (SLAM) had not lived up to expectations, and many did not give the persons whom they saw on the platform that night, much chance for a future in party politics. But one felt that although SLAM cut a sorry picture that evening in Castries that the people would have forgiven them as Jesus had taught them in one of his core principles - forgiveness of wrongs done to us whether intentionally or not.

How I Met George Odlum

*….but Jesus pronounced that her sins had been forgiven,
articulating one of his core principles....*
Bruce Chilton: Mary Magdalene

.

How did you guys meet; I mean yourself and George Odlum? Are all the stories about guns and wanting to take over the country by force, as your friends did in Grenada, true? How did you sustain yourselves and supporters' interests and what would you say was the driving force behind your passion for politics? Did you ever fear for your life especially during the protracted 'leadership struggle'? Is there anything you would change if you had to do it all over again?

These are just a few of the questions I have been asked by friends and others alike particularly in the period following the leadership struggle, after we were out of office. Other questions of a more personal nature were often thrown in seemingly, for good measure.

Sometimes, I merely ignored such questions, thinking that I had said enough to guarantee any interested party a fair and truthful reply, if they knew where to look. However, for the sake of posterity I am happy to make the following observations.

I first laid my eyes on George Odlum at the time he visited Vieux-Fort around 1953, as the goal keeper of a visiting St. Mary's College football team. He stood out then, because many children my age gravitated near the goal area during a match. I noticed the keeper carried a very marked scar, near his left eye. Even as a child I remembered thinking that the man had come fairly close to losing his left eye. I was to learn much later that the scar was a result of a tree climbing accident he suffered as a boy. The other notable schoolboys on that college football team whom I vaguely remember were Desmond Sealy (Sage), Cuthbert Henry (Abdul), Garth

St. Omer, and David Auguste, younger brother of Laurie Auguste, himself an outstanding sportsman and cricketer.

Many years later at St. Mary's College, that same person with his left eye scar, had become a teacher of English Literature. He still played football (soccer) for the school. At that time, he was considered one of the best goal keepers on the island. Still later, after we had both returned from studies overseas, our paths were to cross again. This time it was as members of the Saint Lucia Forum. The details of this long association are recorded in several other parts of this book. They are the basis of what for me and for many others both in Saint Lucia and the wider Caribbean became 'SHATTERED DREAMS'.

I am also happy to say that as far as I am aware there was never any plan by me, or anyone else I knew at the time, for the violent overthrow of the government of Saint Lucia. Any accusations of this nature must have been scaremongering tactics by our political opponents. I have elaborated further on this toward the end of this work. I have also explained in some detail how Foreign Minister Odlum came to approach Prime Minister Louisy for permission to train a small selected group of young men in security matters, in Grenada, during that period, and why he felt compelled to do so. At the time certain policemen were known supporters of the party (UWP), which had just been voted out of office. These men seemed determined to frustrate the work of the new Labour government and possibly pave the way for an early return of John Compton to office. It was therefore for the protection of Odlum and certain other Ministers of the government, including me, that it was felt necessary to hire personal security, outside the police force.

We may however, have unwittingly added to the perception of an armed take over. Our strategy of constantly feeding information on the inner workings of the government may have made us seem too anxious to be in complete control of events. These moves seemed as deliberate propaganda to some, and to others, as a smoke screen for a more sinister move, on our part. Then for still some others, the election campaign and its results had signaled bad news for the island. The early press releases may also have served to remind our opponents that yesterday's villains were now the government of the island - and anxiety showed on some faces. Many had not yet adjusted to that fact and we were perhaps too much in their faces, reminding them we were the bosses now.

Therefore, the stories that one hears about events of the seventies are the result of individual imaginings of those who were not present and who knew little or nothing about me or my politics. Indeed, I have experienced first hand the stories some people tell about me even when they must have known these were pure fabrications. Such persons would go as far as placing themselves near the centre of their inventions, about me. All this they did in my presence. One could therefore only imagine what could (and would) be said when I was not around to correct those fanciful imaginations. Unfortunately, there will always be such stories. Some may even be printed and used as a means of income for their inventors and publishers. Hopefully, those who wish for the truth will be led to this source and to others who were present and are capable of telling the truth.

It is difficult to say with any precision where my drive (and love) for politics came from. Persons from my community who knew my parents and grand parents believe it may have been from my maternal grand father. Gaston Alphonse was a carpenter by trade and one of the best on the island at the time, I have been assured. His paternal grand parents had been brought to the island from India, as indentured labourers. He was therefore conscious of his Indian (Hindu) heritage and may have been more appreciative of politics than he allowed. When we were growing up, his grand children were in constant contact with him. I remember best his peaceful and tranquil aura. He spoke little; he did his job, and he provided handsomely for his large family. He fathered two boys and four girls. His skills were always in demand, even by the Americans then stationed at the U.S air base in Vieux-Fort, who often drove right up to his home to offer him work, while he was engaged elsewhere, and never applied to them for a job. He would often turn them down if he did not think he could spare the time to offer them his best efforts. It was the same with everyone else who needed his services.

My dad on the other hand, from whom some Vieux-Fort elders believed I got my easy-going manner with people, was a more outgoing, jovial and talkative personality. He did not suffer fools gladly and he was often accused of speaking his mind too openly. But that trade mark never faded once he was certain he was telling the truth. It never seemed to bother him that some people were not interested in the truth. He told it as he saw it and he believed wholeheartedly that his trust in God would see him through, whatever the consequences of his words. He prayed often and prayed long. Yet he was not a religious person in the way the plebeian world judges such things. It was impossible for any one to miss his strong inclination towards charity. He gave whatever he had and gave it without the expectation of reward. I often heard my mother admonishing him for giving; sometimes at the expense of his own family. But he never stopped giving even when he was down to his last five dollars.

On the maternal side, my mom was as introspective as her father, Gaston. It is from that side of the family I suspect my introspection and philosophical musings are derived. Her mother, 'Ma Doe', as we all called her, - her name was Edosia Etang - was the hardest working person I have ever known. I also believed Ma Doe was the only person I knew who was all loving and kindness. This is the only person to whom I felt such a strong bond, as a child. I thought at the time I would have done anything she asked me to and perhaps defended her with my life, had it ever become necessary. That is how I felt about her up to the time of her death in the early seventies. That quality of her love shone - and showed - in her eyes and even as a child I was aware of her strong magnetic bond and love. She exhibited strong, Carib-like, facial features. She hailed from the village of Laborie and was of the Etang clan before she married and took her husband's family name - Gaston. There was an ever present bright light which burnt in Ma Doe's eyes. I recall as a young man, I tried several times in playful gesture with her to look and focus my eyes into her powerful penetrating gaze, but experienced great difficulty in keeping my eyes focussed on hers. It was a favourite game we shared. Ma Doe had no match when it came to hard work. She took care of cattle, sheep, goats and chickens. She tended garden, planted sweet potatoes and other cash crops and walked the two miles to the town of Vieux-Fort at least three times a week to buy fresh fish for her family. I never saw her with shoes on her feet except when she went to Sunday mass or on the two occasions she visited us in Castries, when I was a student at St. Mary's College.

A frank and dispassionate assessment should reveal that both my genetic make up as well as my early, happy and secure childhood, were responsible for my passion for fair play, justice and politics. It so happens that I also came to believe that, for these three to prevail in a country, they had to be first created, nurtured and actively promoted at the very highest source of power in that country. Perhaps my participation in politics was a form of representation of all the unspoken dreams and prayers of my parents, grand parents and those of the many ordinary people who may have done a far better job than I did in politics, had they been afforded the same opportunities which I had. For so many of the past generations, their dreams were shattered long before they were afforded an opportunity to bloom.

After my departure from the public service I started a landscaping business which sustained me for a year or two. I had some ten regular clients who paid well and treated me with much respect. So while some may have thought me crazy for giving up a secure civil service job for politics, I was in fact very happy with my independence. Apparently, so too were those who had employed me to care for their lawns and gardens. If these clients were friends or supporters of Premier Compton at the time, they never showed it. I therefore owe them a debt of gratitude for judging me by the quality and standard of my landscaping work rather than by the measure of my political beliefs, back then. They know themselves and they may not be agreeable to seeing their names in this narrative.

This may be somewhat difficult for some people to appreciate, but I never feared for my life even when it became clear to me that certain well connected persons at the time, considered me a threat and a nuisance, to be got rid of. Incidentally, the only time in my adult life I have felt any real fear has been riding the subways of New York, USA, late at nights, after the rest of the city was asleep. And that was mostly about the city and not about the rest of the United States of America. In my early days in politics I took many risks, especially with the police. I am not certain why I felt an obligation to do what I did and how I did them. All I know is that at the time I felt a responsibility to try to change and modernize my island in the same way that other great leaders whom I had read had done in their time. I was aware that the time would come when those who were to follow me into politics would add their own labours to the vineyard of national development. So for me, politics was a way of serving my country and doing so with honesty and integrity. In this, I was so busy, there was no time left for fearing for my personal safety.

I have always believed that the political struggle to raise the standard of education and to liberate the minds of my fellowmen was never about me personally. Of course it would be preferable if at the end of the day something nice was said about one's effort in national politics. Raising the general standard of awareness of self was very important in Saint Lucia at the time when there were still such deep pockets of ignorance, illiteracy and lingering poverty. If I was asked what the greatest contribution George Odlum and I made on the island, my answer would be the raising of self awareness of its people. We taught the people to appreciate themselves and their culture and that being born with dark or black pigmentation was neither a crime nor a barrier to economic success. No one knew before the St. Lucia Forum came on the scene, to what great lengths (and beauty) the 'kinky' African hair on their heads could grow. If the drug cartels and others have targeted the long-haired Saint Lucia youth to use and peddle drugs then surely, this vice cannot be placed at the feet of those who first gave them the confidence to be proud of who they were. The foregoing are the facts as I knew them. I have written and spoken with truthfulness and candour as I have done throughout my life, especially on matters of state and politics. The reason I have always tackled subjects of public policy and politics head-on is I am aware that no one man or person has all the answers to solving social, economic and political problems of a country.

Politics and public policy are therefore matters that are always open to debate, discussion, and refining. To my mind each country must therefore fashion its own economic, social and political pathway based on its natural resources and the intelligence of its people. It is now generally accepted by international economists (and economic historians as well) that the rule of law is the most crucial ingredient - the cornerstone as it were - for economic growth and development.

This chapter on the relationship between George Odlum and I would not be complete however, without the input of deceased friend, Patrick Fell, who passed away in May 2000. Before he died, he often took time to caution me about my relationship with George Odlum. He feared that a free and innocent spirit such as myself was doomed to perish in the treacherous fields of politics. He saw George Odlum as a great speech maker, but not a doer. He also viewed him as a man filled with ideas who would not stay long enough to implement any of them. Patrick often reminded me of past divisions and split-ups in local politics and feared we would repeat the mistakes of the past. He was also concerned that I may be worse off in the long run in the Labour Party. Patrick warned me about some of the persons with whom I was associated in the Labour Party and sometimes he even called names. He never disclosed how he came by the information he shared with me, but his connection with senior Customs officers where he first worked may have held a clue. At the time I steadfastly dismissed him as one who was too blindly supportive of the government side to see any good in the work of the opposition. Patrick and I were friends from age eleven and we remained very close friends until his passing at age fifty eight. Before he died, he persisted in warning me about certain persons within the Labour Party and often fingered George Odlum as one whom he believed was merely using me for his own purpose. I dismissed such claims and just as often reminded him that there was more in the mortar than the pestle. Later, Patrick became a close confidant of John Compton and on reflection I concluded that he may have been trying to get me to do the same.

Patrick was undaunted. He was certain foreign businesses and governments had a hand in destabilizing the island and that I was too much a political novice to see this. All this was coming from someone who had never showed any inclination towards a political career or to anything remotely akin to it. I thought 'scare tactics' at one point but I demurred, favouring my friend with more principles than one who would hit his best friend below the belt.

Yet when the political events of the day forced a parting of the ways between George Odlum and I, it was none other than my good friend

Patrick Fell who agreed to stand for elections in the Castries East seat (Marchand) which I then represented and wherein he was born. I was at the time political leader of the St. Lucia Labour Party in 1982. Back then I had made it plain to Odlum that if the quarrel between himself and Louisy persisted, it would fracture the government. I also indicated that he (George Odlum) would leave me no choice but to stay with the Labour Party that we had both fought so hard to reorganize and build. George finally left to form his PLP, as we shall see later and the leadership of the Labour Party was thrown into my lap. Patrick Fell proved his friendship and loyalty to me and by extension to his country. Of course he was too kind to remind me of his earlier warnings.

Before all of this however, we must return to George Odlum and St. Mary's College briefly. It was a custom at that school for the head master to announce at afternoon assembly, the names of those students who were chosen to play for the school team. One afternoon I was encouraged by friends to stay and watch a football match at the Vigie playing field, near the airport of the same name. I was a little football fanatic at the time so it did not need much encouragement to get me to stay and watch that game. I have no recollection of the outcome of the game but I am happy to recall that it was the same George Odlum with the scar near his left eye who kept goal for the school team. The College custodian had by then made quite a name for himself between the uprights. I was taken aback that I had not seen Odlum anywhere on the school compound before encountering him on the football pitch once more. The reason is that in my first year at the College, Odlum was not assigned to teach any subjects with my class and I was too busy with my friends to have noticed any teacher except those with whom we interacted. Besides, the masters' room was upstairs at the far end of a fairly long building, where I did not visit.

After that initial taste of first division football at the Vigie playing field, I became a regular spectator along with my friends Casian and Karl Emanus, Lennard Cardiff James, (Nard). Sometimes I would stay and watch football matches at that venue whether or not the College team was playing. St. Mary's College was a force to be reckoned with in those days and the team held their own against such formidable opponents as Wolves F.C.; V.S.A.D.C., and C.Y.M.C. The College team was marshalled by hundreds of college boys who cheered their hearts out on the sidelines and who were encouraged to do so at every school assembly, before a game. Not only was the school team imbued with swift and cunning forwards, but its middle and backlines were equally skilled at reading the game and frustrating their heavier and bigger opponents. To top it all off, when the opponents were able to penetrate the College goal area, there was the school's 'Flying Darkie' in the person of George Odlum to thwart any attempt on goal. Odlum was nick named 'Flying Darkie' in England, while he attended Bristol University and exhibited his goal keeping talents to the surprise of many over there. He played semi- professional soccer in England which helped with rent and food. He had a pair of safe catching hands and his rapid reaction time often frustrated many skilled forwards. In his time at goal before he left for England, Odlum was already being compared to the great goalkeepers of the past. His only serious competitor for top honours in the goal back then was Vincent Devaux, alias 'Quayak' who kept goal for VSADC.

During my second year at the college Odlum was assigned to teach English Literature. That year, concern grew among the·young upstarts of form two, who were taking these compulsory English Literature classes, that these teaching assignments may have been taking too much energy from the 'Flying Darkie'. The source of these concerns was that our new teacher, Odlum, seemed forever to be dozing off before his young charges. Sometimes he had these attacks of sleep only moments after arriving to take his assigned subject. Some smart aleck – there were some precocious thirteen year olds back then – opined that, our dear teacher may have contracted the dreaded sleeping sickness which was then known to be rampant in equatorial Africa. Whatever the reasons, it must be remembered that teacher Odlum always took the precaution of giving the class a reading assignment either from 'Julius Caesar' or from 'The Merchant of Venice' whichever one caught his fancy that morning. Of course such readings were to be done in silence as any loudness would have disturbed our sleep-deprived-teacher. Perhaps teacher Odlum's demand for silence was also to avoid his class disturbing other students next door. Years later I learnt from the man himself – after I had asked - that the sleeping episodes were as a result of frequent nocturnal activities all over the town of Castries even on weekdays. It seems at the time that young men of George's age found such nightly escapades irresistible. It helped explain why his body shut down into sweet sleep in class. It was in order to restore equilibrium and strength to our night owl. I learnt the valuable lesson, from the horse's mouth so to speak, that the human body had no way of telling night from day and that it would shut down when it reached the limit of its endurance, regardless of place or time. I was also to learn soon enough that if one was in love with a remarkable lady, one does not regret the reverses and setbacks in life, whether they came early or late.

Soon after our earlier discovery, we were informed that teacher Odlum had migrated to England where he was to continue his studies in English Literature and related subjects. I ought not to close this tidbit by omitting to say that when teacher Odlum had been spared a hard night out, the next day he was able to steer his literature class to a forty-five minute period without dosing off, even once. Then he would be on his feet reciting, gesticulating, walking and play-acting his favourite passages from the works of Shakespeare or some other book of English Literature. In these rare moments, he did try to interest us in developing a liking for the subject and the wonderful usages to which good writing could be put, in order to reflect the full breath and depth of human emotions.

Time flies and before you knew it I too had left St. Mary's College and taken a job at the Government Audit department for one year. The following year (1961) I left the island in order to further equip myself to face the challenges of the world, as my father always reminded me that I should. On my final return to St. Lucia in the late sixties I learned that Odlum had been back on island and worked as Permanent Secretary in the Ministry of Trade. He seemed to have aroused the ire of the powers that be over their refusal to appoint him Education Officer in the Ministry of Education after he had applied for the position. Instead, one Leton Thomas (later, Sir Leton) was preferred. According to Odlum he felt at the time he was more qualified to handle the job of Education Officer, but that he had not really wanted it. The reason, he applied, he said, was to expose the machinations of certain local religious authorities in the affairs of State funded education. He confided in me that these religious types had deliberately kept the island in darkness and ignorance, thereby ensuring control over them. He also believed that it was these same religious people – he did not specify any denomination - that had tried so hard to keep the works of the now famous Walcott brothers – Derek and Roderick - from reaching the average citizen on the island at the time.

Some persons still argue that religious denominations (and religion) play too large a role in important appointments in the public service. Thirty years after political independence these concerns seem to be fading away. With such a reduction of influence, many argue that the island is becoming worse, not better, in its pursuit of academic excellence. At the time of writing, the jury is still out on this particular issue. To this debate has been added the question of transference of the island into the hands of certain leaders and top public officers, whose first language is not English. George Odlum must be turning in his grave to hear the daily slaughtering of the English language he loved so dearly, by those assigned to teach and lead this small nation.

1974 - 1979: Years of Struggle and Change

Beauty is the mark God set upon virtue.
Every natural action is graceful.

Ralph Waldo Emerson:
The Essential Writings of R.W. Emerson

For me, these were by far the most exciting years in the political life of this little Caribbean island. They were also a time of protest marches, fun, joy, beauty and learning all wrapped in one. It was a turning point to which God may have inspired certain persons to inscribe his mark of beauty on this island's politics. We had tested the limits of our democratic freedoms and found them to be largely solid and reliable. For the first time, general elections were to be contested among 34 candidates, in seventeen constituencies - one for each of the two political parties. Another six 'Independents' threw their hats into the ring, seeking personal acclaim.

The elections were held on the 6th of May 1974. Many felt that they were too close to call but most pundits gave the United Workers Party a slight edge in the polls. I was confident of victory in my East Castries/ Marchand seat. The Labour Party felt at the time that it was a better team to govern the island even though it had not sorted out the conundrum of multiple leaders levelled at it by its opponents. By then it had become widely accepted that logic and common sense did not go to the polls to vote on Election Day. Instead it had been observed that people generally voted on their emotions, particularly on their fears, and seldom on the basis of reasoned arguments. We were also aware that the hard core supporter from either party would rather stay home than vote against his or her party. We placed our trust in the newly registered voters and prayed that they would come out to support us on Election Day.

The tactics of our opponent was to either scare away new voters, or to frustrate them by attempting to omit their names from the register of voters and directing others to wrong polling booths on polling day. Scare tactics were being employed even on polling day. The fear of Communism and Black Power which was propagated by the United Workers Party seemed to have worked among some older SLP supporters. The party in power attacked the elections as if their lives depended on winning it. An important side issue for the ruling party seemed to have been to keep George Odlum and myself from being elected to Parliament, no matter what. The only reason I could think for such an opposition to the two of us was that we were not malleable or easily fooled. They succeeded in warding off Odlum in the Castries South East seat. I won the Castries East seat from Joseph Desir, a former Mayor of Castries – by a small margin.

When the final results were in, the government was returned to office with a three seat majority having won 10 seats to the Labour Party's seven. The reconfiguration of the electoral boundaries had apparently helped the incumbent to retain office but the election results proved conclusively that the island was split down the middle as far as the popular vote was concerned.

The winning candidates for the Labour Party were Gregor Mason, Gros-Islet; Jon Odlum - Castries South; Peter Josie - Castries East; Kenneth Foster - Anse-La-Raye/Canaries; Evans Calderon - Choiseul; Allan Louisy - Laborie; and Boswell Williams - Vieux-Fort North. The results for the Vieux-Fort South constituency showed that Bruce Williams of the Labour Party had won by four votes on the first count on the night of May 6th. By next morning that victory margin was overturned, thereby giving his opponent, Henry Giraudy an additional forty votes and a margin of victory of some thirty – six votes. In our first past the post system of selecting a government, one vote can mean the difference between forming the government and languishing in opposition, for five years. Those who were responsible could have given Mr. William's opponent the victory by a much narrower margin but they must have told themselves, why take a chance with single digit margin of victory, and later incur a possible Court challenge and an overturned victory?

Suspense gripped the entire island at the counting of ballots that night. A prominent member of the winning team was heard to say on public radio that evening that the difficulties in Vieux-Fort south constituency would be sorted out and that, it would be all right in the morning. Those words have been immortalized in a book of the same name and written by someone who has made a habit of making 'bread' off befriended politicians with or without their knowledge.

In the Dennery north constituency, in which Frances Michel was the Labour candidate, supporters who were employed as Party Security guards reported seeing ballot boxes taken on devious routes to the police station before disappearing completely and then returning to expose their contaminated and secret ballots. There was absolutely no doubt in the minds of the leaders and executive members of the Labour Party that both Bruce Williams and Mrs. Frances Michel were sidelined and cheated out of a seat in the Parliament of the island on the night of May 6, 1974. Those election results were therefore not a true reflection of the will of the people at that time.

It seemed to the Labour Party that the peoples' wishes were frustrated by the police - the very persons who had sworn to serve and protect. However, to prove our suspicions in a court of law would have meant a pursuit akin to a wild frolic amongst unmarked ballot papers, and thereby tantamount to a waste of time of busy and impatient Justices of the Court. Besides, every one with a law degree had by that time fully understood the full extent and latitude a lacuna in the law offered to Counsel on either side of a legal argument.

The day following general elections we gathered at our usual meeting place in Castries to lick our wounds, to comfort the losing candidates, congratulate the ones who had won and to plan for the future. The more militant persons within the party proposed a five year campaign of attrition, rather than sitting meekly and waiting the next five years for another opportunity to get into Parliament and Government. Everyone gave their assent to the idea but it was clear that the body language of some sang a different tune.

At that meeting we selected Allan Louisy as the Leader of the Opposition. Kenneth Foster, who was still leader of the party and had won his seat, unhappily surrendered to the will of the elected parliamentary minority even though it must have been clear to Kenneth that, in this game of Snakes and Ladders there were more snakes around him then, than ladders. Interestingly, Ken Foster did not put up much of a fight. For a while he was sullen and withdrawn, but then soon settled down to oppose the government at every turn. The writing of his demise (as leader) had been on the wall for some time before the elections of 1974 and he must have seen this coming. The Executive had pointedly appointed an elections campaign committee headed by Louisy, in which Foster had little or no say. The old guard of the party, which had stood with Foster, now switched allegiances to the former judge, Louisy. Perhaps their shared fraternity within the legal profession made it a little easier for Foster to defer to Louisy. Whatever the reason, Foster bowed out gracefully, meekly, even. Compton, the old Fox, read Foster's disappointment and maneuvered to have him elected Deputy Speaker of the House of Assembly. If that move created any mistrust for

Foster within the elected seven of the Labour Party, it did not show. The election results had clearly shown the people were ready for change and that a robust five year political/education campaign would overturn the 1974 result at the next elections.

During the five years spanning those two elections (1974 and 1979) the two issues which held centre stage were the Amerada Hess Oil Corporation Bill (known simply as the Hess debate) and the Government's published White Paper proposing to proceed to seek political independence from Britain. Those issues were, however, dwarfed by the mobilization efforts of more progressive elements of the Labour Party whose ranks were beginning to attract other young political activists.

The trade unions were by that time, fully mobilized. By 1976 St. Lucia was witnessing May Day rallies on a scale never before seen on the island. Odlum, Michel, and myself had taken over and reactivated the Farmers' Union based in Babonneau. They had expanded it to include farm workers and relocated its offices to Cul-de-Sac, Castries, and later to Grand Riviere, in the Dennery North constituency.

Many public political meetings were held under the auspices of the Labour Party, between 1974 and 1979. Those meetings attracted large groups of organized workers, especially from the ranks of the Civil Service, Teachers, Nurses and the Seamen and Waterfront Union and the St. Lucia Workers Union. These meetings were deliberately targeted in the constituencies in which the Labour Party had performed creditably in the 1974 elections. In addition, we continued to target the towns and villages, whence the United Workers traditionally drew its strength and which in the past were neglected by the older Labour Party strategists.

Both the 'Hess debate' and the Independence 'White Paper' debate were to heighten the political divide in the country. For a moment these two gave the governing United Workers Party the opportunity to face the public and to respond to the nightly criticisms of the Labour Party. By then the Castries Market Steps, which was Labour's chief meeting place in the City, was renamed the University of the People in the same way the Woodford Square in Port-of- Spain, Trinidad, was rechristened by the followers of Dr. Eric William, that country's first Prime Minister. He had previously used 'that 'square' to good effect, against both the American base at Chaguaramas and also against British colonialism, generally.

The years 1974 to 1979 were probably my most important (and rewarding) years in politics. This is because that was when I firmly established myself in the consciousness of the people of the island that I indeed had a contribution to make to my country and that I was not to be written off as easily as some who came before me had been. I believed at the time that I was cut from a different political cloth, and that I should prove it. My contributions to debates in Parliament and in the electronic media covering issues of national importance were widely listened to, and often well received. It warmed my heart when the plaudits even came from total strangers who had followed political debates elsewhere. One incident in particular stood out for me after a budget debate in 1977 or '78; in which I had spoken on a wide cross-section of subjects including of course, agriculture. Soon after the House had adjourned for the day, I was approached by two prison officers on the precincts of the Parliament, who confronted me at the same time and in the presence of several persons gathered there for the budget debate. They said that they simply had to tell me that a young Englishman who had been arrested on a drugs offence, and had listened to my speech that day on the radio, could not stop singing my praises. We had never met, but he wanted it conveyed to me that he had listened to other budget speeches before and that he was confident mine was amongst the best that he had heard. The poor fellow I learnt had insisted that I be told this by the prison officers.

By the mid-seventies, John Compton had established himself and his political party as the overwhelming dominant force in Saint Lucia's politics. The island by then had turned almost exclusively from sugar cane cultivation to the growing of bananas. It was experiencing a sort of growth spurt it had not hitherto known from the fortnightly harvesting and shipping of bananas. This regular income throughout the year was a welcome boost to the economy. New houses, roads, schools and health facilities were built around the island. The change in economic fortunes of the island was noticeable by those who had eyes to see. That economic transformation was to seal John Compton as the politician and leader who had supervised the period of most rapid and consistent social and economic growth on the island. It would therefore be true to say that Compton had taken St. Lucia into modernity. Unfortunately, such changes had left the weakest links in the chain of human development, mostly where it had found them. That was to prove the Achilles' heel of both Compton and his United Workers Party.

One can therefore well imagine how difficult it was for the opposition Labour Party which had been earlier characterized (and generally accepted) as the party of the marginalized, the low-wage earner and which had emerged from the trade union 'labourers' of king sugar, historically. It therefore may have seemed rather infra dig to Premier Compton and his United Workers Party that some upstarts would dare to claim credit as the ones who had led the country from darkness and into the bright lights of economic buoyancy and progress. It was a challenge which was countered at every turn by Compton and his UWP as they were determined to safeguard the gains which they had accomplished, by dint of hard work - their words - for the island and its people. If they had listened carefully they would have noted that it was not the material progress which was being questioned, but rather the lack of self-respect and self-confidence, even personal pride, which permeated the society every place one turned.

Anyone who would challenge the status quo at the time not only came up against stiff resistance, but was also treated as though he had committed an offence which was dangerously wrong. Even to be seen to be treated kindly was anathema to those who had given themselves permission to play God. Anyone who sought the empowerment and a more fully integrated society based on sharing the increasing banana prosperity with a little dose of black pride and dignity, was judged as lacking control of his faculties. The contest became even more intense when the divided St. Lucia Labour Party (SLP) was reunited under the leadership of Allan Louisy, and some of the young bloods who had returned to the island from studies abroad were now arrayed beneath the banner of that party.

In the Heat of Struggle

...and that for her to treat me as a human being was not only wrong, but dangerously so.....
Frederick Douglas, on American Slavery

By that time the leadership of the St. Lucia Labour Party had perceived some members of the police force as hostile to the party. Perhaps it was because the experience in the 1974 election particularly in the Dennery North constituency, had not been forgotten. It was for this reason that the party had asked its supporters to prepare for a long 'war' of attrition against the government. We communicated this decision by word of mouth and by use of the Crusader newspaper and the electronic media. We also made it clear that our beef was not against the police force, but against the few policemen who put party politics before duty to the country. We were aware that some members of the police service were sympathizers of the SLP. We were also aware that many in the police service were merely doing their jobs as best they could. Perhaps some may have wished to be elsewhere rather than on the streets facing hostile political picong and taunting, in the heat of the struggle.

Within months of his election victory Premier Compton sprung the notion of political independence for the island. Some claimed that he had made token reference to the issue in his 1974 election campaign, but it was not one which drew much attention because of the dismissive way it was treated by his own political party. To have brought up the subject again so soon after such a hard fought election was too much for the Labour Party to bear. Perhaps it was what it perceived as Premier Compton's underhand methods by which he wanted to proceed to independence, that unhinged the opposition. The opposition therefore decided that before this constitutional change could be foisted on the people they must be given an opportunity to decide the matter through a national referendum. Soon after that declaration the opposition campaign got into high gear. It organized street marches and public demonstrations against the underhand methods of the government. The opposition made it clear that it was not against independence for the island but that the government ought to do it right and follow the correct procedure.

These protest marches were to culminate in a massive show of peoples' power on the William Peter Boulevard in downtown Castries, the capital city. There was one major problem, however: the application to hold such a demonstration was refused by the police on the grounds that it would disrupt business in the city, and pose a challenge to law enforcement. The opposition for its part saw the police refusal as politically motivated and decided that it would go ahead with its planned gathering in the Boulevard. When word of this got to the police high command, it mobilized its entire resources in order to prevent the opposition from having its way. Even the dreaded Special Services Unit (SSU) was mobilized ostensibly to help keep the peace in the city that day. It frightened us that there may have been policemen on duty that afternoon on the William Peter Boulevard, who felt duty bound to defend and protect government parliamentarians only, in exclusion to the rights of others.

The thought had also occurred to me that perhaps among these policemen would be those who had been assigned to transport and protect the ballot boxes in the Dennery North constituency on the night of the 1974 elections. We remained convinced that at the time the ballots in favour of the Labour candidate had disappeared into the still of the dark night without a trace, and that could not have happened without the knowledge of certain officers within the police service.

A crowd of some five thousand had gathered in the centre of Castries that day. Microphones were set up for persons wishing to address the crowd. But before a word was spoken Deputy Police Commissioner Nichols, ordered George Odlum and me, the two leaders of the demonstration, to return to our homes and to disperse the large crowd that had gathered, before leaving the Boulevard. Immediately after this, when it became apparent that we were not moving, word began to circulate among the crowd that the S.S.U. had been called out. It spread like wild fire that the no-nonsense youthful Superintendent Martin Carasco and his feared SSU were already advancing towards the Boulevard. At that time the S.S.U was fast gaining the reputation of shooting first and asking questions later. With such a reputation, word on the ground of their imminent approach heightened the already tense atmosphere. Tension was mounting every minute, and one saw it in the faces of the men and women gathered there.

Another rumour soon began among those near the open stage which had been built for the speakers that the police were ordered to shoot to kill. The crowd grew quiet in anticipation. It would not have surprised me if the elderly then prayed for rain or some sign of divine intervention. It was weird to imagine that that crowd could have resorted to prayers as one felt fairly certain that many in that huge crowd had long abandoned prayers - and religion. Wild rumours kept circulating. New ones were invented even as the old ones were reconfigured and repeated. There was no offer of proof at any stage to any of the wild rumours. The only constant theme was that the dreaded S.S.U. was on its way and that when they arrived, there would be blood - that was their reputation.

Let us turn to Carasco and glean from him his frame of mind on that day. Here is the story as he relates it. 'On my return to St. Lucia, I was invited to undergo riot training under the Deputy Commissioner in the yard at police headquarters. What I saw there during that early morning training convinced me that the methods of the local force were outdated and needed upgrading. Even the equipment which was in use at the time, belonged to the old stock of late forties and early fifties'. Martin Carasco, with the boldness of youth on his side, made his views known to both the Deputy Commissioner in charge of the drill and also to his subordinates who participated in the early morning exercise. By his account, the following weekend he was invited by the Commissioner of Police to take charge of the riot drill on the police compound. His first order of business, he recalled, was to do away with the antiquated practice of policemen charging into an unruly crowd with swinging baton and riot shields at the ready, defensive position.

Caraso continues: 'I completely reversed the practice agenda for the riot drill and instead suggested the formation of a special, well equipped unit of armed policemen within the police force, which would then be specifically trained to handle terror and major public disorders. I named it the Special Security Unit or simply the S.S.U.' In his view that unit consisted of the best trained men (no women at the time) in the force. The equipment he requested was all delivered in quick time, making it appear that Carasco had the ears of the Minister for Finance and National Security of the country.

The specially built 'cage' within the back tray of the SSU pickup truck was designed to hold and transport criminals to chosen police stations on the island. Sometimes, those criminals who resisted arrest or tried to run were taken to the general hospital or even to the mortuary, depending on the severity of the crime alleged to have been committed. Within a very short time, Martin Carasco and his S.S.U. became the most feared (and respected) group of policemen on the island. They were also the most effective crime busters. When the police were informed that armed bandits and criminals were harassing law abiding citizens, Carasco and his crack S.S.U. moved into quick action in response. They often took charge of the situation and took the fight to the criminals. They achieved results, much to the satisfaction of citizens who feared for their lives and whose only recourse was the island's police service. The SSU was the fire power of the local police force. In the eyes of many they seemed determined not to spare the rod and spoil the child. The only difference, if we were to listen to eye witnesses of the period, was that the S.S.U. became not only the rod of correction but also the arbiter of final justice. This did in fact disturb some persons who believed in the judicial and legal processes which the island had inherited from Britain. It was therefore argued that the police ought not to usurp the work of the courts - even in a feeble and effete judicial system. However, justice was quite often delayed, thereby appearing to deny those who sought the protection of the legal system.

That explains why only a few people complained when no court of law or judge was ever needed when the S.S.U. dispensed final justice. Back then, death may have seemed to the law-abiding citizen as a welcome end to those who operated outside the law, and made the entire country seem unsafe. Those who had been terrorized by criminals therefore praised the work of the SSU. Known felons with a history of criminal violence were given short thrift. Few law abiding citizens if any, offered tears for the deceased. Therefore, one may love them or hate them, but one thing was certain, criminals cringed when the S.S.U. was on the beat with Martin Carasco at the head of the squad.

Peace loving citizens felt protected. And at one point it dawned on me that if either Odlum or I was taken out by the S.S.U. there may be some crocodile tears and many more dried eyes, especially among those for whom John Compton was God. Also, it was equally true that no one could tell for certain where such an act of reckless execution by the SSU would end. There were no 'Human Rights' personalities or national 'rights' organizations ready to put their necks on the block for us, who were considered by some diehard political opponents as trouble makers and pests. To be certain, we were never intent on any acts of criminality even though some political foes may have suggested or wished that we were.

Regular police officers were posted on the beat to observe and report on activities in the boulevard, that day. But the job of stopping those activities which were deemed either unlawful or criminal in nature was that of Martin Carasco and his S.S.U. Only the stupid, stubborn drunkard stayed within sight, when it was announced that the S.S.U was on its way. That day no one as far as I could tell left the Boulevard. The people were out in their numbers and they were determined to prevail. Carasco wished it to be properly and truthfully understood that the S.S.U. was a call of last resort. It did not formulate policy neither did it pass laws. It merely executed commands to keep the peace and good order. This meant that on that fateful day, the unarmed police must have exhausted every peaceful means of persuasion at their disposal before 'the death squad' as some locals then called the SSU was called in.

There was no blood letting when the SSU arrived. They arrived and took up their planned strategic positions. Martin Carasco was in charge. This is how he remembers the afternoon: 'Having made a determination that George Odlum and Peter Josie were the ring leaders, I first approached Mr. Odlum (Mr. Josie was addressing the crowd) and cautioned him that this was an illegal gathering under the Public Order Act and that he should disperse and send his followers home. George Odlum pleaded passive innocence bordering on stupidity. As I approached to speak to him I could see that the crowd was closing in around us – a situation not conducive to my own safety. With an air of total innocence which I had not before associated with Odlum, he stared at me with a blank face which I then interpreted to be asking to be helped out of the situation. He seemed to be pleading to be arrested and removed from harm's way. In other words Mr. Odlum, in my opinion, was literally begging for a peaceful way out and to save face'.

In a small island such as ours, the Police were not immune to the political machinations of men and their political parties. Also, it appeared by their conduct that the average police officers' first duty was to the duly elected government. Later we shall see that this was not always the case. By then most people also understood the country's process of democracy. Elections were held, a government was sworn into office, Ministers were appointed to head various Ministries of the government and that they were allowed to settle down and work. But that year would be different. Premier Compton had angered too many people with his talk of independence. The country would therefore not allow his government to settle down. At least not this time!

In such a situation more pressure was brought to bear on the police. Even under such pressure it was still relevant to ask whether their roles in the society had changed and were they now to act more as an army than as a police service. It was our understanding that the duty of the police was to follow the orders of their superiors within the police service. They were not to take sides in political disputes. On the other hand, the opposition also had a constitutional role to play. It may not have determined what that role was, but it could certainly decide for itself how it would oppose the government. It had already made such a determination, and so neither Carasco and his S.S.U. nor any other group, armed or unarmed, could have told us how to do our work. We were aware that they could not have been shielded from the politics of the country, and that at some point they too would be called upon as citizens for an opinion on independence for the island.

However, their first and paid obligation as law enforcement officers was to the constitutional authority of the country. Since it became an Associate State with Britain the island had assumed responsibility for its internal affairs and now the police force was under the full constitutional and legal authority of the Minister responsible for Internal Affairs and Security. The police were therefore expected to demonstrate that they were competent in maintaining law and order. It was such obligation and competence which were to be severely tested in the heat of the struggle for political supremacy between 1974 and 1979.

When the protests and arguments had finally reached a crescendo it seemed that the time for martyrdom had finally arrived. The moment, it seemed, and the man, had finally come together. Carasco swears to this day that in his professional opinion George Odlum did not wish to die for any cause or political party. Neither did he wish to die for any ideology or country. Carasco disclosed that he believed that in Odlum's mind, if there was to be a sacrificial lamb then it had to be either Peter Josie, or someone else. Carasco reported that he felt that 'Brother George' was virtually begging to be removed from the scene by a soft and quiet arrest at the hands of the police. That is before any serious escalation of action that might have ended in bloodshed. So if there were to be any bloodletting, Brother George would not have been around to witness'.

Carasco therefore calmly walked up to George Odlum, spoke to him again, then took another step or two towards Odlum, held him by his right wrist and said to him 'you are under arrest.' That was a very tense moment indeed. There were keen spectators observing from the upper offices of the banks and business houses on the Boulevard. One wrong move, and there would be blood. The young officer's eyes met those of St.Lucia's evangelizing cultural icon and English orator par-excellence, turned politician - Brother George. He may well have been the happiest man in St. Lucia when he felt the firm grip of officer Carasco's arresting right hand and fingers then tightly curled around his left wrist. At the time I was completely innocent of all the play acting between Superintendent Carasco and George Odlum.

However, it often happens that at a sublime moment of soulful introspection (and spiritual bliss) an experienced combatant instinctively knows what is to be done. Odlum must have sensed that he had outrun his course, and that he had played his last card. He knew then he had run out of options, and must therefore have welcomed Carasco's rescuing hand.

The young Carasco, on the other hand, had held his nerve as he walked bravely towards the Jeremie street police station holding Odlum securely at his side. He later revealed how surprised he was that Odlum had submitted so meekly to the arrest, proving his earlier suspicion that Odlum had hoped for such an outcome. Carasco said he knew for certain that he was doing George Odlum a big favour that day, one which he felt certain Odlum desperately wanted. By removing Brother George from the William Peter Boulevard Carasco must have saved himself (and many others too) from the dangers and bloodshed which could have ensued.

That arrest brought a premature end to the day's proceedings. It was well past six-thirty that evening, when Odlum was finally released to his lawyers and close supporters. The next move was to appear on the Castries Market Steps an hour or so later and once more to act the part as the peoples' hero and their new 'Sacrificial Lamb'. It was an act befitting Hollywood's best actors.

Here is Superintendent Martin Carasco again: 'After the arrest of Mr. Odlum, Peter Josie laid down the microphone and the meeting went dead. He started to follow and began a harangue aimed at me. On crossing the street and proceeding east before the Cox building, I asked Mr. Josie to come with me. He followed my orders and he too was arrested. The three of us then marched towards the Jeremie Street police station. Mr. Josie was never charged with any crime but I preferred him away from the crowd where we could keep an eye on him. I charged and processed Mr. Odlum. However, Mr. Odlum's matter never reached the courts'.

Carasco may not have been as innocent as one would make him out to be. That day he must have calculated that by reining in the big bad wolf of St. Lucian politics and his political 'twin brother', he too was playing a role that might fast track his own career towards the office of Police Commissioner. Carasco looked a fit and determined young police officer then with well fitting Khaki uniform, clean shaven face, bearing an alert pair of dark eyes and a serious demeanour. He took on the appearance of someone strutting his measured steps in victory. After his arrest of George Odlum, everything about Carasco seemed changed that day. To a close observer it appeared he had climbed the Everest of St. Lucia politics and had returned to ground zero, with little wear and tear to show for his heroics.

If the arrest of George Odlum had been planned before hand and executed in the way that it happened with me also being arrested, I knew nothing of such gamesmanship or plans. Here is Martin Carasco again: 'As I approached George Odlum that afternoon, my S.S.U. men were strategically dispersed to cover known mischief makers in the crowd, and to quell an uprising, should one suddenly arise. After the arrests and on arrival at the police station, the crowd which had occupied the William Peter Boulevard now found itself on Jeremie Street at the front of the police station. Carasco continued: 'We then had a new situation on our hands. That crowd which had followed me and Odlum to the police station on Jeremie Street also had to be dispersed. Thankfully, Lawyers for Mr. Odlum arrived at the station within an hour of his arrest and were soon able to fix bail.' By the time bail was posted for Odlum, the crowd had started to disperse, and upon his lawyer's advice Odlum encouraged everyone to go home and to return to the market steps at seven thirty that evening for the planned public meeting. Written police permission had already been secured for that meeting. Carasco later confided to his friends that he believed the fact that a police officer would dare arrest the charismatic and well liked 'Brother' George Odlum, Mr. Eloquence himself, was sufficient to send the crowd into a mind boggling, 'Oh-No' moment. That fact he believed, had assisted law enforcement officers on the island, handsomely thereafter. A positive outcome of that arresting episode Carasco believes was that the police were then thought of by average citizens, as being impartial in the execution of their duties. The arrest of George Odlum was perceived by many as proof that no one was beyond the arm of the law, according to Carasco.

To this day, there are persons who had followed these political events very closely and who remain doubtful, even cynical of Carasco's actions. Some believe that he and Odlum may have planned the show before hand. Within months of these events George Odlum became the Minister of Foreign Affairs of the government of Saint Lucia, and Martin Carasco was then transferred from the police service to the position of Foreign Service Officer in that Ministry.

Be that as it may, the facts remain that in times past, only the rich and well connected were treated special. These 'special' citizens functioned well beyond the reach of local law enforcement. In those days local politicians were without independent means and therefore had never seemed well respected. The foreign (and colonial element) always treated the police as overgrown Boy Scouts with little ability to think clearly and wisely for themselves. They were therefore to be told what their duties were, including who they should arrest.

John Compton, who rose from Chief Minister, to Premier and then Prime Minister of St. Lucia, was one of the most successful and longest serving politicians in the entire Caribbean. He too was arrested when he attempted to lead a march of sugar cane workers in a demonstration against the owners of the Dennery Sugar Estates in 1957. To this day, no one in private business, buying low and selling as high as the market would bear, has ever been arrested and charged for price gouging or for any other crime, including corruption or falsifying customs declarations. Today, it seems just as easy for a policeman, especially one who has strong political views, to arrest a practising politician - even a Minister of the government - who is deemed to have run foul of the law. The precedent had been set and precedent is a major pillar of our laws. Surely, it would do local law enforcement a whole lot of good the day they are able to arrest corrupt and scheming business men. And also to do it without any malice or partisan political biases encouraged from behind the scene by bosses who are determined to free such culprits without as much as a slap on the wrist.

For those interested in such matters, it should be repeated that the charges against Odlum never reached the courts. Why? Everyone seemed to have agreed those arrests were executed as an aid to dispersing a large politically motivated and restless crowd. The Odlum and Josie arrests had therefore served their primary purpose - that of keeping the peace.

Obviously, those responsible for wanting a quiet transition to a new constitution for an independent Saint Lucia did not wish to draw too much attention to them. To have the spotlight moved from the public streets to the quieter Courts of law would only serve to enhance the martyrdom that Odlum and others were accused of seeking. One should therefore not be surprised when future politicians decide that the indignity and embarrassment of a public arrest may be worth the end result of power. Certain persons believed that these highly advertised moves by the police on known public figures whose politics they do not like, is a very serious matter. Such conduct can have lasting consequences if not nipped in the bud. Besides constituting unfair harassment of public figures, such arrests can be designed to remove the spotlight from the more dangerous criminals on the island. It is common knowledge that some of the well connected have been known to get away with many serious crimes, - a feature not unknown in other Caribbean countries.

After his release form the Port Police Station where he was detained for about ninety minutes, George Odlum and his Labour Party followers were soon at it again. The 'Do it right' anti-independence protest marches continued to be organized. The difference this time was that the Public

Order Act had become law. It was foolish to continue to disregard the new laws. Unfortunately for the protesters, its provisions were used to control and direct the opposition marches into parts of the island where no one lived. In effect, protesters were sent to march among banana plantations, in the Cul-de-Sac valley, for example. Only the desperate and political fanatic came to these far off people-less places. The opposition was not amused by the police and government strategy in this latest insult. Both entities fully understood that these public marches were meant to demonstrate the resolve of the opposition in its 'do it right' campaign. The opposition would therefore have preferred to march amongst the ready-made audience of curious onlookers in the city, rather than in empty country roads among banana fields.

By then Compton's Government was midway into its five year parliamentary term of office. It was now 1977. In late 1976 the government of St. Lucia laid the proposals for moving the island to political independence before the expiration of the parliamentary term. The 'Ayes' had it yet again. Compton had his way but only after a long spirited debate, which lasted two days, and which went well past 11.30 p.m, on both days. At that debate, the Standing Orders of the Parliament had not yet been amended to place time limits upon the speeches of Honourable Members. Back then, the speaking time allotted to a member was without a limit. Each member was therefore allowed to fully express his views on the independence debate. The Parliament Chamber was packed to capacity as St. Lucians showed their interest in the independence issue. The grounds surrounding the Parliament were abuzz with curious citizens who were unable to find seats in the parliament gallery.

When my turn came to address the House of Assembly that day, I executed a speech I had waited many years to deliver. It was the most emotional speech ever delivered by me during my time in politics. I had by then learnt the art of controlling my breathing and harnessing my emotions to good effect. It was a credible performance even though I say this myself. It was the first and only time I was warmly congratulated by members opposite. When I had finished, I had spoken for a total of five hours, a record for Parliament then, but a pyrrhic victory for those who were opposed to independence. One of the unforeseen outcomes of my marathon contribution to the debate was that soon thereafter the Standing Rules and Orders of the Parliament were amended to allow each Member just one hour to make his/her contribution on any matter on the Order paper. So the one hour speaking time may truly be described as the Peter Josie amendment.

Perhaps in time, that particular standing rule of the Parliament will again be reversed and that each member would be allowed the latitude afforded by the earlier rule. This may well happen when more citizens begin to assume a deeper, more purposeful involvement in the political affairs of their country. My constant prayer is that when the Parliament shall delete the one hour limit and revert to the zero time limit on a member's speaking time, that rule would not be abused. The liberty to speak for as long as one wishes on any matter deemed to be deserving of full analysis and discussion before the peoples' Parliament, should be jealously guarded and cast into clearly written law.

Following the debate on the government's proposal to take the island to political independence, the Foreign and Commonwealth Office of Her Majesty's Government in London, invited a delegation from both sides of Parliament in St. Lucia to talks in London. This was ostensibly to explore whether the island wanted to become independent or not. It was at this stage that the real fun and games began on the road to independence.

Now it was as if all the drama and political manoeuvring had been towards that final step to freedom. But it was a step which had been initiated by the former colonial power in keeping with its new policy of closer unity with its neighbours in Europe.

Invitation to Talks in London

This island is heaven –
away from the dust blown blood of cities…
Derek Walcott: As John to Patmos;
(Collected poems).

At the instance of the Foreign and Commonwealth Office in London, (F.C.O.) the Government of St. Lucia as well as Her Majesty's Loyal Opposition were invited to England to meet with the Minister with responsibility for the Caribbean, Mr. Ted Rowlands. The governing party, led by Premier John Compton, celebrated this invitation as it would an election victory. To hear their supporters tell it in public, one could be forgiven for thinking that independence was a done deal. The date of December 13, 1978 first suggested by Premier Compton was touted about by party stalwarts as the agreed time when the island would be finally set free to manage its external relations and its own defense – independence.

For its part, the Opposition received the news of the invitation with trepidation and foreboding. It seemed to confirm their long held suspicion that someone in the British government had taken a special liking to Premier Compton and wished to entrust an Independent St. Lucia to his continued leadership. The invitation threw the senior members of the opposition party's central executive committee on the horns of a dilemma. The party had long proclaimed in its aims and objectives the idea of liberty and Nationhood - thereby strongly hinting at political independence and freedom. Yet it questioned the undue haste with which Britain now wished to sever its remaining ties with the island and by so doing invited many raised eyebrows from friends both at home and abroad.

The elders did not appreciate the confrontational methods of the young Turks within the party, but reluctantly admitted that, perhaps the time for a more aggressive tactic in its national mobilization drive against the hijacking of the consultative process, was the best approach. It determined that no quiet, give-and-take negotiations were possible in a situation in which only one side was prepared to compromise. It rejected the idea of surrendering ground to the government and risk diluting the principles for which it stood. Still, it knew that without compromise there would be no progress. The game was not cricket, and the British knew it!

The opposition also knew that the dice was loaded against it. It wisely decided on a course of constructive engagement by actively participating in the talks leading to independence for St. Lucia. It feared that any refusal to participate would be interpreted as an abdication of the important duty it owed the people of St. Lucia. It also figured that the moment in history called for a robust demonstration of the views of the parliamentary opposition to the Government and most of all, to the people themselves.

The onus was therefore on the Leader of the Opposition, Honourable Allan Louisy, (later, Sir Allan) to whom Minister Rowlands had addressed his letter of invitation, to decide which of the other six members of the St. Lucia parliamentary opposition would accompany him to London. The invitation had suggested a date in March 1977, and it allowed for two days of discussions. The agenda was quite specific. It was to report progress of the independence consultations at home and any other relevant matters. To this end therefore, the Leader of the Opposition, after consultation, decided that I was the best person to accompany him to London. I did not ask how he arrived at that decision, neither did he volunteer. I also felt then, there was no other who had demonstrated the propensity to debate the issue of independence and to retrace the road we had journeyed as a people, bringing us to where we were then. It took much courage to convince the largely backward, indoctrinated people to see themselves as equal to any other and to appreciate the justice of the educational, public and progressive political stand I had consistently taken on the question of political independence and economic liberation for the people of St. Lucia and the Caribbean. So I readily agreed to accompany Louisy in presenting the opposition's view to Minister Rowlands, on the matter of independence for St. Lucia.

I was of the mature age of 35 and sufficiently familiar with aspects of constitutional, legal, political and moral reform which I thought ought to guide a progressive nation/state. My only niggling concern was whether the leader, Louisy, was up to the task. My detractors, of whom there were many at the time, were spiteful in their concern that I may proceed to bang the polished mahogany at the ornate offices of the F.C.O. with my shoes, (a'la mode Nikita Khrushchev, of the U.S.S.R. at the U. N. General Assembly at the height of the cold war in the early-sixties).

Having accepted the invitation to accompany the Leader of the Opposition to the talks, I found myself confronted with an immediate challenge. George Odlum, with whom I was by that time inextricably linked in matters of local politics, approached me and suggested that I should remain in St. Lucia and not accompany Louisy to London. The reason he gave was that by my presence I would legitimize the process of the 'talks' and henceforth, the call by the opposition to 'do it right' would sound hollow and without merit. Of course I disagreed with Odlum totally and I spared few words to let him know how I felt about his suggestion. I interpreted it as deliberately placing an obstacle in the path which was not completely of my own creation. I felt that the peoples' business came first. I was conscious of the confidence they had reposed in me by their vote in 1974 and that I was now duty bound to honour that trust. I had pledged to serve my constituents and country the best that I could. I also knew that my attendance at these talks was bound to raise a more positive image of me than that I had hitherto enjoyed on the island. I was therefore determined to show leadership when it was called for, rather than to appear in the shadows of those who wished to project me as a bit player in their political show. At the time I was a Member of Parliament and George Odlum was not, so I could not let him or anyone else decide whether I should accept Allan Louisy's invitation to accompany him to London. This was therefore my call and no one else's. Besides, it was a privilege to be selected by one with such vast experience as Louisy, especially when there were three lawyers and other capable men to choose from. I saw the invitation by Louisy as an indication that it was my time to shine.

Furthermore, a change of mind on my part would ring hollow and untrue with the flimsy excuse George Odlum had offered me. To turn down that invitation without a plan 'B' would seem even more absurd given the opposition's stance on the independence issue. Besides, I asked myself who would speak for the leaderless masses on the island if I did not accompany Louisy to London? Who would deliver to Rowlands the sense of mistrust and foreboding felt by so many at the time, given what had taken place at the 1974 elections? If I were to change my mind at this eleventh hour and Louisy was to attend the talks all by himself, he would then look rather silly, since he was the one who had asked to be accompanied to the talks in the first place.

What I did not tell my friend 'Brother George' at the time, was that I thought perhaps he was a little jealous and even a little fearful, that my true worth would be exposed in a positive light without the distraction of his ample shadow. I believed in my heart that each person is presented at least once in his or her life time with such an historic moment. I could not therefore, in good conscience, reject this golden opportunity to help shape what would be forever etched in the annals of my island's quest for political freedom and economic self-determination. I may not have agreed with the method employed by Premier Compton, but I had argued more strongly than most for the total emancipation and conscious elimination of the shackles of illiteracy and ignorance which bound so many Saint Lucians to lives of poverty, hunger, and disease. Only a free and independent St. Lucia could change that. Of course, back then I was seen by many as an incurable radical who might plunge Saint Lucia into the hands of the communist/socialist/black power ideological maelstrom, at any moment. It was a new monster my opponents had invented in order to protect their own narrow financial and political interests. Time would prove that the electorate did not take them seriously. Only the enemies within the Labour Party were able to shatter my dreams - which they never stopped trying to achieve.

Such political opponents were to my way of thinking, only interested in maximizing their profit margins and siphoning these profits as quickly as possible to external banks. It was and always has been, in the interest of such persons to keep the true patriot quiet at best and to silence him in whatever way they could, at worst. To make matters worse there were always pliable and anxious simpletons of dubious character and shady connections who were willing to throw their hats into the political ring, in anticipation of promised rewards. This was a situation which has threatened to become more widespread over time, even as the country offered more opportunities each year to institutions of higher learning.

When all was said and done it could have been truthfully reported that Louisy and I gave a fairly good account of ourselves at the first round of constitutional talks in London. Premier Compton and his friend Henry Giraudy also represented the government's case as best they could. Soon the spotlight was to shift to the second and third round of talks and the entire population waited with baited breath to see where (and when) these talks would all end.

The significance of the moment was not lost on my bias towards history. I kept recalling the words of C.L.R. James in his book 'The Black Jacobins' in which he observed that, 'no mulatto whatever his number of white parts could ever take the name of his father' and wondered to myself what might have been the outcome of such talks had the island been represented by white Englishmen who had settled there and not by the sons of former African slaves.

Preparing for London

...No Mulatto, therefore, whatever his number of white parts,
was allowed to assume the name of his white father.
C. L. R. James: The Black Jacobins.

Once I had accepted the invitation from the Leader of the Opposition to accompany him to London, I began making preparations for the exchanges which were to take place, and which would have to be informed by reason backed up by factual information. Even conjectures and opinions would have to be properly thought out and cogently argued. And I felt supremely confident and up to the task which awaited us. Even my opponents knew I could do this. In preparation I also began to ponder the most suitable dress code for the formal part of the talks as well as for those informal occasions with interested officials and other important British Parliamentarians that had been arranged. The informal sessions were also to include St. Lucians living in England. I also had to think of how I might wish to spend 'free' time with family and friends in London whom I had missed on my first visit three years earlier. The Leader of the Opposition and I arranged private exchanges at which we discussed the tactics and strategies we were to adopt at the talks.

Premier Compton had chosen his trusted friend and long standing party chairman, Henry Giraudy, a lawyer by training, to accompany him to London. The St. Lucia delegation was therefore John Compton, (Premier) Henry Giraudy, (Legal Adviser) Allan Louisy (Leader of the Opposition) and myself (Peter Josie), Member of Parliament. Three lawyers - and an unlikely fourth person who was a young Agronomist - and an inexperienced novice to the parliamentary political stage. 'And yet this young man was fully supported on the ground in St. Lucia by the grass roots he helped empower with information about their past; the uses and abuses of Capitalism and Slavery; and the post colonial difficulties of leaders wishing to cut a new and independent economic and political path for their peoples' as John Francis, a kind soul had remarked at a private party in London. The road ahead would not be easy. At the heart and centre of our imposed political system was the adversarial two-party structure which seemed to have been designed to ensure the frustration of over ambitious leaders by an electorate more concerned with its daily bread, rather than grand plans for the future. I was deeply disillusioned that many of the early radicals and intellectuals of Caribbean politics had openly and meekly bowed to this particular divisive system - in which brother fought against brother - without offering a more suitable adaptation or an alternative. Such a system was to divide families over small crumbs of economic assistance which were often given (and accepted) with reluctance and disdain. This, while those who were the architects of the cunning divisive system, remained on the sidelines and watched native politicians destroy each other - and their country - in the name of democracy. Such divisions were to create more poverty and strife at home from which others with little or no interest in the island benefitted.

Before the St. Lucia delegation left for London, it was reported that on March 15th 1977, a delegation from the Government of Dominica under Premier Patrick John, had entered talks with the British Government in the United Kingdom leading to political independence for that island. A release from the British Government Representative in Castries at the time, Eric Le Tocq, boldly predicted a successful outcome to these talks, leading to political independence for Dominica. He also vaguely suggested that St. Lucia would follow a similar pattern. By then it would have been very difficult to doubt the efficacy of Le Tocq's release, coming as it did, on the heels of the public announcement that a team of four St. Lucian Parliamentarians, two each from government and opposition, were confirmed to visit the Foreign and Commonwealth Office in London for exploratory talks on constitutional advancement for that island. It is of interest to note that the British Government called it 'constitutional advancement' for the island, whilst everyone else in St. Lucia, including both government and opposition, was calling it 'political independence'. We had long learnt that in diplomacy, as in statistics, there are facts, figures and bloody lies.

Meanwhile the opposition-led campaign to 'do it right, let the people decide' continued unabated in St. Lucia. In early March 1977, the government tabled and passed a resolution in the island's Parliament calling on Britain to free the island and to allow it to proceed to Independence. The Opposition St. Lucia Labour Party subsequently boycotted the

House Select Committee appointed to prepare a draft constitution for an Independent St. Lucia. At that time, the Opposition also dispatched a letter of protest to Her Majesty's Government in the United Kingdom, complaining of the manner in which the people of the island were being forced into a situation that had not been fully discussed with them and whose views were never properly sought.

The House of Assembly Resolution seeking Independence for St. Lucia was therefore passed in the absence of Opposition Parliamentarians and then forwarded to Britain by the government.

It may be of interest to observe that the parliamentary resolution on Independence was preceded by a letter in the Voice newspaper of St. Lucia, by a special correspondent, seeking to discover whether plans for independence had been dumped. This was followed by front page news in the same newspaper four days later, claiming that a veil of secrecy hung over St. Lucia's plans to seek full independence from Britain. The newspaper made no secret of encouraging open and swift action on the matter. The politically astute were therefore, to easily connect the dots in the series of 'planted' articles in the island's leading newspaper.

Following the flurry of activities in March 1977, both in the Parliament of St. Lucia and outside in the broader community, and in response to the request from the Foreign and Commonwealth office in London, the time soon came to travel there for the first round of exploratory talks on constitutional reform. On the afternoon of Saturday, twenty-third April 1977, we gathered at Hewanorra International Airport, at Vieux-Fort, in the south of the island (formerly named Beane Field after a United States Army Officer) for a flight to London. The British Airways flight first took us to Barbados, about one hundred nautical miles East/south/east of St. Lucia, the only stop on the eight hour transatlantic flight to London's Heathrow airport.

The atmosphere at the local airport at Vieux-Fort was calmer than I had expected it to be. The handful of supporters from both parties who had gathered to see their 'boys' off to those important talks, kept their respective distances and only occasionally cast side-long glances from deadpan faces at each other as each departing politician made his way to the departure area. The fact that I was still relatively new to politics and that I had perhaps subconsciously taken every opportunity in the past to lambaste the government on its performance, did not help to calm the growing tension between supporters from both parties wherever they had gathered and I was present. Three members of the delegation belonged to the honourable society of lawyers and had known each other before I had cut my political teeth. If Louisy and the government's team seemed especially friendly to each other, that should explain it. Besides, their respective personalities dated back to a time when the people on the island were generally more courteous and much more genteel in their outlook on life. Back then people seemed to be more caring towards each other. Party politics was threatening to destroy this natural bond which a small island people shared with each other.

Whilst speaking to friends and supporters at Vieux-Fort that day, I observed that all four politicians who were about to leave for London were either from the south of the island or represented constituencies there then or previously. Premier Compton's family had lived in the village of Micoud and he later represented that village in Parliament for many years. His friend and colleague, Henry Giraudy hailed from Vieux-Fort and represented that constituency at the time of the talks. The Leader of the Opposition, Allan Louisy, hailed form Laborie, a village three miles west of Vieux-Fort. And I, the fourth member of that delegation hailed from Vieux-Fort, and at the time represented Castries East constituency in Parliament. Such an observation is important to note because it points to slight cultural differences within the island. Persons who are from the south of St. Lucia, traditionally, were more open to working together co-operatively, especially in home construction, gardening, the felling of trees and clearing of land et cetera. They seem to possess in their natures a greater propensity to help each other progress, in a cause they deem worthy. On the other hand persons who are from the northern part of the island seem to prefer to pay for packages, such as house and land deal, for example, rather than building and working co-operatively with family and friends.

On the day of our departure to London, the Leader of the Opposition was accompanied by his private secretary, who worked diligently at his law office in his village of Laborie, where he had chosen to retire after leaving the East Caribbean Supreme Court, as a Justice of Appeal. She was physically challenged, petite, young, apparently very capable, and obviously helpful to him outside the office. For example, she was required to keep watch over the six pieces of hand -held luggage which she and Louisy were jointly allowed to take on aboard that flight. It would not surprise anyone who knew Louisy and his secretary if it was discovered that she had accompanied him on the flight for the purpose of assisting him with his luggage.

During our short stop over at Barbados, I exchanged a few words with Premier Compton to break the ice which I felt existed between the two of us and also to enquire what his expectations were from the mission we had embarked upon. I found him very cagy at first, the quality which those who knew him best had warned me to expect - and almost reluctant to expose his hand, so to speak. After a few minutes he did open up a little, sufficient to repeat his earlier stance on colonialism generally, and in particular of the arrogance of the British government in refusing to set the people of St. Lucia free, to be masters of their own destiny, words one felt certain Compton knew would be music to my ears. The rest of the flight was uneventful. We must have all fallen asleep and taken the much needed rest that we had each, in our separate ways, fully earned. Between bouts of sleep, I caught the Leader of the Opposition on more than one occasion leaving his first class comfort to walk towards the back of the large jumbo 747 jet aircraft to check on his secretary and to see that all was well. A good boss could be expected to do no less. By all accounts Allan Louisy was that and more, as he was later to prove his caring qualities in my presence.

Time appeared to fly by quickly, and soon we arrived at Heathrow airport into a wet blustery morning at around seven and were quickly guided into the safety of a very small lounge that seemed designed for invited guests and other special visitors. We were offered coffee (and cognac) the latter to ward off the obvious chill which had greeted us upon arrival. As we left the aircraft we followed the officials from the F.C.O. into the V.I.P. lounge. After an official briefing which reviewed our timetable in London, we were driven to our hotel in the city. We were put up at the posh Bristol Hotel in London. On the previous trip we had stayed at the Trafalgar Hotel right on Trafalgar Square. The Leader of the Opposition soon announced his preference for a room on the ground floor of the hotel rather than one on the fourth to which he was assigned. This was quickly arranged to his satisfaction. Soon after we had settled at the hotel, friends of Louisy's secretary came to pick her up.

Later that morning I reviewed the entire process that Saint Lucia had gone through since the government had first announced it intended to seek independence. I then slept my tiredness away and, for my sins, missed lunch. But I made up for that lack later that evening as Mr. Louisy and I had dinner together, at the Bristol Hotel. It was April 24 and the time was 7.30. Following this, we reviewed the situation we were to face the following day and retraced the details of the mental road map which we had both discussed in St. Lucia and Barbados. We agreed that the British Government had its own agenda, and possibly, even a time table for setting our island free. We therefore concluded that the F.C.O. would try its best to accommodate Premier Compton's demand for a new 'independent' constitution for the island, even as they did their best to also keep a straight face about it in our presence. The British were fully aware of the conditions on the ground back home, and in our view, they would not wish to be seen going against the wishes of the people. The large following which the opposition had built up in St. Lucia for its case on constitutional reform was well known to those concerned. The opposition had simply asked to 'do it right and let the people decide'.

The following morning we were picked up by officials from the Caribbean section of the Foreign and Commonwealth Office at 9.00 o'clock promptly, for talks slated to begin at 10 that morning. I knew from reading modern Caribbean history and from books written by Caribbean Scholars, that British officials and politicians with whom we were to interface knew much more about the politics of the Caribbean than a novice to the game would imagine they did. Those whose business it was to know, were constantly briefed about the goings on in the region. Their numerous officials and research post graduate fellows, also seemed to hold fondly (and personally) a cultivated love affair with the Caribbean. The region is famous for its excellent blends of rum made from sugar cane, the cultivation of which had brought so many to the Caribbean, in the past and still did. Upon arrival at the F.C.O. at White Hall, it was all very formal and with certain officials displaying an air of importance. The atmosphere, I suspected then was deliberately created to announce without the need for words, that there would be no filibuster and no time wasting. It was all serious business and it was obviously stage managed in order to look that way too. In any event my untrained eyes could hardly tell the difference. We were quickly introduced to Edward Rowlands (who promptly asked to be called Ted) and just as a warning and to show that we, the opposition from St. Lucia were in a no nonsense mood either, I suggested to Louisy that he should question the seating arrangement, rather than accepting it and sitting obediently and quietly on the chairs we were assigned. This was merely a test of the willingness of Minister Rowlands to compromise (and change) if it was proven desirable. There was no intention on my part of pursuing the matter, but it would have been nice to see and to hear the reaction of those present. I had previously read that in the negotiations which took place in Paris between the United States and the Viet Cong and the North Vietnamese, with a view to ending the war in Vietnam, it had taken the parties three hundred and sixty-five days to agree on the shape of the conference table and seating arrangements before any meaningful negotiations could begin. Of course during that time both sides were still trying their very best to win the war and to inflict sufficient damage on each other, perhaps to more easily determine the shape of that table - and the outcome of the war.

Of course we enjoyed no such luxury. At my observation on the seating arrangements, I saw the colour drain from Louisy's face and for a split second, I thought we may have had a serious medical condition on our hands. I immediately dropped the subject and I reassured him that it was all in jest. To be truthful, the idea had only occurred to me on the spur of the moment, and the only reason I attempted to test it was to prove to everyone in that room that there was a new breed of politician emerging from St. Lucia and the Caribbean, and that we were not to be trifled with. Frankly, Louisy and I had not discussed strategy or tactics in any great detail, and we did not have a specific plan-B in case those talks had taken a crooked, unexpected turn. I felt we should have invited professional help in this regard, but immediately decided that this was too preliminary a feeler to waste any sleep over. At the time politics was a part time occupation of amateurs, and politicians loathed seeking professional help when faced with new situations they could not understand or control.

After we were seated, Rowlands again thanked us for coming and then proceeded to introduce his officials. We were now also seated in our assigned places which had been previously determined by our host. The St. Lucia delegation was arrayed across the table from Rowlands and his team. If it had not yet dawned upon us, it became crystal clear at that time that this was us, versus them, and the 'us' was the government and opposition from St. Lucia. The British had made no distinction between government and opposition from the island and frankly, they did not seem to care. That was an important lesson for me. If we were not sufficiently wise to close ranks and fashion the type of constitution for our country which we thought best, then we would be to blame. Neither the British nor anyone else was to be blamed for the final outcome of such talks. This was the lesson I took from this first round of talks on constitutional advancement for Saint Lucia. The British may have invented the idea of divide and rule as far as their colonies were concerned, but now it was up to us to discover the power of unity. If we were so egotistical and power hungry that we were blind to that fact, then this was to be regretted. The British had also exposed us to the best education which their colonial system was able to offer. It was now up to us to get smart quickly in our country's best interest, and to learn the meaning of co-operation and unity. In our hearts we knew that the people were not psychologically prepared to strike out on their own, as a free and politically independent nation. Years of colonialism and learnt dependence had seen to that. We therefore had to stand on our own feet sooner rather than later. The only question was: What was the best time to do this?

The richness and interesting diversity of the cultures of the Caribbean - including St. Lucia - was being rediscovered due in large measure to the rediscovery of things African, including pride in the black race. Earlier, the

St. Lucia Forum had let it be known that pride in one's self did not always come before a fall - at least not the sort of pride the group was advocating. A germ of an idea was perhaps beginning to take root in the minds and hearts of the people, and we felt this should have been strengthened by more updated and revised school syllabuses and support for national and cultural art forms as well as community culture groups. We saw the use of theatre as a learning tool, above all else.

At that first meeting with the Foreign and Commonwealth Office, each side of the St. Lucia political divide put its case clearly and squarely to Ted Rowlands. We had shown at that first meeting that the two parties from St. Lucia were separated only by the approach which was taken on the road to political independence for our country. The opposition was convinced that if and when the broad masses of the population were to unleash their true sentiments in a constitution for the island, the resulting document would be far different from that fashioned and handed down to it by the British authorities. However, this was only the first of what eventually turned out to be three rounds of talks leading to a new constitution for our island. At the end of the first day it appeared that the arguments of the Opposition were well received. We argued that if the people were to be the central force and power in the exercise upon which we had embarked, then the British government had, in our view, a moral obligation, to ensure that some legitimate means was found to educate the people on the process of independence and to test their readiness to proceed to that new status.

Louisy put forward the view that Associated Statehood with Britain should only be terminated through the procedure outlined in section 10 (1) of the West Indies Act. He also re-stated the official position of the Parliamentary Opposition in St. Lucia, which was that the move was hastily conceived and that the people were not adequately prepared nor had they been given an opportunity to comment adequately on the issue of Independence. The government of St. Lucia, through Premier Compton, put forward its case that the island should be facilitated to achieve full sovereignty, and that his government believed that section 10 (2) of the West Indies Act was the most appropriate avenue by which to proceed. He also advanced the broader argument that circumstances had changed since Associated Statehood was granted to the island and that the time had come for full independence.

Following the two days of talks, a communiqué was agreed to by the three parties, and issued by the Foreign and Commonwealth Office. This communiqué indicated that some progress had been made towards the attainment of the goals which the government of St. Lucia had set for itself. It also made clear that on return to the island the Government should hold further consultations with the people. The latter did not meet the direct referendum or general elections which the opposition was demanding, but it had the effect of drawing out the consultative process on the island thereby, guaranteeing a wider cross section of the population's participation in the Independence debate.

The Government of St. Lucia could therefore claim some sort of victory from this first round of talks. Furthermore it was directed by the British Government to prepare a 'Green Paper', stating its proposals for a new constitution for the island, and which clearly opened the passage to eventual full sovereignty. The timing may not have been to Compton's liking but he was prepared to settle for half a loaf than go empty handed. The 'White Paper' which the Government of St. Lucia had previously issued was to state what advantages it saw in independence. That issue was now behind them. The first round of talks saw to that. By then, any fool could have seen that the government was on the way to getting its wishes of independence for the island. It did not matter how nicely and sweetly Minister Rowlands and his officials had smiled with and treated the opposition from St. Lucia, they were determined to be rid of all their Associated States.

At the end of the talks, the St. Lucia Association of London, whose executive members were all unknown to me, and who had faithfully supported Premier Compton's leadership, arranged for the delegation to meet with its Executive and members. One felt quite certain that many who came that day were drawn by curiosity to meet with, and to get to know those whom they had not met before; also to renew old acquaintances. Some interest was also shown in hearing the opposition's case on the issue of independence for St. Lucia. The group was privy to the actions which the government was taking to lead the island to independence and some may even have fancied diplomatic postings and other job offers after the island achieved independence. It was difficult to explain to the gathering the story of the opposition's efforts back home which were aimed at ensuring that full consultation lay at the centre of the process leading to freedom for the island.

Notwithstanding the political support for Premier Compton, the Executive of that St. Lucia group in London, showed much respect for Louisy and myself and offered their personal help to both of us during the remainder of our stay in London. There was certainly no discrimination in the manner and quantity of beverages which were offered to us during that town hall meeting in London. Many interesting questions were asked, the majority aimed at Compton and his post independence vision for the development of the island. By ten-thirty that evening we were safely at our hotel and looking forward to our trip back home the following morning.

The next morning we were checked out of the hotel and driven to Heathrow airport with the same courtesy and efficiency for which the British authorities are well known. Before long we were on board British Airways flight 253 to Saint Lucia. After a brief stop at the Grantley Adams airport in Barbados, we arrived safely at Hewanorra, in beautiful Saint Lucia. Word of our arrival had reached supporters of the two political parties and small curious crowds from each side came to see us as we alighted from the huge jumbo jet which had deposited us back from whence we first departed four days earlier. As much as I enjoyed politics at the time, deep within me I felt revulsion for the divisiveness of our politics which was creating more division, rather than unity, at the time when unity of our people was most crucial for the progress of our country. In my view, the steps towards independence were achieving the very opposite of what politicians should be aiming to do: that of bringing the people together for a massive assault on poverty and for creating a positive and disciplined work force. The deep political division which was then based on personalities rather than on ideology was not helping in the quest for political freedom, economic liberation and prosperity for all.

The multi-party political system had its advantages, but we in Saint Lucia and the Caribbean have not had the courage to streamline it so as to make it less susceptible to willfully neglecting the half of the population which did not vote for a particular political party. And for how long would we continue to blame the British colonial system and everyone else (including our history) for our unwillingness to extend our minds (and energies) towards the idea of meaningful change, was left to be seen. We were all aware that Britain's interest was, and would always be first and foremost - Britain. The small Caribbean islands bereft of natural resources had long ago become a drain on the British treasury and there was no gain to Britain in continuing to hold on to them. And no one could deny that Britain's interest was then best served by freeing herself of all those overseas territories and colonies that were draining her treasury. And that furthermore, these colonies were an embarrassment to her, as she forged a new policy of closer economic union with the rest of Europe.

During this first experience of negotiations with a former colonial power, it was difficult to draw a line between economics and politics. It was even more difficult to tell which part of past economic neglect was due to scarcity of resources and therefore budgetary constraints, and which was due to racism and psychological warfare. Quite often it seemed at such negotiations that one had slipped from the economic field into the field of psychology, as Professor Sigmund Freud had suggested in his book; 'Future of an illusion'.

The Second Round of Talks

*We have slipped unawares out of the economic field
into the field of psychology.*
Sigmund Freud: The Future of an Illusion.

The first invitation to talks in London was ostensibly to determine from parliamentarians representing both sides of the House in St. Lucia, what advantages, if any, they saw in Independence. At the end of these talks the government was asked to prepare a 'Green Paper' to say what changes to the existing constitution would be necessary for an independent Saint Lucia. After a suitable period for such consultation, it was the stated intention of the British government to issue a second invitation to another delegation from St. Lucia to discuss the outcome of these further consultations. To the opposition, this was a very clear signal that the government of Saint Lucia would be certain to be granted its wishes for Independence, once it could demonstrate to the satisfaction of Britain that the procedural efforts at consultation had been fulfilled. Britain clearly wished to free itself of these small and now useless islands, but it also wanted to do so cautiously, perhaps even graciously. In the process she hastened with due deliberation, thereby giving to both government and opposition a sense of fair play. She did not wish to be seen, favouring any particular one of the many little 'tin gods' who the first past the post system of democracy had created in the Caribbean. These small-minded men had learnt well the lessons of patronage and political party loyalty, and believed to a man that in politics, ...'use is all'.

On returning from the first round of talks, both government and opposition continued their separate ways on the Independence debate. The government finally published its 'Green Paper' in early August of 1977. It then went one step further and appointed a constitution committee under the Chairmanship of the Speaker of the House, Honourable Wilfred St. Clair Daniel. The committee was to consult and to prepare a new draft constitution for an independent St. Lucia. The opposition for its part continued its protestations and warnings that independence was not about a person or a political party, but about the future welfare of all the people of the island, - including the unborn. It continued to worry aloud about the approach which the government was taking to this most important endeavour. It repeatedly pointed out that independence could not merely be a token or prize to satisfy the egotistical longings of an individual or a political party.

For its part, the Foreign and Commonwealth Office had stated that 'a further meeting would be convened in London, after a due interval, to review the outcome of this consultation' A St. Lucia government release said that ten thousand copies of the 'Green Paper' were published, and that these would be distributed to schools, youth groups, social and cultural clubs, the commercial sector, professional organizations, libraries, professional associations and the media. Furthermore, it said: 'copies of the 'Green Paper' will also be made available to Saint Lucians resident in the United States of America, Canada and St. Croix.'

By early October 1977, Britain had issued the promised invitation to review the 'Green Paper'. Again both government and opposition were invited to this second round of talks. Upon receipt of this invitation, Premier Compton stated that he was unable to accede to the British government's invitation at the time, due to the pressing work of budget preparation at home. Compton also used the occasion to indicate quite clearly to the British government that 'it was absolutely humiliating and intolerable for a government that has been duly elected by a majority of the people since 1964, to be travelling at great expense of time and money like so many mendicants seeking favours from the master'. That statement, along with that which had been offered for his inability to leave St. Lucia at the time, placed Compton in the higher category of 'Statesman', appearing to put the business of people and country first. In addition, he appeared to be standing up to London as no mere mendicant begging for independence for himself. Taken together, these two statements Compton had set the cat among the pigeons. For a time he appeared to have completely destroyed the opposition's charge that he was seeking independence only for himself and his political party.

The Premier then went on to anticipate the outcome of the second round of talks and suggested to his supporters that he was putting forward the date of December 13, 1978, (St. Lucia's National Day) for achievement of full sovereignty for the island. Compton's exact words to the British

Foreign and Commonwealth Office were: 'when the consultations on the constitution have been complete, a delegation from Saint Lucia will be prepared to discuss with you an agreed constitution for an independent Saint Lucia, which it will be our desire to have inaugurated not later than the 13th. December, 1978'. It appeared that Compton was setting the Independence agenda.

This was politics at its very best, and Compton was proving he was every bit a practiced exponent of the game. Sensing the hard edge to his correspondence to the Foreign and Commonwealth office, Premier Compton quickly added: 'this is not an ultimatum and should not be so considered. It is a realistic date and we hope Her Majesty's government will make it possible for us to meet it.' Compton had previously reminded the British authorities in London, that 'it had been accepted that one of the procedures - that of a referendum - laid down in the constitution for terminating the association is now obsolete and no longer relevant to the present circumstances.' The only other option, he said, is that of Her Majesty's government. The cards were therefore acknowledged to be in the hands of the British Government.

Interestingly, the parliamentary opposition was making that same point with the clear understanding, that if a law had become obsolete and irrelevant, then it should not continue to enjoy the light of print. And once that law had not been rescinded by an Act of Parliament, which had created it in the first place, it remained in force by whatever name one may choose to call it. Those to whom Compton had directed his observations knew their job. They therefore did not need to be reminded of it. The opposition's take on this matter was that Compton, as usual, was attempting to convince the doubting Thomases from within and without. Within his party camp, however, all appeared to be going very well indeed. If he said to jump, his supporters simply asked how high. The second round of talks leading to independence was therefore postponed from the end of 1977 (November 30 and December 1) to a date in March 1978.

During the time allotted by the government for discussions on the Green Paper proposing changes to the St. Lucia constitution, there was much talk and Government public relations information. The government had pointedly invited the contributions of the public on the new constitution. But few persons and organizations took the opportunity to do as the government had asked. Only one source of enlightened learning condescended to shine its considerable luminosity on the proposed new constitution. That inspired source was none other than the local Bar Association. Back then, the legal fraternity in St. Lucia was distinguished more by its silence than by its studied comments on any matter of the law.

One heard from that august body once every calendar year, and only after it had anointed a new president and an executive committee to see after its affairs for the ensuing year.

Certain well placed citizens had proffered the view that lawyers, as a group, were better placed to express an opinion on the new proposed constitution. So there were calls from supporters of both parties for the Bar Association to comment. It finally consented to do so, and it put out a document in which the group recommended the creation of a 'No Party' state on the attainment of political independence for the island. The Bar Association was then headed by Mr. Vincent Floissac - later Sir Vincent, - a former Nominated Member of the House, and Chief Justice of the Organization of East Caribbean States: A legal luminary of unsurpassed excellence.

The document from the Bar Association, however, said that the view prevailed that it would be imprudent to supplant the existing provisions of the constitution by something which was yet to be fully developed in theory and practice. To the layman, that meant that the legal fraternity had given with its right hand and reclaimed with the left, thereby leaving the citizens no wiser. To the cynic, the legal fraternity had too readily aborted an idea, which it had created, not allowing it to see the light of day. And yet, what the people have always needed, both before and since independence, was well formulated and fearlessly advanced ideas for their own improvement. Without ideas to answer the questions: How and by whom; how can we be expected to progress? That was the question on the lips of those who cared enough to speak.

The year 1977 was a very eventful one indeed. Politics seemed then to take centre stage in all the island did and said. The people were animated and many found good humour and even theatre in the politics. Sadly, in July 1977, the St. Lucia Labour Party lost one of its stalwarts and most competent electrical technicians on the island in the person of George Murray, who succumbed to cancer of the liver at age 57, and was laid to rest on Wednesday, 13th July, of that year. He was a former General Secretary of the St. Lucia Labour Party, a one time member of the Castries City Council, and a life-long employee of Cable and Wireless, West Indies. He is remembered fondly by many who have followed the political fortunes of the St. Lucia Labour Party and especially by the senior generation of Labour Party politicians on the island. He was the only person who consistently volunteered to stand in general elections against Compton, when no one else would, for fear of losing their deposits.

At the time of his passing Murray was actively involved in the opposition's stand on the Independence issue. Apart from active participation as a public speaker, Murray repaired and maintained the loud speaker systems for the party. He kept each one functioning and in good order. He did so free of charge and often supplied spare parts with his own money. The loud speaker systems were an important part of the party's ability to communicate to a large gathering. One felt then that Murray's demise could not have hit the opposition at a worse time. At his most active, his home was a veritable archive of tape recordings of public meetings of the St. Lucia Labour Party from the fifties up to the time of his death.

As if to compound the ill luck that had visited the opposition, rumours began to circulate in St. Lucia that Her Majesty's government had informed the United Nations Committee on Small States (group of 24), monitoring de-colonization – that it would soon grant independence to two Associated States – Dominica and St. Lucia. The British government denied the allegation, and said that it planned to issue another invitation to the St. Lucia government and Opposition delegates early the next year (1978) for another round of talks on the island's request for full independence. It would be recalled that the meeting had been postponed from November 30, and December 1, 1977 after Compton sought an assurance that the talks 'would achieve or strive to achieve' independence for the island.

The release from the British government also added that it was possible that a misunderstanding had arisen in connection with a working paper drawn up by the Secretariat of the U.N. Committee of 24 dated October 14, which read in part, 'Dominica has advanced a target date for independence of January 1978 and St. Lucia by the last quarter of 1978'.

The opposition was appreciative of the clearing up of this rumour that had taken on a life of its own in the tense independence debate that had gripped the island. The opposition knew it had its work cut out for it. It was constantly kept on its toes by those wishing to accept independence at any cost and with whatever constitutional arrangements agreed to by London and Castries. The opposition had long felt it understood the historical meaning of freedom to the peoples of the Caribbean. They who had been brought across the Atlantic Ocean from Africa, did not need any one, including the United Nations group of 24, to lecture them on how to guide the people of this island to political and economic freedom. Britain should not be allowed to continue to exploit the colonized peoples of these islands, and then to off load them as she determined, without paying due compensation.

After a period of mourning for the deceased George Murray, the opposition resumed its protests on what by that time it had dubbed 'the backhand method of sneaking political independence' which the government of St. Lucia seemed determined to pursue. It continued to protest and make its voice heard with rallies and public meetings throughout the island.

By agreement between the parties, the second round of talks was scheduled for London towards the end of March 1978. The time soon came for the government of the island to report on its consultations and to present the changes to the present constitution it thought necessary for an independent St. Lucia.

We returned to London by the same route as before. This time the Leader of the Opposition was not weighed down by additional hand luggage and he seemed much calmer and more self assured than on the previous trip. Our arrival at Heathrow was uneventful. Once there, we were extended the same courtesies as when we had arrived there for the first round of talks.

This second round of talks focussed on a report by the government of St. Lucia on the consultations it had carried out on the island and the ideas which it thought should be included in a new constitution for an independent St. Lucia, as requested at the end of the first meeting in London. The Opposition, on the other hand, was asked to comment as it saw fit. It was prompted to offer its opinions and to seek clarification on points that it felt needed to be fleshed out. This time the opposition team of Louisy and Josie included George Odlum, who had a change of heart about attending these talks. He was not an elected member of parliament at the time, so he used all his creative skills to bend Allan Louisy and John Compton to have him attend the talks. By then it seemed that the British authorities had amended the original insistence that members of the St. Lucia delegation be sitting parliamentarians.

In anticipation of a more incisive and detailed discussion on the Independence issue at the second round of talks, the opposition had taken the precaution and prepared its own position on the changes it wished to see in a new constitution for an independent St. Lucia. This constituted a shift in strategy forced upon the opposition by the government's Green Paper. The opposition had made its ideas for a new constitution public in a document which it called 'The Red Paper.' It formally launched this Red Paper on the Castries Market steps on Thursday 22nd September, 1977. That event served to heighten the divide between the visions of the two political parties on the island, on the issue of Independence. There were at least two important differences between the Green Paper and the Red Paper. The Red Paper proposed clear and finite term limits for the office of Prime Minister. It proposed that the island abandon the Monarchical system of governance in favour of a Republican system. This meant that the Red Paper preferred an Executive President as Head of State, rather than a Governor General, representing the Queen of England. It also advocated a unicameral legislative body with Senators elected to represent specific interest groups such as Business, Farmers, Women, and Trades Unions and so on. It also suggested that a third term may be possible for an elected Prime Minister, but only after an absence of ten years from contesting general elections. The Red Paper also proposed a fixed date for the holding of general elections on the island. It did not propose to change the five-year term of government.

It is of interest that neither the government of St. Lucia nor the opposition was able to make any significant changes to the system of government which the British knew and practised. The text of a draft constitution which the British government technocrats had prepared for discussion at these talks was the same old document which they eventually handed down to every former colony in the Caribbean, as far as we were aware. One therefore did it the way the British government dictated, or one took a hike and passed the political baton to someone else, more pliable. To be truthful, there were small and insignificant concessions made to the opposition; as for example, in the number and allocation of seats in the Senate. But the opposition never suggested, nor did it wish for a rubber-stamp Senate.

In its view, the final constitutional model for the island revealed no creativity or significant change for the better. Our ideas were flatly rejected by both the British and St. Lucia governments. We therefore ended up with a constitution which provided for second chamber - the Senate - which in our view was nothing more than rubber stamp, of wasteful expenditure. It claims to be a second review chamber, but it merely masquerades as such. Its status does not come anywhere near to that of the House of Lords in England where the idea for a second chamber first arose.

Premier Compton and his team mates, Henry Giraudy and George Mallet may have gotten their wish for an independent constitution for the island, but the date of December 13th 1978 was roundly rejected by the Foreign and Commonwealth Office in London, who instead proposed a date of 22nd February 1979. It furthermore tied the granting of independence to an assurance of early general elections thereafter. The opposition, which had always advocated elections before independence, did not mind this outcome since it had long gotten into elections mode after studying the outcome of the first round of talks.

At the end of the second round of talks the St. Lucia Association of London, again hosted both government and opposition. This was not unlike a victory rally and an independence flag raising ceremony. That 'independence' fete, pre-dated the actual event by a long way, but as far as I could tell no one complained. Interestingly, that event in London coincided with celebrations in St. Lucia, this time by the political party of Premier Compton, celebrating at the end of the second round and well before St. Lucia's official attainment of Independence.

The time soon came for us to return home. Speaking on his arrival at Hewanorra airport, Compton told the large gathering that his delegation had won last year (April, 1977) and had won again this year (March, 1978). He promised his listeners that 'we will go back again in June or July and we will win again'. He repeated his call for independence by December 13, 1978. Compton's speech at the airport on his arrival did little more than emphasize the deep division over political independence for the island. Not surprisingly, he omitted to say how much time, energy and money had been invested, on the subject. In reality the issue had quite literally become a political football and the worst offenders in the view of many was the government of St. Lucia. It was they who had first asked for the island to become independent from Britain. There appeared to be little introspection and even less serious political analysis of the economic, social and political discipline which this small island nation had to come to terms with if the political Independence it was so determined to gain was to mean anything. The opposition continued to insist that the whole purpose of the exercise was to promote the interests of the people of the country, and that Britain should understand this, though others may not.

Back home, the Government Information Service issued a press release in which it stated that the government was boldly pressing ahead with its Independence plans. To that end, GIS said that the government had sought and secured from the Government of Trinidad and Tobago, the services of Mr. Barry Auguste, a St. Lucian by birth, and a Foreign Services Officer of that country - as an advisor to the government of St. Lucia on Foreign Affairs and International Relations.

In all of this debate, communications and interfacing between the government and the opposition in St. Lucia on one hand, and the British Government on the other, it was to be remembered that in the final analysis, it was only the British Parliament which could finally determine, through its own processes, the constitutional future of St. Lucia. It was therefore no surprise when questions broke out in the House of Lords, about such an eventuality. The questions were chiefly from Lords who either had an interest in the island or who had been lobbied by others, who had. Soon after the second round of talks, news reached the island that the Lords had discussed the St. Lucia independence affair. The information from that body must have been very comforting indeed to Premier Compton and his team. The net outcome of these discussions was that Britain will cooperate under section 10(2) of the West Indies Act if that proved to be the right process. This statement, minus its cautious proviso, had come from the lips of Lord Goronwy-Roberts, speaking on behalf of the British Minister of State in the Foreign and Commonwealth office – Ted Rowlands. In his reply to a question from Lord Segal, seeking greater clarity on the possible date for Independence for the island, Lord Goronwy-Roberts replied that he would not wish to interfere even in an oblique way, with the partisan politics of St. Lucia. He added that he had no doubt that both government and opposition in St. Lucia had the best interest of the country at heart, and repeated the decision to cooperate under section 10(2) of the West Indies Act of 1969. He once again employed caution and this time, he also repeated the proviso.

Lord Walston, a former owner of the three thousand acre Marquis estate in the north east of St. Lucia, asked Lord Goronwy-Roberts whether he was aware that the independence debate in St. Lucia has been going on for a long time now and that there is a widespread desire among all types of the population in St. Lucia that it be speedily resolved. Not to be outdone Lord Hawke, asked 'will an independent St. Lucia depend on the British tax payer for subsistence? To the latter Lord Goronwy-Roberts replied in the negative and to the former, from Lord Walston, he answered in his customary cautious manner, repeating what he had said earlier to questions of the same genre.

Back home, the two political parties continued their campaign to win hearts and minds to their position on the question of Independence for St. Lucia. The Opposition had been convinced a long time ago that Compton would be given independence and that he would sooner, rather than later, become the first Prime Minister of an independent St. Lucia. With this in mind, the opposition changed strategy and tactfully began to focus on the upcoming general elections and concentrating all its efforts at winning it. We were fairly certain that these elections would take place around the middle of 1979, not long after the Independence celebrations were over.

To that end the St. Lucia Labour Party launched its Youth Arm on May 28, 1978 in the village of Micoud. Jon Odlum, later to become Minister for Youth and Sports in a Labour government, was the co-coordinator of the programme. He had the additional advantage of family from the village. A full programme of activities was planned for that day and from every indication it was a near perfect event. It should be borne in mind that at the time the village of Micoud was represented in Parliament by none other than Premier Compton, who by then had successfully contested six general elections in the area and had romped home to victory by convincing margins each time.

The continuous contest of wills over the Independence issue between the government and opposition had unfortunately long degenerated into much more than a political contest. The conduct and courtesies among parliamentarians were beginning to lose the accustomed civility. This was clearly demonstrated when the parliamentary opposition declined to accept an invitation from the local branch of the Commonwealth Parliamentary Association (C.P.A.) and the House of Assembly of St. Lucia, to a dinner in honour of Honourable George Mallet, Minister for Trade, Industry and Tourism, to mark 21 years as a parliamentarian. The dinner went ahead at the Green Parrot Restaurant, on Morne Fortune, overlooking Castries the capital and seat of parliament. At the time, that restaurant was the premier dining place in Castries (and possibly the entire island). It was then owned by the popular Chef Harry, a local, who took great pride in recalling the excellent training he received at Claridges in London. He was truly a man of many parts and accomplishments and the numerous accolades he received from his many international visitors and guests, were ample proof.

Following independence and the general elections later that year, Chef Harry was invited by Prime Minister Louisy to serve in the Senate of Saint Lucia. He did so with some flair during the short two and a half year term of the new government in office.

At the end of the second round of constitutional talks, there was little doubt that some form of concordat or agreement between the Her Majesty's Government in London and the Government of St. Lucia, had been reached. No peace treaties were called for at the constitutional conference and it was hoped that none would be required between the contesting political parties on the island. No one could deny there was a clear contest of wills at these talks, reminding us that treaties were but the combat of the brain, where still the stronger lost, and the weaker gained - as John Dryden might have put it. The opposition was certainly the stronger of the parties on the Independence issue, but they were to lose the battle for a proper and more relevant constitution for the island, because in that particular battle, Premier Compton, the leader of the island, was clearly supported by the British Government.

That was a great pity, and thirty years on, the island is still hamstrung with a constitution which is stifling its economic and political development, by making it extremely difficult to become part of a wider Caribbean construct. Indeed, even a desire for St. Lucia to join the Caribbean Court of Justice (CCJ) as its final Appellate Court, is being frustrated by the constitutional requirement imposed on it at Independence. The irony of this particular situation is that Britain, and in particular its Privy Council, have confirmed their belief that the Caribbean is quite competent - both intellectually and financially - to administer and uphold such a court as the CCJ.

Third and Final Round of Talks

Treaties are but the combat of the brain,
Where still the stronger lose, the weaker gain.....

John Dryden

The third and final round of talks leading to Independence for St. Lucia was called the Constitutional Conference. That name said it all. Both the government and the opposition were again in London at the invitation of the British Government. This time the Government of St. Lucia took along its Attorney General, Mr. Parry Husbands, while the Opposition was accompanied by a fourth member in the person of Mr. Evans Calderon, a Barrister trained in London and M.P. for Choiseul constituency, who was also the acting General Secretary of the St. Lucia Labour Party.

These talks were scheduled for three days but were extended to a fourth, as the three sides argued and debated important elements of the proposed new constitution for the island. Outstanding bits and pieces of refinement, some procedural, were to take up as much time at the conference as other matters of substance. For example, whether there should be an elected Senate or a nominated one was discussed at some length. At times the British authorities would disagree with both Government and opposition on matters for inclusion in the new constitution, claiming a bewildering drafting complication for the legal draughtsman and his team.

Although the government of St. Lucia had earlier indicated the changes it wished to make to the existing constitution to make it more suitable for an independent St. Lucia, there still remained deep division between it and the opposition on certain important provisions. At the debate on the constitution in the parliament of St. Lucia, the opposition had walked out at the commencement of the exercise, claiming the debate to be unconstitutional, ultra vires and without effect since the matter in its view, had not been properly put before parliament.

Unfortunately the idea had gained currency both at home and abroad that the opposition was against independence and wished Saint Lucia to remain as an 'Associate State' of, and with, Britain. The truth was that the more forward-looking anti-colonialist elements within the opposition Labour Party of St. Lucia had long advocated a severing of all remaining legal/constitutional ties with Britain. This was well ahead of the time that independence for the Associated States became a matter of urgent British foreign policy. The open secret was that the same elements within the opposition party had also put forward the idea of a bold new Republican form of constitution for the island, borrowing from the American model.

It urged the people of the island to strike out in a more fundamental way from the constitution of their former colonial bosses by completely abandoning the Monarchy for a Presidential or Republican one. To that end, it even wished to sever the Queen's head from the currency which the island formerly shared with the rest of the English-speaking Caribbean. Many bristled at the idea as it was felt that it would lead to too much fragmentation of currency in the region. The proponents of the idea countered by pointing out that a new currency (minus the Queen's image) could, without difficulty, be adopted as legal tender for the remaining independent States in the Caribbean, if they wished to do so. All sorts of frivolous reasons were hatched in order to frustrate the new currency initiative put forward by the progressives within the opposition. Of course all these ideas on constitutional transformation were to heighten the debate and further examine the question (and purpose) of Independence.

Those who then energetically promoted the idea at last seemed as shallow as the Jordan River, after a very long hot summer. The undue haste, with which they were proceeding with Independence, had many persons suspicious. It was to expose such apparent expediency and what it also perceived as the false and winking camaraderie between London and Castries that the opposition put up such a stout defense of its own ideas, for a new constitution for the island. It wondered aloud, why those who were advocating Independence were so afraid to strike out on their own and leave 'that Europe where they are never done talking of man yet murder men everywhere they found them', as Franz Fanon from Martinique, had earlier observed. The opposition also questioned rhetorically whether such advocates perceived political Independence merely as a convenient escape that would set Britain free to pursue her so called 'European agenda and final destiny'; or was there another hidden and more cynical motive.

So both opposition and government once more proceeded to London for the last time to the all important constitutional conference which would put the seal on independence for the island. We were booked on the same airline and route as before. By then we were familiar with the drill at Heathrow and once British Customs was satisfied we had packed our suit cases ourselves; we were then whisked through the airport and into our appointed hotel in the city. At this final trip we stayed at the Tara Hotel, which one suspects was somewhat more reasonably priced compared to the Bristol of our previous visits.

After settling at the Tara Hotel, the opposition met in the lobby for a final briefing on our approach to that final meeting. We were determined to stamp our presence at these talks even though we were aware that the Independence was a done deal. The talks began in earnest. There were many back and forth exchanges throughout the next three days and the legal draftsman appointed for the purpose returned time and again with the draft wording for a new constitution before it met the approval of the parties present. After much debate and exchange a new constitution began to emerge which seemed to meet the demands of both government and opposition, and with which the British authorities also seemed satisfied.

It was tedious and painstaking work, but the constant exchanges and engaging discussions kept the momentum alive and at a safe distance from boredom. As I sat at these discussions each day, I kept wondering how the outcome would be viewed by our constituents back home, many of whom had placed so much store in our ability to fashion an instrument which would preserve the peace, promote democracy and hopefully lead to greater prosperity for themselves. The opposition was concerned to close any loopholes, perceived or real, which a would-be dictator might find sufficiently attractive in order to keep himself in office, and the people in poverty. The potential abuse of the new Independence constitution was a major concern for the opposition, and it was disappointed that the British authorities did not support its view of a 'two-term' limit for a Prime Minister, after Independence.

The opposition was satisfied that its views were fully aired, listened to and appreciated. However, the British were as interested in preserving their own brand of democracy as they were in securing an appropriately worded document upon which the island was to be set free. They were equally satisfied that the inclusion of certain entrenched clauses in the document were to go some way to appease opposition concerns. These new provisions unfortunately, were also to make it more difficult for the island to amend the entrenched clauses in the constitution in order to allow it to become a part of a larger united Caribbean nation later, if it chose to do so. In fact, these clauses demanded a two-thirds majority in parliament after a national referendum had been held on amending the same. It struck me that the same people who would not grant the opposition its wish for a referendum on the question of Independence were now so adamantly insisting on seeing that provision included in the new constitution. It was worse, that they strengthened these entrenched clauses by the provision of a specific parliamentary majority, before the island could be rid of the new stranglehold, which Britain conspired to impose.

After the lengthy process of constitutional construction, the St. Lucia delegations returned home to overwhelming public welcomes for both the government and opposition delegations. No date was agreed (or given) by the British when the island would be finally set free. The process obviously needed the approval of the British parliament in London. The timing of its final passage in both the House of Lords and the Commons was clearly out of the hands of the elected officials from St. Lucia. The office of the Minister for Foreign and Commonwealth Affairs in London, which had worked very hard to arrive at the new constitution, promised to do all in its power to secure the passage of a bill through the British parliament. Truth be told, it was that body and it alone which held the final card on the timing of Independence for St' Lucia.

After the lengthy negotiations were finally over, an official of the Commonwealth Office came quietly across to George Odlum and me and offered us tickets to the theatre to see an American dance musical, then performing in the theatre district in London, called 'Bubbling Brown Sugar'. We both willingly accepted that invitation and had a very enjoyable night out on the theatre district of London and Leicester square, that evening. On another evening we were also to enjoy 'Evita'- the musical based on the political life story of Evita Peron, of Argentina fame. These shows proved a useful diversion as I had made up my mind that I would skip any celebrations organized for us in London, to mark the end of these constitutional conferences.

I declined to attend any more of the organized celebrations put on by our friends in the St. Lucia Association of London. I needed some quiet down time alone. Later that evening I chose the hospitality of another St. Lucian family who had settled in England a very long time ago. Many St. Lucians living in England, and particularly the friends of Premier Compton, celebrated the end of these talks as if it were Independence Day. Perhaps they saw Independence as a special blessing and I respected their right to celebrate their island's progress.

At the end of it all, we finally headed home with the dubious satisfaction of political independence nearer than when we had left. Notably, there was no sign of an economic plan which one expected to be offered by Britain on setting the island free. Besides, Rowlands and his delegation had omitted to settle some important and outstanding constitutional questions which the parties could not agree on. Instead, he proposed that these be settled in the parliament of St. Lucia. There was only one interpretation for such an action. The British Government had rid itself of one more burden on the British tax payer, and we were left to fight among ourselves if we wished. Thankfully, this Pilate-like washing of the hands was not entirely new to some of us. Its repetition in this modern era, however, still smacked of cynicism and disrespect! Many saw it as a clever manoeuvre in disposing of a matter in which the British had little or no interest. They had seen to it that the basic framework for general elections and the basic freedoms had been preserved, and so they had done what they considered the most crucial job. Their first and foremost task at these conferences was to ensure that the rule of law was enshrined and preserved in any new constitution. Their second was to appear at all times impartial and even handed. The politicians and citizens of the island were to take due notice - if they were smart enough to do so.

We returned home to the usual rousing welcome of supporters from both sides of the political divide. Upon arrival at Hewanorra airport both the Leader of the Opposition and Premier Compton made brief statements to the media. Said the Leader of the opposition 'It is clear that the policy of the British government is to grant Independence to the Associated States – including St. Lucia - as soon as is reasonably practicable. But even in achieving desirable goals it is vital that the method of achieving these goals are plausible, legitimate and that guiding principles are adhered to'. He then added 'In the course of the conference, my delegation has insisted on some basic provisions for the protection of the people. Some were accepted, but others were not. We will endeavour, however, to draw such provisions to the attention of the people of St. Lucia in the months that lie ahead'. For his part Premier Compton told the press that 'We have spent the last four days modelling the new framework within which the people of St. Lucia will soon begin to conduct their affairs as a free and sovereign people'. Compton then added that the goodwill that had prevailed within the Saint Lucia delegation led to the success of the constitutional conference. He intimated that for his part, that goodwill would continue to prevail and then urged Minister Ted Rowlands to do all in his power in light of pending parliamentary elections in Britain, to permit the people of Saint Lucia to enter into sovereignty on their national day, (December 13, 1978).

In anticipation of the above remarks, Minister Rowlands had observed at the end of the Constitutional Conference that 'the constitution which had been agreed is a very good one'. But he also warned that it could not guarantee democracy for the people of Saint Lucia. 'Only the political will of the people, can ensure that real democracy survives'. He then added: 'A constitution can only provide a buttress for a democratic system'. He observed that the significant changes which were made to the draft constitution were in no small part a tribute to the constructive approach of the opposition which he said had proposed many changes to the draft document. He ended by praising the spirit of compromise with which both delegations had approached the last four days of discussions and promised that the new agreed constitution would be sent to the island as soon as possible.

It bears repetition that no agreement was reached at the constitutional conference on whether or not St. Lucia should have an elected or a nominated Senate or whether there ought to be specific term limits for Prime Minister's stay in office or a known date for the calling of general elections, or whether the island should introduce a republican form of government with an Executive leader voted into office by the public. All these issues, important to the opposition, were craftily side-stepped by both the British and St. Lucia governments. It was therefore left to the parliament (and people) of St. Lucia to debate and decide. Framing of this new constitution had taken the better part of one year, and in the process the people were to have been fully consulted on its contents. One was therefore left to wonder whether the proposal by the British that the remaining issues to be resolved in the new constitution for the island be settled locally, was merely time wasting tactics.

By the end of September of 1978, the Government Information Service released the news that the Draft Constitution for an independent St. Lucia had been received by the government. The document, it said, would first be circulated to Members of the House of Assembly and then to the local media. It would afterwards be presented to the House of Assembly for debate. It added that during that sitting and after each member who wished, and had his/her say, a request (and consent) Resolution under section 5 (4) of the West Indies Act would be presented by the Government (of St. Lucia), making a formal submission to the British Government, to make an Order under Section 10 (2) of the constitution, for the termination of Association and the granting of full Independence to the island.

The new constitution was circulated as promised and by the first weekend of October 1978 a meeting of the House of Assembly was called to discuss it. With this development, Compton's patience was to be tested one more time by the Leader of the Opposition who had by then, expertly refined the ancient art of time wasting. He now seemed as determined to use the privileges of parliament to continue his set ways if not to demonstrate that he was now in full campaign mode. By then too, everyone in the opposition had conceded Independence to the government.

Louisy therefore wrote to Compton, seeking a postponement of the scheduled sitting of the House. Not to be outdone, Compton for his part, took the initiative of addressing the nation via radio and television the night before on the planned sitting and of course informed his listeners of the important debate the following day. The Premier, to his credit, and not wanting it to be seen too anxious to celebrate the big day, bent over to accommodate the Leader of the Opposition, one more time. Everyone who followed these events knew of the delaying schemes of the opposition, but they were powerless to do anything about it. The filibuster was just another tool of politics. And in Western democracies one soon became familiar with its use or abuse.

The new date for the independence debate was therefore moved to Friday, 20th. October, 1978. Before that, (around the 13 October) Compton informed the nation and his political party colleagues and supporters in particular, that the date of December 13 – St. Lucia's National Day - Discovery Day would not now be the date for the island's Independence from Britain; he believed the reason was the unsettled nature of Prime Minister Callaghan's government in Britain, which then faced a vote of confidence in the British House of Commons. It turned out that Callaghan and his government survived the 'no confidence motion' in November 1978.

At the sitting of the St. Lucia House of Assembly to debate the new independent constitution, Kenneth Foster, Barrister, stood on a point of order before the proceedings had properly begun. That experienced Barrister, speaking for the opposition, wished it to be known and stated for the record, that the opposition was participating in the debate, without prejudice. He charged that the motion for Independence was unconstitutional, invalid and null and void. Before the words were properly out the barrister's mouth, the Speaker of the House had intervened to deny the motion. Furthermore, the Speaker indicated, persuasively and forcefully, one might add, that the debate would continue, come hell or high water. The Speaker also overruled the charge that the motion as applied for by the government was not properly before the House and that it did not violate any rules for the laying of such papers.

But Foster was not finished. He was soon on his feet again. This time he claimed that the document before the House was not genuine but rather that it was a 'dummy' purporting to represent the real. He affirmed that the 'dummy' was an incomplete document and that it contained so many errors and substantial amendments, that it would, in his view, be more prudent for the government to have it withdrawn and re-laid before the House. Foster could well have been speaking to a dressed-up stone in the Speaker's chair. Having attempted (and failed) in his spirited attack on the method by which government had laid the constitution motion before the House, the debate proceeded without further incident and in a very anti-climactic and lack lustre fashion.

Your humble servant, the M. P. for Castries East, (Marchand) at the time, rose to speak on the motion. I briefly traced the work of the various delegations to London on the subject at hand, and then made what I thought was the important observation that the document which was laid before the House of Assembly for consideration contained matters which were never discussed nor agreed to at the constitutional conference in London. I pointed out that the specific issues which were not agreed to, and which the British government had suggested be settled in the Parliament of St. Lucia, ought to have been matters for further public consultations. These formed the core beliefs and input from the opposition for constitutional change. I did not favour the House with concrete evidence of these feelings being fairly certain that those colleagues with legal training were amply qualified to expand on my proposals for term limits; the character of the Senate; (should there be one), and the dating and calling of general elections.

On that day every Member of Parliament spoke on the issue of a new constitution for the island. That may have been because the proceedings were broadcast live. Politicians from both sides of the aisle seized the opportunity to impress their constituents and others. As usual, members of the opposition spoke at some length on that Independence motion and the record of Hansard for the period should reveal more fully the entire breadth of fancy which took flight in parliament on that day. What remains to be added here for posterity, is the fact that no member of the opposition voted against the Independence motion. In fact, Parliament, on that day appeared to have been unanimous in its support for Independence for the island. Here again, the records of Hansard should verify this. Furthermore, long before the Independence motion was finally laid in Parliament, the opposition had conceded that Compton would soon become the island's first Prime Minister. It therefore determined to focus its energies on making certain that he did not also win the next general elections, due by mid-1979 - four months after Independence.

After a lengthy debate at which no new information emerged to support the case for either side, the Government of St. Lucia duly reported the outcome of the debate in the St. Lucia parliament to the Government of the United Kingdom, in London. At the same time the Government of St. Lucia formally applied to London to sever their remaining constitutional ties, and announce a date by which the island would proceed to political

Independence. Following the formal procedure in the British Parliament, the date for Independence was decided. Later it was announced, first by the British High Commission office in Barbados, and not by the British Government Representative (B.G.R.) in St. Lucia – a point not missed by students of politics and diplomacy.

That announcement came too late for the island to proceed to Independence at the time which Premier Compton had originally suggested. When it became clear that the date set by Compton had been missed, the opposition celebrated as if they had won a substantial political victory. To mark the occasion, they coined the phrase 'we missed the boat' and behaved as if they too were not to ride the Independence boat, whenever it arrived. But ready or not the boat - the "S. S. Independence" was to arrive on the 22nd February, 1979. Perhaps to certain opposition elements at the time, the twenty-second February held fewer terrors than thirteenth December of the year before it. The important point it seemed, was that Compton's preferred timing had gone adrift with the British handing the opposition a dubious victory even as it allowed Compton to proceed to Independence. The phrase 'we missed the boat' had provided temporary and dubious pleasure to the opposition and its supporters. Looking back, it seems all so childish now. Yet that phrase had gained wide currency among the ardent followers of Labour. It would be an understatement to say that it became another propaganda tool in the fierce and narrow partisan politics that had gripped young and old alike on the island, over the issue of independence.

Compton and his team were soon to have the last laugh on that particular issue. By the end of November 1978 the Government of St. Lucia received word of the date Her Majesty's government would set the island free, to take its place among the independent nations of the world. The news from London was that the 22nd February, 1979 was the preferred date for Independence. On hearing this, Compton and his colleagues as well as their party supporters now claimed to the world that they had caught the 'Independence' boat. They jumped and danced (and drank), celebrating as when a great personal triumph had been attained. They celebrated well into the night at all their favourite watering holes around the island. Their teasing of the opposition supporters was to follow in like manner as was done to them when the preferred date was first missed.

Upon receipt of the date for Independence from Britain, Compton addressed the nation on December 5, 1978. He said in part: 'Against the jeers of the faint-hearted and against obstructions, procrastinations and delays, we struggled on until victory was assured. But this is not a victory for party or faction; it is a victory for a people who, throughout this long march have conducted themselves with dignity and maturity. Our debates may have been spirited, but never acrimonious; our differences may appear to be wide, but never divisive; above all, we did not tear apart that under-lying fabric of unity of our people which is so necessary as we venture out into the new wide world'.

The Premier was giving one of the more important speeches of his long political career and he certainly seemed aware of the full import of his words. An impartial, detached listener would conclude that Compton had chosen his words very wisely indeed. His opponents, though, may have had other ideas, even as the Premier continued to wax eloquent and added as if struck by a sudden bolt on heightened statesmanship: 'It is only by looking back through the long corridors of history we can fully appreciate the immensity of this great achievement. And now that victory has been won, let us not tarnish it by continued strife. Let us instead, show the world that whatever our political differences may be, we put on the mantle and accept the responsibility of independence and nationhood, as a united people'.

The opposition listened with interest, and appeared deliberately sanguine in its chosen path as it assessed the effects of the Premier's speech on a divided nation. It also saw that speech as coming from a master politician who was wearing the robes of a fox. He had apparently decided that it was more useful and tactful to put aside the demeanour and roar of the lion and instead to clothe himself in innocence and diplomacy. This even as the fox silently gloated over the capturing of the prize he had most coveted.

It was Compton's best performance by far since the independence issue was first mooted. He had secured the coveted prize and that was all that mattered, at the time. In addition to securing a date, there was the little matter of uniting the nation as one, if Independence was to mean anything. That seemed to have been the entire purpose of Compton's address that evening. Achieving national unity, in the view of many, would be Compton's real test as first Prime Minister of a divided citizenry. At that moment it was to him alone that the island looked for fashioning and securing a path to social and economic progress.

The island was soon to set out on a new and un-chartered journey into political Independence. Its only guide and compass were the scattered remains of certain former colonies which had already travelled that road and had little to show for their journey. Poverty and misery in the midst of their flag waving, their new currency and their precious national anthems were all the symbols available. But these were just a beginning. The advantages of political Independence had simply vanished in many former British colonies, once certain government leaders had rested their sticky fingers on the levers of political power.

By then December 13, which the island calls 'National Day' was fast approaching, and with it the beginning of preparations for Christmas. December 13, also marks the day the island is reputed to have been first set foot on by Christopher Columbus, thereby claiming it for Spain and Roman Catholicism. At the arrival of the Spaniards, the island was renamed 'Santa Lucia', in honour of Saint Lucy, from its original 'Land of the Iguana -Iyanola' as its native people -The Caribs - had first called it.

With the approaching festive season, the St. Lucia Labour Party toned down its public meetings as well as its scheduled indoor political meetings. This was to allow the people time for reflection and for family. The party, however, continued to keep a watchful eye out on the process of registration of new electors. That process was continuously plagued with shortages of necessary material for the complete registration of electors for the highly anticipated elections in mid-1979. The voters list for the entire island was for the first time, being completely renewed under a system which involved the issuance of registration cards/identity cards, bearing the photographs of qualified electors. These new cards contained the holders' social security number, date of birth as well as their address and gender. That national identification card. also held other bits of useful information.

The registration of voters was frustratingly slow; much too slow for the liking of those who feared that their supporters would use this as an excuse not to register. There were constant complaints throughout the island by persons who wished to be registered and who were turned away by those who were hired for that purpose, claiming the lack of registration material or the absence of cameras for the all important photo I.D. For those who were employed, the new process of registering eligible electors was perhaps even more frustrating. Others with the luxury of time and who were determined to be registered, often had their patience and determination rewarded. Still there were many who were not so fortunate. At the end, no one could tell for certain how many electors were left out of the process. It appeared to the casual observer that elections did not seem to matter for those who refused to be registered. Provisions were made in the new legislation for those who had registered under the new system of I.D. cards and who for whatever reason were unable to produce these new identification cards (ID') on the day of elections. The law had determined that a St. Lucian passport or a birth certificate or other suitable photo I.D. would suffice, provided that such a person's name appeared on the new list of electors for the 1979 general elections.

The opposition candidates many of whom were already identified by the Labour Party, but not yet been officially announced, were keeping a constant and watchful eye on the registration proceedings. They were reported to be out walking and driving through their respective constituencies and encouraging persons, especially known party supporters to register, in order to vote. At times candidates and their friendly operatives were seen transporting these would-be voters to the registration centres in privately owned vehicles manned by party volunteers. Notwithstanding these efforts, the opposition still contended that the new registration process never got running as quickly and as smoothly as it would have liked it to. It was difficult to erase from one's mind that this slowing down of the process to a mere trickle, was not a deliberate act, calculated to frustrate persons who it is believed were supporters of the opposition party. It was not difficult to arrive at such a conclusion, after it became known that the registration centres were secretly and quietly issuing the necessary I.D. cards to known supporters of the ruling political party. Such issuing of I.D. cards continued even after the office processing these cards had been officially closed for the day. It did not help that almost every identifiable employee at the registration office and in every constituency, was a known supporter of Premier Compton and his political party.

In early December 1978, the opposition threatened to resign 'en masse' from the House of Assembly should the Order-in- Council granting Independence to the island be presented and approved by the British Parliament. However, the opposition appeared to have had a change of heart. Instead of its planned mass resignation from Parliament, it decided to boycott all further sittings of the House, including the important and historic Independence Day ceremonial sitting. That event was to be presided over by no less a person than the Princess Alexandra, the Honourable Mrs. Angus Ogilvy, Her Majesty's personal Representative, who was to sit as head of parliament that day and to chair the brand new Independence proceedings of the first parliament of an Independent St. Lucia.

In the meantime, the sister Caribbean and Windward Island nation of Dominica achieved political independence on November 3, 1978. That event passed largely unnoticed in St. Lucia. There was no known reason that that island should have attained political independence before St. Lucia. However, both the Government and the Opposition in Dominica were reported to have been equally persuaded that they shared a common and joint interest in political Independence for that island. Dominica now had its new national flag, new anthem and new Coat-of-arms, and was very proud of it all, from reports reaching us in St. Lucia. It even changed its name from the simply Dominica, which Christopher Columbus might have recognized, to the more prideful: 'The Commonwealth of Dominica' perhaps to prove that it too had arrived. It may also have been to emphasize there was little in a name.

Meanwhile, back in St. Lucia the Independence Committee, under the chairmanship of House Speaker the Honourable Mr. St. Clair Daniel and Secretary, Mr. Fitzgerald Louisy, Permanent Secretary in the Ministry of Education and cousin of the Leader of the Opposition Honourable Allan Louisy, were moving full steam ahead with preparations for independence celebrations. A sub-committee under the chairmanship of Honourable Clendon Mason, Minister for Communications and Works and Parliamentary Representative for the Dennery South constituency, decided that the island would keep its Statehood flag, and its coat of arms with only slight modifications to the latter, as their new independence loin cloth and apron. The State national anthem, which was open to competition, was written by Father Jesse, a senior F.M.I priest from Britain who had spent a lifetime on the island planting Roman Catholicism. The lyrics had been put to music by one of the more illustrious sons of Vieux-Fort and St. Lucia, the highly acclaimed musician, Leton Thomas, himself a devout Roman Catholic who had spent his entire life in the field of education both locally and internationally. He was later knighted by Her Majesty on the recommendation of the government of Saint Lucia; and is now properly to be called: Sir Leton.

In early January 1979, and counting down towards the date for Independence of February 22, the Government Information Service reported that Premier Compton was seeking joint overseas representative missions with other East Caribbean territories which were at that time also proceeding to Independence. Later, the Windward and Leeward Islands were to sign the Treaty of Basseterre (in St. Kitts, in June 1981) creating the Organization of East Caribbean States (O.E.C.S.) in which these islands agreed to work together for the common good in matters of economic, social and external relations.

As the new year (1979) began, the opposition renewed its campaign for early general elections. It still kept up the pressure on both the British government and the government of St. Lucia for their mediocre handling of the Independence issue. To this end, the Leader of the Opposition, who was by that time becoming more and more radical in his expressions on the Independence issue, informed a large crowd of party supporters at a public political rally in the southern town of Vieux-Fort, that he had recently written to Mr. Callaghan, the Prime Minister of Britain. The letter urged Mr. Callaghan, even at this eleventh hour, 'to do it right' and repeated the opposition's arguments against the manner by which the British Government was sending the island off, without an appropriate package of economic assistance. That package was by then becoming increasingly important in the opposition's case against both the British and St. Lucia governments. The opposition felt that both governments were colluding in setting the island free on a mere pittance and without a prayer or a hope. In its view, the offer of fifty thousand pounds was worth less than 1% (one percent) of the profits the British had earned from the island over the last fifty years, at least.

Mr. Callaghan's reply to the Leader of the Opposition was read aloud over the microphone by Mr. Louisy at the public rally. In it, he thanked Mr. Louisy for his letter and then went on to urge him to co-operate and unite as the island moved towards Independence. In response the crowd burnt an effigy of Rowlands, the Minister in the Foreign and Commonwealth Office who had conducted the Independence negotiations on behalf of the British government. Mr. Callaghan too, would have suffered a similar fate, had that crowd known him well enough to produce an effigy. The crowd was obviously more familiar with Ted Rowlands having seen his photograph so often in the newspapers and his images on their television screens. That crowd therefore produced a fine substitute for Mr. Rowlands which was to be set to fire that evening. Staunch Labourites later insisted that it would have been far better politics if two separate and distinct effigies were burnt that night; substituting some impression of a demon for Prime Minister Callaghan, and then forwarding suitable images of the entire event to the British Broadcasting Service, in London.

Interestingly, as the Leader of the Opposition and his party colleagues busied themselves with public political meetings and protests throughout the island, the National Independence Committee established by the government was also working at full steam in every village and town around the island, including those represented by the opposition parliamentarians. The political heat created by the opposition was, however, beginning to take effect. That was deduced from the actions of the police. The opposition was frequently frustrated by the police who often refused late applications for public meetings. The police would sometimes change the venues for public meetings which were often applied for in good time. The excuse was that they could not guarantee safety and security in the specific area for which the meeting was applied. The opposition believed that the attitude of law enforcement came from over enthusiastic supporters of Premier Compton within the St. Lucia Police Force. Some of these officers and their families hailed from the then, booming banana belts of Dennery, Micoud and Babonneau. Many of these people had been assisted in one way or the other by John Compton - the politician, and lawyer.

The attitude of the police only served to deepen the already widening gulf and knee-jerk suspicion that had long existed on the island, between opposition supporters and the police. The intense struggle over the

Independence issue, had now dovetailed into the 1979 general elections campaign. This did not make the work of the police any easier. However, the opposition persevered, with the knowledge that both the police and they had their different and equally important roles to play in a democratic system of government. If free speech and free assemblies of law-abiding citizens were to be preserved on the island, as the foundation pillars of our system of governance, then this was to be tested whenever the citizens had an issue deserving of such a testing. It was believed at the time that Saint Lucia was perhaps the only island in the Caribbean where such deep divisions persisted between opposition and the police on matters of such great national importance. The opposition also let it be known that a spirited electioneering campaign was a small price by which to test freedom's promise. The police had to learn to exercise tolerance and impartiality, if they were to develop a professional force which enjoyed the support of all sections of society, claimed the opposition at the time.

To be fair, the apparent political divisions within the force may have been due to differences in age, qualification and training. The young Turks in there tended to be more independent of thought, while the older more experienced heads were proving resistant to change. At a time which called for unity and visionary leadership it was disheartening to witness the arrogance and self-imposed importance of certain senior politicians who were refusing to meet with the leadership of the opposition to discuss, and agree on a way forward, in unity. It was as if they were telling us that the government had not yet realized that politics was not about winning a political game, but about producing better lives as Professor Cornel West had observed in his book, 'Democracy Matters'. Indeed Professor West could have been speaking to the cows at Beausejour; Vieux-Fort as far as the Government of Saint Lucia was concerned.

The police, it seemed, had little choice but to follow the orders of government, and at the time seemed afraid to be seen speaking to the opposition. It was with this in mind that Premier Compton's campaign rhetoric that 'St. Lucia is mine in seventy-nine' delivered in early 1979 prior to Independence, came to be so offensive to so many. That statement only served to further exacerbate the tense atmosphere on the island. This in turn put more pressure on an already fractured police force. Many ardent supporters of the opposition were sincerely frightened by the Premier's words. Perhaps they had come to believe that the man was usually as good as his word. He somehow always seemed to follow them with action. This grand announcement that: 'in seventy-nine, St. Lucia is mine'….. phrase was the straw that finally broke the camel's back; the flame which ignited a highly combustible emotional situation on the ground. These words were interpreted to mean a declaration of war by Premier Compton on his opponents – a war which he apparently thought he would win, whatever the cost. These words unfortunately also meant that the Independence celebrations would pass with at least half of the population staying away and praying for the days to go by quickly and for the next general elections to be held. Many an opposition supporter hoped to answer the Premier's veiled threat on Election Day 1979.

Perhaps what mattered even more than the next general elections was the fact that by that time the politicians on both sides of the House of Assembly, seemed to know intuitively that politics was much more than just winning contested elections? They obviously understood that it was also about changing the lives of their constituents for better. It is an observation which too many supporters of political parties often omit to appreciate and acknowledge in the hurly burly of active political campaigning. Someone ought to say to such supporters that there will be life after the next general elections and that politicians come and go - some even changing sides between elections. The idea of lurking quietly in the dark and then suddenly exploding into quarrel and tearing each other apart for the sake of politics, must therefore be discouraged by everyone who has a voice or a hand with which to write - or both.

*Peter Josie: 'The Diamond in the Star' - symbol of the
St. Lucia Labour Party in the nineteen seventies and eighties*

School friends, St. Mary's College 1960
Standing L-R: H. John, Velon John, Sylvester Dubois, Alfred Gaspard
Front L-R: Desmond George, Errol Hunte, Peter Josie, R. Riley

*St. Mary's College (St. Lucia) sports team at the regional Windward Islands
Secondary Schools sports tournament, 1960. I am at front right standing.
At back, second from right, is Unison Whiteman of Presentation College
Grenada, where the picture was taken. Presentation was our sister college
in Grenada although it was the Grenada Boys Secondary school (GBSS)
which participated in Inter-schools tournament, in 1960*

*Kenneth 'Ken" Morgan, Victor Ludurum (St. Lucia) winning the
800yds race in the 1956 Inter-School Windward Islands Tournamant*

*Augustus 'Pan' Andrew represented St. Lucia in Football and Cricket.
Here he is receiving the baton in the 400yds relay at the 1956
Inter-School Windward Islands Tournamant*

My immediate family: Left to right; Carol, Lance, Me, Petra and Beverley. Children (and spouses) of politicians often suffer for sins they did not commit. I owe my children a special debt for bearing my public life with all the pain it often brought.

Final year (B.Sc.) class (Agriculture) St. Augustine Campus University of the West Indies (UWI) Trinidad, 1968. I am standing at the back, five from right.

*For over fifty years   Bro. De Lellis, a son of Ireland helped to
educate and train the sons of Saint Lucia*

*Her Majesty and Prince Philip acknowledge warm welcome
on Campus (St. Augustine) 1966*

May Day rally with three main speakers of the Seamen and Waterfront Workers Trade Union. Left to right H. Deterville, Peter Josie and Marcel Thomas: a stalwart of the Union and labour movement generally.

Banana farmers visit to London with me, Minister of Agriculture, St. Lucia to learn first hand the value of producing top quality bananas for an increasingly competitive and globalised world market.

A public meeting of St. Lucia Labour Action Movement (SLAM) comprising members of the former St. Lucia Forum and disgruntled Labour party supporters.

The Honourable Peter Josie, Minister of Trade, Industry, Tourism and Foreign Affairs (Saint Lucia) welcomes his counterpart Mr. Jose Velasco Zambrano, Foreign Minister of Venezuela, on an official visit to the island. During the visit a bilateral trade agreement was signed between Saint Lucia and Venezuela.

Students of Advanced Level College (St. Lucia) paying a courtesy call on the Minister of Foreign Affairs (St. Lucia) 1981.

Jubilarians with His Grace, (L-R): Bro. De Lellis O'Sullivan, Bro. Clement McCarthy, Bro. Liam Quirke, Bro. Matthew Feheney, Archbishop Kelvin Felix, Bro. Benildus Fenton, Bro. Gerard, and Bro. Robert Fanovich (Regional Leader).

Maurice Bishop left and I, in Cabinet room (St. Lucia) 1980.

Mr. Martin Carasco: The Special Services Unit (SSU) was his creation and he used it to put criminals away.

Frances Michel: She was a formidable political campaigner for the rights of women, farmers and the underprivileged.

There was much rejoicing and positive anticipation during the 1979 campaign. The people knew instinctively that positive change had finally come to the politics of the island.

Calixte George (right) and I. Calixte, an Agronomist by profession, had worked both at the Caribbean level and at home. Together we prepared what may have been the first comprehensive land use map of the island, but frustration over the unscientific and opportunistic approach to land use on the island by reckless politicians, soon led us to seek new pathways.

35th International Transport Federation Congress, Luxemberg, 1975
L-R: Sir Roy Trotman (Barbados Workers Union), Francis Mongroo (Seamen and Waterfront Workers Union- T'dad), PeterJosie (Seamen and Waterfront Workers Union - St. Lucia) and Ottiwell Simmons (Bermuda Industrial Workers Union)

Peter Josie in Constitution Park near to the precincts of parliament,
a place where Angels feared to tread. The ensuing political turmoil helped
bring down the Louisy-led Labour government, and saw the return of
John Compton and his UWP to political office.

A working lunch of the Farmers and Farm Workers Trade Union - 1977.
L-R: George Odlum, Frances Michel, President, Peter Josie is not in picture.

Hurricane Allen 1980
Volunteer workers clean-up and clear roads

George Odlum; restraining an animated supporter in another display of street theatre. Politics was an extension of the theatre which Odlum loved so much. Every street was a stage and the men and women there (including the police) merely props and bit-players to the one who had mastered English Literature early and had pursued it all the way to Bristol University in England.

From Left Joseph Lawrence, senior civil servant Ministry of Agriculture, Father Theo Joseph, Roman Catholic Priest (Saint Lucia) Peter Josie (pointing) and Calixte George – perhaps discussing the way forward.

Right to Left: Sally Shelton United States Ambassador to Barbados and the East Caribbean, Peter Josie (Minister of Agriculture, Saint Lucia), His Excellency Sir Allen Lewis and two other officials discussing assistance for the island following its destruction by Hurricane Allan, in 1980.

My maternal grandmother, Edosia "Ma Doe" Alphonse
formerly Etang from the village of Laborie

Jouvert Old Mas 1980

155

Regrouping after the SLP Government self – destruction.
Peter Josie is seated at extreme left. Behind him is George Odlum and
to his right is Dave England whose family were true friends and
supporters of George Odlum, Saint Lucia.

Former Speaker of the House of Assembly
Hon. Wilfred St. Clair Daniel

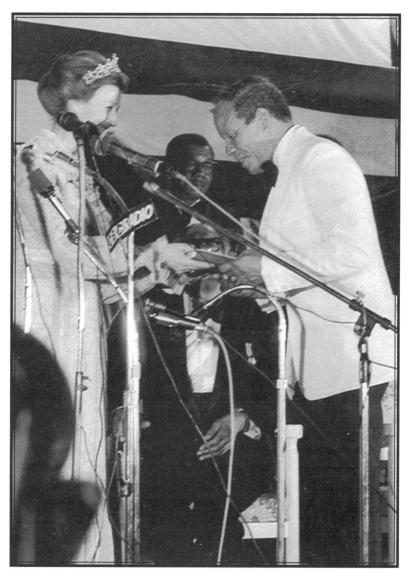

First Prime Minister of Saint Lucia, John Compton, receiving the instrument of political independence from Her Majesty's representative Princess Alexandra, the Queen's cousin.

A Dinner with the Queen

We long for a politics that is not about winning a
political game but about producing better lives.
                              Cornel West: Democracy Matters

When I was a child in Vieux-Fort the school children there looked forward to the celebration of 'Empire Day' with feverish glee and innocent joy. On Empire Day our school joined with others in the town to parade with the boy scouts and girl guides and afterwards to enjoy the treats, including unbelievably creamy ice cream served to us by the American base, near the town. The imminent closure of that air base in the early fifties was a pain to the entire town's population. Many St. Lucians and other West Indians were employed there and had established themselves on the island. In anticipation of its early closing, one noteworthy Vieux-Fort politician, seeing well the inevitable economic hardships that would follow its closure, was moved to ask publicly, 'after de closing of de base WHAT?' That question became the popular phrase for several generations of persons from Vieux-Fort who were made aware of the benefits of that base long after its closure. The school children were also saddened by the closure because unlike other schools on the island whose Empire Day treats were supplied by the local administration, and were limited to a small coconut cake and soft drink, ours on the other hand, was a real treat. We had tasty goodies of all descriptions and in addition each child received a full bottle of soft drink, (soda). In addition, the extra creamy vanilla ice cream brought out the nicest smiles and joyful glee to each little face. Back then, my grandparents owned a few cows and sold milk in Vieux-Fort and Castries as an important source of income. Delicacies such as ice cream were unknown except at Christmas, weddings and First

Communion. It was popular among school children and adults to regard the Americans as generous and the British as less so, particularly at the celebration of Empire Day. It was common knowledge that the children at Vieux-fort were better treated by the Americans, and therefore considered themselves luckier than others around the island.

I can not explain why the statement on the closure of the American Air base at Vieux-Fort made such a lasting impression on my mind. Neither can I explain why I remember so well the characterization of the British as stingy and the Americans as generous. At the time I certainly had no idea that we were citizens of the British Empire even though some kind teacher may have mentioned it. I also remember that the currency we used back then bore the head of King George the sixth of England. Only after his death and the coronation of Elizabeth the Second, did the currency change to display the images of the new Queen.

At that time the centrepiece of Empire Day activities was the lusty singing of the British National anthem and I remember it being sung with much conviction and fervour by all and sundry. As we sang, there was very little room left for insincerity among my school friends, even though I was aware there were some adults who disputed our status, as citizens of the 'British Empire'. Those adults were adamant that we were nothing more than mere subjects; a quite different matter they claimed, than citizenship. As I have said, none of this early debate, if we can even call it that, interested me then. We sang lustily and sincerely, even as we used our wits to shelter from the burning sun. I imagine there must have been some children who grudgingly went through the outdoor programme as a sacrifice, knowing what was to follow the singing and marching in the streets of our little town.

It seems such a long way from those colonial days. One would have thought that in time, every colonial subject would readily jump on the bandwagon to political independence. It must therefore have come as a complete surprise to many St. Lucians as well as our Caribbean brothers and sisters, that the political party then in parliamentary opposition was demanding that the British government 'do it right and let the people decide' instead of jumping with both feet into the proposition.

It was now March 1977, and much water had by then flowed under the bridge, as they say. As fate would have it the members of the opposition delegation to the London constitutional talks that year included that same little boy - now no longer a child - who had sung 'God Save the Queen', so lustily. The others were Allan Louisy, Leader of the Opposition in Parliament, John Compton, Premier and Henry Giraudy, the Premier's adviser. At the time, I may have stopped visiting the Roman Catholic church in which I grew up but I still remembered a favourite character from the Holy Book - all the letters of Paul - and therefore thought that the invitation to the London constitutional talks had been my own special 'Damascus moment'. As fate would have it, the closing of the American Air Base at Vieux-Fort was to become an important side issue at the Independence talks. Of course the British demurred when I proposed a package of special assistance for Vieux-Fort and to assist its many citizens who had been displaced by the war effort, some becoming poorer as a result. Such special assistance as I had proposed had also become the consuming passion of Bruce Williams, alias 'Daddy Bruce' who, at that time, had the ears of both members of the opposition delegation. Indeed it was Bruce Williams who was later to become parliamentary representative for the town of Vieux-Fort, who had first convinced me of the need for special assistance for the people there. 'Daddy' Bruce was loved by all Vieux-Fortians and he jealously guarded that love.

The thirty–year gap between that Vieux-fort school child and the person who eventually left with the Leader of the Opposition to represent the other side of the independence debate in London, was filled with many wonderful blessings and many more interesting stories from the politics of the past. The many lessons, both formal and informal, throughout those thirty years between leaving Vieux-Fort for St. Mary's and up to the time of my departure for London could be distilled into one or two sentences namely: that the greatest education of all is self knowledge, self discipline and self-confidence; that the process of learning never ends. Secondly, parental love and caring is the surest foundation on which to build trust and self confidence. With a solid foundation based on sustained love, a child can achieve his or her highest dreams, no matter what challenges that child faces in life.

The details of those constitutional talks are a matter of record and are available at the Foreign and Commonwealth office and hopefully at the national archives in St. Lucia. By the end of the formal talks in London there was much conviviality and rejoicing among delegations. After the formal proceedings the established protocols were observed.

The Boy Scout rule of learning to smile and whistle under all difficulties, which I had learnt as a school boy at Vieux-Fort, came in very handy then. With hearty handshakes and smiles all around and a cocktail or two, we were becoming impatient for the next event. We soon left for our hotels where we refreshed and prepared for the main event of the evening - a dinner to be hosted by Her Majesty the Queen.

The three-way political tussle (negotiations) was now over. It was now time for reflection, planning ahead and a breath of heightened civility.

More importantly, it was time to find the courage to unite the people of St. Lucia behind what we had done together, however much these meetings may have fallen short of our expectations. Perhaps the night's dinner with Her Majesty would set the tone for a more proper and civil way forward, I thought, as I got ready for that final farewell dinner, and the return trip home. Whatever else tried to intrude on my thoughts at that time, I kept returning to Empire Day and to the 'God Save the Queen' anthem we sang so merrily in my youth, at Vieux-Fort.

This was the same Queen to whom the school children of my generation had sung their lungs out on Empire Day beseeching God to 'Save the Queen,' the British national anthem which had become ours too. Soon Saint Lucia would have her very own anthem, and it was my sincere prayer and hope that one day a new generation of St. Lucians would learn to sing their anthem as lustily as an earlier generation had sung, 'God save the Queen', beseeching the Almighty to protect Britain's Great and to save our own Great Majesty.

Our political battle for our country was now put aside, at least for the time being. On that evening it was not easy to tell who was with the opposition and who was with the government. Of course we were briefed on how to bow and curtsy and the proper manner to shake the gloved hand of Her Majesty the Queen, as we were introduced to her. We soon made our grand entrance into the ornate and beautifully appointed dining area. It was a delight to be in the midst of such opulence; such majesty, such ceremony! It was a setting truly befitting the images one paints with such vivid imagination if one has had the benefit of reading Royalty in children's classics. The food of course was as excellent with early spring 'Irish' potatoes. I was assured the potatoes were really from Ireland, after I had made discreet enquiries. They were the main source of our carbohydrate offerings that evening. There were perfectly cooked fresh-water fowls and young ducklings - the main source of protein. Of course, there were also red and white wines in addition to other drinks which one fancied. The excellent cucumber salad was a specialty of the English which I had the privilege of sampling elsewhere before that evening.

The main thing of course was the atmosphere and the moment which would forever be captured in history. The atmosphere was tranquil and civil. One could often pick an occasional ripple of subdued jollity and controlled effusiveness. A more perfect dinner setting with such a high historical figure of renowned excellence and in a setting equally famous in the annals of Saint Lucia parliamentary politics, could hardly be surpassed. I felt then that this opportunity would not come my way again, any time soon. However, it was not the last time I would have an audience with her

Majesty the Queen, as we shall see. After that dinner we said our goodbyes and were soon whisked away to our respective hotels.

In all their tough talk and unbending countenance, the British Government had granted one concession to the opposition. General elections were to be held within six months of independence. We were not exactly excited over the outcome of those constitutional conference talks but we were aware that things could have been worse. So we accepted what was in reality a fait accompli. We therefore left London uncertain of the role which the Opposition was to play in the formalities leading to Independence. I was certain that we all loved our country dearly and that we wanted Independence and all that was best for her. No one had the monopoly on ideas, but we had history to guide us. And history does not lie - only those who interpret it, do.

When we touched down at Hewanorra airport Vieux-Fort from the constitutional conference in London, we were met by party stalwarts who were determined not to let the government use the granting of Independence to their advantage. Right there and then the decision was taken to continue the political campaign through to the next general elections which thankfully was not too far off.

Independence came and went and it did so sadly, without the full participation of many who could have helped to usher in a better day for our country. One felt certain that serious mistakes were made due to the mishandling of events by both political parties. The democratic vote in the hands of the poor and marginalized is an attractive commodity not only to drug barons and unscrupulous religious types, but also to con men posing as politicians. We were aware there would be disagreements in future but we remained hopeful that our country would be considered first, at all times, and certainly before personal ambition and greed.

It is said that a man's first charity should be to his own family, especially if poor. But no one ever said that any leader should take care of himself first before seeing after those who had put him in power and with the clear mandate to help the poor and suffering. A leader's first charity should therefore be to the poor of his country. Those who finance political campaigns should remind those whom they fund that the first responsibility of a parliamentary representative is to the people who elected him or her into office. It has become too apparent of late that he who pays the piper calls the tune. Our objective, whatever the colour of our party political T-shirts, must remain, strengthen the rule of law, the education and training of our people, and the empowering of each citizen to be the best that he or she can be.

The end result should always be that our people shall control the commanding heights of the economy and that social progress will be planned in an orderly manner thereby allowing the country to progress relentlessly forward to better and brighter days. The economic, social and political life of our island - and our Caribbean region too must be secured by each leader for the next generation. The slogan 'forward ever backward never', in my estimation was never meant to be used for political trash talk. It imparts a serious political fervour and even a spiritual and religious one. Each 22nd of February as we observe our political Independence from Britain, we must remember the road we travelled from Crown Colony, to the present. We must therefore, wish each other Happy Independence and pray that our people continue to strive for progress and unity as we move forward. As a people, we need to reach a consensus on the development agenda for the next twenty years or more. There is therefore increasing need for consultation, as we move forward.

We must learn to think (and act) beyond the next general elections, whenever these may be called. At this juncture, I should say thanks for the privilege and honour that I have been afforded in representing my country - Saint Lucia - at all three rounds of the talks (and negotiations, in England) which finally led to the island's achievement of political independence. As no country can truly be said to be totally and completely independent, Saint Lucia will learn soon that its progress will depend largely on the skills and resolve of its citizens and its friends, all working together as one.

I know that I stood on the shoulders of early pioneers, such as Geroge F. L. Charles, Martin 'Oleo' Jn. Baptiste, Burke King, Charles Augustin, Allen Lewis and Allan Louisy and many others on whose labours the first political parties on the island saw the light of day. To those early pioneers we owe a special debt of gratitude. More than this we owe it to them to make the dream a reality. The struggle is not over. The work of building a better country with stronger, more educated and committed citizens therefore continues. Our ultimate goal must be to create a united, proud, Caribbean people, each contributing to the growth and development of the whole. As we have agreed earlier, politics is not about winning a game; it is about producing better lives, and that the first charity ought always to be to our own family (and citizens), especially the poor.

The Hess Oil Debate

A man's first charity should be to his own family, if poor.
Allama Sir Abdullah:
The Wisdom of Muhammad

This account of the Hess Oil debate in the parliament of Saint Lucia is not an exact blow by blow description of the events leading to the debate and the establishment of the company's 'oil-tank-farm' at Cul-de-Sac in Saint Lucia. For this, one ought to consult the minutes of the parliament for that debate. These are recorded in 'Hansard' - the parliament's official record keeper. Also the newspaper reports of these specific events may furnish information which I may have missed. The reader should be warned, however, that neither newspaper reports nor recordings in Hansard provide the social, political and economic background against which the Hess oil debate took place. Neither do these sources observe and record for posterity the emotional and psychological state of parliamentarians and the people whom they represent in office, at the time of this, and other similarly emotive debates.

The Hess Oil debate was a hotly contested and argued issue. The proposal was brought to parliament at about the same time as the emotional issue of political Independence for the island had opened itself up for scrutiny and public discussion. Soon, both debates became embroiled as one and the same national issue. Emotions were running high on the Independence issue and many persons were suspicious that the timing of the Hess investment deal was a plot to save face for the government. That explains why the latter was initially regarded with so much disfavour. Perhaps only the few who were at the centre of the Hess political storm or who were close confidants of the government are sufficiently equipped to describe the emotional roller coaster ride of that period, with accuracy and with candour. The following is therefore an honest attempt by someone who was a major participant to capture for future generations the story of those tumultuous days in the history of a small island.

At the time of the presentation of the Hess Oil Bill to Parliament, St. Lucia was an Associated State of Britain: meaning that she was responsible for her internal affairs, while Britain continued to be in charge of external affairs and defense. The island was at the time slowly emerging from years of colonialism and neglect. The education of its citizens was then a priority of the island's government, which was expressed in its yearly expenditure on education. However, the island was still a very long way from universal secondary education; or compulsory corrective adult literacy. Besides, at the time, it needed better quality roads and bridges as well as a better health service. Those who had missed out on primary schooling were rarely given a second opportunity at educating themselves in those days. There was no second chance except for the very few who were able to escape overseas.

It is therefore fair to say that the island was emerging from many long years of backwardness, poverty and even disease. There were still only a handful of secondary schools to serve a growing population of some 110,000, in 1979. Only a measly 35 or so of its students gained the required passes each year to qualify for entrance into tertiary institutions. Of these a minority left home for further studies at the University of the West Indies. Loans for education were not yet available through the local banks, or anywhere else. Students wanting to pursue further education therefore had to look to government bursaries or make their own private arrangements. Access to the single scholarship that the U. W.I. offered to the island each year, was also very limited. That competition was open to the entire Caribbean, so it was tough going all round for anyone who wished to pursue university education.

The banana industry, which had replaced sugar, was quickly establishing itself as an important and regular source of income benefitting more rural peasants and small farmers than sugar ever did. The reality remained, however, that the majority of its citizens never learnt to read or write. Thankfully, continued regular income from the banana industry was changing things around. To be candid, the island had come a long way, but it had miles and miles to travel on the road to social and economic progress. It therefore could not afford to rest, even for one moment. It is against this dire search for economic growth - made more urgent by the high rate of unemployment - that the country learnt of the intention of the government to strike a deal with Amerada Hess Oil of the USA. That announcement of a promise of an oil refinery and the creation of thousands of jobs on the island should have been greeted as the best news since the opening up of the United Kingdom for immigrant labour from the Commonwealth around 1950. But that bit of good news with its prospects for jobs and economic progress was soon polarized along party political lines. The real benefits and long-term interests of the company were then openly questioned not only by opposition politicians but by many others demanding more concrete information on the proposed investment. Soon the question: 'What were the real long-term benefits' was on many lips throughout the island. For a brief moment following the initial announcement, all systems were going, and things looked good and positive even to the opponents of the government. But all that was about to change; and change fast.

When therefore, the Government of St Lucia carefully leaked information that the island was to become the new St. Croix of the southern Caribbean, the news generated quite a stir. The excitement was palpable. The anticipated positive economic outcome became the shared currency of the time. The salivary glands of the nation were fully titillated. No one had read the details of the deal struck between the Government of St. Lucia and Hess Oil, but the people supported it anyway. Excitement ran wild. Environmental impact studies did not seem to matter then. Those who took a long-term view of development and cautioned against the possibility of permanent long term damage to the island's fragile ecosystem were summarily dismissed or cowed into silence. 'Let the oil flow' became the popular cry of the common and educated alike. Before this, that slogan had also become a political party line for those who had squeezed through the 1974 general elections. For a time though, the government seemed to have received some respite because of the Hess Oil announcement.

At the time, the Independence issue was at the centre of the island's concerns. The frequent public meetings of the opposition were gaining momentum and sidelining the government propaganda machinery into silence. Information on the proposed refinery travelled quickly through the Caribbean. Unfortunately, because of the prevailing hostile political climate within St. Lucia at the time, such information soon became tainted and twisted into all manner of shapes and fashion. Supporters of the government began to inflate the figures on the quantum of the investment and then proceeded to fabricate new stories each day, about the new Oil Messiah who was coming to save the island. Opponents of the government then retaliated with invented, negative stories of their own. The informal but popular grapevine of the opposition seemed then to take over the Government Information Service - GIS. It did not help matters that the G I S only broadcast what it deemed the public ought to know, and quite often much less than that. The policy of the news media was to support the government of the day.

The sure way in which people showed their discontent was to vote with their feet - by leaving the island. At one point in the mid-sixties St. Lucians left in droves for the island of St. Croix, about one hour's flying time from Saint Lucia. The reason they chose St. Croix was that Amerada Hess was building an oil refinery on that island. St. Lucians therefore had first hand information on Amerada Hess (Hess Oil) long before the news of the company's interest in St. Lucia. It was well known among St. Lucians that that company had changed St. Croix for better. So everyone became excited when it was first announced that Hess Oil intended to invest in Saint Lucia too. Soon the promoters of the St. Croix model began reminding the people in St. Lucia of the many ways in which their families had benefitted from Hess investments on that island. They also reminisced on the contributions of St. Lucians who had planted mango, breadfruit, plum, citrus and even ornamentals soon after they had arrived in St. Croix. Some even boasted that they had made St. Croix a green island, long before going green became a new political football. The propaganda to 'let the oil flow' was so intense at one point; it must have turned off even those who were inclined to support it. For others of a more skeptical bent it was too messianic for comfort. The Hess oil divide therefore began more and more to resemble the political divide on the question of independence.

In such a charged atmosphere what, if anything, was a young politician and first time Parliamentarian (in opposition) to do? Should he forget that in his judgement the whole of the Hess deal had not been fully revealed? Was it sensible or wise to support legislation embracing long term development projects that had not been fully ventilated? Should a young parliamentarian be guided by his conscience and vote no, if he lacked information (and confidence) in the details which were being presented to him for a vote? Or should he instead, vote yes, in order to appease those in his constituency anxious for work? Was he sufficiently brave to vote no, and risk the hostility of the crowd that had gathered on the precincts of the parliament building for that important debate? There were certainly more questions than answers that day for me and I suspect for many others in the opposition. Perhaps I should have taken my cue from the local environmentalists who went silent on the day of the debate. Their silence was deafening. Others in leadership roles were too busy registering new companies to capture the anticipated spill-off business anticipated from the oil refinery project, to care about the details of the Hess deal.

Where then should anyone with misgivings about the advertised benefits of the proposed oil refinery turn? Should he accept the proposal by the oil company that the parliamentary vote on the matter should be unanimous, if the project was to be implemented? Or should he as a matter of principle, defy the dictates of big petroleum money and refuse to subject the fledgling island democracy to such crass bullying and abuse? Do principles always apply in parliamentary debates or were they convenient tools which could be dispensed with as the issue dictated? Was it all right in times of hunger and poverty, to forgo the finery of dignity, self-respect, and conscience, and vote instead for bread as any layman or beggar would do?

In short, should I vote yes and 'let the oil flow' as the government propaganda of the day had insisted that all seventeen elected members of Parliament do? And if I did, and voted yes, how then would I explain afterwards to my children and grandchildren that, at the hour of trial I failed to stand up for what I believed was right? How does a man of honour not stand on a point of principle but instead condescend to bow meekly to the dictates of cheap political mischief? At that time, even the prayers which parliament invoked at the commencement of each sitting were being made a mockery of, as far as I was concerned. Each had sworn to serve his God and his country faithfully, but on that day whose God were we serving? Before the House met for debate on the Hess Oil bill I meekly recited my own prayers. I fell on my knees as any thoughtful person would. I truly repented for my acts of transgressions and omissions. In focussed meditation I invoked the names of every saint my religion had taught me could intercede, on my behalf. Who was I to talk to God directly? Saints were therefore important to persons like me, as intercessors. And it was the prophetic miracle worker, St. Jude, to whom I finally turned, hoping to find strength to die for what I believed, if it came to that. 'To hell with everybody else', I thought. No leader had ever made a name without challenging common wisdom and standing against the establishment, and for a set of principles he deemed inviolable.

I therefore determined to vote against the Hess Oil Bill when it came up for debate and voting in parliament. This I decided on my knees, in prayer. I would not let an angry mob stop me. More than that, I also decided that I would express my displeasure with some of the provisions of the Hess Oil Bill by dramatically tearing up that document whilst I was on my feet and making my contribution to the Hess Oil debate. That simple act should send the most powerful signal, of my defiance against bullies, I thought. It would teach would- be investors not to trifle with emerging political progressives as I fancied myself then. It would instill also in local and foreign investors that every politician is not a squirming coward carrying a concealed price tag; a few stood for honour and virtue, and I decided to make that point in the most dramatic way I knew, on that day. Yes, I may have been only one of seventeen, but throughout my life I had heard and seen one or two persons who had made a difference to a community, a country and at times even to the world. So yes, minorities matter very much. Real change often began with only a few good (and bold) men - and women too. Such has been the hidden secret of real change from time immemorial.

St. Lucia needed a miracle of enlightment - and I needed guidance and courage. For further assistance and perhaps to prove my deep faith in him, I cut the prayer to St. Jude from its folder. I still carry that prayer in my wallet thirty plus years later. Back then I was concerned that desperate political party hacks would harm anyone perceived to be standing in the way or blocking large investments such as Hess had offered. I had made up my mind that no matter what the political future may hold, I would say and do what in my heart I knew was right, and it did not matter the consequences. It may have seemed foolhardy, but that was my stance then. This debate was a test I should not fail. Let ignorance crucify. 'History will absolve me'. I thought, recalling Fidel Castro's famous lines from one of his early speeches following the success of the Cuban revolution. The people had chosen me to lead and I must point the way no matter how strewn with obstacles the course.

I offered earlier the period 1974 to 1979 as the most exciting of my political life. The Hess Oil debate was the zenith of that period. It caused the greatest anguish within the breast of a young parliamentarian determined to establish his mark. It brought to the fore the most fundamental questions of governance which young emerging democracies like ours face. Should the elected representative always abide by the wishes of his or her constituents or should his gut-feeling and judgement prevail? How does one reject arguments that are without merit and at the same time avoid offending long and valued friendships? Should one bow to information that has been deliberately skewed to produce a specific, desired political result regardless of future consequences for the country? And should one also humbly accept the dictates of the poor and unemployed anxious for work, knowing that when the project materializes, there would not be the number of jobs for the marginalized that had gathered in Constitution Square that morning? Grappling with these questions I recalled the book entitled 'The Loneliness of the Long Distance Runner' but I could not put my hands on it when I needed to review it, for 'Dutch' courage.

At the time of my involvement in the 1974 general elections, I had made the decision to devote 20 or so of the best years of my life to serving my country at its highest court and forum – its parliament. The Hess Oil debate was an early and severe test and threatened to scuttle that ambition.

I felt then that the people were convinced by what they had been told by the government that the economic benefits of the project were all real and that it therefore ought to be embraced by everyone. To vote against the bill for whatever 'academic' or frivolous reason would be tantamount to ending one's political career before it had properly got off the ground.

On the day of the debate, the ruling party had quietly invited its supporters to Constitution Square, the minuscule green space that sits between the parliament building and the judiciary across from it, in Castries. The park itself is no more than one hundred by ninety feet in area. It sits at the eastern head of the William Peter Boulevard, the main shopping rectangle in the city. That town plan was as a result of the 1948 Castries fire which almost completely wiped out the capital.

Today, anyone looking at the layout of the city of Castries, would surely appreciate the short sightedness of its planners and designers. The people who live there have learnt to live and work with such planned incompetence. What has been done is done, seemed to be the common wisdom. Successive governments of St. Lucia have announced plans to redesign and build a new city. Hopefully such plans will materialize in the not too distant future.

During the days leading up to the Hess Oil debate, the opposition held several public political meetings. They were intended to present a united front on the issue and to inform the public on all aspects of the agreement. I attended meetings to which I was invited, including those called by my concerned constituents. The week before the debate, the seven elected Opposition Members of Parliament met with the Chairman of the Oil Company, Mr. Leon Hess, at his request. Hess implored us to trust him, 'He was a man of his word', he said. We were concerned however, that trust was a two-sided affair. I pointed out that everything the company wanted from the members of Parliament was all written down in black and white and was to become law. On the other hand we, the representatives of the people of St. Lucia, were being asked to take a leap of faith by a transnational corporation. Why our concerns shouldn't also be put on paper and made law, I asked. Everyone in there fell silent. By the sixties and early seventies, such transnational corporations had unfortunately become the scourge of developing third world countries. It also occurred to us that at the time trust was an important consideration of the Chairman of Amerada Hess Corporation - Leon Hess. Other American transnational corporations such as Chiquita and Dole were lobbying in order to deprive us of the special privileges which our bananas enjoyed in the United Kingdom market. Trust was good; if only it could be verified. Everyone there that day understood that legally binding agreements only reinforced mutual trust and were much favoured in business over nice sounding words.

By the time the opposition parliamentarians met with Leon Hess, I had successfully kicked the smoking habit, a gift from a young parliamentarian to himself. The zeal and fidelity, with which I tackled my important parliamentary duties and indeed politics in general, were to deter me from accepting the gift of cigars and a gold Cross ball point pen which Leon Hess offered each person present at that meeting. That was not easy to do. One did not wish to seem hostile or inhospitable to someone who had promised to do so much for the island. Yet accepting the pen and cigar seemed at the time as gift trinkets to 'the native Indians of old'. However, if the gifts were larger it would surely be construed as a complete buy out, or sell out of one's integrity. At the time, I kept thinking that this was the very thing that members of the St. Lucia Forum had warned against in past years. I therefore determined to treat this Hess issue as a test of principles. It was not easy to tell what, if anything Hess learnt from that encounter with the opposition. But I thought he gave his hand away somewhat, when within a few days he invited George Odlum and me to breakfast at La Toc hotel. That hotel was his home in St. Lucia.

Leon Hess proved a most gracious host. He was even more forthcoming and explicit in his plans for the island than he had been in that cabinet room. I had to keep reminding myself that no one loved this little Caribbean rock of an island more than I did. If Hess wanted to share it with us then perhaps we should be polite and gracious and allow him. Both George (Odlum) and I listened to what Hess had to say. At one point he offered to fly us to any of three named destinations within the U.S.A. including Puerto Rico to see the standard of hospitals his company was offering to build in St. Lucia. We were also welcome to tour St. Croix at his expense, any time we wished, to see for ourselves the social infrastructure he had built there for his employees. George Odlum and I advised Hess that our top priority for our people was to educate them; so if there was any voluntary investment to be made by his company in St. Lucia, it should be in the construction of schools, and the training of teachers. We were not the government of the island at the time, and neither was Odlum a Member of Parliament, then.

Leon Hess did us the courtesy of listening to us, as we had, him. Towards the end of breakfast, we were again invited on another occasion to dine with the Chairman of Amerada Hess. That gentleman had certainly earned our respect especially when he showed us that he was to change his focus of assistance for the island from health care to education, as we had proposed. He also gained our respect because he proved he knew where the pulse of power lay in the island at that time. I learnt from Leon Hess that a wise investor always read the political climate (the political tea leaves) with fair accuracy.

Leon Hess later proved to be a man of his word. Today, the green and white colours of the Hess Corporation, adorn the Leon Hess Secondary School in the East Castries (Marchand) constituency, which I represented in parliament at the time of the Hess Oil debate. Also, there are several other schools in St. Lucia built by Hess Oil and which wear the Hess green and white colours with pride. For me, the Hess Oil debate proved a defining moment in parliament. That day if ever a voice resonated, it belonged to the Member for Castries East - and I say so with humility. I may have been the only parliamentarian, who questioned the miniscule throughput charges in that contract between the company and the government of St. Lucia and I say this with pride - and not shame. I also challenged the length of the contract (49 years) among other things.

The Hess oil debate is recorded in Hansard of the Third House, Fourth session (1977-1978) and my contribution is at pages two to sixty-nine. It would be impossible for anyone reading my contribution to miss the number of times that I was challenged by the Speaker and equally the number of times I stood corrected as I was certain that there was a plan that day to frustrate my contribution to that important debate. I said in part: 'I see the Premier came well prepared and I must congratulate him for this. It is the first time since elections 1974 that he has come so well prepared. He was not that well prepared in his last budget presentation neither in the presentation of his national plan for the country. He said earlier that oil don't come without grease. I have never worked in the industry so I am in no position to make such a statement. But if oil does not come without grease, then it appears that that grease can work miracles'.

At the voting stage (of the Bill), as expected, the 'ayes' had it! Leon Hess got all that he had asked of parliament. Soon after the vote the large crowd that had gathered outside erupted in celebration. Passing near my vehicle, some shouted in jest 'Peter let the oil flow'. I did not acknowledge those who wished to be heard on the issue. It was too late for that anyway. However, I tried to mark their faces but quickly dropped the idea when I saw the majority seemed over thirty-five years and most, I judged, did not seem to have darkened the walls of any school here or elsewhere.

One of the lessons of life I learnt is that people cannot hide behind their professions. Journalists are no exception. There are persons who are 'professional' at what they do; others are merely mediocre. People often seem to come to their life's work carrying their personal baggage with them. What some may have wished to consider objective reporting at the time was more often than not a projection of their pet peeves, hang-ups and fears. The nationalities and political persuasion of owners of media houses complicate objective reporting sometimes even more than is acceptable; allowing for the broad freedom to speculate. The media is therefore seen by many in St. Lucia and the Caribbean as a tool for promoting a certain way of thinking - and acting - which is often anathema to breaking new ground, moving forward.

They seem to reason that advertisements are more important to the media's bottom line than what it says in its mission statement. So if one can withhold or bend the truth a little and perhaps to accommodate large advertisements, then why not? All this is not to deny journalists a right to their opinions. However, when such opinions are promoted as fact and even defended as the truth, then it becomes a very different kettle of fish. The deliberate distortions of the truth - as opposed to outright lies - is now becoming a problem of the wider Caribbean and those entities and persons that are adversely affected by false reporting, are growing.

The Hess Oil debate was never about the Chairman of the Hess Oil Company, or any individual parliamentarian as far as the opposition was concerned. Neither was it about whether the parliament and Government of St. Lucia wished to welcome foreign investors or to otherwise promote job creation on the island. Every parliamentarian is expected to want progress for his or her constituents and country, too. Indeed many wish and work for a better life for themselves and their families. It is the duty of politicians to educate their constituents (and their country) that every investment comes at a cost. It is for our leaders, including an objective press, and environmentalists among others, to help point the way in choosing the correct (and safe) investments for a country.

Not to put too fine a point on it, that Hess Oil debate was also about the little boy David standing up to the Goliaths of the world. In this fragile ecosystem of ours, we need to think long and hard before we give the green light to projects that may create a few temporary jobs, while on the other hand permanently destroy our island heritage and environment. We know from experience that job creation always comes at a cost. Even the banana industry which did so much good for so many and for so long, destroyed much of the island's natural rain forests and water catchments. It is therefore for us to calculate the cost of development carefully. What costs may be too high for long term sustainability is to be determined by us and no one else. No one should be allowed to bully our elected officials into making hasty uninformed decisions about investments vis-à-vis the long term implications for sustainability. We have to constantly remind ourselves that man does not live by bread alone.

Since that debate, I have often wondered what became of all those who had dreams of making something of themselves from the oil which they wanted to flow so badly, and so freely. Perhaps those dreams and many others at the time have been utterly shattered. "Shattered Dreams" may well capture the pervasive feeling on the island in those bygone days. One learnt that many of the heavy equipment operators preparing the foundation for the project did in fact fare better than most. At the start of construction the Hess Oil company introduced a savings plan for its workers. From each pay cheque it deducted an agreed sum which was then placed into a savings fund in the worker's name. This savings plan was an idea which George Odlum and I had discussed with Hess and to which we lent our full support. The accumulated savings were paid in full to each worker at the end of the construction period. One imagined that it would be difficult to squander such large sums of money all at once. It must therefore be assumed that some of that final pay packet went into purchasing house and land and also to the educating of these workers' children. These were the fortunate ones.

After the dust had settled on the Hess Oil debate and sometime after his meeting with George Odlum and myself, I was invited by Hess to visit with him and an official from the United States Embassy in Barbados, who was visiting St. Lucia at the time. By then Hess had charmed his way into our hearts and after consulting with some colleagues from the U.S. I decided to accept his invitation. The official drove with me in my pick-up truck and we were followed by Leon Hess and his driver. We visited the Conway area in Castries and we also paid visits to my Marchand constituency. I pointed out the several social pressures, including the disposing of garbage in the Castries River, which were all crying out for correction. It may have been as a result of that visit that several years later, Sally Shelton then the United States Ambassador to Barbados and the East Caribbean, invited me to participate in the United States Visitors programme. It may also have been that invitation and my ready acceptance which created the jealousies that eventually took me along a different and separate political trajectory from whence I had started. I shall return to this later.

I am not quite certain what it was about me that Leon Hess liked. I knew he was impressed with the leadership of John Compton. On the other hand he may have admired my forthright honesty and candour. He probably also saw something in me that recommended itself for a future leadership role. I never asked any questions then. He, however, must have noted my determination to put country first, and my resolve to refuse all personal gifts, no matter who was offering. But as fate would have it, around that time the Marchand Improvement Committee was formed in my constituency, by a group of residents who got together to work for the general improvement of the community. A member of the group, whom I knew, asked whether I could help with some seed money. 'The group had planned fund raising activities but it needed a push start' he said. By the time of my election to parliament I had known Francis 'Mindoo' Philip for at least twenty years. He was a national icon and perhaps the greatest cricketer St. Lucia has ever produced.

Soon after that quiet conversation with 'Mindoo' I left for a planned trip to North America. I called Leon Hess at his New York office as he often asked me to do and asked if he could help the Marchand Improvement Committee. He then invited me to breakfast with him at his Park Avenue apartment, a couple days later. I went. I again put the request to him on behalf of the community group. He said that I should see Michael Gordon when I returned home. Michael, a lawyer among other things, was the Leon Hess point man in St. Lucia at the time. Leon Hess did not appear to do anything without Michael Gordon's input. I duly visited Gordon's office on Bridge Street, in Castries, upon my return to St. Lucia. At that office I was handed a cheque in the sum of twenty seven thousand dollars East Caribbean dollars in my name. I duly cashed it and then arranged a meeting with the Marchand Improvement Committee. At that meeting, I handed the Chairman the twenty seven thousand dollars (cash), a gift from Leon Hess. I think the Chairperson of the group at the time was John Moise Calixte, a Civil Engineer by profession and one who has given many years of loyal and professional service in the island's public works department and later at the Water and Sewerage Authority (WASA).

On reflection, I felt very badly that on the morning of the breakfast with Leon Hess at his apartment that I had to turn down an offer of brand new suits which were made in order to replace the long-sleeved shirt jacks I wore at the time. My regret was based on the assumption that Mr. Hess still saw some leadership qualities in me and that the need to dress me up appropriately to that potential, was all he cared about. I confess I saw value in what he was saying at that time but I had boxed myself so firmly into the afro and shirt Jack (Guyaberra) corner, I couldn't help myself. I may also have vaguely calculated that time would transform both style and politics, and that I had time in which to change when I deemed it fitting. Even the great revolutionary leader, Fidel Castro Ruiz himself eventually dropped his army uniform and wore a three piece suit when he addressed the United Nations General Assembly, in his latter days. I think that visit and my refusal of his offer to dress me in some classy suits, marked the end of the formal and distant relationship I enjoyed with Leon Hess. I left his Park Avenue apartment feeling that he had given up trying to make me what at the time I was not yet willing to become. Unfortunately, when I finally was, the tide had receded, taking my would-be ventures with it. But as the saying goes 'one is never ready until ready'.

On reflection, I think Leon Hess saw in me the same zeal and fire that burnt in the breast of John Compton. Left to his own devices, who can tell for certain what the three of us could have accomplished for St. Lucia, working together. He did not seem to remember my rejection of his offer earlier. I regret he passed away before our paths had crossed again. He was a man who seemed to know instinctively the right psychological moment when to say nothing. Perhaps, one day when we have matured beyond our pettiness and stupidity we will find the courage and grace to plant a tree and build a suitable monument in honour of one who asked St. Lucians to trust him and who has delivered far beyond what any of us imagined he would.

At the time of the first draft of this writing, thirty years have sped by since the Hess Oil debate in the parliament of Saint Lucia. Sadly, both Sir John and Leon Hess have gone to their respective resting places. Before he departed, Sir John had been returned to office in December of 2006 and stayed with us as Prime Minister long enough to sign a new agreement between the Hess Oil Company and the Government of Saint Lucia. This time the baton has been passed to Leon's son John, to seek to push Saint Lucia forward with new investments. I met the younger Hess at the funeral reception for Sir John at the Sandals Grande Hotel. I summarized most of what I have written here about his dad to him. I then wished him well with his new investments in Saint Lucia. I know he has a tough act to follow. His task will be made more difficult because there are so few politicians left who will work as hard as Compton had done to achieve the school building programme that has produced so many exemplary young citizens of this fair land.

History is certain to determine that the Amerada Hess Corporation served Saint Lucia best by the voluntary contribution it made to the education of her youth. It should therefore come as no surprise that an increasing number of Saint Lucia nationals are continuing to benefit from the investments Leon Hess made in the construction of the schools on the island. If there is one parting word of wisdom one may suggest for the benefit of the many young people who may study at one of the Hess-built schools on the island, it is that their benefactor always seemed to know the precise psychological moment when to say nothing. It is a quality of silence the entire island may do well to copy. Talk is cheap. Too many people abuse it because they believe freedom of speech means a right to talk whatever foolishness that enters their minds. The talk show hosts in Saint Lucia and elsewhere in the Caribbean often prove as guilty as the clueless that must have their few seconds of fame.

At the time of the Hess oil debate I was familiar with the work of certain Cuban poets including Nicholas Guillen. I particularly like the witticism of the poem that he called simply: 'Traveller'. And every true traveller who lives long enough will one day discover that there are no paths - paths are made by walking. And if there is one parting lesson in the Hess episode it is that we ought never to be afraid to stand for what we truly believe, even though the whole world is opposed to our position at the time. Making a difference is always a difficult road to travel because there are so few road signs and so many obstacles determined to challenge one's fortitude, courage and strength.

During the Hess Oil debate, the following persons were present and took part in the proceedings of the house of Assembly:

1   Mr. Speaker.............................W. St. Clair Daniel
2. Premier.................................J. G. M. Compton
3. Min. of Trade..........................W. G. Mallet
4. Min. of Education......................J. R. A. Bousquet
5. Min. Communications & Works........C. H. Mason
6. Min. of Housing ....V. H. Rock
7. Min. of Agriculture. ....Ira d'Auvergne
8. Acting Attorney General ..............L.A. Williams
9. Parliamentary Secretary. ....H. D. D. Bristol
10. Member for Dennery North...........Dr. V. G. Monrose
11. Member for Micoud North ....R. A. Jn. Baptiste
12. Member for Soufriere ....C. C. Alcindor
13. Leader of the Opposition..............Allan Louisy
14. Deputy Speaker ........................K.A.H. Foster
15. Member for Castries East ....Peter Josie
16. Member for Vieux-Fort North ....Boswell Williams
17. Member for Gros-Islet ....C. G. Mason
18. Member for Choiseul ....Evans Calderon
19. Member for Castries South ....S. N. J. Odlum
20. Nominated Member ....Ms. Lucille Lorde
21. Nominated Member ....Murray Thomas.

Independence at Last

The consequences of universal law lie scattered before
our eyes in apparent confusion....
James Joyce: Ulysses

Political Independence is serious business. It is also difficult business. It is considered even more serious if it can trace its origins from slavery to colonialism, then to neo-colonialism and its Legislative Council, and to partial independence before the full constitutional transfer of power. It is difficult business because few, if any, of the leaders who were to guide the nation at, and after Independence, were specifically trained to lead and manage social and economic growth. To be successful at it one needs a complete and transformational change from a colonial mind-set into a new and revolutionary type of thinking. There can be no progress without such fundamental change in the way leaders think and encourage their citizens to do the same. One needs to be constantly reminded that independence is above all a never-ending mental process. Independence therefore takes time. It also takes a certain calculated effort and preparation. It has a foundation in formal education and academic training although knowledge and experience are often more important than mere academic qualifications. In order to acquire a wholesome spirit of political independence, one needs in addition, a spirit of abiding nationalism. If we accept knowledge as the accumulation of useful information as one journeys through life; and education as a systematic, deliberate imparting (and receiving) of information, whether useful or not to one's interest, then clearly, both knowledge and education are useful to an independent people. Independence often makes strenuous demands on those who lead. Others of a more adventurous nature may choose to create a new and different path of leadership, rather than be led. For the many, independence requires a rebirth of the personality, a new psyche, sea-change - from ignorance and illiteracy to awareness, knowledge, and wisdom. It is also a daily struggle to set aside the learnt dependency syndrome of the past. It means above all, self-reliance.

Political independence makes great demands in ordinary situations. It makes even greater demands in times of crises and difficulties. It cannot be achieved overnight or by the mere raising of a national flag or the singing of a national anthem; no matter how lustily the latter. To top it all, internal dissent, wars and natural disasters, famine and religious strife seem to be constantly conspiring to erode political independence and national cohesion. Furthermore, history teaches us that wealth, size of country, even recognizable and acceptable national boundaries are no guarantors of political independence and sovereignty.

Independence often means citizens standing together in a national cause. People may not agree how best to achieve national unity, but the more perceptive understand that when the independence of their country is threatened, a call to national unity ought to be obeyed by everyone. Independence also means putting one's shoulders to the wheel and encouraging others to do the same for one's country. True independence, for many older and more experienced people the world over, also means the exercise of full personal responsibility as one continues a quest for personal development and true freedom. It recognizes the nation as being greater than the sum of the individuals who live and work within its national borders.

For the people of Saint Lucia, independence ought also to mean the building of the spirit of the 'coup-de-main' through volunteerism and national service. It is the strengthening and refining of the spirit of thrift (savings) through the use of the cultural heritage of the 'sou-sou'. It means building the institutions which strengthen both our independence and our inter-dependence. Wise leadership, impartial justice based on the foundation of law, equal opportunity and equal protection for all, protecting the island's fragile eco-system, whilst rejecting the negative influences of greed and avarice, are all sure ways to promote and enhance national independence. A country can progress towards independence if its citizens are prepared to work towards it as a united people with an agreed agenda for social and economic development and progress.

The trick for successfully emerging from a state of dependence to one of independence appears to be in part, the ability to observe others who have gone that route before and to copy what in them we observe praiseworthy, practical and workable; and to amend in ourselves what in them may appear defective. Each person therefore has a special gift to contribute to the common good. Ours must be to continue the pursuit of excellence by building desirable attributes into a more wholesome and complete personality, through life-long learning. Volunteerism and national service ought to be an essential and necessary part of one's life in an independent country. These two, national pride and volunteerism, are ingredients already present in many a St. Lucian breast. They therefore need to be nurtured and mobilized and placed at the forefront of our national agenda for youth development.

The 22 February 1979 was Independence Day for the island of Saint Lucia. The day finally arrived when the Union Jack of Britain would be lowered on the island for the very last time and the cerulean blue banner of the island with its overlaying triangles of black and white mounted upon its yellow triangular base would be raised to signify the island's new status. But all was not well on that day. It could be seen that many citizens and guests thoroughly enjoyed themselves especially at official government functions. On the other hand, there was a sour mood of discontent amongst the other half of the population. The government largesse for the celebrations had seen to it that each of the various constituencies and communities around the island were presented with suitable treats and entertainment to mark the occasion. It is also noteworthy that the opposition did not participate in any of those planned official activities; neither did it organize any of its own. Perhaps it feared being misunderstood by persons whom it perceived were out to twist every move which it initiated at that time, to the advantage of the new Prime Minister, and his government and party.

Notwithstanding their resolve to refrain from participating in the proceedings, the official parliamentary opposition continued to receive each official document produced by the Government Public Relations Service, and circulated with great care to the opposition in parliament by the Independence Committee. The opposition continued to hold firmly to its stance of non-participation in the celebrations. During that time there was one small gesture which was interpreted by some as a measure of goodwill, by the government towards the opposition. The police case against three members of the St. Lucia Labour Party (SLP) for taking part in an illegal march was dropped. This action by the police and the Director of Public Prosecutions was widely reported by the leading newspaper on the island, and of course by the Government PRO.

The three who were afforded this special treatment were Winston Cenac - QC, his brother Neville Cenac and his cousin Carlisle Jn. Baptiste. The others against whom police charges were not dropped and who were therefore prosecuted for participating in an illegal march were: Evans

Calderon, Boswell Williams, Michael Pilgrim, George Odlum, Kenneth Foster and Peter Josie. The newspapers also reported that the SLP had launched its election campaign with a 'meet the people tour' motorcade starting at Marchand grounds. It was reported that the motorcade made brief stops to explain the party's stance on Independence and ended at Bexon where all seventeen party candidates for the upcoming general elections, were presented to the very large crowd. In the immediate period leading to Independence, several acts of lawlessness were reported by both the electronic and print media.

At that time, to say that the island was on edge, would be putting it very mildly indeed. Political Independence seemed then to suggest much to certain persons and to others it mattered very little. Some people have claimed that the lack of emotional connection to Saint Lucia by the persons who promoted its independence may be gleaned from the fact that, no street was renamed 'Freedom Avenue', no building was called Freedom House; no community or group arose to mark any special understanding of their new status, by a gesture of service or sacrifice to mark the new day. It is noteworthy that certain media personnel did refer to Independence Day as 'Freedom Day'. Some persons wrote emotional letters to the local press using 'Freedom Day' in place of the words 'Independence'. However, the government itself never used the word freedom, or liberation, or any other such synonym in any of its speeches or community rallies. That was a most revealing aspect of the celebrations for those who are capable of reading meaning into simple gestures. The same old worn out clichés were reworked by the leadership of the country. One therefore never got a sense that a new and brighter day had actually been born, in this land of hills and valleys.

An important feature of the Independence programme was the opening of the first session of the new parliament by Her Royal Highness, Princess Alexandra, on Thursday, 22nd. February 1979. The event began with the swearing in of Senators in the chambers of the Supreme Court and the selection of a President of the Senate. The Senators then proceeded across the narrow green to the Parliament buildings to join the elected members who were to have taken their seats, by 10.35 that morning. Absent from that list were the three Senators appointed by the Leader of the Opposition, Allan Louisy.

.

The first Senators to serve an independent Saint Lucia were:

Governor General Selection:
>Ms. Lucille Lorde
>Cornell Charles
>Elijah Greenidge

Government Senators (UWP)
>Vincent Floissac *(President of the Senate)*
>Ira d' Auvergne
>Murray Thomas
>Edsel Edmunds

Opposition Senators (SLP)
>Bruce Williams
>Winston Cenac
>George Odlum

Although the three Senators appointed by the Leader of the Opposition were absent from the first sitting of the first House following Independence, they were all present at the next sitting on 27th. March 1979. It would be observed that at the very first Senate the Governor General appointed three Senators and only appointed two Senators subsequently as the independent constitution envisaged.

Four months after the first Senate was appointed, general elections were held. The government changed hands and so did the composition of the Senate. The following is the composition of the Senate after the Labour Party came to office in mid-1979.

Governor General appointed Senators:
>1. Ornan Monplaisir
>2. Dr. Joseph Edsel Edmunds

(UWP) Opposition
>1. Bryan Charles
>2. Winhall Joshua
>3. Romanus Lansiqout

(SLP) Government Senators
1. Calixte George
2. Charles Augustin
3. Lydia Beryl Edwards
4. Frances Michel
5. Thomas Walcott
6. Hamilton Vitalis

By 10.40 that morning, the Sergeant - at -Arms had left the Robing room of the Supreme Court followed by Mr. Speaker and the Clerk of Parliament. The crème de la crème of Saint Lucia were all seated in the Parliament chamber by 10.00 a.m. Their Excellencies, the Governor General and Lady Lewis, attended by their ADC were prominently seated. Diplomats and others of high rank were likewise present. For the record, the following were the members of the House of Assembly the day of Independence, February 22, 1979:- The Honourable W. St. Clair Daniel, CBE, OSTJ, JP, MJI, Speaker; Hon. John G. M. Compton, LL.B, Premier and Minister for Finance, Planning and Development; Hon. George Mallet, Deputy Premier and Minister for Trade, Industry and Tourism; Hon. J.R. Allan Bousquet, JP, Minister for Education and Health; Hon. Clendon H. Mason, B.Sc., Minister for Communications and Works; Hon. Heraldine Rock, JP. Minister for Housing, Community Development and Social Affairs; Hon. Ira d'Auvergne, Minister for Agriculture and Lands; Hon. Parry J. Husbands, MA, Acting Attorney-General; Hon. Hollis D.D. Bristol, JP, Parliamentary Secretary; Dr. The Honourable Vincent Monrose, MD, B.Sc, Member for Dennery North; Hon. E. Henry Giraudy, LL.B, Member for Vieux-Fort South; Hon. Rodney A. Jn. Baptiste, Member for Micoud North; Hon. Christopher C. Alcindor, Member for Soufriere; Hon. Allan Louisy, Leader of the Opposition and Member for Laborie; Hon. Kenneth A. H. Foster, LL.B, Deputy Speaker, Member for Anse-La-Raye and Canaries; Hon. Peter Josie, B.Sc, Member for Castries East; Hon. Boswell Williams, Member for Vieux-Fort North; Hon. C. Gregor Mason, Member for Gros-Islet; Hon. Evans Calderon LL.B, Member for Choiseul Fond-St. Jacques; Hon. Jon Odlum, Member for Castries South; Hon. Murray Thomas, JP, Nominated Member; Hon. Lucille Lorde, MBE, Nominated Member, Mrs. Doris Bailey, Clerk of Parliament. At 11.35 the Saint Lucia Equerry handed to Her Majesty's Special Representative the speech from the Throne which was then read and broadcast live throughout the island.

At the end of the speech, the President of the Senate and the Speaker both rose and collected a copy of the speech from Her Majesty's Special Representative and returned to their places to listen to the first speech from the first Prime Minister of St. Lucia. In this short address, the former Premier (now Prime Minister) was effusive in his praise for all who had helped to make that day a reality. The meeting ended soon thereafter, and Members and invited guests proceeded out of the Assembly in orderly fashion, led by the Sergeant -at- Arms and followed by Mr. Speaker and the President of the Senate and then by Her. Majesty's Special Representative, then His Excellency, the island's first Governor General, followed by Members of the House and Senate. The majority were expected afterwards to repair to the expanded and renovated parliamentary facilities upstairs for drinks and hors d'oeuvres.

In all this the opposition was nowhere to be seen. They were sticking to their pledge of non-participation. They claimed that political Independence had been handed down unfairly, to a favoured person, whom Britain wished to reward, with the accolade of Prime Minister before he was voted out of office. The opposition had chosen to 'celebrate' Independence not as a united entity but rather each was allowed the freedom 'to do their own thing' in their various constituencies. The party had made absolutely no plans for that week of official celebrations.

To get some idea of what these elected representatives did on that historic day we must now take a closer look at their activities. There may not be another English-speaking island in the entire Caribbean which arrived at its political independence with so much division and bad blood within its population as did St. Lucia. The road to freedom was not made easier by that island's founding history of strong and passionate struggles between the French and British for supremacy and ownership. After the French, the rebels had overthrown the monarchy and declared Liberty, Equality and Fraternity, (1792) and they had set the slaves in St. Lucia free. Historians tell us that St. Lucia was the first French colonial outpost to support the rebel revolutionaries in France, in declaring a Republic. The British later recaptured the island from France and re-introduced slavery. There are many recorded battles and skirmishes between the enslaved Africans and Caribs on St. Lucia on the one hand, and those who would use force to keep them enslaved on the other.

The spirit of independence and freedom therefore ran deep in the former inhabitants of the island, and especially in the south and west of the island from Micoud village in the south east to the town of Soufriere, in the south west. That spirit was particularly strong in the south and south-west of the island. It seemed the people from those parts of the island knew instinctively of their history of struggle against British rule. They seem to understand without being told that independence was a right to be fought for; and not a gift to be bestowed by anyone. By the signing of a document (instrument) declaring the island independent, some persons on island without formal education, were to see through the sham and duplicity. The latter was seen as a merely agreed procedural shenanigan in place of a willingness to force the colonizer to release her grip on power. Liberty, Equality, Fraternity were not mere words to be sounded aloud but rather ideals to be vigorously pursued - and die for if needs be.

This may therefore have been good reason the date of the twenty-second of February 1979 was treated with less than heightened emotional regard and respect. That date bore no relevance to the earlier struggles of the island and its people, for liberty, fraternity and equality. Except the timing was meant to correspond with the beginning of the carnival celebrations which were to be followed by the Christian season of Lent - and there was nothing else to recommend the date. In time, it can be clearly seen that it was not a day or year of the peoples' choosing. One ought therefore to appreciate the reasons that opposition parliamentarians who understood the history of their peoples' struggles wanted no part of these sham celebrations on the 22 February, 1979. St. Lucians from all parts of the island, especially from the south and rural St. Lucia stayed home, and refused to participate in the celebrations. The Labour parliamentarians did likewise. Of course there were many persons who took their cue from the island's parliamentary opposition, and the sour note of their absence from official functions, and stayed home themselves. Perhaps the country will be more united when it debates a new constitution and declares a Republic. History is indeed a very good teacher and those who forget the mistakes of the past are condemned to repeat them.

At that time persons interested in the annual carnival celebrations on the island were in full preparation mode. For many the first Independence Day became lost in the carnival celebrations which by then had become deeply rooted in the culture of the society. That fact was acknowledged some time later when carnival activities were forced down the calendar in order that it did not detract from Independence Day activities. Carnival now takes place in the month of July each year. It has unfortunately lost its historical pre-Lenten roots when Catholic Christians recoiled from the flesh (and carnival) into the forty days of prayer, introspection and fasting. When we are sufficiently at a distance from the events of February 1979 we may be then capable of seeing them for what they were: a desire by Britain to move forward with Europe and the willingness to trust a conservative government whom they knew - and respected - and led by a Prime Minister they wished to reward for his civility and stewardship of the British way of governance.

Nomination Day June 6, 1979
Time of Reckoning...

Traveller, there are no paths; paths are made by walking.....
Nicholas Guillen:
The Great Zoo and other Poems

Before the big day, Parliament first had to be dissolved; afterwards came nomination day, when candidates tendered their nomination papers signed by constituents as the law required. Nomination fees were then paid to the Returning Officer between the hours of nine in the morning and twelve noon. The sum required to be paid by each aspirant was two hundred and forty East Caribbean dollars (approx. $96.00US) If for any reason that requirement was not met by a candidate wishing to contest the elections he or she forfeited the opportunity of contesting. This procedure was to be followed by each candidate whether contesting as an 'Independent' candidate or as a member of a political party. Each candidate was to organize how and when he or she did this. He or she had to organize the time and place to meet the seven or so electors who were to sign the nomination form, certifying that the candidate was known to them and that he or she had qualified to stand as a candidate for general elections on the island.

On nomination day, one secretly - and quietly - wished that one's opponent would, by some miracle, forget to turn up at the correct polling station or that he or she would turn up later or without the necessary deposit. If that were to happen it would mean that such a candidate would most likely be debarred from that particular contest and would have to wait until the next elections. As far as I am aware, no candidate for a general election has ever admitted nursing such secret and perhaps selfish thoughts but if it were ever to happen that in a two-candidate race one was to disqualify himself or herself on nomination day, it would mean an automatic victory for the other contesting candidate. This has never happened in Saint Lucia or anywhere else in the Caribbean as far as I am aware. But if it were to happen in Saint Lucia for example, the declaration of a victor would have to be made by the chief elections officer and that would most likely be that, once the law was obeyed to the letter and intent.

However in such a situation questions were sure to be raised especially by supporters of the party whose candidate had defaulted at such a crucial moment. The procedure for nomination was basically the same in each constituency. The sum of two hundred and forty East Caribbean dollars was to be deposited with the returning office in the exact amount. Some candidates have been reported to make such deposits in coins rather than the simpler and more expeditious paper currency. I have never quite understood why anyone who is sufficiently sensible and of the age to qualify for elections should descend to such idiocy and childish conduct. Once that amount has been paid by legal tender however, it has to be accepted by the returning officer who is to deposit all such monies into the national treasury at the earliest convenience. After the elections are over the deposited sum is returned to the contesting candidate as long as he has received not less than ten percent of the votes cast in that particular constituency.

On rare occasions persons who had earlier announced an intention to contest general elections have been known to withdraw such intentions on nomination day, perhaps saving themselves embarrassment and the loss of over two hundred dollars. One such example was reported on nomination day leading up to the elections of 1979. It was reported that one Lennox Laurencin, who had earlier announced his intention to contest the Soufriere seat, a town in the south west of the island, arrived after nominations were closed. He was therefore unable to proffer either his nomination papers or the required deposit in order to be a candidate. Election watchers however believed that, at the time the man had done absolutely nothing to canvass that particular constituency and that there was probably no intention to contest the elections.

For the elections of 1979, each of the two parties endorsed candidates for all seventeen electoral seats. Doctor Vincent Monrose, a physician and former parliamentarian for the Dennery North constituency for the ruling party and who had been overlooked as a candidate, decided to contest that seat as an independent. The favoured candidate to replace Dr. Monrose was Ferdinand Henry, a friend of Prime Minister Compton, who hailed from the constituency. Mr. Henry was a well liked young man from the constituency in which his family had strong roots. We were school mates at St. Mary's College at a time when it was the only secondary school for boys on the island.

The only other event of some note, which was confirmed on the day of nomination 1979, was that concerning the former representative for the Vieux-Fort North constituency, Boswell Williams who had decided against contesting the elections on the grounds of poor health. There is always an air of excitement surrounding nomination day. In the past most candidates were required to walk or drive to their respective places in order to make the necessary arrangements to register as a candidate. Since the late nineties, however, there has developed a new style of certain candidates being accompanied by a large delegation of some fifty or more persons. I am not certain what purpose this serves but persons who carry their ignorance with them wherever they go, have been known to throw snide remarks at opposition candidates and their supporters. This is a development which probably needs looking into with a view to correcting the conduct of the more exuberant party fanatics. As nomination day progressed the excitement appeared to have reached fever pitch when the news hit the airwaves that each of the selected candidates from the two parties were duly nominated and were therefore officially announced as candidates, in the race. The election horses were now lined up, so to speak. At that point bettors and electors alike were overcome with excitement. The election bell which many had impatiently anticipated had been rung about ten days or so earlier and nomination day signalled the official start of the election contest which electors had patiently awaited for.

A proclamation from Government House, followed by the publication of an extraordinary issue of the official Government gazette, informed all interested parties that on Wednesday June 6 the Parliament of Saint Lucia was officially dissolved. It was further announced that the government was to continue to serve until a successive one had been elected and sworn to office. That period also marked the official end of Prime Minister Compton's third consecutive term in office; viz: 1964-69, 1969-74 and 1974-79. Although these elections were constitutionally due in September of that year, (1979) Mr. Compton addressed the nation on the night of the dissolution of Parliament to say that he had called early elections because the period of uncertainty was delaying the progress of the island. Investors, he assured were awaiting the outcome of these elections before making a final decision to set up shop on the island. Of course the words were spoken in such a way as to imply that the opposition would not attract new investments if it were to form the next government. At the time the announcement made it appear that attracting investors to the country was a secret art known only to the Prime Minister and his friends in the UWP. In any event, opposition supporters were no longer listening to Compton. For all they cared he could be speaking to the wind. And, judging by the election results in 1979, it appeared that some supporters of his party had also stopped listening too. The general feeling within the camp of the opposition was: "Why wait till June or July for fresh elections"; so ready were they.

The formalities of the laws governing general elections on the island required notices to be issued and published in the official Government gazette as well as in the leading newspapers on the island. This was in keeping with section 42(2) of the House of Assembly (Elections) Act 1979. The Act also required the publication of form No.10, for each electoral district showing the polling stations, the names of the contesting candidates as well as that of the Returning Officer. The latter was the person legally responsible to the Chief Elections Officer for ensuring a fair and orderly ballot, within the allotted time, according to law - on polling day.

The night before the big day, the opposition party decided that each of its seventeen candidates should hold public meetings or engage their constituents in some activity. I held an indoor meeting of my constituency group that afternoon at the residence of Mr. and Mrs. Mauricette on the Marchand main road. All twenty or so persons who formed the core of that group turned out. The group selected from amongst those present eight of their number who would accompany me to the designated polling station the following day in order to deposit my nomination papers. At the time of the meeting I had purchased several copies of the voters list for that particular constituency and I ensured that each person who was selected to sign the nomination forms was duly registered as an elector as the law required.

I also had in my possession the other documents such as nomination papers and forms for the appointment of poll clerks and agents. Having selected eight persons to sign the document the following morning, we then decided on a place and time of meeting. My policy in these matters has always been to get them out of the way as early as possible after the official start of business. We therefore agreed to meet downstairs of our usual meeting place at Marchand Road, at nine o'clock the following morning - Nomination Day. The evening before Nomination Day the Castries East (Marchand) constituency group organized a large public meeting on the main road in front our usual meeting place. The purpose of the public meeting was to keep our supporters informed of progress towards elections as well as to assure everyone that the process had been going smoothly as far as my group was concerned and that the party had reported similar progress in other constituencies. That public meeting also served as a great morale booster for those who may have had lingering doubts about our ability to defeat the experienced fox - John Compton - at the polls that year. In addition we did not wish our supporters to be attending meetings of the other side on the final run to general elections for fear that a last minute desperate throw of the dice, or some outrageous promises and unbeatable incentives would cause them to switch sides. It was not unknown in local politics for enticements by way of suitable incentives to be offered to certain important campaigners in an attempt to execute last minute change of loyalties. This was often desired more for psychological purposes than for any votes such a person may persuade to switch from one side to the next.

By the time nomination day rolled around, the opposition St. Lucia Labour Party was pretty confident of victory. The party had predicted that it would win not less than ten of the seventeen seats. But everyone knew that before that final day in which the people of the island were to be given an opportunity to decide who they wanted to govern them, there had to be the formalities of nominations, according to law. So although everyone looked eagerly to elections, those who were in the bosom of the beast, so to speak, fully understood and appreciated the significance of nomination day. That day was usually two weeks before elections so as to give the authorities sufficient time to prepare the necessary ballot papers and other notices which were required to show the names of contesting candidates.

In 1979 there were some candidates from each party who had not contested elections before and I volunteered during the campaign to ensure that every candidate of the Labour Party was duly informed of the forms which were required on nomination day. I also encouraged each candidate to purchase as many copies of the electoral lists as possible for his particular constituency, so that as many helpers as possible could scrutinize such lists, identify as many of the electors on it as possible with a view to getting them out to vote on election day. I confess that I rather enjoyed the campaigning and the general preparations such as the printing of posters and T-shirts leading up to general elections. For me, once that has been done to the best of my ability and I have been afforded ample time to ventilate my views and vision for my country, then I feel fairly certain I have done my duty and in the process contributed to the survival of democracy as we know it on the island. I have therefore always told myself that unless there is a clear case of fraud or glaring irregularity at the polling division in which I am contesting, I will never challenge or question the decision of the electorate. Besides, I remain convinced that people vote their fears and their passions and that both these states of mind are subject to change over time.

One of the concerns I experienced during the period of nomination was the exhibition by certain party stalwarts of an attitude which judged the successful nomination of his party's full slate of candidates as a reason for uncontrolled celebrations. I always found it difficult to ask grown men to control themselves by modifying their drinking and behaviour or otherwise and cease behaving as though some great victory had been won, by the simple fact of a successful nomination day. So while some of the Labour Party supporters drank and celebrated on the evening of nomination, I was worried sick as I began to doubt the party's ability to meet the high expectations of the electorate, and perhaps continue the drive to victory, without too much casualty between nomination day and polling day.

Perhaps as a young politician I had taken this obligation which ought to devolve on every contestant for political honours of delivering a better life to my constituents, and also to the national community, much more seriously than many may have given me credit for. But then, who can tell for certain the cast of mind of a young, untried politician? In the island's culture there are certain emotions and feelings a man is expected to keep to himself. I was constantly reminding myself that it may be a supreme act of arrogance for a person to take it upon himself or herself and believe that people need their help in order to progress and prosper. On the other hand perhaps such young (and new) politicians may have known all along, perhaps instinctively, what others of a more artistic bent such as Nicholas Guillen had previously discovered. That secret which was shared by that great Cuban poet has been left as a legacy for all who wish to discover a new and perhaps better way of bringing peace and prosperity to their people. Nicholas Guillen wrote in the collection which he called - The Great Zoo and other Poems - 'Traveller, there are no paths; paths are made by walking'. It is not a too subtle way of inviting everyone who dares to set off on a journey as exciting as that of politics to dare to break new ground through innovation, imagination and courage. The problem with every politician with whom I have been acquainted - including Brother George Odlum - was their inability to change the old way of doing things in order to make life happier for the people whom they serve - in other words an inability to change the way people think of themselves and acted based on this new self-worth. An example which jumps to mind is the procurement of important documents from a department of the government. It does not matter in what part of the island one lives, one is often told to return in two or three days in order to collect such documents. Why hasn't anyone thought of fixing the machinery of government so that it delivers to the people a much more efficient service than it has done since the days of colonialism?

Such inefficiency in government simply says that we as a people are not yet ready to walk (and create) paths that have not been previously trod by some person who came before. Such thinking is passé and archaic and needs to be replaced by new and more modern management whose emphasis ought to be to deliver to the public a more efficient public service. After nomination day the election campaign continued full steam ahead. There was no rest for any contestant during the last two weeks leading to the really big day - elections 1979. Soon all the talking and arguing would be over. Nomination Day would have been forgotten as the Election Day drew nearer and last minute checking of the voters' list continued at a frantic pace. By then the majority of electors seemed to have decided which way they would cast their ballot. People were generally quiet on nomination day and many waited until nightfall to attend public meetings of their favourite party. Although the air of expectancy persisted until the day of elections, those who had made up their minds seemed then to withdraw to a normal life, leaving the talking and shouting to the minority. Indeed, it may well have been said of many electors at the time, that they knew the precise psychological moment when to say nothing, if one were to borrow an adaption of Oscar Wilde in a 'Picture of Dorian Gray'. Soon it was general elections and the people would get their opportunity to speak through the ballot box with their precious votes.

General Elections 1979
SLP in Landslide Victory

He knew the precise psychological moment when to say nothing
Oscar Wilde: The Picture of Dorian Gray.

By the end of December 1978 and soon after Premier Compton had missed his preferred date of December 13 for the island's independence, everyone in the opposition - perhaps in Mr. Compton's party too - felt certain that the governing party's goose was cooked and that at the next polls, due in six months or so, a new group of people would be voted into office, to govern the island.

The leadership of the party in opposition at the time had done all it could to cause Her Majesty's government in London to hold either a referendum or a general elections before granting independence, but it soon discovered that London was perhaps as keen to set the island free, more than the local politicians had   imagined. Its avowed policy to become an integral part of a new Europe was evident to all who cared to look. With President DeGaulle of France safely out of the way, the doors to the European Union was now seemingly thrown wide open to Britain and others desirous of joining the European experiment.

By the time Her Majesty's representative handed Premier Compton the instruments granting the island political independence on the night of February 21, 1979, the opposition party had long dissolved its protest marches and theatrical (some say hypocritical) *'do it right, let the people decide'* campaign against independence, into one of open electioneering for the June 1979 general elections. Mind you, the date for these general elections had not yet been announced, but this date was the only date that year which meant anything to those who where intent on seeing the back of the ruling regime. There was therefore very little rest for the candidates of the opposition party who had all been selected by the end of December 1978.

The election campaign continued in earnest and after the formalities of Independence celebrations, Premier Compton's party went full steam into electioneering mode. The methodical approach and even handed thoroughness with which each of the seventeen constituencies on the island was treated by the government, was laying the ground for the official start of its efforts to retain power. Premier Compton and his top advisers were past masters in the art of political campaigns and they threw everything at the opposition in the months following independence and leading to the general elections. They built footpaths and connected electricity in communities and hamlets where the people had long suffered from busted shoes and toes for lack of these basic amenities. They opened health and community centers. They arranged these in such a way that persons whom many had been quietly informed were the government's candidate for a particular constituency, was often invited ahead of the parliamentary representative. It did not matter that such persons had no previous connection with the communities in question. To add insult to injury, opposition politicians often did not bother to show up when invited to speak at such events, even in their constituencies. That was not cricket. In fact nothing was, and everyone knew it. Could anything have been done about it? Where and when will it all end?

In the heat of the campaign in 1979, no quarter was given and none asked. The government threw everything it had at the opposition, as we have seen. The opposition was accused of fostering violence and of planning to stage some sort of military-style coup, as its friends in Grenada had done in deposing Eric Gairy, that island's Prime Minister.

It was also accused of nursing Communist tendencies and prone to promoting disobedience, the terror of religion and to the Monarchical system of government based as it then was on the old colonial system of colour and class.

Of course no one was allowed to use the publicly funded media to refute such claims, even when payment was offered for its use. Interestingly, the case of the young man held in Castries with three sticks of dynamite after several loud explosions had rocked the city that year was never prosecuted and no one can tell for certain what became of that person. The most telling and effective accusation leveled at the opposition, if we were to poll the voices of our supporters, was that it was a multi-headed animal which would destroy itself and the island with it. That accusation had probably arisen much earlier, when certain members of the St. Lucia

Forum, who had later joined the Labour Party, where they were known to have refused to accept a conventional structure for that grouping; such as President, Secretary, Treasurer, for example. That had raised a few eye brows to put it mildly and their presence within a political party did not help dispel their previous aversion to the old 'structure' and way of doing things. We had earlier avoided such offices which were associated with the conventions of the time for political organizations. It may be recalled that earlier, the Forum tried very hard to distance itself from party politics and it had accused its practice and participation thereof as 'papyshow politics, to use a local phrase.

On the other hand, the opposition accused the government party of being arrogant and distant, not listening to the voices of the people and going as far as putting foreign interests ahead of those of its own people. It feared loudly that the additional power which the attainment of political independence had conferred on their political leader, would lead to dictatorship if the opposition were not vigilant, careful and fully engaged. These tendencies, it claimed, were already evident in the manner the registration of electors had been designed, added to the frequent shortages of registration materials resulting in the frustration of persons who did not support the government, perceiving some sort of trickery. In addition, only its hand picked State functionaries, were given official duties at election time and this, added to its already tight control of the publicly owned electronic media, amounted in the eyes of the opposition to something very sinister and dangerous.

So if indeed there was to be a dictatorship, it argued, it was preferable to have that of the many over the few, than that of one man, over the entire island. The opposition's problem was that it tried too hard to explain and rationalize its position on the political social and economic situation of the time, seeing the education of the masses as an essential and necessary element in the economic development of the island. Politics, it argued, was only a means to an end and that means was determined by culture, experience and the yearning of the human spirit for justice, and not cast in stone anywhere.

Apart from the recent attainment of independence and the role it felt the British authorities in London had played in facilitating the ruling party, the opposition also remembered the elections of 1974, which it believed was taken by stealth and sleight-of-hand, using its allies in law enforcement to do its bidding under cover of darkness. It also believed that a few of those who had sworn to serve and protect were confusing party for country, and were therefore a scourge on the democratic rights of the people to choose their representatives in free and fair elections. In the end, such persons create more problems than they solve.

It would be a gross understatement to say that the elections of 1979 were very heated. They were much more than that. Often, the opposition seemed to be skirting the very brink of irregularity as it determined to do everything in its power to stop any planned mischief this time around. Public political meetings of that group were often laced with threats and incendiary remarks, all seeming to confirm, rather than dismiss, the Government's accusations of violence and anarchy, which they claimed were all aimed at achieving the communistic ambitions of the opposition. The Government went as far as to resuscitate a meeting of like-minded West Indians which had taken place at Rat Island off the north-west coast of St. Lucia in the early seventies, and which it claimed was called to co-ordinate the taking over of these islands by force, and with the help of Cuba. Poor Cuba! Of course, none of this was true.

The incidents of excessive heckling by rowdy supporters of the opposition were reported each day in the electronic media. The more severe cases of such conduct were also reported by both police and government Ministers, speaking in their official capacities. All this reporting seemed to confirm the accusations leveled at this association, and its conduct became cause for closer scrutiny by the conservatives in the society. The Government swore to put an end to the heckling. It did not succeed.

An incident of severe heckling was reported from the village of Canaries (in the Anse-La-Raye/Canaries constituency) where it was alleged that the Labour party candidate drove his vehicle alongside a public meeting of the ruling party and used a loudspeaker, mounted on his vehicle, to motivate his supporters to disturb and eventually cause a stoppage of the said meeting. Later, it was discovered that the opposition candidate was no where to be found and that the heckling was started by a tape recording of the candidate's voice, apparently switched on by an over enthusiastic foot soldier driving the vehicle. But nothing could stop the march of the opposition to victory. Meetings of the ruling party were more difficult to conduct in the economically depressed (and neglected) areas of the towns and villages where the mass of humanity that was left behind by the scourge of colonialism and its scheming capitalist system had relegated such individuals to a life of illiteracy, joblessness and crime. Reports on crime and criminal behaviour had earlier concluded that the greater the concentration of such masses of people on the fringes of society and the closer they are to the centers of business and affluent populations, the higher the propensity for disturbance and for sudden eruptions of violence. The political campaigns were excuses used by such idleness for mischief. These idle hands were often available to the highest bidder, not caring with ideology or platform or the vision from either side, for a better constituency community and country.

There was one particular case of stone throwing which was widely reported in both electronic and print media, and for which a popular candidate for the ruling party had to be treated for wounds sustained during a particularly hostile encounter in Central Castries at the junctions of Chaussee and Marchand roads.

The general elections of 1979 were both interesting and memorable. Interesting, because it was the first time any elections were contested on the island with a clearly defined ideology differentiating the two contesting parties. True, the line became blurred in the candidacy of certain individuals, from either side. Some effort was made to heighten the ideological differences in the 1974 contest. Generally speaking however, it was clear that in 1979, the opposition party advocated a parting of the old ways and an empowering of the ordinary man and woman; a clear departure from the politics of the past which had only offered to dictate how the island ought to be developed by persons arrogantly claiming to know more of what was good for the electorate and the population at large.

Perhaps the attainment of political independence had sharpened the rhetoric of the opposition party with regards to fashioning a new path to social and economic development. However, engaging the people at the grass roots level was never easy. It had never been done before and politics to them was more about theatre and 'big' often well connected men making fools of themselves and their opponents – the latter much to the bemused and straggling crowd who often gathered as detached and uncaring witnesses – to listen, laugh and then later, gossip, at the display of such public street theatre.

The general elections of 1979 also proved very hard work indeed. The public address system was often our only means of getting to the electorate and by then both parties had apparently stumbled unto the idea of mass rallies and bussing their supporters to a central location on weekends as the preferred way of energizing their respective bases for the coming vote. To be truthful, the ruling party at the time was a little ahead of the game and had before (1974) attempted these mass rallies, on the advice of foreign experts brought in for that purpose. Big money had also begun to show its ugly head in local political campaigns. Handsome financial contributions were known to come from certain foreign political parties, wishing to influence government policy. Today these rallies have become the central campaign focus not only in St. Lucia but in every other political campaign throughout the Caribbean. Too often however, people are drawn more by the entertainment and the carnival-like atmosphere rather than by a need to listen, perchance to vote for the better, more progressive ideas and economic and social policies for the country.

The more dynamic platform speakers were always in demand not only in the near-by constituencies but throughout the length and breadth of the entire inland. The charismatic public political speaker is still a very highly valued commodity in this part of the world. Our politicians have discovered that, the best ideas, when not properly articulated can go up in smoke even before they are properly examined and discussed. And whereas, everyone on the island understands the native Creole language, if one were to create the best possible impression, as a future Parliamentary representative and political heavy-weight, one must first prove his or her quality in speaking English correctly and not punctuated by too many… ah's…ah's..m's…ah's..ma's..s's. If his English is found wanting with poor diction, bad grammar, wrong choice of words - even inappropriate pauses - the politician will be laughed at openly by his friends as well as by his opponents, even those who are no better than himself but who are smart enough to appreciate their own limited abilities, in the speech-making business. With the passage of time one observes that standards are being gradually lowered and the use of faux pas in English are not laughed at or even corrected, by those who know better. Certain local University graduates are known to pay scant attention to spelling and constructing basic English sentences in their jobs, and elsewhere. And this is a whole other tale to be carefully analyzed and properly documented, in the not too distant future.

During campaigning, great demands were made on a handful of candidates as well as on the better known and articulate platform speakers such as Robert Sandiford, Hilary Vidal, Vic Fadlien, George Goddard, Karl Pilgrim, Joseph (Joe) Daniel for the public meetings of the Saint Lucia Labour Party, especially in the Castries basin. The same was true of several noted speakers of the ruling United Workers Party, as well. Those talented spokespersons also campaigned for their respective parties throughout the length and breadth of the island. Often, political meetings started at 7.30 in the evening and ended at ten-thirty; often going past that in the rural communities. A speaker in high demand would often speak at three political meetings per night, returning at the very end to close the one held in his own constituency, This, many candidates were expected to do.

As we burnt the midnight oil, and fully extended our energies to help our candidate colleagues of the Saint Lucia Labour Party, we also had to keep a close eye out in the day time on the voter registration activities at the polling stations which were on-going. Happily, we were receiving less and less complaints each passing day, and so we began to relax and to believe that the register of voters would allow for a fair general election. We had however, one final hurdle: that was the publication of the final list of voters which was expected well before the June elections. We needed ample time for each interested voter to peruse that list and to make certain his names and that of his family was registered, addresses correctly shown, and that the Identity Card number matched that on the list, with his name. Again, this was a monumental task. Even in a small population such as Saint Lucia's with just under one hundred thousand registered electors in 1979 the continuous monitoring and checking of the voters list was tough.

Towards the end of that campaign, we in the opposition Labour party had satisfied ourselves that we had answered every accusation the government had thrown at us, met every challenge of citizenship and our island identity which some had dared to question; and even answered the challenge of irreligion and ungodliness. Our opponents even accused us of some of the sins for which they themselves were best known.

Land Reform Commission

A Prince is further esteemed when he is a true friend or a true enemy... This policy is always more useful than remaining neutral.

Niccolo Machiavelli - The Prince

I was appointed Minister for Agriculture of Saint Lucia in July 1979 and on assuming office I immediately sought and received Cabinet's approval for setting up a Land Reform Commission. That Commission was headed by Professor George Beckford of the University of the West Indies, a renowned Agricultural Economist who had researched and written numerous papers on aspects of land tenure in the Caribbean. The other members were Dr. P. I. Gomes, an Economics Professor and Social Scientist, Dr. Nick Liverpool, a Law Professor, Ms. A. Cole, a Sociologist, and Mr. Calixte George, a former Senior Research Officer in the Ministry of Agriculture, St. Lucia, and member of the St. Lucia Forum. Calixte George was included with specific instructions to guide the process along the ideas on Land reform which had been discussed at some length at meetings of the St. Lucia Forum. It was the government's stated purpose that the work of the Commission should eventuate in the total and the complete revisiting of the difficult land issues resulting from the island's French heritage of undivided property rights (land) amongst families. Land reform was an issue which I was determined not to pass to the next generation of Saint Lucians, or to leave for someone else to resolve, if it could be helped.

That Land Reform Commission reported its findings six months after it started its work. Cabinet reviewed the report and it decided to implement its proposals.

The report pointed out in part, what was widely acknowledged in St. Lucia: that the largest agricultural estates were inefficient producers; that undivided family land was a deterrent to agricultural production; that many persons who claimed ownership of lands had no title to such lands; that ownership of certain lands was in dispute and the heirs and families would not agree on a solution. The most glaring examples of the former were the Geest estates at Roseau and Cul-de-Sac. The report also revealed that small farmers, who were either landless or farming very small patches of land, were very inefficient producers and were therefore unlikely to make farming a viable proposition in their existing situation. The more thrifty persons within certain rural households were reluctant to farm undivided family-owned lands since the lazy and less cooperative in the family were entitled to harvest without planting, or working. It was the view of the government that a suitable mechanism ought to be found to consolidate fractured family lands, and to sub-divide the large inefficient estates to make them more pliant, manageable and productive. Such a policy, as far as we were aware, had never before been enunciated on the island.

The Ministry of Agriculture therefore set about its work with the full support of the Government and Cabinet. The main point-man and former fellow Forumite, Calixte George, was in the vanguard of implementing the Ministry's vision. I knew at the time that I could rely on him for the speedy implementation of the Land Reform policy as he was the only other person within the ranks of the party who, in my view, was seized of the necessity for land reform in Saint Lucia. He understood its far reaching impact on agriculture production and productivity, and how it would be used to guide the agricultural development of the island. A most rewarding aspect of this huge land reform undertaking was the solid support the Government of Saint Lucia received from the United States International Development Agency (U.S.A.I.D.). We also received the support of the Inter-American Bank for Development (IADB) in pushing ahead with land reform. Another source of surprisingly unfailing support was from John Hailwood, who was at the time Managing/ Director of Geest Industries Ltd. and Geest Estates Ltd. based in Castries. These were the owners of the estates the government wished to purchase for sub-division and sale to farmers.

Hailwood served that company for many years in St. Lucia. The entire farming community as well as the Government and opposition on the island, held him in very high esteem. Many persons with whom the Geest Company did business in the Caribbean found him a very tough and a very fair Chief Executive.

I recall with some satisfaction that at an earlier period when the St. Lucia Forum called for sensible land reform on the island, Hailwood was the only Chief Executive who bothered to invite some members of the group to discuss the issue in some more depth. Of course this must have been with a view to ferreting out additional information from the group which hopefully would help guide his company's policy on the island. The process of consultation continued when I became Minister of Agriculture in 1979. That the Land Reform proposition became nationally acceptable was due in large measure to the understanding and co-operation of Hailwood and USAID. Looming world events such as The World Trade Organization (W.T.O.) and the removal of the protective tariffs for Africa, the Caribbean and Pacific (ACP) bananas in Europe were already being discussed by the major importers of bananas. The question was: 'would increasing competition in Europe for Saint Lucia and Caribbean bananas harm the island's land reform programme'?

Unfortunately, the comprehensive clear title to land and the reform scheme envisaged by the Government of Saint Lucia was only partially implemented due to its very short stay in office. The governments which followed from 1982 onwards did not implement the full range of land reform measures which had arisen from the Napoleonic Code (Laws) or (Code Noir) that had been imposed on the island when it was a colony of France and which I, as a Minister of the then government, had envisaged correcting once and for all. The truncated term of the government (1979-1982), had also put paid to the other visionary long-term plans of the government especially in the field of Education, Health, Sports and Culture, to name just four. The sub-division of the Geest Roseau lands resulted in an increase in banana productivity there from three tons per acre to up to sixteen tons to the acre on these same lands. A few farmers reaped a harvest as large as twenty tons to the acre, in the same location. These results therefore led many to see (and believe) that increased agriculture productivity would have resulted from land reform, if such a policy had been earlier implemented by former governments. I have derived great satisfaction from the portions of land reform which we were able to implement because I think in the end the island was much better off for it. There was in particular an obvious benefit to banana farmers, and to persons island-wide who now had clear land boundaries and title, through the land registration and titling project - LRTP - which was continued by the Compton government between 1982 and 1992.

The national Land Titling and Registration Project was later to bring still more benefits to the people of St. Lucia. For the first time in its history, many of its citizens received clear title to land and became proud and secure owners of that valuable national asset. An important offshoot of land reform was that Government officials in countries friendly to the island, such as in London, Washington, Paris soon became favourably disposed to St. Lucia's development needs as they began to see the positive benefits of land reform. To his credit one ought to add that after the Labour government collapsed, the incoming Prime Minister - John Compton - saw to it that the land titling aspect of the Land Reform programme was successfully implemented. It did not matter that land titling and registration was the easier part of the vision to implement. The tough task of tackling family land issues has unfortunately been shelved or otherwise passed on to future generations, to do as they will. It is an unnecessary burden that has been passed on due to the laziness and cowardly attitude of past government leaders.

By the time the Labour government was unceremoniously kicked out of office in January of 1982, it had laid the solid groundwork for the complete and total revamping of all the major land reform issues with which the island had been burdened for so long. Land fragmentation; unmanageable large farm acreages; the disincentive to farming jointly-owned family farm lands, were just some of the problems militating against a modern, rational and scientific plan for increased agriculture productivity.

The Land Reform Commission recommendation to tackle the 'Title to Land project' was facilitated by financial and technical support from the Inter-American Development Bank and USAID, as mentioned earlier. The more difficult task of settling family land problems and disputes was, however, left unresolved. Unfortunately, it was not undertaken even by a new Labour Government when it was voted back into office in June 1997 with a most convincing mandate. Interestingly, it included in its ranks the likes of Mr. Calixte George.

Calixte and I had also worked on preparing a Land Use Map for St. Lucia when we were both public servants, employed at Union Agricultural Station, Castries. At the time Mr. George Mallet, later Sir George was Minister for Agriculture and Tourism. Mallet was a politician who said all the right things such as the necessity for a dynamic agriculture sector and the diversification of this sector. But every agriculture officer knew the over arching power of the banana lobby at the time militated against even the use of the word 'diversification'. It was clear to us that agricultural diversification would have been a very tough programme to implement. In fact, banana cultivation became so synonymous with total agriculture that every aspect of government as well as the local private sector seemed geared at the time, towards its cultivation. In addition, marketing, research, fortnightly payments to farmers, procuring of fertilizers, pest and disease control and insurance, together formed an interlocking whole, ensuring the all-inclusive nature of the banana industry.

The government's efforts in supporting banana cultivation were rewarded by the involvement of a majority of the island's farmers, in its production. The economic activity which it generated touched the lives of people over the entire island. Merchants sold more of everything when bananas were at peak performance. Motor vehicles and other consumer durables as well as better and stronger houses began to dot the island's landscape. Building materials left business yards like hot bread from the Amur's Central bakery in Castries, on a busy Christmas Eve. And of course Compton harvested all the credit, even claiming full ownership of the economic boom which accompanied banana production. Many of his friends believed it was a well deserved accolade, but those who were knowledgeable in such matters knew his efforts fell short of the vision of a diversified and more scientific agriculture on the island. It was obvious even then that more fruits and vegetables for local consumption and export would have bolstered farm income and reduced imports of food. With the fall in the banana market and the concomitant growth in tourism, it has now become crucial for the island to diversify its agriculture in order to better feed itself and its visitors, while ensuring a more balanced land use as well as better overall nutrient supply, to Saint Lucians.

I remained convinced that the pressures to feed ourselves both in Saint Lucia and in the wider Caribbean - and visitors to the region as well - coupled with the need to garner foreign exchange for consumer durables, will one day force us to revisit land reform issues in order to better allocate resources based on a national land use plan for the island. Such an approach would hopefully lead to greater overall production and productivity in agriculture, while setting aside clearly demarcated areas for recreation, housing, schools et cetera. To this may be added the caveat: 'Provided the demand for house lots does not continue to devour scarce agriculture lands, as it has done in the past forty years or so.

Following the early exit from office of the Labour Government in early 1982, the dream of long-term land reform planning and execution aimed at the orderly development of agriculture seemed to have come to an end. Those who were returned to office in 1982 did not see it fit to define a clear vision for agriculture - and for bananas - even though it was obvious at that time that world market conditions were about to change. That situation was widely accepted and shared by banana producers throughout the entire Caribbean region. The continued marketing of the island's bananas was largely left to the goodwill of certain large supermarkets in Britain as well as to the dexterity and marketing skills of Wibdeco, the Windward Islands marketing company in England. Of course the continued assistance and negotiating skills of the British and French Governments were welcomed by Caribbean governments, some of which still refused to face the music of the increasing threat to their once protected banana markets. We continued to rely very heavily on these two to help us make our case for continued protection and reasonable prices within the ever growing threat by the World Trade Organization (WTO) in the European Community market. The record of government in agriculture after 1982 is there for all to see. It tells the whole story of refusing to take on the difficult challenge of speaking to banana farmers honestly and directly on the difficult challenges which they faced in the global banana market.

When therefore, New Labour was returned to office in 1997, with the overwhelming mandate of sixteen for and only one against in a House of Asssembly, one fully expected that the Land Reform policy of its former colleagues would have been pursued with deliberate vigour and purpose. The early success had helped fashion a new awareness of property rights in St. Lucia. It had also boosted agriculture production and productivity especially in the banana sub-sector. So the need to pursue such a programme was still fairly urgent.

To a political novice looking in from the outside, one expected Calixte George to have been appointed Minister for Agriculture. However, the word around was that certain deals were made with the loud-mouthed banana lobby which had supported the government's campaign, in 1997. The Banana Salvation Committee had arched its back against the appointment of Calixte George to head the Ministry of Agriculture, as Minister. It appeared that the leader of the government at the time was either too coward or that he did not think he had the legitimacy to stand up to the thugs in the Banana Salvation Committee. The use of George's talents in the field of agriculture and land reform was therefore lost to agriculture - and to Saint Lucia. In his place was appointed a baker - one who kneaded bread for a living - and whose claim to fame may have been he started doing this business in England, in addition to holding some pure bred sheep given with Canadian assistance to young farmers in the Micoud south constituency, some years prior to his entry into politics. Strangely, those who had no constitutional authority to act within the new Labour government seemed to have been the ones calling the shots, following their 1997 victory. The cracks within New Labour therefore became obvious very early. Political observers then insisted there were at least four competing elements within that new government.

The four elements which made up the new and unhappy New Labour government were: the embattled 'old' guard some of whom had earlier left to form the Citizens Democratic Party (C.D.P.); then there was the George Odlum faction which had ten years earlier, left and formed the Progressive Labour Party (P.L.P.) and there was also the discarded shell of the original Labour Party which owned the symbol and the name that so many were after, at the time. Finally, there was the new kid on the block - banana farmers demanding, through the Salvation Committee, a much larger say in the affairs of government for the frank support they offered the 'new' Labour party in the 1997 general elections. Neither faction would self-start, or go anywhere, on its own. The four needed each other more than a fish needed water to survive.

It was obvious to casual observers that these elements within the new Labour Government had come together to promote their own narrow interests and were therefore determined to endure that as long as the harvest was good they would stick around. However, the moment it appeared that things were not going the way they planned, the game began to unravel. Old Labour was determined to prevail by clinging to their previous symbol and red party banner. The party constitution had been trampled upon willy-nilly in the past, so what mattered at that stage were the party name and its symbol - a five-pronged star. Little else seemed to matter, then. Those who were pledged to cling to the past glories of labour were doomed to failure.

The outstanding issues of family lands which Compton's government did not tackle were crying out for attention. That cry fell on the ears of New Labour and then fell off it as water off a duck's back. Persons who were expected to take a stand on land reform appeared mute and powerless, in New Labour. Perhaps that should not have surprised anyone for reasons of differing perceptions and the consequent misguided agriculture policy of those who were insisting that they be allowed to handle the entire agricultural future of the island, as pay back for their banana followers' support in 1997.

The Labour government of (1979-82) of which I was Minister for Agriculture had envisaged the orderly and legal consolidation of family lands to boost agriculture production. It passed relevant legislation in order to facilitate a sensible and humane way in which to empower families who were already cultivating these lands, to procure title to them. This it hoped would have resulted in each family member entitled to a share of that land being adequately compensated for such shares. The sole rationale for land reform was to give deserving persons (and families) suitable legal title and to allow for the orderly development of such lands.

Several other benefits were realized from the earlier land reform policy. A comprehensive land survey, mapping and registration of lands throughout the island was carried out. Land boundaries - both private and public - were identified and mapped, throughout the island. Additional surveyors, mainly from Trinidad, were employed in order to speed up the process of surveys and mapping.

There was at least one new development in the New Labour Government which threatened to put paid to the original land reform policy. This was the sale of fertile agriculture lands in the Dennery Valley (Mabouya) to a private Insurance Company ostensibly for home construction, and resale to the Saint Lucian public.

The former government of Sir John Compton had purchased these lands for agricultural expansion and rationalization on the earlier recommendation of the Land Reform Commission, and as the Louisy government had done in the Roseau valley in 1980. Unfortunately, most of this land passed through all sorts of shady deals before it finally fell into the hands of banana farmers (through a local banana company) which then failed to make a commercial venture of the opportunity afforded it. By then Tourism had become touted as the island's new cash cow and economic saviour. It formed the centre piece in the all new development mantra of the Anthony Labour government.

With its emphasis on tourism, the focus of New Labour's policy seemed to have a connection with the complete annihilation of the banana industry. New Labour obviously felt that the banana industry had sustained the United Workers Party and its leader John Compton in political office for too long. Now if New Labour had to firmly establish itself in power, and bury Compton permanently, then the banana industry which reminded so many of him had to go. The idea was that there would no longer be a viable banana industry - or any kind of banana production, for that matter - to remind anyone (especially, Compton's supporters in the villages of Dennery and Micoud) of the good old days of 'Daddy' Compton, and the green gold, he so loved to claim.

It was also my vision as Minister of Agriculture to establish a Land Bank in St. Lucia. The Labour Government of 1979-1982 had sought to create a Land Bank to facilitate persons who may have suffered loss of entitlement to their small portion of family lands. Such persons would have been entitled to purchase land from the land bank at agreed market prices. Such an institution would be charged with giving priority to persons who may have lost out on the sub-divisions of family lands and who had made a claim for purchase of land from the Land Bank. It was hoped that such a bank would be supervised and managed by an independent government agency, with private sector expertise on its Board of Directors, to help guide its commercial activities. From the above, it may be discerned that these land reform proposals were likely to eventuate in more, not less, conveyance fees to the legal fraternity. Since more vibrant land transactions were anticipated throughout the island more money was expected in circulation, all other things being equal. We were hopeful that these ideas would have provided the necessary 'oxygen' that nourished the legal, banking and business fraternity on the island.

The dream of pursuing a resolution to the problems faced by agriculture due to family land issues dating back to the French, as we have seen, was to my mind, one worthy of pursuing by any decent government or Minister of Agriculture. In time the island's biggest challenge could well be how to produce more and better quality food for its growing population and how best its farmers could benefit from the increasing number of tourists who visit the island. As we vector onto our development needs, a strong and determined land policy will necessarily be made to underpin our efforts especially in the area of tourism development. In time therefore, this country may have to revisit the land reform policy which was established by the Labour Government of 1979-82. The present family land system inherited from the French is too well known to merit further analysis. Only swift and concerted action will do at this stage of the development game.

Rather than use their experience and talents to tackle the important national development projects crying for attention, too many new entrants into government and politics wasted precious time down-playing the role of the previous regime in the development of the island and arguing uselessly, amongst themselves, perchance to discover the best way forward. They were incapable of praising the past and went as far, in certain instances, as claiming the better achievements of the past for themselves, even though some were nowhere around when the past was being built. They never mentioned Land Reform even when they knew it had originated from a previous Labour Government. Their plan was to re-invent the wheel and no one would stop them in their reckless spending to build a square circle. Someone ought to tell new politicians and governments in the Caribbean that development is a continuous process and that when they are elected into office they are supposed to continue the positive changes and programmes instituted by those whom they had replaced in office. It makes no sense for these poor backward countries to be forever starting from scratch. On the other hand, perhaps this is easier to do than to suggest that those who they have replaced were in fact working to a plan, in the interest of developing the people and the country.

The conduct some people, including this writer, found even more appalling after New Labour was voted out of office was their total lack of repentance and hostile unapologetic stance for their mismanagement of the economy'. The huge cost-over runs they incurred on every large construction project on the island, during their nine and a half years in office should be cause enough for true and faithful repentance. Instead of being grateful for the punishment of being voted peacefully out of office they were instead demanding another term in office when they should have been falling on their knees and clamouring for forgiveness. They never suggested that their acts of betrayal and their glaring mismanagement of the national economy were deserving of a more severe reprimand than merely being voted out of office. To prove their contempt, once they got into opposition they immediately began to behave as though the electorate had committed a grave and unpardonable error by voting them out. Theirs was clearly case of a lack of prudent management of the economy which in the thirty years before their time had been associated with Premier Compton, and his several governments.

The Land Reform Commission and the policy of the Labour government of 1979-82, was a complete departure from business as usual. It aimed to correct past historical mistakes and set the island on a new path to regularizing the old French laws - including the 'cinquant pas de la Reine' -the Queens chain (fifty steps from high water mark), which the French crown had claimed for itself around each French colony.

Unless this old French law is finally rectified, Saint Lucia will be faced for a very long time with its outdated Napoleonic code, which militates against the development of undivided family property. It is doubtful that those of the legal fraternity who are also politicians will want to change things around; as such complicated land matters only guarantee a steady stream of income into the various bank accounts of the country's rapacious lawyers.

Prudent Economic Management

It was madness, and it required a madman to succeed in it
D. H. Lawrence: Lady Chatterley's lover.

It soon became obvious that the division within the Labour Government of 1979-82 was negatively impacting the robust growth which the island was set to experience after the important contribution the banana industry had made to the national economy. In fact many believed at the time that the direction in which the country was headed would lead it into the stern clutches of the International Monetary Fund (IMF). That possibility worried the more independent and apolitical business community out of its wits. It was also troubling many other citizens and spreading anxiety across the island. That thought may well have been responsible for the early graying of the new and younger politicians and of the drooping shoulders of their seniors. The IMF had developed a very poor reputation in the Caribbean (and elsewhere) for the harsh economic packages which it forced on certain of the region's governments, after their economies had been run down by imprudent management. Although world-wide condemnation of its harsh medicines had forced it to take a closer look at its seemingly punitive policies, it remained for many countries a feared institution of last resort, for budgetary and economic support. The increasingly heavy debt incurred by the government of the island for programmes of questionable merit began to create a panic in both the private and public sectors. Certain expert economic advisors then suddenly and without notice began to bolt from the establishment; in an apparent attempt to distance themselves from the gathering economic melt down.

The population grew progressively restive and agitated as they watched the country decline. Some chose to keep a discreet distance and watched in silence. Others went about stone-faced and sullen like disoriented sheep which had lost their bearings in a storm. Many banana farmers cried openly for salvation when prices for their produce fell on the European market, but they were to discover that none would come any time soon. Senior personnel at the island's main banana corporation were observed to have sat in their offices twiddling their thumbs as the industry continued its downward path.

Several years later the country was to experience the same trauma with the New Labour government, seemingly without the distraction of a leadership struggle, but so bent on deception that it soon began to tinker with the names of well established institutions, even privatizing government properties and pretending these were their creations. WASA -the Water and Sewerage Authority - was changed to WASCO, (Water and Sewerage Company) and the long established government printery became National Printing Corporation Ltd. Apart from these and other cosmetic changes, everything else remained the same; little of substance had changed. Not satisfied with such apparent deceit they began to apply other cosmetics such as the painting of certain doors within the government offices which a previous government had built, in fire engine red - their party colour. So pervasive was their little Machiavellian mischief that their less timid opponents were forced to enquire aloud about the state of mind which then seemed so determined to impose such monumental deceit (and disrespect) for the intelligence of those who they had sworn to serve, in the name of God and country. Even in this acknowledged half literate society, many were moved to wonder at the origins of such base conduct. Some suggested it was politics as usual, while others thought it a matter of character defects in the new politicians.

It did not pass unobserved that nothing radical by way of change in economic policy for the island had been tackled by New Labour. One clearly expected the new government to tackle certain issues of poverty, but they only skirted the surface without confronting the historical causes of the problem. It was sadly transparent that no changes necessary in certain land laws pertaining to sale and title of land would be tackled as long as New Labour was in office. In this regard they were as conservative and careful as Compton's government, and at the same time more timid and uncertain than Compton had ever been during his long career. It also did not go unobserved that amongst the new government there was a substantial number of persons from the rural communities in which family land problems still existed.

On that point it may prove interesting to draw comparisons between New Labour, (1997-2006), and that of the short-lived Labour Government of 1979-82. The earlier Labour government, having obtained a handsome mandate from the general elections of 1979, was soon faced with an internal division - the leadership struggle. Even in those circumstances it was still able to push through major programmes, such as Land Reform, rural road construction and rehabilitation of many health facilities on the island and a school construction programme.

One is aware that comparisons of performances between governments of different time periods are not easy to make. In the short stay of the government of 1979 - 1982 the entire nation became seized of the necessity to grow more food and to diversify its agriculture. There was willingness by farmers to participate and even persons who lived in the city and had never farmed before, collected fruit seeds, and delivered these free of charge for propagation at the several government propagation units around the island. At that time the call for the nation to join in the diversification effort resulted in thousands of avocado seeds being offered by citizens and presented to the agriculture station at Union where they were propagated and then distributed to farmers for planting. The challenge which hurricane Allen posed after its passage in 1980 was met head-on by the island's farmers and by the wider community. Frequent radio talks and addresses by the Ministry of Agriculture as well as the early (six o'clock) visits to farmers, island-wide, helped create the right atmosphere in which agriculture could grow and thrive. That approach also demonstrated a level of commitment which the farmers of the island had not previously experienced as far as one could tell.

In addition, following the passage of Hurricane Allen the government collected planting material for sweet potatoes from the nearby island of St. Vincent. As the Government Minister in charge, I travelled on a very small single-engine aircraft to St. Vincent for that purpose. The pilot and I arrived there after what seemed an eternity. Before our departure from Hewanorra airport in the south of St. Lucia, the pilot and I had removed the two rows of seats on the tiny aircraft to make space for the potato vines we were to collect. We loaded our gift onto the aircraft assisted by two young Vincentians from the Ministry of Agriculture on that island. When we had finished loading our precious cargo, we immediately taxied and made for Saint Lucia. I was pleasantly surprised to find on arrival at Hewanorra close to one hundred farmers waiting for those sweet potato vines anxious to plant their respective farms. We distributed these planting materials amongst those farmers as best as we could.

In those early days I was very energized and my drive was focussed on seeing the farmers of St. Lucia come alive and ready to work again. I believed that at that time the leadership quarrels had dampened the enthusiasm of our hard working farmers and I was determined to do whatever little bit I could to change that.

In comparison to the rigours of 1979 news reports from the Ministry of Agriculture between 1997 and 2001 made the job of economic development seem like a lethargic afternoon stroll in the park. There was by then, a better foundation on which to continue progress. Unfortunately, as is the case with all things that are got without sacrifice and hard work, farmers' enthusiasm soon fell apart and after nine and a half years in office, New Labour was subsequently banished and put out to pasture.

Too often in the politics of the Caribbean (and also in the so called 'Third World' countries) the point regarding the centrality of wise, professional, economic management is often lost on the leaders and politicians. There is quite often a rush to provide essential services to their citizens without first determining how the monies which are to be expended are to be raised. Even when financing may be scarce, certain Ministries of Finance in the Caribbean have gone ahead with the building of fanciful projects, including high rise buildings, and spending scarce or limited financial resources which could have been applied to more productive uses. It is a continuing debate in the Caribbean that the eternal symbols of development such as high rise buildings are more important to most politicians than providing their people with the best hospitals, schools, roads and recreation amenities, for their development. Such politicians obviously believe that concrete and steel rather than people are the stuff of true development.

There may be several reasons some leaders and their friends in the public service find it difficult to build a more solid economic foundation before proceeding with social projects, no matter how desirable. The main one, of course, is the undue haste and indiscipline of first-timers to public office, who are too anxious to please every demand of constituents, no matter how undeserving these demands may be. In an election campaign, many wild, and sometimes ill-thought out promises are made, that on assuming the reins of government a new group even when there are sensible persons amongst them, immediately finds itself under enormous pressure to deliver, particularly that which they had written in their manifestoes. In addition to the pressure which the government exerts upon itself, the new opposition, especially that which had come to believe the seat of the government was their private property to hold and to keep until the end of times, gives the government little or no time to settle before it begins to attack.

In such an atmosphere of political pressure and the haste to ensure their respective constituencies are taken care of, the new government begins - slowly at first - to set aside the sound economic advice of its trained technical staff, for the exigencies of politics. The delivery of the goodies promised on the public political platforms and in party manifestoes, can be an attraction to the unscrupulous business person. The fly-by-night entrepreneur, for example, can quite easily step in and offer to speedily implement government projects, and in the process, incur huge cost over runs and thereby further deprive the State of scarce financial resources. The government soon becomes a sitting duck to wild and fanciful schemes proposed by both local and foreign business people, seeking a quick buck. By the time the new government becomes aware of its mistakes, it has also become too arrogant to admit it has been fooled by persons it thought it could trust. Governments ought to learn very quickly that they will be deceived by friends and acquaintances if they open themselves to such nefarious and deceitful persons. They must be constantly aware that they ought not to embark on an investment programme which they know cannot be sustained unless they tax citizens out of their salaries and investments. In this hole which they have dug themselves, the national debt begins to mount and rather than acknowledge the criticisms of the opposition and perhaps quietly consult external aid, (including the former Minister of Finance, if needs be) and in the process raise the level of politics in the country, the new Prime Minister and Minister of Finance does the exact opposite. He often begins to lambaste the former Minister of Finance pointing to him or her as the one responsible for the economic problems which continue to bedevil the country. At that time, those who are close to the government, seeing the writing on the wall, begin to siphon off larger and larger chunks from the economic pie. Soon there is so little left that the country begins to stagnate, and thereafter the slow decline towards financial ruin and economic doom.

Perhaps the most fatal error which one observes with newly elected governments which had all clamoured for political independence is the lack of continuity from one government to the next. There are certain emerging political personalities, certainly within the Caribbean, who would do almost anything rather than continue along the lines of a worthy and useful development project which was started by the former government. It has been observed that the projects which a new government does not dismiss completely are those designed and sponsored wholly, or in part, by international development agencies of the United Nations or similar other world bodies of outstanding merit. Other than a handful of such high profile cases, projects started by the former government are often discontinued without a second thought whatever of the merit or their value to the national economy. Of course this is bad governance. In some instances it may well be said to be madness because of the large amount of taxpayer dollars wasted. Unfortunately unlike D.H. Lawrence's observation in 'Lady Chatterley's Lover', such madness at the national treasury does not require a man to succeed at it. There are some, of course, who will challenge such an assertion and say that only a mad man can succeed at such madness as displayed by certain ministers of the government, in place of prudent management of the economy.

It is for those reasons and more that many sensible people, with experience in both the private and public sectors of the society, are now convinced that the entire Caribbean (and many third world countries too) need to take another long hard look at themselves. At the end of it, they need to change the politics and the governance of their respective countries in order to give priority to long term economic development goals, rather than to hasty disjointed schemes which only benefit a few people. Saint Lucia and the smaller states in the Caribbean region need to adopt a new approach to politics and economic development even more quickly and urgently - because small may be beautiful, but one is also much more exposed to the hostilities of the outside world with minuscule size - than other former colonies which are more endowed with land, natural resources, and a larger population.

If one were to summarize in any objective manner the methods of these new governments seemingly anxious to please everyone and at all times, it could be captured in one simple sentence. It was madness and it required a mad man to succeed in it. Indeed it may be observed that that was true of other aspects of the new politics. Not only were the new politicians and the new Ministers of the Government incapable of viewing the development of their countries in a holistic and objective manner; some were prepared to bend long established rules of procedure within the public service, to get whatever they determined was urgent and necessary. In such a case prudent economic management often went through the window of expediency, as politicians and their foot soldiers pressed the public treasury for more and more funds, for social projects which were a drain on their resources. Such madness was to continue until the people again revolted and voted out their previous mistakes for a new and at times even larger one.

Jon Odlum

Those who cannot remember the
past are condemned to repeat it.
- Santayana, LIFE OF REASON

Three decades after the leadership struggle and subsequent fall of the Labour Party government, several of the principal characters in that long-running drama are still with us. For the purposes of this book, two of them were contacted for their reflections on that episode in the political life of Saint Lucia, especially given their close association with George Odlum.

Jon Odlum was George's younger brother and was deeply involved with him throughout the 'struggle' from pre-independence to the election victory of 1979 and what followed immediately afterwards.

Mikey Pilgrim was a close friend of George Odlum from the St. Lucia Forum days and made the entry into party politics early in the 1970's. He featured prominently in the leadership struggle and went on to become Interim Prime Minister after the fall of the Labour Government.

The role which Jon Odlum played in the politics of the island probably began before the year 1974. For convenience, and because that year marked an important turning point in the fortunes of the St.Lucia Labour Party, it is a good place from which to examine, however briefly, the part which Jon, the quieter and perhaps less well known of the Odlum boys, played in politics. For this reason therefore, we return to the year 1974 and we are now full swing into the general election campaign in Saint Lucia. The election is billed as one of the most important on the island by both government (UWP) and opposition (SLP) parties.

Unlike previous elections, the 1974 contest is for seventeen electoral districts, or constituencies. That number was arrived at when the former ten constituencies were increased to seventeen by a Boundaries Committee set up by the government of Premier John Compton. Jon Odlum had by the date of these general elections, spent fifteen years working at the Ministry of Social Affairs - a job he says he thoroughly enjoyed - and would most likely have stayed there until retirement. Unfolding events, however, were to pressure him into joining his brother George, who by then was a member of the St. Lucia Labour Party.

The following is how Jon described his journey into party politics and to his campaigning as a Labour candidate for the Castries South constituency: 'After my brother George decided to join the Labour Party, he encouraged me to come with him. My father, who always supported and encouraged George, suggested that I would be a good foil to George because of my calmer, more laid back nature, and my ability to work with people from every stratum of society'.

'I still resisted the idea of entering party politics. However, what neither my father nor George my brother could get me to do, Minister J.M.D. Bousquet (Social Affairs and Sports) was destined to achieve. It happened like this: 'The youth of the Windward Islands had gathered in St. Lucia for their annual cricket tournament and I was asked to prepare a welcome address for my Minister. I spent a long time reading and explaining the high points of the speech to him at his office. On every occasion the Minister fell into a deep snoring sleep. On one of those occasions, while he slept, I left him and ran over to the Treasury Department next door, in order to collect a voucher. Whilst I was at the Treasury, the Minister called and he berated me for neglecting my duties. So I returned for a fourth time and tried to explain what I thought he was to say at the opening of that tournament. He soon fell asleep again but I continued speaking, disregarding the Minister's disturbing snoring. Back then, there was a 'teenagers' fete' every Sunday afternoon at the Palm Beach Club which the organizers had dubbed 'Sunday School' and to which I made reference in the Minister's speech, in an attempt to bring him up to speed with the language of the day. Of course in his address the Minister "ad-libbed" just enough to make 'Sunday school' seem like a trip to a Sunday church service, thereby causing a hearty laugh among the gathered sports enthusiasts. Even our visitors from the other islands knew that 'Sunday school' meant party time at the Palm Beach Club.'

That incident was to mark the beginning of the end for Jon Odlum as a Community organizer and sports development officer. He soon discovered that his free of charge nightly appearances on local television, where he read the sports news was soon to be a thing of the past. Certain politicians it seemed, had registered Jon's close resemblance to big brother George, and were determined to erase that image of 'George' from T.V viewers. They could not chance the softer, kinder image that Jon presented on television being mistaken for that of George. They were determined to destroy big brother George and they feared that Jon's nightly visage on the television militated against their dirty political plot. So Jon was forced out from television….and sports suffered in the end. (Sounds familiar?) He also resigned from his job at the Ministry of Youth and Sports. That move was to eventuate in his giving to the Labour Party and the constituency of Castries South, one of its longest serving and most likeable Parliamentarians.

Jon picks up the story again.

'My first task after making up my mind to enter party politics was to speak to Mr. George F.L. Charles who was then the Parliamentary representative for Castries South. I wanted his endorsement for the seat. George Charles and myself were close friends and neighbours in the C.D.C. buildings on Jeremie Street, opposite the Castries market. He seemed enthusiastic when asked, but said he needed more time to think about my request. One day, whilst visiting Mr. Charles' home, his wife fell ill and I had to rush her to Victoria Hospital. News of this reached Charles and we crossed each other as I was rushing his wife to hospital. He turned his vehicle around and then followed me there. On arrival, I explained to him as best I could the circumstances that led to my helping his wife to hospital. Charles called me later that day and promised to support me fully in the Castries South Seat - he himself having decided to quit politics. Later, he disclosed to me that the illness of his wife and the incident I have described was to him an omen that I was to take over the Castries South constituency from him.'

According to Jon Odlum there were only six weeks left before the general elections of 1974 after he received the blessing of George Charles and the promise of support in his election bid. Primrose Bledman, a Barrister by training and one whose first love was music - specifically the standing bass guitar - was Jon's opponent in Castries South that year. 'Prim,' as he was known to everybody, had been one of the quieter, gentler members of the St. Lucia Forum. His was always the voice of reason. He consistently advocated gradualism. Incremental change was therefore his mantra. Prim had spent many years in England in the fifties and sixties; at a time we are told, when racial discrimination was rampant in that country. That he returned to his homeland without any signs of mistrust or animosity for anything British (or white) was attributed to the many social contacts he is alleged to have made and cultivated in the world of music, including the London clubs of that period. When I first met him in mid 1969 he was married to 'Picky', a French national, born in Algeria, by whom he fathered a son, Eric.

Jon easily won the Castries South seat in 1974. He, however, lost to Prim in the Fou-a- Chaud polling division, an area south/west of Central Castries, where George Mallet of the United Workers had once firmly held sway. When asked what, in his judgement, was the most enduring memory from that first election contest, Jon said:

'One of my fondest recollections of the 1974 campaign was the moment I was whisked away from Maynard Hill, in Peter Josie's Castries East constituency, where I was all alone addressing a public meeting. Peter arrived in a great hurry, wound up the meeting, and asked me to accompany him to La Clery, where Labour's Neville Cenac was holding a public meeting. La Clery was then, a vibrant sporting community, and the young people there requested to hear from me. My good friend Hollis Bristol was the candidate to contest the La Clery seat for the United Workers Party, against Labour. My loyalties were split that night and I approached La Clery with great anxiety. I could not think of anything to say against Hollis Bristol.'

Jon disclosed to me that he had no idea what he was going to say when he arrived at La Clery and he felt very nervous as a result. He said that his prayers were answered when the rain which had been threatening all night, finally burst free from the night sky and gave the whole of Castries - including la Clery - a thorough wetting. The La Clery meeting was aborted and poor Jon was free to exhale.

When asked about his preparedness for Election Day 1974, Jon had this to say: 'My family has always been my greatest support. On the day of the poll every member of the Odlum family who was able to, came out to help me. They were deployed inside the polling stations, at the 100 yards marker, and as drivers, to help get people out to vote. Of course Mona, my wife, was a tower of strength. She stayed home to cook for the entire army of helpers.

I also asked where he was on the night of elections when the ballots were being counted. Jon: 'I was at Fou-a-Chaud – in which polling division I lost that day. I spent the time playing dominoes with my friends. We had just tuned in to listen to the election results, when Primrose Bledman, my opponent, came into the yard to congratulate me on my first electoral victory. I must say that the victory in 1974 was not a total surprise to me. It should be of some interest to note here that Jon was never seen as a front line parliamentarian - along the likes of Josie, Michel and Pilgrim. He certainly was not as vocal as these three or as his brother George during the leadership struggle. He was, however, a leading member of the Progressive Labour Party (PLP) which George formed with Pilgrim and others when it became obvious that they could not have their way within the Labour Party or the Labour Government of 1979 to 1982. Jon Odlum, along with sixteen other candidates, contested the 1982 general elections as a PLP candidate. He was the only successful PLP candidate in those elections. He therefore represented the Castries South constituency from 1982 to 1987 as a member of the PLP.

In 1987 he contested that seat as an Independent candidate, but this time he was unsuccessful. He contested the 1992 general elections as an Independent candidate and with the same results as in 1987. He therefore spent ten years out of parliament 1987 to 1997 after having been elected in 1974 and 1982. Notwithstanding the many obstacles, Jon soldiered on and in 1997, when all the disunited and scattered elements of the opposition SLP were pulled together under a new leader, he was again chosen to contest the Castries South constituency which he easily won. Indeed, his victory that year was just one of the sixteen seats won by the St. Lucia Labour Party out of the seventeen constituencies. After that victory, Jon was named Parliamentary Secretary in the Ministry of Social Affairs and Community Development, and Deputy Speaker of the House of Assembly. He was again given the nod by the SLP to contest the 2001 general elections for that party even though elder brother George had by that time also formed another political party which he called 'The National Alliance'. Jon was again successful at the polls and he was appointed Parliamentary Secretary in the Ministry of Health and Human Services. During his political career, he spent the first ten years or so as a SLP parliamentarian representing Castries South constituency. Then he spent the next ten years outside parliament, perhaps in part due to the division within the ranks of the opposition between 1987 and 1997. He returned to parliament for a further ten years representing the same constituency, again as a member of the St. Lucia Labour Party.

After all those years in politics and in parliament it may be surprising to hear Jon Odlum say he never considered himself a politician. He says: 'From the inception I always saw myself as a representative of the people rather than as a politician, per se. My interest has always been to develop a happy people. My political aspirations were therefore limited to making my constituents and those whom I serve as a Minister of the Government, as happy as possible'.

When asked what he considered his greatest achievement in politics, he says nothing gave him more satisfaction than the many self-help community projects which he built all over the island, often with very little help from the government but with maximum community participation and also with gifts of materials from several friendly organizations, both local and foreign.

Jon added perhaps with a bit of nostalgia that 'one never gets everything one sets out to achieve, but I also believe that nothing happens before its time. I have tried to live my life that way and be guided by such understanding'

I did not ask him to comment on the life and passing of his brother George, but he volunteered this bit of family folklore. He told me that both his parents regarded George and himself as a 'Rat Attack Team'. When asked to explain, he said his parents always saw George as the aggressor that would 'bite' whereas Jon was the one who came around to soothe and blow the bite so that it became tolerable (and less painful) to those who had the misfortune of suffering from George's 'rat-attack-bite'. In the culture of the island, rats have always been looked upon with suspicion since they are known to spread leptospirosis in humans. It is also widely believed that they attack the human feet - and toes - when one is asleep. They are said to keep their victims from waking whilst they nibble and feed, by blowing on whatever part of the foot they happen to be feasting upon, at the time. A team of two doing the rat attack can pose a serious challenge, wherever they happen to operate.

Jon has now handed the Castries South seat to new hands in the person of Dr. Robert Lewis - who won the December, 2006 elections. Jon believes the decision to replace him was not a popular party Executive decision, nor was it a popular decision of his Castries South constituency. But he accepted the decision with grace as he personally believed that his replacement was a fine young man who had much to offer the constituency and perhaps even Saint Lucia.

Jon would not end the conversation before repeating what he considered to have been his role in the public life of his country. He said: 'I was never a politician as such, and I only learnt to cope after I became involved in politics through the encouragement of my brother George and my parents who wished me to be near George to help keep things steady. In my early days in politics I depended heavily on Frances Michel, Peter Josie and of course my brother George, as my platform spokespersons as well as for their political savvy'.

Perhaps a nice way to recall the services of one such as Jon Odlum to the people of Ciceron, Castries South and Saint Lucia is to recall the figures, ten, ten, ten (10-10-10). The first ten represents his early parliamentary life with the St. Lucia Labour Party. Then the next ten were with big brother George and the PLP. The final ten years were as a Minister in the government of the new Labour Party - between 1997 and 2006. I think it will be very difficult if not impossible to see the likes of a Jon Odlum again in the politics of this country.

28

Michael Pilgrim

I am in love with a remarkable lady...I don't regret the reverses and setbacks because late in my life I am blooming like a flower Anthony Sampson ... NELSON MANDELA.

By the late seventies, the anti-colonial movement had gained a sufficient foothold at the United Nations General Assembly, it's 'Decolonization Resolution' demanding the political independence of colonies had garnered wide international support. It may have been a happy co-incidence that at the height of the decolonization debates at the U.N. the countries of Western Europe were themselves moving towards greater union with each other. These European powers may therefore have been happy to support such a move as they no doubt wished to relinquish the financial burdens which these far off colonies were placing on their national treasuries. At the time, Britain seemed to carry a heavier burden of colonies than others and she was therefore more anxious to grant political independence to those who asked for it. It was clear for all to see that Britain's many colonial outposts in the Caribbean and in the South Pacific had become a drain on her economy, as each colony seemed to be demanding increasingly more from the mother country than their products were earning.

There seemed to have been an unwritten understanding that Saint Lucia may be ripe for political Independence if the parties desired it and made it a manifesto item for the general elections of 1974. Grenada with the stylish Gairy was proof of a desire by the colonial power to set these islands free. Sadly, no one in authority seemed bold enough to have been forthright with the citizenry in Saint Lucia. In anticipation of a move for Independence the opposition SLP proposed that a referendum be held on the issue.

Prior to that United Nations decolonization resolution the former colonies of Europe in Africa, the Caribbean and the Pacific were already marching towards full sovereignty. In the Caribbean, Jamaica, Trinidad and Tobago, Guyana and Barbados had each proceeded separately to collect their instruments of Independence from London. Even Grenada, an island in the Windward's group, with no more than 90,000 souls at the time, was to claim Independence from Britain, under Eric Matthew Gairy, its charismatic political leader, in February of 1974.

Against this anti-colonialism movement we may, if we wish, superimpose the on-going ideological (cold war) between the Union of Soviet Socialist Republics (U.S.S.R.) and China on one hand, and the United States of America and Western Europe on the other. By 1970 that ideological struggle had come to a head in Vietnam where the North Vietnamese and the Vietcong revolutionary fighters, backed by the U.S.S.R. (and China) were locked in a fierce combat against South Vietnam and the West. That conflict was framed by the north as a struggle to reunite their country and to free it from the clutches of American imperialism and western cultural infiltration and dominance. Their Vietnamese brethren in the south on the other hand, saw it as a conflict to stop the spread of Marxist/Leninist proletarian dictatorship - Communism, from China and Russia - to the entire region to the south and east of China.

Closer home in Latin America, reports of armed struggles and wars of liberation were a constant diet of the western news media. Armed revolutionary struggles, a la mode de Castro and Che Guevara, were reported from the hills of Peru, Chile, Bolivia, Nicaragua, and San Salvador - South and Central America. Even in Trinidad and Tobago, a former British colony with a history of democracy and political stability had its own brush with armed insurrection. In early 1970 that country's army appeared to have mobilized certain disgruntled elements within its ranks who plotted to take matters into their own hands. These rebels were already advancing from their Teteron Bay Army Headquarters and into Port-of-Spain, the capital city and seat of government. However their advance was stopped by the Coast Guard which had remained loyal to the government.

It was against this background and the general awakening of the people of St. Lucia (and the Caribbean region) for a greater stake in their country's economy that young progressives such as Michael Pilgrim aligned themselves to the St. Lucia Labour Party. The U.W.P at that time was seen (and portrayed) as the remnant of the old plantocracy which had continued to hold onto political office after several general elections between 1964 and 1979. To persons such as young Pilgrim it must have appeared that the old order was refusing to relinquish state power. It was believed then that certain of the operatives of the old plantation system had aided and abetted the disunity of the St. Lucia Labour party. However, with the addition of young vibrant voices such as that of Michael Pilgrim the opposition Labour Party was soon on the ascendency. At the time it was generally agreed that with the introduction of new and better candidates into its ranks, the SLP would soon be on its way to forming the government of the island as it had done between 1951 and 1963.

The on-going feud between Kenneth Foster and George Charles (leader and former leader respectively) within the camp of the SLP had threatened to destroy the very fabric of that party, when it should instead be rebuilding. Although personalities such as Compton, Mason, the brothers J.M.D. and Allan Bousquet, and Dr. Monrose, were long gone from the SLP, the party still seemed blighted with internal division and unable to unite and get its act together. Now with the introduction of new blood particularly that of former Justice Allan Louisy, the very top brass of that political party seemed poised to be set aside in preparation for winning general elections.

By joining the Labour Party when they did, the young progressives such as Michael Pilgrim, Jon Odlum and George Odlum, Frances Michel, Peter Josie and several others breathed new life into the organization. Together with the experienced and conservative Allan Louisy, the SLP boasted the nucleus of a formidable political team. To this day, many still argue that the coming together of this particular group of candidates may well have been the real turning point in the fortunes of the St. Lucia Labour Party. It has been claimed by many that the party may have reached the zenith of its popularity during the 1979 campaign. The new life which the new membership brought into the Labour Party could have sustained it for the next fifty years, if it had been properly harnessed and managed. But to have managed such energy and ideas one needed political skill, dexterity and above all, legitimacy.

When the 1974 general elections were called, Michael Pilgrim had just established himself in his accounting profession on the island. He therefore declined to contest elections that year. However, he was so deeply involved in the campaign and worked with so many candidates, that it was easy to overlook the fact that he was not a contestant. He played a crucial and dynamic role in the rallying of support for the St. Lucia Labour Party in the Castries Basin, both as a public speaker and as a door to door (house to house, as we say in Saint Lucia) canvasser of voters. He was also active in the Dennery North constituency in which Frances Michel (Sister Frances), a close friend of his during his student days in England, was the Labour Party candidate.

When asked about his memories and what stood out for him in that campaign of 1974, Pilgrim had this to say: 'During the build up to the general elections of 1974 I was still employed with the International Accounting firm of Peat Marwick Mitchell. I was based right here in St. Lucia. Before returning to St. Lucia I studied in England where I met and befriended Frances Michel and her husband 'Brando'. I visited them regularly and I was well looked after by both. On returning to St. Lucia I followed the public meetings of the St. Lucia Forum and I was impressed with what the group had to say. I was, however, not interested in party politics and was focussing on a career in my chosen field – Accounting.

By the early seventies, however, Frances Michel and her husband had returned to St. Lucia. They were also close friends of George Odlum and the Odlum family. Perhaps it was our frequent social visits with each other that led to my growing interest in politics. I recall that I started becoming more vocal in defending and promoting the ideas of the St. Lucia Forum (and later the Labour Party) in private conversations. And that, of course, led me into the Labour Party after Frances and George' had joined it.

Following a brief pause for recollection Pilgrim continued: 'I worked with that Accounting firm up to early 1975. After this, I worked as Manager of the St. Lucia Housing and Development Bank, from 1975 to 1977. All that time, I was quietly following the politics as an interested St. Lucian who wished to see his country prosper. Following my stint at the Housing Development Bank I became Financial Controller at Lucelec (St. Lucia Electricity Services Limited) where the working conditions were superior to those at the Bank.'

Mikey Pilgrim was by then fully seized of the need to participate more meaningfully in party politics so we must now examine more closely his efforts in the 1974 general election.

'I think it is true to say that I managed the election campaigns of both Peter Josie and George Odlum in 1974 and I also helped out as often as I could in the Castries South seat of Jon Odlum and also in Dennery North where Sister Frances was the candidate. My job was mainly that of public speaking from political platforms and I targeted the younger voters in each constituency with whom I had a rapport. During that 1974 campaign I lived at Black Mallet Gap about 120 feet from the Marchand main road. Peter Josie lived another 120 feet higher up that same road. At that time my younger brother Karl was also deeply involved along with Tyrone Maynard and George Goddard. The three were young trade union activists at the time. They asked nothing in return as far as one could tell. These young men along with many others did their bit for the St. Lucia Labour Party.'

As we have seen, the 1974 elections were followed by a five year campaign of attrition against Compton's government. That campaign led to victory at the polls for the St. Lucia Labour Party in 1979. Michael Pilgrim became a Minister within the office of Prime Minister Allan Louisy. He shared a large part of the responsibility of bringing the first National Commercial Bank into existence. Such a bank was the jealously held vision of some new entrants into politics who nurtured and expounded in the St. Lucia Forum, the vision for a different and better Saint Lucia.

Unfortunately, Michael Pilgrim fell out of political office with the rest of the Labour Party in 1982. He contested the 1982 elections as a candidate of the Progressive Labour Party (PLP) but he was one of the sixteen unfortunate candidates who lost out that year. Only Jon Odlum won his Castries South seat for the PLP.

Michael Pilgrim again contested general elections in 1987, as a candidate of the PLP, in the Castries North/ East seat. He lost twice to Stephenson King. The second general election of 1987 was called by Prime Minister Compton within thirty days of the first in order to seek a stronger mandate than the nine seats to eight seats the electorate had handed his party. Pilgrim lost both these elections. His loss may have been due to the three cornered fight in the Castries North/East constituency. By then he had left the PLP and returned to the SLP and so to punish him the PLP sent a popular young candidate making it a three-cornered fight and ensuring victory for the UWP candidate, Stephenson King.

By then Pilgrim had set up his own Accounting Firm on the island, but he could not stay too far away from politics. He therefore contested the 1992 general elections as a candidate of the United Workers Party (UWP) in the Gros-Islet seat but lost to the leader of the SLP at the time, Julian Hunte. Before he finally threw in the towel Pilgrim again contested the Gros-Islet seat for the United Workers Party but was again defeated at the polls, this time by Mario Michel who had by then risen to deputy political leader of the SLP.

It may be said of Michael Pilgrim that he was in love with a beautiful lady - Saint Lucia - but that he had many disappointments and failures. However, he may one day quote Nelson Mandela and say that although he had many reverses and setbacks, he does not regret any because late in his life he is blooming.

It was very difficult at the time when our political journey was evolving, to tell exactly how much of our involvement in politics was driven by genuine love of country and how much by youthful emotion and enthusiasm for politics searching for a cause to pin our energies on. After all these years, it appears a light still shines within the breast of many who are alive at the time of this writing and whose concerns for the country still burn brightly, in their aging eyes. Some of these patriots remain in the eyes and hearts of many of the people of the island as the true political soldiers of their generation. Many agree that this island shall not see their likes again. New circumstances call for new politics and a new way of doing things, so it may well be a waste of time comparing mangoes and cellular phones. In time persons such as Michael Pilgrim may well be recognized for the work they did against so many odds, and negative outside interferences.

The Valhalla Epistles

*The sons of Aaron, the Kohanim, shall sound the trumpets and
it shall be for you an eternal decree for your generation.*
Torah: Numbers; Ch. 10 vs.8.

This chapter - Valhalla Epistles - was at first intended merely as a recollection of the more interesting highlights of the political life of George Odlum as I experienced them. It started off as weekly newspaper articles published each Friday in the local Mirror newspaper following the passing of 'Brother George' as he was popularly known and shortly after the elections of 2001. They were intended to be a sort of memorial to his efforts at establishing a more just society. It was a life which many right thinking persons who knew him would agree deserved to be celebrated and remembered. With time these weekly pieces attracted the attention of certain trusted friends who encouraged me to place them in the broader framework of a book describing the social and economic realities of the time that 'Brother George' lived for: 'the struggle'. Back then he and others similarly inclined were at the very summit of their political game. I too, claim inclusion in that lot.

The Chapter took its name, as did the series of articles in the Mirror from that which Odlum had chosen to call his dream home - Valhalla. The house was located at Marigot Bay which, at the time, was a beautifully wooded yachting haven on the west coast of the island, some seven miles south west of Castries, the capital. It was purchased in the early nineteen seventies through a friend who later became a close political associate of Brother George. At the time of purchase that female friend worked with a Real Estate agent on the island. The house was previously owned by a well-to-do Canadian citizen who had built it as a winter retreat.

About seven months or so before Brother George bought that house I travelled with him to London and we were accompanied by the female realtor, from Saint Lucia. The ostensible purpose of that trip was to seek sale for a house he then owned at Muswell Hill, in north London and which that same young realtor, was to help him dispose of. The year was 1972. It was my first visit to England of which I had by then read so much. It was that country which had given Saint Lucia its official language, its constitution and its laws. On that first visit the three of us stayed at the house of Mrs. Bledman, (Picky) at Filey Avenue, in North East London. Picky, I discovered was born in Algeria of French ancestry and had accompanied her husband, Primrose Bledman, to Saint Lucia in the late sixties. Primrose had earlier been called to the bar, in London. On his return to Saint Lucia he became a staunch member of the St. Lucia Forum and a popular cultural activist as well.

I had been previously informed by Brother George that the sale of the London property was to raise the necessary capital to purchase Valhalla. He previously lived at City Gate, on the outskirts of Castries with his lovely wife Fleur, a Barrister. The two had met in England to which Fleur had travelled after winning the St. Vincent island scholarship, in the late-fifties.

At the time he lived at City Gate Brother George was employed as Permanent Secretary in the Ministry of Planning and Development, which was then headed by Premier John Compton. The name 'Valhalla' was not chosen lightly. Its origin was of Scandinavian mythology and means a place in which heroes, killed in battle, feasted in eternity. Such a selection coming from someone who fully understood the power of words, confirmed that the name 'Valhalla', was no fluke. It seemed certain he had chosen it with care and without whim or fancy. Indeed, it is true to say that in his lifetime, that house was to serve as the planning headquarters of a handful of selected strategists and warriors, of his political battles. His companion political warriors were to gather there at his call, to discuss, analyze, plan and strategize, in the name of country and politics. Such discussions often included lengthy dissertations by those knowledgeable worthies who had also been especially invited to participate and lead a discussion topic within their expertise.

It is therefore not that difficult to see the reason I have added the word 'Epistle' to that of 'Valhalla' in the series of articles referred to earlier. That word was not meant to import a religious (or Christian) ethic into the text. It was meant instead, to convey a link between lifting the poor and disadvantaged and of charting a new political pathway by which to achieve the empowerment of the powerless, as Odlum and his mates had planned. From this perspective, therefore, the meetings at Valhalla became sanctified with a special quality of grace, I thought. Such a high calling sprung in large part, from a deep love of country, and for this reason I imagine that many who attended these meetings must have felt a special and divine call to service.

In addition to its title, the quotation bearing the reference to the sons of Aaron and Kohanim are merely reminders that we were all in this search for a better, more peaceful and happier life together. It is also a reminder of Brother George's four brothers and the deeply religious father who cared so much for the Odlum clan. The admonition to the sons of Aaron and Kohanim in the Jewish Torah is not new even though it preceded those of the other monotheistic religions. The book of Proverbs in the Christian Bible is also filled with similar advice to the youth (both sons and daughters) of Christians - and to all who may read it.

George Odlum was born in the mid-nineteen thirties, at a time when British colonialism reigned supreme in Saint Lucia and the Caribbean. Class and colour prejudices were accepted as if they had been decreed by God rather than the result or consequence of man's inhumanity. His father had migrated from his native Antigua at a tender age, and later took a wife from the scenic town of Soufriere on the south west coast of Saint Lucia. George was the first of nine siblings, of which four were girls. He developed an early liking for reading and English Literature soon became his favourite subject at school. He was encouraged in this direction by the Castries savants who had the benefit of education and who gathered each week at Odlum senior's barber shop for the compulsory weekly haircut. George acquitted himself well at St. Mary's College in Castries and liked to remind his friends now and again that he was the first student on the island to pass the advanced level Cambridge exams in English Literature. He left unmentioned the performance of Derek Walcott, (Nobel Laureate) who was a form or two ahead of 'Brother George' at the same secondary school.

For all his efforts though, his application for a job at Barclays Bank (D C O) in 1955 was turned down because the bank, as everyone at the time knew, did not employ dark skinned people. From that experience it was difficult for 'Brother George' to have developed a positive attitude or assessment of the system of colonialism (and racism) which he was certain had denied him the job for which he believed he was qualified. It did not help the young Odlum when it later came to his attention that certain less competent school mates of a lighter complexion were employed by the same Bank, soon thereafter. Such a slight could have broken the spirit of lesser men - and women. He never forgot that slight even though the bank's rejection may have led him to a teaching job at St. Mary's College and soon thereafter to Bristol and Oxford universities in England where he pursued courses first in English, then Politics, Philosophy and Economics (PPE) at Oxford.

Brother George belonged to that class of Caribbean personalities who, whatever their difference with their fellows nonetheless fully exhibited the precise correctness of the language and mannerisms of the colonial elite. This wholehearted acculturation was to set him and his ilk apart from the local country bumpkin whose only language was the French Creole, and which was still considered by many persons as 'broken' French. Creole is now more widely spoken in public than before and it is recognized, officially, as a second language, on the island. He seemed at first disdainful of the class of people who recklessly butchered the English Language that he loved so dearly, at every street corner, wherever they gathered in Castries. He never seemed to doubt his own superiority in speechifying (in English) and the poor diction of those who attempted English in his presence was a deep hurt to his feelings for precision, tone, inflection and delivery. The reckless intruding and the gradual creolization of the English he loved so dearly were to confirm what he already deeply felt - that there was a certain colourful vulgarity of language which belonged to the streets and which appeared patented by those who habituate there. He occasionally insinuated a superior learning, but he was always careful where and when he displayed it. He had an insatiable appetite for enjoying himself and his early morning slumbering as a teacher at St. Mary's College, at the front of his class and in full view of his students, may have been only a foretaste of that earlier lifestyle and what it portended.

Sometimes he tended to exhibit an impatience and boredom with the tasks at hand. On other occasions such impatience would extend to those near him, whom he considered as dull and uninspiring. No one knew for certain the precise source of such fixed uncertainty and child-like impatience. The word on every pair of lips at one time was that he was not able to finish anything which he had started, especially in political office. That of course was not completely true, but even his best friends never bothered to defend him on that particular accusation.

In his political life, his meetings at his 'Valhalla' home with friends and family were always a high point of his day - or night. Sometimes his invitations there reached beyond the realm of politics. They appeared at such times intended merely to titillate and to excite one's intellect and thereby providing food for thought and debate, on a wide range of subjects.

The frequent calls to meetings at Valhalla seemed at the time not dissimilar to that of regular religious calls to prayer. There were no specific days or times for such meetings. However, on Good Fridays which were the holiest in the Christian calendar, one was certain to receive a telephone call from Brother George the day before, (Holy Thursday) to come spend the day at Valhalla or such other place, as he may have suggested. Sometimes, I declined, thinking that the stated purpose of the meeting did not seem to me to warrant a drive to Valhalla or indeed to spend time with anyone, outside my home, that day. But I often went upon being invited because I thought it a way of extending myself, in personal sacrifice, for a greater good, one that my family would one day come to appreciate. Back then, Brother George seemed to experience a sort of vicarious pleasure in gathering his friends and political pals around him, especially on such Good Fridays. Perhaps this was his way of emulating the breaking of bread and the passing of the goblet of changed water, as he imagined it to have happened by Christianity's great Emmanuel, over two thousand years before. Who could tell for certain? He once told me that his father had challenged him to read the Holy Bible from cover to cover, for the reward of a bicycle. I did not ask him how long it took him to do this or how long his prized bicycle lasted.

The Valhalla meetings also served to identify prospective candidates (and helpers) whose names were pencilled into a list which Brother George carried with him at all times. The drill took the form of each person present at the time, suggesting the names of other suitable prospective candidates (or platform speakers and helpers) - in sum; persons who may be a useful addition to those engaged in the political cause - the 'struggle'. It was always, the struggle!

By midday on Good Fridays after (each of) these intense discussions were deemed to have exhausted their run, the group was fed and watered until the gathering lounged, sated with pleasure around the small asymmetrical swimming pool on the sloping ground nearby. The idea of evangelization was not one which was associated with the politics of the day. Quite the opposite was true. Yet here we were breaking bread and drinking pressed grapes from famous vineyards the world over, and doing so, as persons who had been called to a higher evangelization may have done at an earlier time. It was therefore to our deep chagrin that many persons who called themselves 'Christians' at the time, went out of their way to make our politics seem like an evil enterprise - the work of 'the Mr. Evil' himself. One can therefore well imagine how the good people on the island felt when these regular, innocent Good Friday meetings, became common knowledge, especially among strict Roman Catholics.

No one knew for certain the true terrain of the minds that gathered at Valhalla. Notwithstanding this, an effort was made to invite the new persons on Brother George's upgraded list, to subsequent meetings. In that way our numbers grew, but it did so, ever so slowly. Some persons never returned after they had paid their first visit to one of our little gatherings at Valhalla. Those who belonged to that set, never bothered to offer any explanation or apology for their absence, as far as I could tell. Perhaps such dropouts felt no inclination for the difficult political journey (and thankless task) they may have perceived lay ahead. A dubious political lifestyle could have been their lot had they agreed to persevere and take up that heavy burden of a political cross, to be weighted down by people who did not seem to care or had found other less demanding 'religion'. Yes, Brother George always appreciated the marriage between politics and religion.

It was well known that there were persons who knew of these indoor meetings and who did not support the politics of Brother George and the group. Such persons put the word out that the meetings at Valhalla were 'for Odlum to surround himself with fanciful nutcases of his dreams' as one of those types said to my face. Such disparaging remarks were from his more charitable 'friends'. Others, less friendly, and of a more cynical bent, let it be known that Brother George and his group seemed to live in a state of perpetual denial and in the dream-like fantasy of the insane, or otherwise mentally challenged. They opined that invitations to Valhalla were to those seen by their host as pliable play-things on the chess board of his unfathomable mind. Still some others, seemingly without charity (and concrete evidence) observed that the gathered brethren at Valhalla may have been the source of the leaks from government offices which Odlum's weekly Crusader editorials (and bold headlines) used at that time, to highlight and expose some 'secretive' government dealings. The paper's scathing attacks were an embarrassment to those in power. Sometimes the truth was embellished in order to enlist greater animosity against the government and its friends. At the time, that paper seemed to shed considerable light in places where no others dared to venture. If there were any glad tidings to be dispensed in the local weekly newspapers, one would have had to look elsewhere, other than in the Crusader. Even when that paper became part of the government, through Odlum's election victory in 1979 and again in 1997, it continued to be the bearer of all that was negative and off-putting about that Labour government. It appeared the Crusader newspaper had assigned unto itself, the work of the opposition and seemingly, for all time.

Those who thought the Valhalla meetings were a continuation of the Forum groundings of the early seventies were to be sorely disappointed. These meetings were different. Sometimes the assortment of personalities that had gathered there ostensibly for serious discussions seemed more like the tired remnants of a long weekend of unbroken feting. Others, more sober, seemed then to be nursing certain fanciful political notions of an egalitarian Welfare State in which they were to play an important role. To dare to disabuse such reverie was to risk exposing oneself to a cut-eye and tongue lashing of the worse kind. It was far better to allow such minds to dream undisturbed. Perhaps theirs were not to be seen as shattered dreams - as so many others were to become, in their own time.

Everything which I have said thus far in this 'Valhalla Epistles' belongs to a period in the middle to late nineteen seventies. It was a period in which those who were more politically inclined and who attended these regular group exchanges dreamt of playing a role in the future governance of the country. That period may also be counted as the first of three distinct time lines of meetings; what some called 'group therapy' at Valhalla.

There was no agreed time table which identified the beginning and the end of each process. However, it is fair to say that the second phase of these meetings commenced in 1979, after the St. Lucia Labour Party became the government of the island. At that time group meetings were also held at the offices of the Ministry of Foreign Affairs. Brother George was the Minister, there. Unfortunately this second series of meetings was to eventuate in mild chaos before too long. Within a year they had descended into full blown division following the pattern within the government. It was also noticeable that the meetings at Valhalla became less frequent and more irregular. They were then held mostly on Sundays. The only new feature of these Sunday meetings was that, on occasion, a total stranger was to drop by seemingly out of nowhere and without anyone, except Brother George, knowing of such a visit or the stranger's whereabouts. At such times, regular members of the group would exchange furtive glances but no one said a word, perhaps remembering they were all guests.

Once in a while a Sunday meeting would dove tail into a planned birthday party for a member of Brother George's extended family. So after the business of the meeting had ended the brethren who attended were invited to stay and be part of the ceremony. As the music played and more family and friends arrived, Brother George would display an animation and hospitality with which many may not have at first associated him. None could scorn the benevolence he displayed then or indeed at other times when he was in a celebratory mood and the atmosphere was just right. Afterwards, when the crowd had gone home, the music would be lowered and those who lingered there to talk and drink some more, would be treated to Brother George's selection of fine music from Tchaikovsky to Bach and Beethoven, and other past masters of the art.

The more perceptive were then to observe that whatever finery he displayed in his choice of wines were also to be matched by his choice of music. One therefore came from there with the distinct feeling that 'green figs and salt fish' a national dish loved by locals, did not make a suitable match for fine wine, neither was it to be served with such classical 'European' orchestral music. As the night wore on Brother George would suddenly throw himself into an exaggerated up-tempo waltz, having first ensured that he had only minimally raised the volume of his Japanese made stereo system.

That pattern was repeated every Christmas as I recall. He once confided that he rose early in the month of December and immediately switched on his stereo set with the great classical Christmas masterpieces, set to play without interruption between the hours of four and five in the morning. After these early morning renditions of soothing Christmas classics, Brother George, - the energized bunny - then left Valhalla for his village butcher, well before first light. On arrival there he would pick up his choice cuts of beef, pork and lamb which he had previously paid for and secured a week or so before Christmas. At such occasions (and also nearing Christmas) his largesse was boundless. He seemed then to take care of as many family and friends as his wallet would allow; sharing drinks generously, to those who may happen by to say 'Hi' and 'Hello'. It was therefore difficult to scorn such planned benevolence even when one may not have been comfortable with the invading tribe, or their politics. At such moments Brother George seemed to profit from the mannerisms and social finesse he had picked up at Oxford and London. He also seemed more in his element then, than when he was bursting his lungs on the Castries market steps - the University of the People - in trying to convince those who refused to see, that a new Messiah had come to set them free and to make them prosperous. They did not seem to understand when he quoted with proper pause that, 'they should take up their beds and walk'.

Occasionally, the success of these Valhalla parties seemed to entice a certain 'puffed up' exuberance in Brother George which many were quick to put to the contents of the silver chalice from which the products of his chosen vineyard cellars flowed. He never claimed to have blessed either the wine or the bread at these parties, but the symbolism, of drinking from the silver chalice did not escape the curious 'Christian' observer. At such moments he seemed to display the reckless levity of youth in the manner he danced with the younger damsels at the party.

In all this jollity, however, the island was soon to discover that the leadership problem within the government of which Brother George was a Minister, had long begun to fester and would soon drain all the fun from those who frequented Valhalla. It would not be overstating matters to say that even Valhalla began to sour. Yet the general disposition of the Valhalla group at the time was to see how best it could mend the division within the government as quickly and as quietly as it could.

As 1979 turned the corner to usher in 1980 it had become apparent to some regular attendees at Valhalla that the indoor meetings summoned by Brother George were beginning to more and more resemble a gathering of hand-picked acolytes and 'yes-men'. Then by the early eighties, men (and women) who had previously exhibited a propensity to rational thinking, almost overnight, began to speak as supporters of this side or the other within the Labour Party and the government, thereby fuelling the senseless 'leadership struggle'. At its early stage, I confess that, I too could be numbered among the guilty.

However, I also confess that it was in this period that the long political road which Brother George and I had travelled together, forked. We each ventured into separate paths along that forked road, not knowing where it would lead or whether they would ever converge again. That period of travel could be truthfully described as one in the proverbial wilderness. It was a time when neither of us won the privilege of a seat in the island's parliament. It was also a period when we went at each other in public, as by then I had decided to remain loyal to the cause of the St. Lucia Labour party, as Brother George went his way, ending up with his very own political party - the Progressive Labour Party (PLP). It was not to be the final Damascus of our wanderings. In time, I too would be forced to walk away from the Labour Party.

At the commencement of 1997 - which was to mark the end of another period in his checkered politics, Brother George was still in the political wilderness. He had by that time contested the general elections of 1982 and 1987 - both as leader of his Progressive Labour Party (PLP). His party was badly defeated on both occasions. It may have finally dawned on him that both himself and his PLP would be permanently grounded. Sensing this, he soon abandoned his PLP adventures and then seemingly faced a very bleak future. He no longer had the love of his life – a political platform and a working, public address speaker system, to keep him occupied while at the same time offering comfort. It appeared at the time that all Brother George had ever desired in a public, political-life was a suitable stage, a working microphone, a crowd and one or two supporting speakers - bit-players. In the meantime, Prime Minister John Compton – a sworn opponent - was planning to come to Odlum's rescue. After winning the elections of 1992, Compton's third consecutive five-year term of office, he called upon Brother George to serve the country as Ambassador to the United Nations, in New York.

But before Brother George accepted the offer, he made certain to neutralize as many of his more hostile opponents whom he had earlier roundly condemned for associating with Prime Minister Compton. In his earlier campaigns he had called John Compton and his supporters all manner of names which are now better left unwritten. It was perhaps with that sort of former treatment of his opponents in mind that, I received a telephone call from him one morning, seeking my opinion on the offer. Of course I unhesitatingly gave the whole enterprise my blessing seeing it as an opportunity for Brother George to rise again. By then I had been re-elected to parliament for the constituency of Vieux-Fort South and on a Labour Party ticket. I was at the time deputy political leader of that party but it seemed that there were certain influences both inside and outside the party who wished me gone, and which undermined me at every turn. Such persons never made their accusations in my presence, so I never had an opportunity to defend myself.

At the time of the offer from Prime Minister Compton to Brother George, the latter had not regained a seat in parliament. The looming end of his political life seemed then to mock him in the open, and at every turning. He had himself fine-tuned the art of ridiculing his opponents and now the tables had been turned. In essence he was now in a political wilderness of his own making, as they say. Those who were concerned with Brother George's future did not have long to wait, before his fortunes were to change. After making certain his former PLP supporters (or what was left of them) and other trusted family connections were with him on Compton's Ambassador offer, his mind was made up. Brother George accepted the offer, and this was announced on radio and television. He left shortly afterwards for New York and to his cushy UN Ambassadorial sinecure. I was one of those he had invited for a farewell drink at Valhalla before he left for New York.

Although we had not yet reclaimed our former close friendship, I felt certain that those who considered themselves as the 'progressive left' - his former comrades - were also pleased to discover that I was fully supportive of Compton's newest appointment. Everyone it seemed wished to see Brother George emerge from the quagmire into which he had found himself. He therefore had broad national support in his new role as the country's Ambassador to the United Nations.

A few of his unforgiving opponents were critical of the offer, and his acceptance of it, noting that it did not enhance his reputation as a progressive left-winger in the eyes of principled persons - his foes. Some went out of their way to remind those who would listen that this was the same Odlum who had spent the past decade and more denouncing John Compton as the epitome of everything that was wrong with Saint Lucia politics. Compton, it was pointed out had also said some mean things about Brother George. But that was politics, even though Compton's offer was a bitter pill to swallow. But it was a cup which Odlum had to take to his lips, if he wished to breathe new life into his political agenda. So he took Compton's bitter-sweet medicine, and was soon settled in New York. Before he left Saint Lucia, Brother George's family and friends had assured him that it was far better to eat humble pie than to rot slowly away at Valhalla. There simply was no other life line left at the time of the Prime Minister's offer. Knowing Brother George, his opponents' criticisms that he was some sort of paid mercenary must have weighed heavily on his nimble mind. However, if they did, he did not explicitly share his thoughts with anyone I knew. He therefore brushed his opponents aside, as he determined to become the new poster boy for Saint Lucia, for Oxford University, and for Prime Minister Compton, all at once. If Compton's friends believed the 'Fox' had played trumps by plucking Brother George out of his misery at Valhalla with his latest appointment, Brother George was determined to prove that he was also the absolutely best man for the job, at the time.

During his two-year stint at the Saint Lucia Mission in New York, he seemed to have made a fair impression on those who witnessed his performance. Soon after settling into office he started the publication of a weekly newsletter in which he covered the activities in New York, of the four Windward Islands - Dominica, St. Vincent, Grenada and Saint Lucia. I was to visit him twice during his stay in New York and on one occasion he invited me to his well appointed apartment on Third Avenue, a short walk from his Number 800, Second Avenue Suite - the address of the Permanent Mission of Saint Lucia to the United Nations, in New York.

Towards the end of 1993, one year after John Compton had won his third consecutive general election on the island, local banana farmers began to misbehave. Banana exports were facing increasingly severe competition from Latin American fruit in Europe and as prices fell, local protests rose. The Compton government became the target of willful no-cut strikes by banana farmers. Their stated aim was to show the government how vital farmers (and banana farmers in particular) were to the national economy. They were soon joined in their efforts by none other than the opposition St. Lucia Labour Party, which by that time had lost three consecutive general elections under the same leader and who seemed condemned to pasture on barren ground for many more years, once that leader persisted.

At the time it became impossible for Prime Minister Compton to hold any sort of dialogue with the striking banana farmers. Encouraged by the opposition Labour Party, these banana farmers stepped up their protests over the next three years and demanded the resignation of Prime Minister

Compton and his government. Compton, of whom it can be said, always seemed to have had his ears to the ground, particularly in such a political maelstrom as this, had apparently seen the writing on the wall. He therefore took the unprecedented step, and resigned as party leader. Weeks later, he also resigned as Prime Minister of the country. But rather than call fresh elections, as the farmers and their friends were demanding, Compton then invited the former Director General of the Organization of East Caribbean States - Dr. Vaughan Lewis - to replace him. Lewis therefore soon became party leader and shortly thereafter, he won the by-election in Castries Central and became the country's sixth Prime Minister. That election was occasioned by the resignation of George Mallet, Compton's long-serving deputy, from the UWP government, thereby rendering that Castries central parliamentary seat vacant.

Such a move did not sit well with Brother George who, from all reports, was following events on the island very closely, from his New York office. Neither did it please the protesting banana farmers or the opposition S.L.P. At the time of his being hand picked by Compton as the island's Ambassador to the U.N. it must have occurred to Brother George and some of his friends that perhaps Compton's offer was a signal to groom him - Brother George - as Compton's political replacement, some day. With the emergence of Lewis, all this theory and guesswork had been finally unravelled, and thrown out the window. Brother George did not like what was emerging on the political landscape of the island. Indeed it would have surprised only a handful of Brother George's hard nosed supporters, if it had been proven that Compton had deliberately offered him the Ambassadorship in order to get him out of the way, and smooth the passage for Lewis' ascendancy. Whatever may have been in Compton's mind at the time, the move to raise Lewis seemingly out of thin air, proved too much for Brother George to handle - or to accept?

Within days of the announcement of the by-election in Castries Central, Brother George vacated his Ambassadorial posting in New York and returned to the island in order to contest that seat against the new leader of the U W P. He fought that by-election as stoutly as one could have expected him to do in the circumstances. He hurriedly registered a political party which he called 'National Front' and took an umbrella as his party symbol.

As fate would have it, some of his former admirers chose this unguarded moment to proclaim that they believed all along that Brother George was afflicted by a loose screw, (or two); meaning his senses may have taken leave of him. Notwithstanding this cutting criticism and taking into account the native cynicism, Brother George soldiered on, and in the end was able to attract a handful of public speakers to his campaign meetings.

Many more were invited to shelter beneath that political umbrella but they seemed reluctant to do so, perhaps fearing it could disappear whenever Brother George got the itch to travel again. The by-election came and went and it left Brother George, unhappily, in the same place he had been before Compton's call to service. Lewis was duly sworn in as Prime Minister, the sixth since the island became independent in 1979. The year was 1996.

Soon thereafter, I was invited to serve as Minister in the Ministry of Agriculture by Prime Minister Lewis; an offer I gladly accepted. In so doing I had also calculated there was very little chance of reconciliation between myself and the Labour Party. In any event I had also determined to serve the constituency of Vieux-Fort South in the best way that I could, after it had elected me a second time, (1987 and 1992) - to parliament. It was after all, the people of that constituency who had voted me in order to bring relief to them. Lewis' invitation allowed me an opportunity to serve my constituents more effectively, just as Brother George's call by Prime Minister Compton had allowed him to serve the people of Saint Lucia. Lewis soon named Compton as Senior Minister, and the three of us - Lewis, Compton and I - were to work very closely together to help clean up the town of Vieux Fort; open up the Mangue area by building a road through it - which was later named 'Shine Road'. Someone must have forgotten to put the 'Sun' before shine in order that the new name should bring fresh hope to the people who lived there.

In the meantime Brother George and I had continued the friendly relations we were nursing soon after he was called by Compton to serve. It was a slow period of fence-mending for both of us. It was not lost on anyone that the election of Lewis in Central Castries and his ascendancy to the chair of the Prime Minister in Castries did not have any marked effect on the disgruntled banana farmers. They had all paused to watch and study the process which was taking place in Castries, beyond their banana fields, and had apparently decided that the more things changed the more they seemed to have stayed the same. So within hours of his assuming the office of Prime Minister, Lewis was being bombarded by all sorts of frivolous requests from the leaders of the unhappy farmers. Of course even as they were requesting an audience with the Prime Minister, their leaders were also announcing publicly their determination to continue their no-cut strike and street protests, if their demands were not met.

By then no one knew for certain what those demands were as they had become so inextricably mixed-up with opposition politics. The word around was that the leaders of the striking farmers were employed and paid handsomely by agents of certain large US banana corporations who desired to sabotage the banana industry of the Windward Islands. Saint

Lucia was the largest producer of bananas in these islands. Lewis did his best to bring the warring banana factions together, but it was clear to those who would see, that the farmers' representatives did not wish for an amicable settlement to their protest. Both the local banana association and Wibdeco, the purchasing and marketing company, remained distant and stone-faced as if they did not understand each others language.

During that emotionally charged period, I, as Minister responsible for the banana industry, held several meetings with banana farmers. Many of these meetings were between 6.30 a.m. and 7.30 a.m. - something that I had previously done during Hurrican Allen. Other meetings were held between 5 p.m. and 6.30 p.m. at community centers and school buildings. Interestingly, after no more than three or four persons had spoken, it became clear to me that each speaker was merely regurgitating what he or she had been told at public meetings of their leaders a day or two before. The farmers' protests were to continue until general elections were called in 1997. By that time, the opposition St. Lucia Labour Party had found itself a new leader, and had declared itself ready to form the next government. It used disgruntled banana farmers, and the ugly mood they had generated in the country, to calmly stroll to victory in 1997, taking sixteen of the seventeen seats in the elected House of Assembly.

It was widely believed that the re-admittance of George Odlum into the ranks of the St. Lucia Labour Party at the time may have been partly responsible for the sound beating it inflicted on its opponents, then. Of course there were many others within the party who did not trust Odlum and who wanted nothing to do with him. Notwithstanding such strident attitudes the new Prime Minister, Kenny Anthony, appointed Odlum as Minister for External Affairs and Foreign Trade, in the new Labour government. Odlum had in fact revealed to certain close friends that he had secretly canvassed that position among certain of his newly elected 'colleagues' before the group had officially met in the first Cabinet following Labour's victory. Almost immediately, the Taiwanese representative on the island was shown the exit door and Beijing, which had been courting Odlum for many years in New York, was welcomed to Castries, replacing Taiwan. That move was largely engineered by Odlum and everyone on the island knew it. Days before the 1997 general elections he had even boasted how much aid money the government of Taiwan had offered him in order to curry favour with the incoming Labour Party whose victory at the time seemed certain. His friends had it that during his stint at the United Nations Odlum had cultivated Communist China as a true friend and he may even have gone so far as to guarantee them recognition, if they would help finance the S.L.P.'s campaign in 1997. That was the reason, those who had been following closely, had suggested he turned down the offer from Taiwan and then to openly boast about it - Beijing had apparently offered a jucier deal.

Word soon made the rounds at social gatherings and private conversations that the diplomatic recognition of Beijing did not sit well with certain members of the new government, particularly those members who had allegedly opposed the re-introduction of Odlum into the party. But it appeared the guarantee of huge campaign funds was sufficient to quiet those who were not impressed with Odlum's shenanigans. Local mischief mongers even contented that Odlum had sweetened some SLP candidates with the largesse from his new found friends from the Far East.

It did not take long for the nation to discover at least two fascinating and crucial bits of information which would later impact the country. First, there are some persons in the field of politics, who cannot be bought. Second, those who had opposed Odlum's re-admittance into the party and later on, his China policy, were secretly plotting to get him out of the government. It later transpired that some of Odlum's more determined opponents were in the bosom of Anthony's Labour government of which he was a Minister. As soon as it appeared so to Odlum, he was to prove once again that he had no time or patience for the business of governance, and even less for neophytes playing with political power. Besides, opposition politics seemed to have served him much better financially in the past than had any office within a democratically elected government in his political sojourn.

By the second year in office he was to oppose the budget of his own government in open parliamentary debate, much to the embarrassment of the government and, of course, rekindling memories of the leadership quarrels within the Labour government of 1979 to 1982. Before he finally parted company with Anthony's new Labour government, I received a telephone call from George Odlum, in his role as Minister for External Affairs. He invited me to his office in order that he may hand deliver a diplomatic note from the government of Israel, via its representative in the Dominican Republic, to me. It was a personal invitation from Jerusalem for me to visit the Agriculture exhibition in Haifa, Israel. The invitation had offered to pay my living expenses while I was in Israel and I was to foot the air ticket to and from that country, if I accepted. My first reaction was that this was a once in a lifetime journey, I could not afford to miss. Growing up in the Roman Catholic Church as I did, one could not help noticing the centrality of Jerusalem in the foundation of that faith. Religion aside, I had always admired the young radical Jew who challenged the hypocrisy he saw within his own nation's teachings and practices and decided on a path to make all men acceptable in the eyes of the Most High, regardless of religious persuasion. As a former Minister of Agriculture in Saint Lucia, I was aware of certain assistance which the government of Israel had donated in irrigation and soil conservation to the island. Further, I had long decided, even before politics, that Jerusalem was one of the 'must see' places on my wish list of places to visit before I too, was called to the great beyond. I therefore gladly accepted that letter, thanked Minister Odlum for it and immediately began preparations to collect my Israel visa in New York, and proceed from there to the Holy Land; that place which continues to claim so much of the world's attention.

Soon after our meeting at his office, Odlum resigned from the Labour government. It was the second time in two decades (1981 and 1999) that George Odlum had made himself the centre of political debate on the island. He was then to return once more to his old nemesis - Compton - who was still very active politically, and who was frequently in the news. There was much excitement all over the island (and possibly around the Caribbean as well) when it was announced that George Odlum and John Compton were to appear together at a public political meeting, in down town Castries. I was off island at the time, but the buzz was so great that I decided to call home to enquire what the fuss was all about. I was informed that people had gathered there from every corner of the island to witness the spectacle for themselves. The night of the public meeting the crowd was so huge that every vendor around the William Peter Boulevard, in Castries, was completely sold out of water, drinks and food, by nine that evening - the meeting was scheduled to end at 10.30 p.m.

It turned out that John Compton was not quite ready to accept Odlum as a major player in his party and so the two soon parted company – again. Odlum this time also went on to form yet another political party which, this time he christened 'National Alliance'.

Prime Minister Anthony, perhaps recalling that Lewis may have lost the elections of 1997, by procrastinating in ringing the election bell, and not wanting to seem uncertain himself, did not give Compton and Odlum time in which to reconcile their differences and to consolidate their political bases. He rang his election bell in December of 2001, well before the five year period was up.

The United Workers Party for its part was also on the move, trying to rebuild and recapture the government. To that end, they brushed aside Lewis and proceeded to the 2001 elections with an even greener and more innocuous novice in the person of Dr. Morella Joseph, from the town of Vieux-Fort. I had joined the UWP on the invitation of Dr. Lewis and I felt I owed him my personal support and loyalty while he served the party and country. When therefore Dr. Joseph emerged as party leader, I had little hesitation in putting on the yellow, red and green T-shirt of the National Alliance of George Odlum and throwing my support behind Brother George, once more. It was the last political hurray for both of us, and I felt it deep within me at the time.

My family and friends thought that that was one of the most foolish things I had ever done, and they did not keep these very emotive thoughts to themselves. The majority were of the view that Odlum was going nowhere, very quickly, and that everyone else seemed to notice, except me, and a handful of renegades. Why didn't I do like so many others and simply potter around the Executive of the United Workers Party, of which by that time I was a member, and see what came my way, they asked. But how does one communicate to people who one loves and respects that we each have our roles to play in life, and that at times, the agenda is set not by ourselves, but by the Great Architect of the Universe. Of course it is always a greater challenge when one is not singing from the same hymn book as his peers and colleagues. On reflection, I can only put my actions down to the deeper calling (and loneliness) with which the long distance runner is so often cursed and afflicted.

During that 2001 campaign I could have seen that the fire had gone out of Brother George although he did try very hard at times to recapture the performance of his glory days on the Castries market steps. That campaign proved disastrous for both the U W P and the National Alliance, although the former captured two seats in the banana belt between the villages of Dennery and Micoud, on the East coast of the island.

Within a year of those elections the country was hit by the most devastating news it had received in many years. George Odlum had been struck with pancreatic cancer and he was being treated at the private hospital at Tapion, Castries. He revealed to me, when I went to see him at Valhalla that he was also being cared for in Martinique, by highly trained French doctors on that island. Many persons afflicted with cancer have been known to put a brave face to the illness, and Odlum was no different. Sadly, I had not heard of anyone who had survived this particular type of cancer and I felt in my heart that his brave battle would likely be Odlum's final performance.

It was indeed a performance in every sense of the word. Even as it became obvious to everyone including 'Brother George' that this was another battle he would not win, he strode manfully into the deep un-chartered future as any tried and tested warrior would have done. He brought Leila Haracksingh and me together one morning at Valhalla to discuss the future of the Farmers and Farm Workers Trade Union. He also invited the top guns of the National Workers Union to see if there was any way the two organizations could assist each other to grow and prosper.

During that period, I visited Odlum at his Valhalla residence as often as I could. At these visits I met people from all walks of life who came to see the slowly departing warrior. Persons I had not at first associated with prayer and divine worship were driven to their knees in prayer with 'Brother George' at his bedside. Those whom he had earlier wronged with either his incisive pen or razor sharp tongue and on whom he may also have inflicted many a painful political punch in the height of his staged performances on the market steps, came to see him. Perhaps such visits were in order to offer to the slowly departing Brother, an opportunity for quiet contrition, and apology. One of the most deeply spiritual moments I was to experience during one of my visits to the ailing Brother, at Valhalla, was the day I met Dr. Vaughan Lewis conversing softly with the fading voice seated on his well-made bed opposite. Lewis had borne the brunt of Odlum's fury after he had accepted to stand as party leader and Prime Minister, for the foxy Compton. It was the first and last time I was to experience two people speak so deeply, soul-to-soul so to speak, with hardly a word uttered. It was a moment of great surrealism for me, and I figured it must have made both Brother George and Vaughan Lewis contemplate their inevitable destinies, as it did me, of my own inevitable demise.

George continued his regular visits to Tapion hospital Saint Lucia one month and then at the Lamentin hospital in Martinique, the next. The time soon came however, when he became too weak to travel to Martinique. He was confined to the Tapion hospital where he would spend his last days. During the last month of his life the disease had eaten all it could of Brother George's flesh until there was hardly any more of him left. Even his once booming voice had also by then deserted him and he was little more than a whisper to normal hearing. By then, I could no longer bear to witness the callous disregard with which he was being ravished by the cancer. I therefore left for New York to visit family and friends, knowing in my heart that I would never see the likes of him again. That market steps thunder which once boomed from that man-made stage 'I am as constant as the northern star of whose true fixed and resting quality there is no fellow in the firmament' was not to be seen there again until he finally passed lying horizontal in his wheeled mahogany casket - built to suit the political warrior which it held.

He passed away on the 28th September 2003, two days after my birthday. I was saddened by the news but happy to be able to return home for his funeral and burial. His was an open air event at Mindoo Philip Park at

Marchand Road, which Fr. Patrick Anthony had re-named the Cathedral of the people – in order to celebrate the life of the island's great orator. Father Anthony may not have quoted Longfellow that afternoon, but he said enough to remind those listening to him that; 'Life is real! Life is earnest! And the grave is not its goal'.

At the time, I wondered had Brother George to do it all again what, if anything, would he have changed? But then this may not have been a fair question for one born a restless warrior, a political animal and an amateur stage actor, all at once. Such a question may also not be fair to those who may have dedicated their lives in the cause of introducing political change to the country and people he or she loved. The fight against injustice and oppression is a never ending one, because the world had made an industry out of advantage, deceit, and injustice. Perhaps the last word here is to suggest that these are the reasons the struggle must never end until the world is refashioned so that each of its citizens may have an opportunity to evolve into a more beautiful and more perfect work of divine art. Then perhaps we may say with conviction that the grave is not the end - or the goal - of all art or of all things beautiful, meaningful and profound.

Beyond 1979 Elections

The idea of progress is closely associated with
the rise of Secular Humanism
..........Ferdinand Mount: The Theatre of Politics

Unfortunately, there were no lists of names recorded anywhere; no printed documents of achievement and no photographs of the former party faithful of the St. Lucia Labour Party, who worked so hard in the past to keep the party going from strength to strength. Only a minority of those who had been in the vanguard of the early labour movement survived the huge Castries fire of 1948. In that sweet moment of victory in 1979, stories were told of the party's vision of West Indian nationhood whose vague form had been earlier described by such men as Marcus Garvey of Jamaica, Marryshow of Grenada, and Bird of Antigua. Amongst these early visionaries of Caribbean nationhood were the foundation members of the St. Lucia Labour Party such as Charles, Lewis, Degazon, Louisy, Augustin, Cragwell and Collymore.

All this jubilation and reminiscing and the taunting of supporters of the opposing party was not to last very long. Soon the sweet victory of the St. Lucia Labour Party would be soured as a long and bitter internal struggle took centre stage in the party's affairs. That struggle would eventually end with the demise of both government and seemingly the political party as well. Those who reported on the quarrel at the time had framed it as one between two men for ultimate control of the government and the party. But the leadership struggle was much more than that.

That quarrel within the government of the St. Lucia Labour Party was much more than a personality conflict. It had arisen after the victory of the 1979 general election. There is a long story preceding it. Certain persons within the trade union movement on the island had questioned the credibility of George Odlum, and claimed him untrustworthy because no one, as far as they were concerned, had ever before abandoned their Oxford and Cambridge University status (and their international recognition and earned social standing) in order to work amongst the poor and struggling masses of this or any other poor country. The same concerns were raised by others when Allan Louisy left his acting Appeals Court Justice bench for local politics. Many believed both men - Allan Louisy and George Odlum - were too distant and disconnected to the reality of the marginalized and struggling youth, for participation in party politics.

Be that as it may, the point remains that few, if any, political observers had anticipated or properly analyzed the infighting within the government and placed it within its proper global and ideological - cold war - context. It turned out that the older heads within the party, assisted by certain younger trade unionists at the time, were suspicious of both Odlum and Loiusy in the party as well as when it formed the government. Some of these folks viewed Louisy and Odlum as likely messengers or agents of foreign governments, who were sent to calm the radical upstarts threatening to enter the political arena in Saint Lucia. From that viewpoint the older stalwarts saw both men as a step backwards in time, from the more committed and genuine George F. L. Charles, the first political leader of the St. Lucia Labour Party. The better educated and more articulate youth on the island, however, were at that time more inclined to support George Odlum rather than Allan Louisy, to lead the party and the country. They loved his mastery of the public platform and on several occasions Odlum was to mesmerize such persons with his tone, voice modulation and delivery, as well as with his theatrical prancing and gesticulating. His well rehearsed speeches, his green, ex-army political costume, his cloth cap and his market steps semantics and the stage management and acting out his many Market Steps speeches, were also to capture a wider audience than the idealistic youth in search of a hero. His opponents had earlier described his style of dress and his general military-type appearance as merely 'masquerading', but his supporters did not see it that way.

Compared to Odlum's performances at public political meetings Louisy sounded dull and uninspiring. True, he had a strong booming voice but the rhythm of his speech and the things he said were no match for the George Odlum style of delivery. Both were well trained in their chosen fields of endeavour. Odlum was an English major who had also read Politics, Philosophy and Economics at Oxford University. Louisy had read law in England and was highly regarded by the Caribbean Bar. He became a Judge of the Court of Appeal of the East Caribbean and before that had served as Crown Counsel and held other senior positions in the British

Colonial Administration in the Caribbean. He left the Appeal Court of the East Caribbean to join the St. Lucia Labour Party in early 1974. Many persons were surprised when Odlum had so willingly embraced Allan Louisy in the St. Lucia Labour Party, praising him at every opportunity. It did not escape attention that Louisy never seemed as generous in his praise for George Odlum back then. It seemed a sort of balancing cat-and-mouse game between the two, which some people suspect may have started long before these two were elected into government.

Soon after the 1979 Labour victory and long before the dust had properly settled, a meeting of the winning candidates was held at the law offices of Evans Calderon, one of the victorious candidates. The office was situated in Castries, at the corner of Manoel Street and the Brazil Street extension. The purpose of the meeting was to discuss the results of the elections and to decide on the formation of a new government. That meeting, it was later stated may have been the first of several early mistakes of the victorious party. The candidates had unwittingly bypassed the party central executive committee, who many later argued, ought to have been present at that first meeting. It was the central executive which had sanctioned and approved candidates for the election. Besides, the rules of the party had offered clear instructions and guidance on how the organization was to conduct itself after a general election, whether it had won or lost.

Another mistake may have been to have invited certain persons who did not contest these elections or who may have contested but did not win a seat. The purpose of the meeting was to sound off winning candidates only on the way forward. The rules of the party had provided for a parliamentary caucus so the newly elected parliamentarians were breaking no party rules. That first meeting soon turned into a contest of wills between the younger elements within the party led by George Odlum and the more seasoned politicians led by Allan Louisy. The conversation soon turned to a discussion of who should become Prime Minister. A long debate followed in which the position of Governor General of the island came up. The majority at the time seemed to think His Excellency the Governor General ought to be replaced. It was generally agreed that Allan Louisy would be the person to replace him.

My recollection was that that first meeting was conducted in a very amicable manner indeed. After a long discussion I left with the clear understanding that Louisy would become Governor General after six months in office as Prime Minister although the meeting left hanging on who exactly was to replace him as Prime Minister. There was therefore no clear agreement as far as I remember on a deputy political leader to take charge as soon as Louisy was gone. There may have been some feeble reference offered by someone at the meeting against replacing Louisy with a person who may appear too haughty and radical for the likes of the more conservative society. I don't recall anyone answering that it was that same society which had only hours earlier elected the Labour team to office. Of course everyone knew that some of the statements made at that meeting were a lot of lame excuses by apologists who were yet to accept their effeminate selves as full human beings, and were therefore forever in hiding behind a closet of denial. Such people were never up to any good and obviously were not capable of helping their poor selves whichever way one looked at them. As far as I was concerned, the outcome of that first meeting left much to be desired, because too many decisions were left hanging and without clear words and resolve from the grown hard backed men who had just presented themselves to the people of Saint Lucia as some big time leaders of men. These guys almost to a man were nothing - speaking politically. I would be disinclined to take any of them into my confidence, having lived and worked with some of them. Indeed I would give an untested youth a chance before many of these psychologically damaged imposters who continue to offer themselves to the people at general elections. Let me assure everyone who reads this that it has not been written in anger. Indeed, this writing has been more than four years in the making, and many more after the events of 1979-1982, which was sufficient time in which to change an opinion which had been formed between 1974 and 1979.

George Odlum's understanding that Allan Louisy was to vacate the office of Prime Minister after six months, and that he was to be replaced by none other than Odlum was the miss-step that may have broken the back of the Labour government. No sooner had that news reached the general public, than a technical difficulty which may have been left opened deliberately showed its ugly head. Prime Minister Louisy pointed out (correctly) that he had never agreed to step down specifically to be replaced by Odlum. Louisy did not deny that he had agreed to step down. But although no specific person had been mentioned the day of that first meeting, Odlum had begun quietly putting word out to close and trusted friends that he was the heir apparent when Louisy left the Prime Ministership in six months time.

An important aspect of the debate which had been played down from the very beginning was that Allan Louisy had differences with Sir Allen Lewis since the two had served as judges of the Court of Appeal of the East Caribbean Supreme Court. Sir Allen Lewis was then Chief Justice. It was believed that the two men did not see eye to eye on the law and perhaps many other matters. The reasons for their differences were never revealed. All I know for certain is that there was no love lost between the two, highly regarded Justices. Louisy made no secret of wanting to see the back of Sir Allen soonest. That desire however, was a separate and completely different matter from leaving the government in the hands of George Odlum or what was widely considered the left, radical-wing of the party.

There were other old scores to be settled, some personal, others political and historic. These, coupled with suspicions and mistrust regarding the reckless manner in which certain characters, now elected parliamentarians, had conducted both their public and private avocations, left much room for speculation as to the final composition of the new government should Louisy leave. There were politicians in the Labour government who were mortally afraid of George Odlum. More than fear, they also did not trust his holier-than-thou rhetoric and may have actually feared for their freedom and safety, in an Odlum-led government.

Let it be clearly stated that I feel certain that everyone present at that first caucus following the party's victory knew full well that a moral agreement had been reached, though it was not clearly spelt out. Prime Minister designate Louisy would replace Sir Allen as Governor General in six months and the elected majority of Labourites in parliament would choose a new Prime Minister from amongst themselves, to replace Louisy. That was simple enough for any ten year old child to understand. What the party and country did not cater for were the number of agents of foreign governments based on the island and who had spent a large chunk of their waking hours fighting the changes they saw coming. It must have frightened some people that some sort of bad wolf as our opponents had portrayed us, was about to capture their little island and take it into the hell of black power and communism. Even people within the Labour Party sometimes seemed uncertain of the Odlum/Josie, agenda.

It is important to repeat here, for clarity and emphasis that no votes were taken at that first meeting, but a consensus, had clearly been arrived at, as stated above. A successor had not been decided, but many people, including a majority in the country, were led to believe that the next Prime Minister after Louisy was most likely George Odlum. At the time the long hands of the anti-Castro propagandists both within and without, were frantically at work, aiming to render the progressive left of the party, innocuous. Louisy was widely quoted as saying that he had never agreed to, nor did he ever vote for George Odlum to become Prime Minister of the island, or that he would be prepared to step down as Prime Minister, for Odlum. Every part of that statement of course is correct. It is equally true there was an agreement for him to step down. Only the 'for Odlum' part renders the statement different and false, but nevertheless, still a little tricky and perhaps even a little deceitful in the eyes of a strict constructionist especially bearing in mind the full extent of those internal discussions.

It was generally agreed at the time, that George Odlum did not help his cause or that of his more progressive brethren in the party and government by the hasty and unprovoked manner which he leaked to the press, the nature of the deal that was struck at that first meeting. In this, and in many other ways, George Odlum was his own worst political enemy. Many have opined without a shred of evidence that the real reason Justice Allan Louisy vacated the Appeal Court Bench prematurely and entered elective politics, was to assist in frustrating the progressive left-leaning elements on the island. It has been further argued that, had Odlum, Josie and company remained in the St. Lucia Forum and contested elections under its banner, Allan Louisy may still have emerged to help the SLP and frustrate the work of the more militant in that party as well. But we will never know the truth unless those who were involved let us have it.

In the eyes of the progressives, therefore, the former Judge was not the first; neither would he be the last to enter politics with an agenda aimed at reversing the tide of change sweeping the old conservative Caribbean mindset aside. Ever since the advent of adult suffrage there were people who believed that the only road to economic development was to follow slavishly the dictates of former colonial masters in Europe and their cohorts elsewhere. That may well have been true but, it is equally true that home-grown Caribbean intellectuals have long contended that in the new Caribbean, there must be room for all ideas to be debated and exposed to scrutiny and discussion. In other words, every idea must be allowed to contend.

As far as progressive thinking and political change were concerned the entire Caribbean seemed to have had its eyes focussed on Saint Lucia especially after the overthrow of Eric Gairy by Maurice Bishop and his New Jewel Movement. The reported excesses of the former eccentric Eric Gairy were deflected and passed over as the work of an egocentric megalomaniac, whilst that of Bishop who was later deposed by his own military, was seen as the work of outsiders aided by certain over-indulgent Caribbean leaders.

At the conclusion of this first caucus of the victorious Labour candidates, it was agreed that these internal discussions should be kept secret. Even the party executive was not to be told of the decision that Louisy would soon become Governor General. So the staunchest supporters knew nothing of what lay ahead for them and the country. On reflection, it seemed that one needed to confide at least in the party hierarchy and perhaps also in a handful of party faithful who had worked so hard to help the party to victory in 1979. We ought to have kept confidence with the party's stalwarts if we wished to return to them for further advice and support, at a later period or for another general election.

Unfortunately, by the mid-seventies, big money of doubtful origin, was already creeping into the decision-making apparatus of political parties in the Caribbean. Many wise observers predicted that in time, such foreign investments in local politics would further corrupt the fragile two-party system of democracy, and thrust the wider region into confusion and disunity.

As if to prove a point, no sooner had the Ministers in the Louisy Government been sworn into office, the country began to observe all sorts of dubious characters visiting. Many were from North America and claiming an interest in the establishment of gambling facilities and casinos on the island. A few weeks earlier and before the 1979 elections, the SLP had opposed the establishment of casinos on the island, when it was first mooted by the former government of John Compton. Gaming and casinos were anathema to the Christian community. In opposition, the Labour Party had heavily criticized the former administration for merely suggesting the introduction of casino gambling. These Casino 'investors' seemed either not to have heard or their cynicism was so deeply rooted it did not permit them to care about how the new government (and the people) felt about gambling as an industry for the island.

Every week it seemed there was some hair brained proposal brought to Cabinet by some of the newly elected Ministers of the Government. None of these proposals seemed to fit into any long term social and economic development strategy for the island. None guaranteed any sustained or meaningful income for the island. None were to be controlled or operated by Saint Lucians. None provided any linkages to other sectors of the economy. Some party stalwarts were concerned that those Ministers who were so keen on the casino proposals had to have received handsome rewards for their efforts. As usual no one could prove that incentives were offered or received.

The casino issue was not the only one which embarrassed and threatened to derail the Labour government of 1979. There was also the issue of certain 'investors' proposing to drain and reclaim mangroves and other low-lying protected coastal areas on the north east coast of the island and to construct new hotels there. Of course these planted provokers (and would-be destabilizes) were no accidents. They had their fingers on the weak spots within the government and they knew which carrots to dangle, when, and to which Minister of the government. Each scheme promised to create a load of new jobs. Once such promises became public property, principles were thrown out the window and people began to put pressure on their parliamentarians, to allow the investor the concessions for which he had applied. But these would-be destabilizers did not get very far. Some of us immediately saw these 'projects' as having only one purpose in view: that of spreading chaos and confusion within the government and perhaps in the wider society, as well.

This wide array of questionable schemes also had the effect of widening the gap between the progressive wing of the government and those who were anxious to grab at every straw to satisfy their rapacious constituents. There were several other more ridiculous proposals which, thankfully, never saw the light of day. Some of those were presented to the cabinet by average Saint Lucians who seemed to be fronting for other persons, from outside the country.

Early disquieting whispers which had been in circulation soon metamorphosed into loud allegations of horse trading for juicy paying government contracts amongst those who did not support the party when it was in opposition. These were being spread not by the opposition but those who were out to make a killing from the available government jobs and contracts. Those who were willing to offer bribes for such contracts were often assisted in their design. It was in this early confusion and the reach for personal gain that the Leader of the Opposition, former Prime Minister Compton (whose party had just been soundly trashed at the polls) was seeking to hold a 'Thank You' meeting in Castries. The opposition politicians who planned addressing the meeting were the same persons who had found great difficulty in holding a peaceful public meeting anywhere on the island, mere weeks earlier. Now, with the full weight of an electoral victory behind it, the rank and file of the Labour Party was in no mood to be lectured to by former Prime Minister Compton or any other person in his party, for that matter. Even an apparently harmless 'thank you' meeting by the opposition was viewed with suspicion and disbelief. Some people expressed amazement at the gall of the opposition. I was one of those, who believed that such a 'thank you' meeting was bound to end in chaos given the unsettled state of the country so soon after the general elections.

I was supported in this view by many in the vanguard of the Labour Party who expressed similar concerns. Some felt that such a meeting was a deliberate ploy intended to spread chaos and confusion - even destruction - in Castries which it hoped would lead to doubts about the Labour government's ability to administer the country. They may also have reasoned that the people were in too much of an ugly mood to permit such a public meeting, and perhaps even dared them to stop the proposed public meeting. The pervasive hostile elections temperature had not sufficiently cooled, so the meeting was seen by many Labour stalwarts as a deliberate act of provocation by Compton and his party.

On the other hand, word was out within the government that the police had taken the precaution of first consulting the views of Prime Minister Allan Louisy who, to his credit, had then put the question to certain of his Ministers seeking their opinions, before he addressed the police. I communicated to Prime Minister Louisy my views on the matter. At the time, I also made my views known to other persons who were in a position to influence the final decision of the police - on whether or not a public political meeting at that time was advisable.

At the height of these discussions I found myself one day at the office of the Minister for Foreign Affairs, George Odlum who was himself in discussion with several persons, including one Rick Wayne, a local publisher who had written extensively on the subject of local politics. The other persons whom I remembered seeing at Odlum's office that morning were Titus Francis, a former Trade Unionist and Labour Party supporter, Vic Fadlien, a D.J. and fanatic follower of George Odlum and Mervin Johnson, a well known private bus operator, from Castries, who was employed at the time, by Fletcher's Touring Service. I was frankly taken aback to discover that George Odlum was supporting the granting of permission for that 'thank you' public meeting. At first I thought I misunderstood his reasons for supporting such a meeting, feeling certain he had not correctly read the danger signs on the ground. But his words and facial expression, soon said that he had correctly calculated that the meeting would end in chaos and perhaps even violence. Yet, in our presence, he communicated his concurrence for the meeting both to Prime Minister by telephone and to the fully aroused media, who were anxious to know his views on the matter.

Time was to prove that the Prime Minister (and the police) were ill advised. Those who had offered the freedom and democratic rights of the opposition as reason to hold such a meeting had sorely miscalculated. That is, unless it could be proven that such persons had foreseen the chaos and destruction which were to take place in the city on the evening of the said meeting. Perhaps there were other persons who also felt that there was going to be some sort of reward to be harvested from the chaos and destruction of the city of Castries, which the wise had anticipated. Permission was granted for the thank-you meeting that evening, perhaps with the winking understanding that there would be trouble. I had suspected there may have been trouble and so I took the precaution of staying far away.

When trouble broke out that evening it was reported that the police did nothing about it. It was alleged they were rendered powerless by instructions from George Odlum, a Minister in the government. The enraged crowd, which had just rid itself of fifteen years of Compton and his party, could not take such blatant chaffing and provocation anymore. It erupted in a manner which those who had advised the public meeting, may well have anticipated, perhaps not in their final outcome. It still puzzles me that anyone in their right mind could not have foreseen the trouble which lay ahead. It was worse that no one could have correctly predicted where such destruction would end. That night Castries became 'Plywood City' a name given to it by none other than former Prime Minister John Compton, who had ordered the meeting.

Perhaps there were others who may also have fancied a military coup of sorts, perhaps by armed, reckless and undisciplined youth, in the deliberate confusion - who knows? The predictable chaos of that meeting may have been planned and proposed with such an end in view. But as we shall see later, there were some light arms which had entered the country from Grenada and Guyana, and which were in the hands of certain supporters of selected Ministers of the Government. That came at a date following the chaos in Castries when it was believed that the opposition (acting with the police) could have staged a coup d'état.

It is my considered view that neither the government of Prime Minister Louisy nor the police was completely blameless for the destruction which took place in Castries that evening. And neither was the opposition! Those who remained silent, timid or fearful, when they were earlier consulted with regards to affording permission for the said meeting, were as much to be blamed for what happened that night, as those who applied for, and received such permission. From the benefit of hindsight we now can tell with certainty who benefitted from the chaos, and who lost out.

Persons with an interest in politics should study these events carefully and also the cross-party collusion between the Leader of the Opposition Compton and Prime Minister Louisy, some of which I was privy to.

One month after the disturbances in Central Castries, Prime Minister Louisy held his first press conference. The entire press corps turned out, perchance to seek answers to questions which were in wide circulation at the time. Interestingly the main concern of the local press was whether there was going to be established an army for the island. Prime Minister Louisy admitted that his government should have done more; although he did not volunteer more of what he was talking about. He of course vehemently denied that his government wished to establish an army for the island.

He also volunteered that: 'it was totally wrong to say that the government which he headed was leftist' and then he quickly added, 'if Christianity and equitable distribution amount to a leftist government, then we are leftist'. These observations may have hinted at something sinister in the man, but it did not prove anything which should worry the people of the country. He said that he had discovered no connection between the so-called progressive left of the party and a military force on the island. I felt certain at the time that the press must have left that press briefing in a more stupefied and confused state than when they first walked into the conference room.

Notwithstanding the Prime Minister's assurances, rumours kept circulating of the formation of an army for the island to complement the local police force. There were persons who were bent on making a link between the Grenada Government of Maurice Bishop and that of the Labour Government of Allan Louisy and the procurement of arms for a local army. Looking back we can see with the clarity of hindsight where such propaganda originated and why they were so persistently portrayed by certain owners of the local press who were undoubtedly in cahoots with the Secret Services of certain foreign governments.

In early August 1979, St. Lucia was to suffer yet another major item of sad and disturbing news which threatened to destabilize the government. Police Superintendent Etienne Alphonse, who had served with distinction in the police service and who had climbed through ranks by dint of hard work and perseverance, was shot at close range in his back, as he sat in a pub on Mary Ann Street, Castries. That event threatened to plunge the entire island into a new calamity. As the news of the early morning shooting reached other members of the police, they gathered in the yard of Police Head Quarters and refused to work until they had met with the Prime Minister Louisy, and other high ranking government officials.

Senior members of the force were addressed by the Prime Minister. The lower ranks were also addressed by other Ministers of the Government. The meetings were intended to assure the police that the government recognized their hard work and that they were indispensable to the continued maintenance of law and order on the island. Whether they were all fully convinced, or not, we shall not know. The evidence suggested that the police were willing to serve and protect the citizens, the government and the country, as a whole. However, suspicions remained that there were within the ranks of the police certain officers who felt a stronger obligation to the UWP (and to Compton, in particular) than to the country and the Louisy Labour Government. Such police officers unfortunately, were still to be found many years later within the ranks of the local police service.

Following the murder of Police Superintendent Alphonse, the Odlum brothers, George and Jon, volunteered to assist the police in the recovery of missing arms and ammunition. This they did by encouraging young thugs in the Castries basin holding unlicensed fire arms to turn them in to the police. Curious eyebrows were raised when Jon Odlum, Minister for Social Affairs, returned to Police Headquarters one morning with an escaped felon (a dangerous convict, to be more precise) and with the Minister carrying an illegal firearm which that criminal had surrendered to him. It is alleged that this particular criminal had surrendered to the Minister on condition that that particular Minister of the Government would accompany him to the police station. The criminal was reported to have feared for his life, and did not chance going to the police unaccompanied. Funny, I thought that, such men should fear for their lives when they show so little respect for that of their fellow man.

Prior to the shooting death of Superintendent Alphonse, it was reported that in an attempt to calm the air of hostility which prevailed on the island, towards Compton, Prime Minister Louisy said that he would be prepared to resign from the government, if any hecklers attempted to prevent the Leader of the Opposition, and other members of the opposition from taking their seats when the first meeting of the new parliament was called. Mr. Louisy's statement had infuriated many Labour supporters. Young men who never had the benefit of education were heard to ask: Why the' Prime Minister wanted to protect Compton so badly, that he would even resign to get his way; and yet that same man would not resign for Brother George who did so much work in the campaign'? It was as ironic a moment in local politics as any I had known before or since.

It is said that politics makes strange bedfellows indeed. Often times it elicits even stranger vocabulary. As strange as this may seem, it was evident for all to see that as Prime Minister Louisy was threatening to resign in order to protect the Opposition leader; the opposition for its part, was using every opportunity to inform whoever would listen to them that Louisy's party had hijacked the country. In other words he did not win elections fair and square. It was clear that the opposition were very unhappy with their new and unaccustomed role in the new parliament. Their clear and consistent inference whenever they spoke or issued a press statement was that the opposition was concerned that something ought to be done to save Saint Lucia, from Allan Louisy and his Ministers. No concrete proof was ever offered by the opposition and often in the politics of these Caribbean islands, perception leaves little room for proof. It assumes the mantle of truth, and no one knew this better than John Compton.

Compton and his colleagues knew they were not required to do anything for the moment, except create doubts in the minds of the people regarding Louisy's ability to govern. Mind you, this was the same man who was always in secret telephone conversations with Prime Minister Louisy on the goings-on in Grenada and elsewhere in the Caribbean. Compton then appeared to have been appointed Louisy's guardian, protector and teacher, whilst he awaited the correct moment to reclaim the government. Such men were past masters at playing political handball. Yet it was those same men for whom Prime Minister Louisy's heart bled, so passionately. Although Prime Minister Louisy appeared to have gone out on a slender limb in threatening to resign if members of the opposition were not allowed peaceful entry into the House of Parliament, he was observed to be less strident in other areas of governance needing attention.

Prime Minister Louisy got his wish. The new session of Parliament was duly opened in peace and quiet with the new Speaker, Mr. Clarence Rambally, a former candidate of the United Workers Party who had earlier switched sides, occupying the Speaker's chair. Mr. Rambally was nominated by Prime Minister Louisy and seconded by none other than George Odlum, Minister for Foreign Affairs. Honourable Cecil Lay, the Representative for Vieux-Fort North was nominated by the Prime Minister and seconded by Attorney General Winston Cenac, to the position of deputy Speaker of Parliament.

Following the early excitement of the 1979 general elections, the government appeared to be settling down to business. The police too, seemed willing to do their jobs in the recovery process after the mischief which had been visited on Central Castries continued to heal. Small confidence-building measures began to take root. The political tension was gradually being relaxed and people settled down to work and to observe the actions of the government.

However, it was also manifest that those who had become used to political power were growing more determined with each passing day to regain control of the Government. Some persons opined that such restlessness was a sign that the demons of politics were then at large and that they were working full time to bring down the new Louisy government. Very little however, was done or offered by which to engage or challenge the opposition in matters of national economic policy, social development or its policy on agriculture or education. This clearly pointed to the fact that the Labour government either lacked a leader along the lines of Sun Tzu's description of the virtues of a good leader and commander or if there was one then the rules by which it governed were not known to politics. The sad part of all this is that John Compton, that political fox, knew all of this from day one. He may be one of those who might have worked his fox-magic to ensure the Labour government got a Prime Minister which he could have manipulated, at will.

According to Sun Tzu the virtues of a commander are wisdom, sincerity, benevolence, courage and strictness. Funny, I thought that Allan Louisy seemed to possess all of those qualities. What then was his problem? The answer may be to be found in education, culture, religion, age and family.

From every appearance, the opposition was experiencing much difficulty coping with their new status. So they persevered in creating political turbulence, seeing the weakness of the leadership of the government. They held two party conventions within a short period - the first in Micoud, in the South East of the island, and the other at Babonneau, in the North West. At both these gatherings, the Leader of the Opposition and the Chairman of the party assured their listeners that their party would soon be back in power. Such a statement in certain democratic countries would be interpreted as a threat to the State, and possible grounds enough for an arrest to be made and charges laid. The Opposition did not volunteer the sources of its information, but they seemed confident that the government would not hold, and therefore, their supporters would not have to wait long before they were returned to office.

For many ordinary citizens, some of whom may have quietly set aside early misgivings and had voted for the St. Lucia Labour Party, the time had long passed for regrets. For such persons the cat was openly out of the bag, and it was time to review their priorities, as the leadership struggle had now taken a turn for the worse, and was no longer an in-house secret.

The Leadership Struggle

*The Commander stands for the virtues of wisdom, sincerity,
benevolence, courage and strictness.*
Sun Tzu's: The Art of War

The members of the Saint Lucia Labour Party celebrated July 2, 1979
election victory until they were drunk with joy. Their overwhelming
success at the polls had been a long time coming. Many party stalwarts
were reported to have taken that victory a little more stoically, spending
the time in quiet reflection and prayer. For the latter group which included
such long serving members as Whitney Mauricette, George Murray,
George Charles, Charles Augustin and Martin (Oleo) Jn. Baptiste, it was
a time to savour once more the sweet taste of victory. To such men, that
Labour victory meant a major step in the continuing struggle to overcome
poverty, ignorance and disease, which the party had as one of its main
objectives since its founding. To some older stalwarts it was sweet revenge
after years in the political wilderness after certain key members had left
the party to chart a different path. Since its loss in 1964, the Labour Party
had suffered major setbacks, the worst of which was the split between
Kenneth Foster's supporters and those of its former leader George F. L.
Charles.

The 1979 victory was also welcome as a moment to pay tribute to the
founding fathers of the Labour movement, such as Allan Louisy (later, Sir
Allan), Sir Allen Lewis, Sir George Charles and Charles Augustin, Roy
Skerritt and George Murray among others. To be sure many more had
played their part in the early development of the St. Lucia Labour Party,
but they can't all be mentioned here. By the end of 1973, there was little
doubt that a new dynamism had been injected into the born-again Labour

movement. It was perhaps on such new dynamism and youthful vigour that a new Saint Lucia had been promised, according to some pundits accustomed to reading the political climate. But the island's French ancestry, its Creole heritage and language, its mixed Carib/African blood and its inclination towards English culture plus its youthful dynamism, was a potent calalloo and therefore a condition ready made for confusion.

Following its near disastrous errors and the shaky assurances to the press by Prime Minister Louisy, the party and government would soon begin to unravel. It was now just six months since the party was returned to office and it seemed unable to settle down, as its supporters wished it to. Even the bold efforts of the Minister for Agriculture, who had settled down to the task of engaging and energizing his former colleagues in that Ministry, as well as many sympathetic farmers island-wide, could not avert the growing concern felt by many citizens that the government was poised to self-destruct. The flames of propaganda were well lit and the country was becoming noticeably more anxious with each passing day.

By then it was too late to calm the fears of those in the media and elsewhere who had apparently lost confidence in the government or at least pretended to be that way, for their own reasons. The media seemed at the time to have decided that the Labour government had to go, perhaps in anticipation that matters would get worse before they got better. It clearly wanted a return of John Compton and his UWP into office. The fresh air of change which had accompanied the Labour Party victory a mere six months earlier, had by then been largely polluted, with the revelation of the 'six-month-deal', as well as the lies about arms, army, coups and such like. Those in the Labour Party who had vowed that Compton and his friends would never hold the reins of government again were now beginning to doubt their own words. It appeared that certain persons who had been accused of tolerating and looking away at all forms of wrong doing, deceit and wasteful expenditure were once more in the ascendancy.

Prime Minister Louisy had continued his pious platitudes by letting it be known in a second press interview that although his government was under an obligation to right the wrongs of the past and to bring those guilty to justice, he was also under duty to do so in accordance with the law. That statement must have been music to the ears of his opponents. Those who either refused to accept they were no longer in office were thrown a lifeline of unimaginable good fortune and their past record in politics had proven that they would use it to good purpose. It was the experience of these former colonies in the Caribbean that the law had been historically used by the strong to steal from and oppress the weak. So when a conservative former Justice speaks of acting according to law, the poor and marginalized know instinctively that the outcome may or may not be in his or her best interest. The reason for this is quite simple to grasp. The law has seldom in the past been seen as a friend of the poor and the disenfranchised.

It was in the midst of this lingering uncertainty that manufactured rumours moved very swiftly in the still of the warm Caribbean nights. Such rumours were to add to the confusion that had already hit the island, since Labour assumed office. By mid-November, 1979, as supporters were looking forward to the holiday season and Christmas under their new government, the people of Saint Lucia were greeted by a headline in the 'Voice' newspaper, which shouted in bold one-and-a-half inch print - 'LOUISY ASKED TO QUIT.' Its sub-head read: 'Odlum sends P.M. a letter; deputy wants deal confirmed'. After that headline, all hell seemed to break loose. In its aftermath telephones from far and wide began to ring off their cradles. Such frantic communications were to continue for many days afterwards, with everyone seemingly wanting to know what was going on. Slowly, at first and then followed more rapidly each minute, after painful minute. It appeared that the truth of the 'gentleman's agreement' which had been wrought at the very first secret indoor meeting of the winning Labour Party candidates, had not only become public property, but was being kicked around as some muddy football in a Caribbean school yard during the rainy season.

The emergence of a secret deal in the bright glare of public mistrust rocked the government. Foreign Affairs Minister Odlum had leaked a letter which he had written to party leader (and Prime Minister) Louisy to the Voice newspaper. Odlum had done so without informing any of his Cabinet colleagues, including this writer who had in fact supported the 'deal'. Soon people began to speculate whether such a release was the work of a mad man or one who was desperate to become Prime Minister. In a telephone conversation from his home in Laborie, Louisy confirmed that he had in fact received a note from Odlum, but that it was marked 'Private and confidential'. He then refused to disclose any further information.

Pressed for an answer about the newspaper article, Louisy first confirmed to the Voice during an interview that should the paper get the Foreign Minister to declassify his letter then, he Louisy would talk further. The paper went on to remind its readers that Louisy was first elected political leader of the Labour Party in 1977 and that George Odlum, now Minister of Foreign Affairs was its deputy Leader. The exposure of this bit of very confidential information had taken everyone by surprise especially those who were present at that first meeting of victorious Labour parliamentarians. It was my understanding that as the time approached for Louisy to move up to Government House, a meeting would have been called of the persons who first brokered the deal. By then it was too late. Everyone, it seemed, was aware of the person who had leaked that explosive bit of information to the Voice – and thought him a mad man.

When Odlum was confronted by those who still admired and supported him, to explain the reasons for his actions he could not provide any sensible and rational response. The entry of Justice Allan Louisy into Saint Lucian politics may have seemed logical and reasonable to some supporters of the Labour Party but many others, myself included, were baffled. Such an entry was viewed with suspicion by certain progressive elements within the SLP. In the aftermath of the overthrow of Prime Minister Gairy of Grenada in a military-style coup, the entire English-speaking Caribbean appeared to be tilting towards a socialist/progressive ideology. Maurice Bishop, who replaced Gairy as Grenada Prime Minister was well known to have friendly relations with the Caribbean left and with the Government in Havana.

A victory at the polls by Messrs. Odlum, Michel and Josie on the heels of the events of March 1979 in Grenada would have appeared to some opponents as the ascendancy of the left-leaning politicians in the south Caribbean. That certainly was not the wish of the establishment or that of their principals and fellow conservatives in London, Washington, Paris and elsewhere. Others with interest and influence in the Caribbean would by then have begun to connect the dots within the wind of change, and may not have liked what they saw emerging. They may also have concluded that a further radicalization of the Caribbean, from Burnham's Guyana, on the north east shoulder of South America, to Castro in Cuba in the far west corner of the Caribbean Sea was not to their liking, or, in their best interests. The facts surrounding the success of The New Jewel Movement in Grenada and the Labour Party in Saint Lucia were very different. Although both were popular victories, that did not matter to the people for whom democracy means getting the government which one can then manipulate – and corrupt – into office to be used as and when needed. There were many external interests who had been observing the changes in Caribbean politics.

Those who wished to overturn these popular victories in Saint Lucia and Grenada were very careful how they executed their nefarious plans. It therefore did not help matters when, in a flight of fancy, and before thousands of Grenada citizens at Queens Park Oval, St. George's, the Prime Minister of Saint Lucia declared: 'viva la revolucion' in clear reference to the success of the Grenada situation. The language must have surprised many who heard it. It surely did me. Such language may well have been interpreted as paying tribute to Fidel Castro - a huge surprise there, for many of Allan Louisy fans. That 'viva' speech may very well have sealed the fate of those who were sympathetic to Maurice Bishop, and his government – and that of Louisy too. Notwithstanding the popularity of Odlum and company at the time, it appeared that a palace coup within the Labour Government in Saint Lucia would have been very unpopular had it been attempted. Odlum must have known this. Besides, had the young and the restless Labour support succeeded in replacing Louisy by force of arms, it was the consensus amongst the concerned that the dice was by then too loaded against the success of another military coup, in the English-speaking Caribbean. America, England and France may have already decided that Maurice Bishop and the PRG had to go and that there would be no more military overthrows of another government in the Caribbean.

In the case of Grenada, there were many in the Caribbean who thought Gairy had invited his own demise by the dictatorial-style treatment he meted out to certain citizens and political opponents alike. It was widely believed that the Leadership of the New Jewel Movement which had deposed Gairy had done so for his excesses over many years of rule. The opposition in Grenada had consistently criticized Gairy for his rough tactics but over many elections it had chosen the ballot instead of the bullet. Matters had obviously reached a point at which it decided otherwise.

It had been the judgement of the more perceptive youth within the rank and file of the Labour Party in Saint Lucia that at the time those who had successfully climbed up the ranks of the Colonial structure were more likely to be restricted in their thinking - as far as the national anti-colonial movement was concerned - and therefore less likely to support serious and radical change at the attainment of national independence. The suspicion that those who had served the Colonial powers could not easily turn around and then serve a new nationalist agenda, may not have been properly founded. Yet that feeling persisted in some quarters. Indeed one may even say that it was a suspicion which lingered long in the minds of young political activists of the sixties and seventies.

It was in such a mindset that the young political activists of the period were to observe persons such as Prime Minister Louisy so closely. At times he seemed a man out of his depth and at others he would cause people to stand and pay attention by what he had said or done. It is for this reason that I remain convinced, up to the time of this writing thirty odd years afterwards, that the man who had emerged as Prime Minister of Saint Lucia following the 1979 general election, was a unique case, meriting closer study. It was a widely held view of many political observers that the Labour leader and his friends (from both sides of the political divide) seemed to have been united in one thing – that of frustrating the likes of George Odlum, Peter Josie, and Frances Michel, thereby rendering them innocuous. Even after his Grenada speech, his apparent mission 'to save Saint Lucia from radical change' did not seem to have altered. As a consequence of these observations the issue (and question) remains: Who did Louisy really come to serve? And however much the uninformed may wish to personalize the leadership struggle in Saint Lucia; it was in the final analysis, a struggle about political ideology, not personalities. Hopefully with the passage of time, people will get over their little personal family concerns and focus instead on the broader global and Caribbean politics.

New ideas about empowerment of the ordinary citizen, especially women, were willfully frustrated by the self-interested press and others and were not allowed to take root on the island at the time. Diversion was achieved by channeling the core arguments to the outer margins of reporting and by reducing the salient points in the debate about self-reliance, discipline and hard work to relatively trite conclusions concerning investor confidence and maintenance of low wages in order to compete. Any concept which appeared to challenge the old political, economic and social order was ridiculed even by elements in the media from whom one expected better. Valid ideas for social advancement too often became caught up in petty party politics. The prickly little Caribbean mulatto with a steady monthly income and dependable connections in politics were the hardest to convert to the new politics of liberation. In all this, the 'Genie' which came to be known as the 'leadership struggle' was now well and truly out of the bottle and no amount of trying and persuasion could get her back from whence she came.

Such differences grew and soon became the wedge that finally split the P.R.G. in Grenada. This led to the deaths of Prime Minister Bishop, his Ministerial colleague and friend - Unison Whiteman - and several other innocent citizens of that island. Those who cared to look at the events in Grenada more closely would soon discover that the Monroe doctrine, rooted as it was in the United States dictum declaring the entire Western Hemisphere its zone of special interest and influence, was still functional, and still a key plank in U.S. Foreign Policy. However, the U.S Government did not initiate military action of its own accord. It was invited to intervene in Grenada by the Leaders of the East Caribbean Governments fearing for their own skins, following the overthrow of Gairy.

It should be mentioned here that Bishop's promise of early general elections did not fully pacify the cynics in the region or outside. Persons who were adept at spending money at elections to get what they wanted

- and perhaps even manipulate the electoral process to their advantage - had no need for revolution, or radicalism. Such persons were therefore determined to keep the Caribbean within their sphere of influence, by using the system of general elections to throw up whoever was needed at the time, especially the pliable who were willing to play ball. Bishop and his men may not have fitted such a profile, so they immediately came under suspicion. Besides, they had announced their seriousness by risking death in a cause which few others had dared.

Slavery and colonialism may have disappeared from the region, but clearly, the Caribbean would not be allowed to chart its own 'independent' destiny. It appeared to some Caribbean scholars that had the region chosen to masticate its chewing gum in a manner somewhat dissimilar to the way Americans did theirs, it would be unacceptable to Uncle Sam. Everyone had to chew the same way at the same rate and if needs be, repeat the same empty words about liberty and freedom, even as they were being spat upon because they were different. The Caribbean had produced its fair share of brilliant scholars of both sexes and the global reach and achievements of its sons and daughters are sufficient testimony to their hard work, and independence. It is therefore a matter of time before the entire region will speak again as one voice in the important fora of the world.

America's self imposed right to intervene in any country in the Western hemisphere, to stop the spread of ideas it deemed hostile to its interests still forms a cornerstone of its foreign policy. At the root of its most serious warning to Europe, the Monroe Doctrine is also a clear declaration of war to any power messing around what America considers her sphere of influence. Clearly, such a declaration was also to be interpreted by her 'friends' in the region who wished to flirt with outside influences. How else could that country maintain such a doctrine if it were not prepared to use force? Might is Right! Every school child soon learns that. Our political leaders too have learnt that lesson very well.

Before the invasion of Grenada, there were several war games played out in the Caribbean, especially off the island of Puerto Rico. The U.S. Army and Navy to their credit let everyone in the Caribbean know their intentions. Clearly, they did not expect to meet any opposition in Grenada. That explains the preparations in Puerto Rico and the reason the invasion was given the sobriquet 'Amber and Amberines' perhaps sending the message to - Grenada and the Grenadines. The English–speaking Caribbean was divided over the issue of an American invasion. However, it seemed that no one could, or would be prepared to do anything about it. So the code 'Amber and the Amberines' became an open secret of locating the attack; only the timing remained undisclosed.

There was other evidence of war games being practised by U.S. armed forces in the Caribbean Sea and on various islands in the region, sometimes at the dead of night. Such manoeuvres have largely been taken for granted by those who are aware of them and are often interpreted as friendly, and not hostile to the islands or the region. For example, in the late seventies and early eighties, police insiders were certain that there was evidence of U.S. army personnel movements between the islands of Antigua and Saint Lucia at all hours of the night. This was executed without the knowledge of certain Ministers of the Government or of the lower ranks within the local police force.

In addition it has long been known in the region that in certain training programmes undertaken by the Special Services Unit (S.S.U.) of the Saint Lucia Police Force, certain law enforcement personnel have been flown to the United States and upon arrival these men were then blindfolded and flown on various unmarked aircraft to unannounced destinations within the USA Once there, these officers became the official property of the USA government. Although no one will ever admit to it, the first call on such 'trained' officer's time - and his loyalty - seemed to be the United States of America. The leaders of these Caribbean islands have little control over such police officers who are regularly briefed and debriefed by USA intelligence personnel. Apparently, only a handful of Americans in the various Secret Services of that country know about these special Caribbean operations.

That should come as no surprise, considering the uncoordinated and divergent ways the security services in the USA had been known to operate, especially at the time of the 911 terror attacks. Incidentally, does any one know how many Caribbean Leaders secretly work for US intelligence because they have either compromised themselves and their countries by being caught smuggling prohibited and dangerous drugs, or because they hold dual citizenship?

In such an environment and with the opposition politicians in Saint Lucia and their friends sensing that all was not well within the newly elected government, it was only a matter of time before one was to witness the complete demise of the new radical politicians in both Saint Lucia and Grenada. In hindsight, and viewing the entire Caribbean from the perspective of the cold war, one can now fully appreciate the reasons that certain political parties and their trade union allies were so closely monitored by the external powers in Europe and America. This was obviously to ensure that the region remained safe for Capitalism and the Western way of life which was often presented as free speech and regular elections, while not bothering to analyze how its practice impacted the lives of those in abject poverty and who will not vote.

It can therefore be seen, then, that there will always be very powerful forces arrayed against any political party wishing to alter the status quo in these islands. Any serious attempt to reverse the excesses of history for example, as far as land ownership is concerned, as in the case of Saint Lucia, is bound to be met with threats against one's life. Former Court registered documents are available which prove the legal ramifications and difficulties faced by persons holding land titles written in French and others holding deeds for the same lands written in English.

In such a situation a politician who sets about empowering the poor by attacking the irregularities (and the old French code which was still a part of the island's land laws) immediately exposed himself to all sorts of speculation. But how else was anyone who spoke of change and knew of what he spoke to regularize the system and empower his people if not through a thorough investigation of land and property? How else can a people take control of their destinies without the ownership of land and the control of production from such land?

At that point only a few progressives in the Caribbean had gone as far as suggesting that an enclosed economic system such as had been devised by Jewish people in the Kibbutz of Israel, should be replicated in the Caribbean, at least on an experimental level. It had become clear to those who wished to see that whosoever attempted to unite the African Diaspora within the Caribbean; such a person was heading for a confrontation with mighty forces with vested interests in the region. Time had already proven that these vested interests were the same kith and kin to those who had fought the black man ever since he first laid eyes on him. Some have predicted that the black man, over time, would prove to be the all powerful and might of God, of which all other races seem afraid. Any talk of wealth redistribution; compensation for the wrongs of slavery or the return of stolen cultural artifacts and national assets are therefore deemed radical, communistic, or perhaps something worse, and were not to be allowed to see the light of day, if possible.

It should therefore have been clear from the outset to those who called themselves 'progressive' that a life of politics was one of great sacrifice and pain. Quite often even his own family will deny him if he decided to set himself up as an agent of radical change. The progressive's only sure guide was to copy the path which others such as Gandhi, Garvey, King Jr. and Mandela, and other heroes of the struggling masses had trodden in order to set their people free and on a new path to progress and happiness. The political visionary ought therefore to be informed by constant vigilance and caution. A person with such a vision has to guard against the intrusion of his private space by others whose motive may be to frustrate his ideas from taking root and therefore prevent his work from bearing fruit. For this reason it may be advisable for new candidates who wished to join a political organization to be carefully screened and examined before acceptance. This ought to be the case even at the most junior level of the organization. Only persons who are determined to transform their people and help take them from where they found them to a better place spiritually, socially, educationally and economically should qualify as leaders, in my book. The trick is to detect from early the genuine from the imposter, since so many now come with fine words. Persons who attempt to ingratiate themselves on the body politic by smarting and canvassing their way inside the party hierarchy and executive sub-committees and who demonstrate little or no skills, must be kept at a far distance from the party and the government at all times - if possible. Further, political parties ought to be compelled by law to develop strict guidelines for national security, for fighting corruption within their party and in government and for fighting crime at every level in society, from petty ones to more serious ones of drug trafficking and treason.

That the Labour Party government (1979-1982) was allowed to disintegrate and fall out of grace was perhaps the most amazing event I have ever experienced in my entire political life. Had I been asked what was the most frustrating experience I had as a young politician it would have been what I had discovered about human nature - about persons whom I thought were genuine, honourable, and unimpeachable and above board, and to find them quite the opposite. It was also the discovery of man's insatiable instinct to be acceptable to his fellow man and often to receive honours conferred on him, some of which were clearly undeserving. The study of oneself may therefore be the greatest study of all. Looking back, it seems clear now that there were persons who entered the field of politics with only one purpose in mind, which was to frustrate the forward march of the progressive movement of Saint Lucia and the wider Caribbean. It would not surprise me the least if this remained a motivation of certain persons, even today.

Another aspect about politics in a backward salt fish society, is that for every hundred thousand in the population only one person in every twenty years or so, will rise and take a stand against the things he or she perceives to be wrong in the society. There are unfortunately, so few real leaders that quite often such lack is made up by persons setting off to deliberately mislead the population and bleed the national treasury for themselves and their close friends. Sometimes, such men make such a convincing show of it that even when they are caught; there are some who would deny the evidence and even attempt to rescue such rogues.

In this Caribbean region we are woefully short of Commanders; leaders who demonstrate the qualities of leadership alluded to earlier by that great Chinese warrior Sun Tzu. Too many persons who offer themselves for political service are lacking in the virtues of leadership. Worst of all these political novices have apparently not studied in any great depth the sacrifices, hard work and dedication which are required, in order to build a better country.

We need leaders who would no longer consider the slave trade and the morality, or lack thereof - and the social responsibility which it still imposes on some nations - as a thing of the past. The consequences of that abuse are still all around us. Yes, I agree it ought not to be used as an excuse for our lack of progress. Equally, we ought not to deny the fact that part of our problem is the huge backlog of poverty and ignorance and the indoctrination of religion in the programme of slavery. If there were any lessons to be learnt from the leadership struggle in Saint Lucia, one must certainly be the total and complete waste of human resources which may otherwise have been usefully engaged in a wider Caribbean nation, where there should certainly be more room for such wide disagreements. The other lesson is that persons of such diametrically opposite views will never form a strong and united bond unless there is some other stronger force binding them together. In such an atmosphere as existed at the time, and without a concrete plan to stop it happening again, how can we be certain that this island has learnt anything from the mistakes of the past? How can we be certain that things (and people) shall be afforded their real value unlike what obtained in the days of which Eric Williams writes in his book 'From Columbus to Castro'.

Shattered Dreams

And here, shipmates, is true and faithful repentance;
Not clamorous for pardon, but grateful for punishment .....
Herman Melville: Moby-Dick (the Sermon)

The revelation by Prime Minister Louisy of George Odlum's 'confidential note' to him had apparently started life as an inconsequential telephone conversation between the Voice newspaper and Mr. Louisy. This was perhaps on the heels of an equally innocent leak from Odlum to the same newspaper, but which at the very early stages of the game had not yet been revealed. The three parties must have quickly realized the full import of the 'confidential note', and may even have pondered the reason it was handled the way Minister Odlum had chosen. The fact that the writer had not consulted any of those who were present at the initial meeting when the deal was brokered was a question which the note writer never properly addressed when he was later confronted on the matter. As the contents of the note became public property - by its headline news in the Voice - the question which was on the minds of the public was: 'How did that newspaper come by such a confidential note and why'? The answer to the first part we learnt later when some of us put the question squarely to Odlum. What was the purpose of that intentional leak? Was it to stir a hornet's nest or was it perhaps to ensure that Prime Minister Louisy -and the Voice too - were to regard him (Odlum) as heir apparent if Louisy did in fact decide to become Governor General? Soon, the revealed facts became the property of the entire Caribbean and Saint Lucians all over the world. The local, regional and even some western international media were having a field day. They soon took the simple spark of Odlum's apparent hasty disclosure from his untimely note to his Prime Minister, and fanned it into the all-consuming flame it soon became. That political flame was to ignite passions across Saint Lucia and the Caribbean and would eventually consume everyone who dared to have witnessed its igniting. It was both the fall out of the disclosure and the manner in which it was handled by both warring sides, which finally led to the shattered dreams, of so many Saint Lucians and Caribbean people, at that time.

It was no doubt as a result of the evolving drama from that revealed note that, one newspaper headlined on Thursday November 29, 1979 screamed at its readers; 'LOUISY ADMITS'. It said that Louisy had replied to Odlum's note saying that he had agreed to vacate the post of Prime Minister, but pointed out that the move was not agreed to by some of the party's elected twelve. He also told Odlum that he did not think the move opportune in the light of current circumstances coupled with public opinion on the issue. Prime Minister Louisy is also reported to have pointed out that he would be prepared to step down if that was the wish of the Central Executive of the party. However, he also warned Odlum that he, Louisy, was prepared for any eventuality. If any undemocratic means were used to remove him from the office, said the Prime Minister to Odlum, it would fail. That proved too much of a poisoned sting from the scorpion's tail for the latter to accept meekly. Odlum lost his cool and composure and some argue he may have lost much more than that when he received Louisy's rebuttal. Had Odlum remembered my caution about the acceptance of persons into the Labour Party, or any party for that matter, as leader, without any evidence of political credentials at the time, he did not say. But it was clear that a huge chunk of his personal dreams had been shattered right there and then. Only pride kept him going and as he was to quote so often, 'pride comes before a fall' but he failed to see its application when it was his turn, to be cautious. Indeed, part of the sad downfall of the Labour government in 1982, was the fact that so many grown men were unable or unwilling to put the country before their pride and their egos.

Before Mr. Louisy's private telephone conversation with the Voice and the subsequent public outcry which followed, Odlum had a few days earlier – perhaps in anticipation of the public's reaction to the disclosure of his letter to Louisy - told the Chamber of Commerce in Castries, that Saint Lucia needed leadership which was 'bold, competent and efficient'. He also suggested to the Chamber at the same time that it was not in the interest of the commercial sector, to have a weak and vacillating government in office. Did everyone at the Chamber luncheon that day hear Odlum correctly? It was barely six months since the people of Saint Lucia had voted the government - of which Odlum was its Minister for Foreign Affairs - into office. Even Louisy's opponents within the Chamber of Commerce must have been awestruck at Odlum's disclosure. Perhaps to smooth the rough edges of his observations, certain members of the Chamber were to quietly observe that Louisy was soon to turn 63 years - by his next birthday in 1980. Age may therefore have been advanced as a reason for tolerance or perhaps the reason he should leave. Louisy did not make it easy on himself. In the five and a half months since the Labour Party had come to power in 1979, he had kept a very low profile, at a time when the country most needed a dynamic leader to point the way and to establish his authority on the island; perhaps even the Caribbean. The blind could see poor Prime Minister Louisy was not up to it. He was certainly not filling the shoes left by John Compton; and that was very troubling indeed.

By then the private media had begun to openly question whether Allan Louisy was up to the job of Prime Minister. The press then began to suggest, as the Leader of the Opposition had done previously, that 'Louisy must govern or leave'. It appeared from these exchanges, that there was a growing consensus among George Odlum, (The Minister for Foreign Affairs); John Compton, (The Leader of the Opposition) the St. Lucia Chamber of Commerce and Agriculture, and of course the press - a potential poisonous brew.

Louisy, not to be outdone began to fight back. His first line of attack was to use his trusted friends within the executive of the Labour Party, and wherever else they were to be found. By mid-December 1979 therefore, he sought and received the endorsement of the Central Executive Committee of the party to stay as leader and also to continue as Prime Minister of the country. Unfortunately, that endorsement did nothing to embellish his leadership qualities. The uncertainty which had cast a long shadow over the island therefore continued to spread far and wide. Odlum on the other hand would not keep still. By then he was at full throttle and on a wild rampage taking down everything in his path. He was attentive and even respectful at times, but in truth he listened to no one. The proverbial bull in the China shop had gone wild and nothing would calm it down. To add to the island's dilemma and confusion, Prime Minister Louisy seemed powerless to dismiss this, or any other of his wayward Ministers, of which I claimed membership, at the time. The Government was split right down its middle and it was an ugly and vulgar wound.

The festering and ugliness displayed itself more reprehensibly each day to a dumfounded public, now running to God – and John Compton – for help. Each day there was new drama. No day was to pass without some hurtful exchange within the government which was then broadcast by the media. The media at the time seemed to also reveal a macabre and sick indulgent quality about itself that one day ought to be properly questioned and analyzed. Everyone saw where this was heading. But no one seemed strong enough to stop it. The rapid slide and the eventual wreck would lay shattered for many years and only a handful of those who formed the government at the time, were ever returned to parliament. Legitimacy is the word which comes to mind in the face of such vacillating and weakness by a political leader. It was even more despicable when such a leader had no agenda or plan for those whom he was supposed to lead. To such persons, the badge of leadership in my opinion represents an accolade wrongly offered, yet one which has been accepted even as the recipient knows he or she is undeserving and that such gifts are more suited to other hands. But it appeared then (and now) that, few people think about such things.

The controversial leadership issue continued to burn even more brightly after the party executive's endorsement of Louisy. All that support seemed to have accomplished was more intransigence and inaction on the part of the Prime Minister, and an equal determination of his opponents to be rid of him. It was clear that he had been ordered to stay put by his superiors (both local and foreign), and that if needed they would use force to defend and support him. There would be no experiment along the lines of the Bishop regime in Grenada. Come hell or high water, the country would continue along with its cautious baby steps, until the WTO and international conspiracy took everything away. Those who feared the progressive left Caribbean nexus now had new reason to regroup and to throw their full support behind Compton and his party. It became clear that all Louisy was doing was blocking the way, so Odlum and his mates could not advance. Many believed this to have been the real role Justice Louisy had been made to vacate the East Caribbean Appeals court bench, to play. And he was proving as good a blocker in politics as he was in blocking his opponents' double sixes in their hands, at the game of dominoes which he loved so much. He performed his role excellently, and rendered the progressive left of the party (and government) innocuous and effete.

It was also clear to everyone that silence in the face of mounting protests and questions were not an option for Prime Minister Louisy. Yet that was the exact thing the Prime Minister chose to do. He had let it be known on more than one occasion that to do nothing was itself an action; in other words, doing nothing was similar to doing something. It was an idea which one imagined students of philosophy were happy to spend many weeks and months mulling, discussing – even arguing - over. No one seemed to have told the Prime Minister at the time that developing countries could ill afford the luxury of leaders who only seemed to act, by doing nothing. The island had by then been forced to face yet another intriguing question. What was this mess of pottage which the plotters and dissemblers had presented to the Labour Party and to Saint Lucia? That may well have been a question on many lips. At a time when Saint Lucia and the entire Caribbean was crying out for bold and visionary leadership, and when so much was at stake, the caterpillars of the commonwealth had chosen this moment to undermine a government which had the potential to deliver a better, more progressive society through a better, more enlightened governance.

Of course by that time, the leadership struggle had assumed a life of its own. I recall sharing with friends how disappointed I was to discover that there were members of the executive of the Labour Party, who were more inclined to support John Compton, in a crunch, than George Odlum. I had no doubt that it was the weapon of fear (of communism) and the way it was spread night and day by Odlum's opponents, which had affected the minds of his own party colleagues. Surprisingly, these accusations of communism were coming at a time when the Soviet Union was near its end. Interestingly, the same accusation had been levelled against John Compton at the beginning of his political career. But why did it work so well against Odlum and not so against Compton? Compton was a red Negro who attended any church, whereas Odlum was an exponent of black power and that negro did not see the need for church except where it may have been politically expedient. That may have been the crucial difference between the men and their politics.

When I first informed Odlum of the reaction of the party executive towards Compton, I was surprised he remained silent and offered no opinion on the matter. Perhaps his thoughts were already racing ahead to the next public move he intended. It was unlike him not to have anything to say on such a matter. It was therefore a rare silence for one, whom many believed came into the world fully affected by the angel of speech. However, I felt certain that he understood the depth of his predicament and that some radical remedial action was called for in order to correct the situation. I felt certain he understood what he now faced within the St. Lucia Labour Party and also what it portended for his struggle with Allan Louisy – Prime Minister. Given the poor quality of leadership of the party at the time, coupled with the high rate of illiteracy on the island, we finally (and reluctantly) concluded that we were in for the long haul, and that there was no guarantee of success. The level of illiteracy, ignorance, obeah and general backwardness we had already discovered during our groundings with the grass roots in the St. Lucia Forum, seemed to have now found its way into the executive of the party, and perhaps even within the government. I concluded at the time that every party and government built on such poor foundation would always be one step away from having its worthy dreams shattered.

Perhaps the entire episode of that sorry and reckless, leadership struggle was best summarized by a young journalist at the Voice newspaper - Guy Ellis. In an article entitled 'Mr. Louisy's night of folly' published in the Voice of December 23, 1979, Ellis captured, for posterity, the essence of political folly, pantomime, drama, and intrigue that plagued the disparate group of men that formed the government of the island at that time. The central thesis of Ellis argument was that having been elected both political leader and then Prime Minister, Louisy should not have made any deals with any one regarding the leadership of the country, during his term of office. Historians would wish to go one step further and examine the reasons Louisy might have felt the need for such a compromise, in the first place. Unless we understand the power relations which existed on the island at the time, and the role which outside influences played (and continue to play in local politics), we are apt to miss the essence of that struggle and worse, dismiss it as a mere quarrel between two hard-headed male egos, purposely colliding in combat in order to prove their survival skills, and macho stubbornness

By January 1980, it was disclosed that George Odlum, had secretly negotiated with the Peoples' Revolutionary Government in Grenada, the training of certain Saint Lucian youth, in military and police work. That training, Odlum said, was for a fixed period and for a total of twelve young men whom he claimed were to be special body guards of the new Labour Ministers. When confronted by the press with this information, Prime Minister Louisy claimed surprise at the number, but admitted knowledge of the scheme. He then disclosed that he had given permission for only two such persons to proceed to Grenada for training, a la George Odlum style.

Louisy's disclosure did nothing to calm the nerves of those with the most to lose on the island, from such a scheme. The fact that it confirmed the suspicion of the opposition regarding certain persons' love affair with guns as a tool of politics, was to further divide the party and the government, and the country. It also sealed the fate of the Louisy administration. It was now clear to everyone except the party gargoyles who saw no evil, heard no evil and spoke no evil, that Allan Louisy could not measure up to the task of leading the country. He seemed not only incapable of dismissing anyone from his government, but equally damning was the fact that he also seemed to waver from supporting Odlum one minute and opposing him the next. That was perhaps the final straw which broke the back of the Labour government, and shattered the dreams of so many of its loyal supporters.

Soon after the news of the training of youths in Grenada became public, Compton and his United Workers Party upped the ante by calling for fresh elections, and threatening street protests and demonstrations. Already, he was attracting much larger crowds to his public political meetings. A former confidante and working colleague of Odlum was spotted at one of these opposition demonstrations holding a large placard which said: 'V.I.P. - Vagabonds in Power'! That for Brother George Odlum may have been a deeper cut than any Louisy had inflicted on him.

By then the writing was clearly on the wall. However, the actual demise (and shattering of the dream) of the party and government may have been precipitated by the announcement of the resignation of Attorney General, Winston Cenac from the government. This was followed two weeks later by the resignation of the then youthful Minister of Education, Kenny Anthony, who had earlier been brought into the government through the Senate. At the time Anthony was made a Senator the Constitutional requirement for such an appointment had to be amended in order to lower the age limit to facilitate the move. Frankly, the majority of elected members at the time saw Anthony as a creation of George Odlum, and kept him at a distance. Prime Minister Louisy for one did not like the idea of tampering with the constitution and neither did some of his friends. Louisy later supported the constitutional change and thereafter, wholeheartedly embraced Anthony, perhaps after consultation with certain persons in his Laborie constituency.

I was quite disturbed to discover that certain Ministers were whispering their suspicions about the new Minister of Education, to certain supporters of the party. Senior Ministers of the government had earlier criticized Anthony's (caucasian) father for the way he had treated the workers on a certain large estate in the south/west of the island, where he was the manager. These Ministers acted as though the younger Anthony was guilty of the same grave offences as his father. However many listeners did not believe the son should pay for the sins of the father. Others, including some politicians behaved as though all such attacks on an aspiring politician were fair and square especially in a salt fish and green figs society. These, plus the fact that many saw the Labour government headed to self-destruction - and shattered dreams - may have been behind the resignation of the young Minister of Education.

Following the Cenac and Anthony resignations Bruce Williams of Vieux-Fort South constituency and Cecil Lay of Belle Vue, Vieux-Fort North constituency, two persons who had steadfastly stood at Louisy's side, were appointed Ministers without Portfolio. The earlier resignation of Winston Cenac - an elected Member for Soufriere - had further weakened the government.

When the island reached its first anniversary of independence on 22 February, 1980, no one was celebrating. Few seemed at the time concerned with anything other than the pending fall from office of the Louisy Government. The problems there had taken centre stage and things had deteriorated so much that people were wagering when it would fall. The official opposition, which had fought so doggedly for political Independence for the island, was now totally oblivious to its first anniversary. They were instead totally focussed on bringing down the Labour government. Only the return to office - and soon - would do for them. This was yet another lesson in party politics, for those who cared to learn. Yesterday's issues belong to yesterday. Today is a new and different day, with new issues calling for new solutions.

At the first anniversary of Independence, Sir Allen Lewis, Governor General, tendered his resignation. This opened the door for still more political comedy and drama. To fill the gap left by Sir Allen, Prime Minister Louisy appointed Boswell Williams the former representative for Vieux-Fort North, to act as Governor General. Everyone waited anxiously for what was to follow. People were now openly asking how long the agony would last. How long before their dreams were to lie completely shattered? How long before the country would be returned to the polls?

By then the annual budget was due for presentation to Parliament. Even before the ink had properly dried on his Budget address, it was publicly criticized by both the Leader of the Opposition, Compton, and by Odlum who at the time was still a Minister of the Government - but also in a sort of alliance with the opposition. The Leader of the Opposition called the budget 'Empty and Bogus' - a favourite phrase of his. Odlum referred to it as 'A Robin Hood budget' which aimed to take from the 'haves' and give to the 'have nots'. By whatever name its opponents chose to call it, Louisy's first ever budget to parliament was approved, by that body. Odlum had kept to his word of not wanting to thrust the island into fresh general elections and had therefore not voted against the budget, then.

Following his successful budget, Louisy received another confidence booster in the form of a very successful May Day rally involving all the major trade unions on the island. The Trade Union membership had been fully mobilized through the efforts of the National Workers Union, the Seamen and Waterfront Workers Union, the Teachers, Civil Service, Nurses and several other unionized groups and from the inspiration earlier provided by personalities such as Frances Michel, George Odlum and myself. I had previously served (early seventies) as President of the Seamen and Waterfront Workers Trades Union and also as Secretary of the Civil Service Association. Prime Minister Louisy attended the public rally at Mindoo Philip Park in Castries – formerly Victoria Park. Midway in the celebrations, one enthusiastic supporter of the party, a lawyer, jumped onto the stage in broad view of everyone present, and got Louisy's right hand into that of Odlum, forcing the two men into a handshake. For many the leadership battle was by then too far past the point of reconciliation and a simple, forced handshake, would not change anything. By that time few seemed to remember that the Leader of the Opposition was a blinkered workaholic who loved political power. The leadership of the Labour government on the other hand did not appear to show such focussed and undivided need for political office. Sadly, it continued with full vigour soon after that May Day rally.

Around that time, the main commercial house in downtown Castries was put up for sale by the Devaux family which owned it. The government immediately expressed an interest in purchasing the property. I was taken aback, however, when one of the major trade unions on the island voiced opposition to the government's idea for such a purchase. The government's stated intention was to convert that building into a mall and furniture display centre for all locally manufactured wood, pottery, paintings and handicraft, arts and crafts produced on the island. What could be so wrong with that, I asked? Of course such a thing had never been tried before on the island and thus the knee jerk reaction of those of our friends who were wary of the unknown - as were perhaps our greatest opponents who rejected the idea.

It should be noted here that Courts Ltd., with Head Offices in England, was established on the island soon afterwards and doing basically the same thing for local furniture manufacturers, which the SLP government had planned to do. The major difference was of course, the profits would now go to Courts or rather to shareholders in Europe and not in the pockets of local craftsmen and artisans. It is a matter of record that thirty odd years later, there is still no national co-operative which markets locally made furniture, or any national co-operative exporting any local products, save bananas and ornamentals. As for the M&C building, it was purchased by the National Insurance Corporation (NIC) many years later, and converted into a mall, called the Blue Coral, in which Courts St. Lucia Ltd. may well be the most dominant tenant.

As the first anniversary of Labour's victory at the polls approached, the opposition planned to 'celebrate' with a mass rally seeking to bring down the government. The rally was held at the Vigie playing field, a stone's throw from the city centre where many political rallies were held. At that rally a resolution was adopted demanding that the government call fresh general elections within 90 days.

By that time the church leaders seemed to have had enough of the leadership quarrel. They volunteered prayers to heal the nation. For a while afterwards, things appeared to have calmed down. One could be forgiven for thinking that the prayers had worked against the opposition which it had intended to help. As if to break the blessed covering of sanctified silence, Odlum loudly accused the opposition of harbouring armed followers at their last rally. The opposition's response was to challenge Odlum to prove his allegations. Nothing further was heard from either side. At that moment the prayers seemed to be holding, and citizens breathed cautiously if a little uneasily.

As if to make certain that the energies of the government would be focussed on nation building rather than on the leadership struggle, the island was visited by one of the most devastating hurricanes experienced in living memory. Hurricane 'Allen' struck on August 3, 1980 and almost ripped the island apart. Few private homes were spared. It destroyed roads and other infrastructure. Electricity was off for well over a week. Many bridges either collapsed or were made impassable by debris accumulated upon them. It wrecked the entire banana industry which at the time was responsible for some seventy percent of the island's exports, the Gross Domestic Product (GDP). Roads were made unmotorable by strewn rocks and fallen trees. For a while after the storm's passage, the entire island seemed to have experienced a sort of hushed stupor. Every politician went silent, even the most vocal ones.

Many were happy that hurricane Allen had intervened, where Prime Minister Louisy could not, or would not. That force of nature was chalked down as an act of God. The people and the government had no choice but to concentrate on rehabilitation work, after the hurricane. That event may well have inadvertently prolonged the life of the Louisy Government. There were also supporters of the government who interpreted the visit of the hurricane as a sort of blessing in disguise! They reasoned that, if anything could have brought an end to the senseless leadership struggle, it would take only such a force of nature, as a hurricane, to do it. Where man had failed, nature would prove its power. To many Saint Lucians, it was the hand of God himself which had intervened.

For some time following the passage of that severe hurricane, all hands were on deck. Even the print media which at first seemed to have taken a special delight in fanning the flames of division and keeping the bickering within the government alive, had now fallen into a constructive phase.

The island regained its composure more quickly than many had expected, thanks in large part to the prompt and timely assistance from countries far and near. One remembers in particular the efforts of Venezuela's Ambassador Senor Rodolfo Molina Duarte who went far beyond the call of duty and visited many parts of the island which were damaged by the hurricane. The many persons who Senor Molina visited had suffered loss of homes and other valuables. His government in Caracas not only provided replacements of lumber and zinc (galvanize) sheets for re-roofing, but also lent a helping hand with labour, for the reconstruction effort. It also paid for the transportation of building materials to communities where they were most needed. In addition, both Ashley Wells of the US Communications Agency in Barbados, and Sally Shelton, US Ambassador responsible for Saint Lucia did their part to ensure a speedy recovery from the devastation of Hurricane Allen. The government of Grenada gave a vehicle and food items. Hess Oil provided food and materials for the rebuilding of schools. The British and French governments both helped by sending army personnel to rebuild the public communications systems destroyed by the hurricane.

Perhaps the most outstanding work and one which has to date remained under reported and perhaps not fully appreciated was that of the field staff of the Ministry of Agriculture, then headed by Mr. Laurie Auguste, who has since passed away. The extension division of the Ministry of Agriculture worked tirelessly with farmers, who had for the most part lost everything. His work and that of others in that Ministry ensured farmers' morale was high and this aided in a speedy recovery, especially in the banana sector.

In the immediate aftermath of the hurricane when most people were hard at work rebuilding, Odlum leaked word to the press that he had discovered massive fraud and corruption within the Ministry of Communications and Works. It concerned the procurement and distribution of lumber and other building materials for the reconstruction effort, following the hurricane. The Minister serving there was none other than Kenneth Foster with whom Odlum had more than just political reasons for observing very closely. It was also public knowledge that the matter over which the two differed was a very delicate affair which had little or nothing to do with politics.

On the corruption charge, no evidence was ever presented against Foster or his Ministry, as far as I recall. The accusations continued nonetheless. It grew both in intensity and viciousness. Other departments of government and Ministers close to Foster were also accused of complicity and wrong doing. In time, such prolonged finger-pointing, without a shred of evidence, was to earn Mr. Foster much sympathy, especially amongst the hard core stalwarts of the Labour Party. George Odlum was again seen as the fault. Even the Minister's political opponents in the opposition camp appeared to be siding with him against Odlum, on the charge of corruption. Not surprisingly, the crocodile tears shed on Foster's behalf by the opposition only served to infuriate Odlum. Nothing became of the charge except that Odlum lost the respect and admiration of Evans Calderon - a barrister and Cabinet colleague of Ken Foster at the time, but one who had also admired Odlum's talents. 'It was at that time I made up my mind that I would no longer be part of Odlum's quarrel with Louisy'. Now, for too many people, this was the moment the dreams became truly shattered. The bond between George Odlum and myself had given many people reason to hope for a better day. Once it was broken, all dreams were shattered.

To no one's surprise George Odlum had found a way to be heard and seen. If not Louisy then Foster would have to pay. By then my patience had run out with helping Odlum win a battle in which he was determined to snatch defeat from the jaws of victory. I felt in my heart and mind that this was no longer about the people. It was a one-man show with a willing and youthful cast of characters, and the show was the thing - the fallout from it no longer mattered.

Another side issue which developed as a result of the fall out between Odlum and me was that I, who had been a long and a vociferous critic of Louisy, was now prepared to join with him to save the Labour government. Of course Odlum and his friends did not see it that way. I had two other choices. I could have resigned from the government and party or I could have left politics, altogether. Of course I could also have joined the United Workers Party. At the time I decided not to quit. Clearly, the problem was not politics. Instead, it was the quality of some of the people who used politics for their own aggrandizement and to the detriment of the people. Having chosen to stay with the Labour Party, I immediately became a marked man. Of course Odlum and his friends soon branded me a traitor and turncoat. Some of his apostles called me 'Judas' but when I asked which Jesus did I betray, they looked back at me, with ignorance etched all over tense facial muscles. At the time I felt up to the challenge and I felt certain that Brother George knew that too. I also felt certain there would be no one else among his novices, including his new hobby horse, Mikey Pilgrim, who were prepared to take me on. They all knew I could go toe to toe with the very best of them and would most likely emerge triumphant, whatever game they chose.

Fortunately, I had long determined that it was a time for true and tested leaders to rise above the party political fray. The petty personal politics that was tearing the island apart back then had to be stopped at all costs. Although I still did not quite understand what made Prime Minister Louisy tick, I wished to give his office the benefit of the doubt. Odlum had given me cause to believe that he too had chosen a personal path to destruction of which I wanted no part. It was obvious that my advice no longer mattered to him. I felt hurt and insulted by such an attitude and it therefore remained for me to do what any man of dignity and honour would have done. The time had come for bold initiatives and firm patriotism, and a new politics, I told myself. I believed then that our people were prepared for the Labour government after John Compton was voted out in 1979. But the leadership struggle had by then depressed the entire citizenry at home and abroad, and had shattered the dreams of many persons both nationals and residents.

The leadership quarrel was so distracting it often diverted attention from our friends in Grenada. On the other hand that may very well have been a reason it persisted so long. It was perhaps to destabilize the entire Caribbean region that it was continuously fuelled by those invisible hands (and mouths) to which only the main plotters were privy. Were the Labour Party in St. Lucia to collapse, one felt certain that Bishop's Government in Grenada would be next. Such an eventuality did not seem to faze their cousins in the SLP. The possibility of a shattering of Louisy's government in St. Lucia before its five-year term was up looked more likely with each passing day. It should be recalled that the Labour government of Saint Lucia had proven a true friend of Maurice Bishop and his P. R .G. Grenada, had also been the seat of the Appeal Court of the Organization of East Caribbean Supreme Court, and as such, was home to Justice Louisy, before he resigned from the bench for politics. Justice Louisy was therefore well known to many of the political actors in Grenada - including the young attorney, Maurice Bishop.

I first met Maurice Bishop while visiting Grenada as a member of the Saint Mary's College inter-secondary schools tournament team in 1960. According to practice (and tradition) the four Windward Islands (Grenada, St. Vincent, Dominica and St. Lucia) met each year in rotation to participate in competitive sports, including athletics, football and cricket. Our official host in Grenada that year was the Grenada Boys Secondary School (GBSS). Notwithstanding this, the St. Lucia tournament team took time to visit our 'sister' College in Grenada - Presentation College - at which both Maurice Bishop and his Minister of Agriculture, Unison Whiteman were students.

Later, the three of us were to cross paths again; they, in their New Jewel Movement in Grenada, and I in the St. Lucia Forum. By the time we got into political office, Maurice by means of the Grenada 'revo' and his comrades in Saint Lucia by means of the secret ballot had developed a fairly cordial and respectful rapport.

It was my understanding that we were to work as closely as possible towards a Caribbean Economic union, and later to develop a new political vision for the region. It was our understanding that the purpose of regional politics was to bring about a revolution in the lives of the masses of the people who participated in such action and who it was meant to serve. We shared the belief that we each owed a special duty to lift the poor and downtrodden masses that were still languishing at the bottom of the social and economic ladder in the Caribbean, to a new level of self-respect, dignity and economic empowerment. We saw the task of educating and liberating the masses as essentially one project - one for our time.

Since our future was so inextricably bound, it was incumbent that we in St. Lucia assess the repercussions of any move we made and how it would affect other governments in the region particularly that of Maurice

Bishop, in Grenada. To his credit, even Prime Minister Louisy whom many persons (including me) had branded a conservative was prepared to support the Bishop Government, up to a point. How far that point was, we were too naive to have allowed it time in which to be tested. Fast moving events were to eventuate in the demise of the Labour Government in St. Lucia, and to the subsequent internal strife and brutal execution of Maurice Bishop.

Before his passing, the more perceptive had observed that Prime Minister Bishop in the several speeches which he gave during his time in office and specifically on the issue of construction of the Point Salines International Airport, never failed to mention the technical help which his government received from the Air Ports Authority of St. Lucia. There were others in the Caribbean just as capable of giving such help, but Bishop knew he had trusted and reliable friends in Saint Lucia, including Prime Minister Louisy.

However backward and conservative we may have thought Allan Louisy to be during his stint as Prime Minister of St. Lucia, it is still my conviction that he would not have readily given his consent for the invasion of Grenada, as other mendicants in the Caribbean had done. Besides, he was more likely to be firmer had he been guaranteed the support of George Odlum and the Ministers and officials who still supported him. It has always intrigued me that political leaders who have read Eric Williams and other modern Caribbean history, and who see the evidence of past neglect and abuse wherever they turn in the region, can be so negligent in their duties to the people they were elected to serve. Observing such leaders reminds one of the simple people who themselves had no idea which way to turn for support and sustenance. Such leaders needed to be led more than the people they pretended to lead. Sadly, the poorer the constituents the less capable the representatives they seem to throw up.

The more capable (and valuable) the constituent - like a slave ships' cargo - the more care it received and the less neglected its residents should the political weather ever turn unfavourable. The psychological and material support which Allan Louisy's government had given to Grenada during his stint at office is a matter of record. He visited that island on the first anniversary of the revolution, along with Odlum (his Minister of Foreign Affairs, International Trade and Tourism) and myself, (his Minister of Agriculture, Forestry, Lands and Fisheries). There may have been talk among his contemporaries that he was being used, but such persons seemed to have forgotten that Allan Louisy was a founding member of the first Trades Union movement in Saint Lucia as well as a very early member of the St. Lucia Labour Party, long before he became a lawyer and a Judge.

I have earlier referred to the 'viva revolution' speech given by Mr. Louisy during that short visit to Grenada. The speech had helped cement our friendly relations, and had also made it clear that the Prime Minister of Saint Lucia was not prepared to toe the old colonial line of being dictated to if he could help it. As usual, Odlum had given a rousing speech befitting the occasion. As if to prove the bond of friendship was mutual, here is a quotation from Prime Minister Bishop in reply: 'We are also still hoping that a joint application of Grenada and St. Lucia in 1980, for communications equipment assistance of this project (the Point Salines Airport), will be approved in due course by the ten member states of the European Economic Community'. In that statement, Prime Minister Bishop went on to assert that he had received valuable cooperation from St. Lucia and Aruba through their respective airport authorities. These governments granted tours of their facilities and their technocrats held in-depth discussions with their counterparts from Grenada. Such information was used by Bishop to refine his plans for Point Salines airport. To further elaborate the point regarding joint application by Grenada and St. Lucia for airport communications equipment, it will be recalled that at the time, the European Community had in place a policy in which the Community would look more kindly at financing capital projects which were jointly presented to it, by two or more governments from the OECS. In the eyes of the European Union, such external aid financing would only be considered, if (and when) it had been jointly applied for. For example, the Roseau water dam in St. Lucia and the only airport on Canouan Island in the Saint Vincent Grenadines were two such projects financed under such a policy.

The Labour government continued to limp along. It was by that time severely wounded. Everyone knew instinctively that it was only a matter of time before it finally fell and imploded (thereby shattering the dreams of many), and with little hope of a quick repair. Perhaps, the only matter yet to be decided by those planning and plotting in the background was who would replace Louisy, after he had been removed from office. The plan had obviously been to replace him with someone who would ensure that the Labour government resigned from office as meekly as possible. There was to be no shedding of blood. No half-crazed political rebel to sow the seeds of revolution and disappear. The whole system was to be carefully manipulated to bring about Labour's downfall. This was to be done in a manner that was in keeping with the letter of the constitution.

It appeared to many younger supporters of the Labour Party that some deals were made by senior lawyers in the party and behind the backs of of other Labour parliamentarians. The transition from Louisy to Cenac was seen by many as merely cosmetic and perhaps only a time wasting interlude before the 'corrupt hounds of war' would return to demand the government which they believe was theirs to enjoy.

The important point here was that the so called radicals of the Labour Party had been manoeuvred out of the leadership of the party and this in the final analysis may have been the point of the entire leadership struggle. These plotters and manipulators who were working quietly in the background could easily have given Hollywood's best directors a thing or two to think about.

The fact of the matter was the handing of the Labour Government to Winston Cenac in 1981, was in reality just a holding sort of half-way house tactic. The people obviously had to be given some more time in which to be psychologically prepared for the return of Compton, which was in fact the end result of the games which were being played. Cenac represented a breather. But with a majority of one and the lack of fight in the man, he was picked for failure. The prediction must have been that by the time Cenac threw in the towel, the people would have been so fed up; they would be prepared to accept the former government they had only recently kicked out of office. Poor Cenac had accepted the poisoned goblet, but I often wondered whether he ever knew that in that poisoned chalice were the shattered remains of the dreams of two - perhaps three - generations of Saint Lucians.

It did not seem to matter to the main players how many innocent voters would have lost out when the Labour government fell. There were obviously no morality or high ethical principles at play at the height of the struggle. No one seemed to have spared a thought for the descendants of those who had made it through the middle passage and who seemed just as lost today as when they first arrived in these new lands. Perhaps this explains the focus and growth of religion. It may help stay the hands of the unhappy who are poor as well as the poor who are unhappy and even divert their attention from politics and armed rebellion. But for how long can the neglect and the deceit of man using religion continue?

Swearing in as elected MP for Castries East, 1979

*These two may have shaken Saint Lucia from its long
slumber of blissful innocence.*

Peter Josie gives a formal bow to Speaker Wilfred St. Clair Daniel upon entering Parliament chambers in 1987, as Member for Vieux-Fort South constituency. Mr. Josie had previously represented Castries East constituency in Parliament.

Opening OAS Conference - Saint Lucia 1981

OAS Conference - Saint Lucia 1981 - Hon. Peter Josie

Peter Josie, Minister of Foreign Affairs Saint Lucia, (with ear phones assisting in automatic translations of languages) chairing a plenary session of the OAS General Assembly held on the island, in 1981.

OAS General Assembly Saint Lucia, 1981. Left to right, OAS Secretary General, Peter Josie Minister of Foreign Affairs (Saint Lucia) and Winston Cenac, Prime Minister of Saint Lucia.

Michael Pilgrim: Dubbed 'Mr. Clean' by George Odlum and his political admirers, perhaps to better use him for their various secret agendas.

Jon Odlum: A former Community worker and Minister of Community Development, Youth and Sports and one who many believed was the real worker and thinker of the Odlum brothers, in politics.

Relaxing at Jon's residence at Marisule
L-R: Jon Odlum, Peter Josie, George Odlum and 'Pan' Andrew sitting

The SLP seemed equally certain to retain its hold on power in this 2001 photo
on the Castries Market steps the favoured platform of that party in Castries.

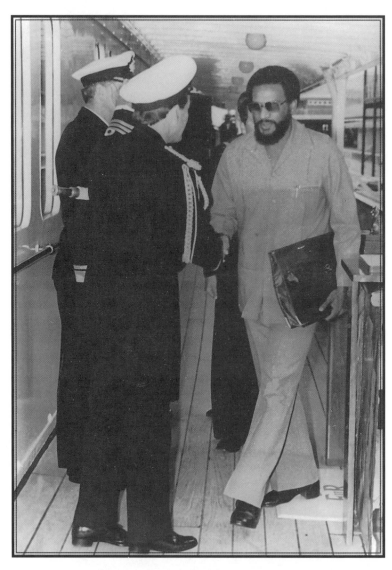

Following Independence, I represented the Island at the Heads of Government Commonwealth Conference in Australia, 1981. Here I am being welcomed on the Royal Yacht Britannia for private talks with Her Majesty the Queen of England and the Commonwealth

Allan Louisy, Leader of the Opposition (St. Lucia) and myself a Member of parliament, (1977) at the first round of constitutional talks in London leading to political independence for St. Lucia

Hewanorra International Airport (St. Lucia): supporters of the two political parties (UWP – United Workers Party and SLP – St. Lucia Labour party) welcoming their delegations back home after independence talks.

Swearing in of George Odlum at Government House, Castries, after his return to the SLP following his failed Progressive Labour Party (PLP).

Allan Louisy thinking about his next move?

*George Louison; A soul mate and Minister of Agriculture in the
Maurice Bishop-led Revolutionary government of Grenada.
Following the collapse of the 'Revo' George read law in England and
later returned to the Caribbean and practiced in Trinidad.*

*Peter Josie: another day, another address.
The message was self-reliance, community action, mass-political-education,
continued struggle for economic liberation and true freedom.*

The baton has been passed. Vaughan Lewis (right) replaced
Honourable George Mallet centre, as the Central Castries representative
for the United Workers Party. Lewis also replaced John Compton as leader of
the party and Prime Minister of Saint Lucia in 1996-97. At left is Mrs. Mallet.

At the Mount of Olives in Jerusalem (Israel) 1998
with the Dome of the Rock in the background

Odlum and his side kick Newman Monrose at Saint Lucia Jazz 2002

John Compton left with A.N.R. Robinson then Prime Minister of Trinidad and Tobago. They were close friends from the fifties when they both read law in England. In 1990 Prime Minister Robinson was injured during an attempted coup in Trinidad, whilst in Parliament.

*Romanus Lansiquot right and I in happier times. We were once rivals for the
Castries East seat (1979). After the bitter leadership struggle (1979-82)
I left to contest the Vieux-Fort South seat and Lansiquot easily won
Castries East in 1982. He held that seat from 1982 to 1997.*

*Exchange of a hearty handshake between Bishop Senior (left) and son
Maurice Bishop Senior was killed by police in 1974 during a protest
march in St. George's Grenada. His son Maurice was killed in 1983
when the "REVO" turned on itself.*

George Odlum left, with his mentor Hunter J. Francois right. At Francois' left is former Permanent Secretary Education Mr. Leton Thomas (now, Sir Leton) and between Odlum and Francois is renowned Saint Lucian artist, Llewellyn Xavier.

Like minded comrades and patriots; pioneers for a new Caribbean
L-R: George Odlum, (St. Lucia) Unison Whiteman (Grenada),
George Louison (Grenada), Peter Josie (St. Lucia), Maurice Bishop (Grenada)
– all Ministers of their respective governments in St. Lucia and Grenada.

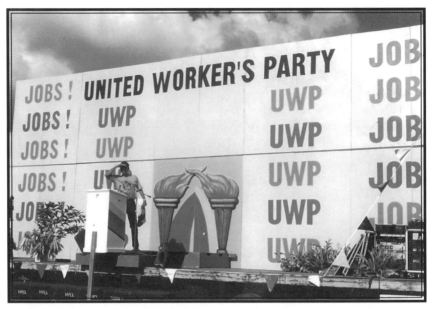

One of the more striking messages posted by the United Workers party (UWP) in one of its political campaigns of the nineties. A fifteen- year UWP – rule came to an end in 1997, when Dr. Vaughan Lewis who had replaced John Compton as political leader was comprehensively beaten by the returning prodigal – Kenny Anthony.

The election campaign is on: A constituency group makes its way south to assist a candidate of the party. It is a common scene in elections in Saint Lucia and in the entire Caribbean whenever general elections are expected.

Victory for the UWP looks quite certain in this 2001 political rally.

'Saved' with his fishing rod in hand on the beaches of his native Canouan Island (St. Vincent Grenadines) he was sent to school in St. Lucia. He lived there with his uncle, Mallings. Later he worked in the oil fields of Curacao, and then migrated to London, picked up a Law Degree and Basic Economics at London University, before returning to Saint Lucia to practice law part time - and politics full time.

John Compton, at the height of his political power. Many considered him the father of the nation and the architect of Saint Lucia's economic and social-progress. He was certainly the preferred Saint Lucian leader in Washington, London and other European capitals.

Preparing for Armed Take Over?

The morality of the Middle Passage was regarded merely
as an unfortunate trading loss, except for the fact that
Negroes were more costly than cattle.

Eric Williams:
From Columbus to Castro

Looking back on the events which led to the rise and fall of the Labour Party between 1974 and 1982, one may be persuaded to sympathize with those who believed that there were certain elements within the Labour camp preparing for an armed take over of the island. To be certain, there was plenty of loose talk thrown carelessly around from public platforms in that period. This, added to, and the ex-army uniforms worn by the more outspoken leaders of political opinion at that time, may have inadvertently helped to confirm the propaganda spread by the party's opponents. It was therefore our fault that we seemed then to confirm the mischief created and spread by our foes. It was bad politics on our part and we should have known better than to continue along that path. As rational men are often able to explain their actions, it is not too late to point to the reasons which informed our actions at the time.

Like the rest of the Caribbean, Saint Lucia had suffered through two hundred years of slavery and colonialism. The pace of social and economic progress at the time seemed deliberately calibrated to stultify and frustrate the social, economic (and intellectual) growth of the people of the region. In addition, class and racism still played too prominent a role in the distribution of wages, the dissemination of education and other social amenities across the island and the region. It was time for change and no piecemeal - 'wait your turn nigger' - attitude would do for us. There had to be a physical whipping of the money changers from the temple and it would take only a handful of determined men under a special leader to take us to the new Promised Land where everyone would be served according to his needs and give back to society according to his or her ability. The social and economic situation was there for all to see - and it was crying for change.

At the time, democracy was being touted as the best form of government. But whereas the island's constitution guaranteed the vote to eligible adults, it also reposed almost total power in the hands of a single elected official - the Premier, later rebranded as 'Prime Minister'. The script written by our former colonial masters by whom we were to be governed therefore had to be changed. Left to themselves they would always grudgingly amend and tinker rather than make a quantum leap forward, so to speak, that was necessary and essential if the island was to extricate itself from poverty and backwardness. In short, we needed a revolution, whereas the colonial power wished for gradualism, regardless who suffered in a state of despair and hunger on the journey to the Promised Land. We therefore had to learn to think and act for ourselves and to do so quickly.

That in itself was a revolution, and it had to first take place in the mind. At the time it was also obvious that the former system of colonialism (and British democracy), - including financial management of the economy - had bequeathed little to the sons and daughters of former slaves and the indigenous peoples of the Caribbean. Dr. Eric Williams, one of the great scholars of the region had argued (successfully in my view) that the business of slavery was an economic enterprise which was reluctantly abandoned when it proved unprofitable. That may have been the point at which the Negro slave became more expensive than cattle. Many have also argued that the psychological damage inflicted on descendants of former slaves persists to this very day. Be that as it may, there could be no pussyfooting nor playing around with half measures in tackling the problems of psychological, social and economic development in Saint Lucia and the rest of the Caribbean, or indeed of the rest of the undeveloped world.

I first learnt of the seriousness with which America viewed the Grenada Revolution after the St. Lucia Labour Party took office in mid-1979. One morning, without previous notice and before the 9 o'clock start of the weekly Cabinet meetings, Prime Minister Louisy invited George Odlum and me into his office. It was a relatively small office adjoining the Cabinet room to which there was an inner access door. The main entrance to the Cabinet room could have been accessed through a main door which led to the outside through a corridor which also led to other offices within the building. That morning I arrived early to Cabinet meeting. So did Odlum, who was not always punctual at these meetings, perhaps because he was usually accompanied by his Permanent Secretary, Mr. Edwin Laurent who presented important documents to the meeting, for Cabinet discussion and conclusion, and on behalf of his Minister.

That morning, Ms. Gloria Menal, the Prime Minister's long serving Secretary, ushered us into his office. She left shortly thereafter. Without warning and with little introduction, the Prime Minister proceeded to pull open a drawer on his desk and pulled out a bundle of eight by ten inch photographs which he then passed to Odlum and myself. He said he had found these in his desk drawer and had been informed they were aerial pictures of Grenada, showing large clearings in certain forested parts of the island. He said the photos were recently taken and that they showed the extent of arms and ammunition build-up on that island since Maurice Bishop and his friends had overthrown former Prime Minister Gairy.

The clearings seemed obvious enough from the photographs which we were shown, but one had to look long and hard to discern what appeared to be the outlines of crawler tractors and large tarpaulins which appeared to be covering some sort of cargo; large wooden boxes lying partly covered in the open where the tractor had cleared. We were informed that beneath the tarpaulin were hidden huge anti-aircraft guns which we were told Grenada did not need to defend itself at the time.

Soon, the Prime Minister's Secretary pushed her head through a side door and signalled to him that it was time for his scheduled cabinet meeting to begin. He therefore retrieved the photographs and put them back into the same desk drawer from which he had taken them. At that point Odlum and I then left the Prime Minister's office and without discussing the photographs we had been shown. Later that day when we met casually, Odlum did not ask my opinion on the photos we had been shown and neither did I raise the subject. I was fairly certain, however, that even though the matter was not discussed these photos were on his mind. They certainly had not left mine. Prime Minister Louisy knew of my support for Maurice Bishop and the New Jewel Movement of Grenada as I had made no secret of this. In addition, it could also have been seen from the evidence of his weekly writings in his Crusader newspaper plus his political rhetoric on public platforms that Odlum was also supportive of Maurice Bishop and what he had done in Grenada to be rid of Gairy. It would therefore be correct to say that both Odlum and I fully supported the ideals of the New Jewel Movement in Grenada and the charismatic Maurice Bishop, in particular.

I cannot say for certain whether Odlum and Prime Minister Louisy ever discussed the photographs between themselves after that morning to which I have just referred. However, when Odlum and I accompanied Louisy to Grenada on the first anniversary of Bishop's Peoples' Revolutionary Government (PRG) we were invited to inspect certain defensive positions the government had built. They reminded me of the photographs I had seen in Louisy's office. We were told by our hosts that they were necessary in case 'Gairy and his Mafia friends tried to hire mercenaries and attempt to overthrow the PRG'. By then the news throughout the Caribbean and the world was that Bishop and his friends were being assisted by Cuba's Fidel Castro who was in turn acting on orders from the Kremlin, to destabilize the entire region. Those who were familiar with western propaganda knew the origins of such talk. In reality however, Grenada was seen by London and Washington and their friends as a Communist beachhead in the southern Caribbean. Unfortunately for Bishop and the Labour government in Saint Lucia, persons who remembered the meeting of the Caribbean left (and progressives) at Rat Island in St. Lucia in 1972, began to make connections between that meeting and the events which had led to the armed overthrow of Gairy, and with possible links elsewhere in the region. These people began to wonder aloud which of the Caribbean Prime Ministers would be overthrown next. And some spoke as though there was confidential and accurate information from that Rat Island, Saint Lucia meeting, to confirm their fears. My position was: 'Let them tremble if they wish', I would not confirm or deny anything. It was my ardent wish and prayer to see oppressed people everywhere, particularly the black man, throw down his yoke and burden and rise up to fashion a new nation by whatever means possible.

By then the army in Trinidad had attempted to march into Port of Spain with a view to overthrowing the government of Dr. Eric Williams. They were frustrated in their efforts by forces - including the Coast Guard - which had remained loyal to the government. The story of Maurice Bishop's success in Grenada following the failure of the attempted military coup in Trinidad in 1970 is instructive. Eric Gairy, whose early politics is best remembered in two words 'Red Skies' had earlier returned from labour in the oil industry of the Dutch Antilles - Aruba and Curacao. The code 'red skies' referred to the menace the young Gairy posed to the owners of large sugar estates in Grenada, upon his return. His threat to turn the night skies over Grenada red was understood by his listeners as an attack on big sugar in particular and the colonial system which supported it. Gairy's Grenada United Labour Party (G.U.L.P.) triumphed in early elections on that island after adult suffrage. The rank and file of the Grenadian population had been granted the vote as a result of the Caribbean-wide disturbances of the late thirties and early forties. This followed, as did the rest of the Caribbean, from the Moyne Commission report on the workers' uprisings and its recommendation for a solution.

As the GULP continued to win general elections in Grenada, Gairy's propensity for showmanship, style and excess, increased. His extravagance and show also seemed to have affected the administration of the island. He was accused of spending budgeted funds from the British Treasury with less care than was expected of leaders thrown up by the democratic vote. He was therefore arrested in 1961 on squandermania charges by the British Government law enforcement officers and detained on a British warship anchored just outside St. George's harbour, in the capital. Reports confirmed that he was released two weeks later, without much incident. The electorate seemed to have gotten the message that the arrest was meant to convey. He was therefore voted out of office at the next general election and replaced by his counterpart and the less flamboyant personality, Herbert Blaize, who was born on the island of Carriacou, a tiny island just fifteen miles north of Grenada and administered from St. George's. He was leader of the Grenada National Party GNP) at the time. Soon, however, people appeared to tire of the lacklustre Blaize and Gairy was voted back into office.

Before Gairy's return to office, Grenada had been granted a slightly more advanced constitution, wherein the island was in charge of all its affairs, except external relations and defense. Blaize was therefore credited for taking Grenada from colonialism to Statehood or semi-independence. In this more advanced constitution the Chief Minister was restyled as Premier. The new constitution afforded the government full responsibility for the preparation of the island's annual budget including taxation, and without Britain's right of veto.

Some Grenada watchers believed that 'Uncle' Gairy must have felt peeved over the honour denied him, of being the first Premier of Grenada. He may also have decided there and then that he would become the first Prime Minister of Grenada when his GULP returned to office, regardless what anyone said - or did. That he succeeded in his ambitions was in large measure a testament to the man's grit, determination and political savvy.

It had also become an open secret by that time that Britain was studying a destiny within Europe and for this she would have to be rid of her colonial appendages. The granting of political independence to her former colonies had therefore become a priority of the British government. To this end it appeared she wished to jettison these small dependencies in the Caribbean Sea as soon as it was practical to do so. Besides, these colonies had become a drain on the British purse as sugar consumption fell. The desire to free itself of its colonial appendages was therefore an idea whose time had come. Britain was assisted in this policy by the United Nations anticolonial lobbyists in New York, which may have had its own epiphany.

It was during the years leading up to political independence in 1974 that Gairy faced his greatest challenges as a leader. By then he had declared his intention to take his 133 sq. mile island into political independence. Blaize, leader of the Opposition in Parliament and of the Grenada National Party (GNP) opposed the idea. Blaize's opposition, however, was confined to debates in Parliament. He did not take to the streets of St. Geroge's as Bishop and his New Jewel Movement had done or, as the opposition Labour Party in St. Lucia did four years later. Gairy was reported to have ridden roughshod over the gentle and self-effacing Blaize. Later, when Premier Compton tried the Gairy tactic in Saint Lucia he was met with stern opposition - on the streets. Besides, Compton lacked Gairy's flamboyance and dexterity and he faced a more determined opponent in Louisy (and the SLP) in the parliament of Saint Lucia.

By 1974, a new generation of University trained graduates had returned to the island and they too became embroiled in the politics of the day. Enter, Maurice Bishop, Unison Whiteman and Kenrick Radix and their New Jewel Movement. In Saint Lucia and the rest of the Caribbean the same phenomenon was being played out. A number of Saint Lucia graduates returning home had become embroiled in this island's politics. The heat had been turned up several notches on the independence debates in most countries within the Caribbean. The British government would not be allowed to shed her responsibilities to these neglected colonies so lightly or easily. Peter Josie and George Odlum were to lead the charge in Saint Lucia while Bishop, Whiteman, Radix and Coard led the opposition charge in Grenada. By then key persons within the NJM - Bishop, Radix and Whiteman - had been elected to parliament in Grenada. They swore to deny 'Uncle' the accolade (and crowning glory) of first Prime Minister. The battle for political Independence in both Grenada and Saint Lucia had seemed to have followed a similar pattern.

In Saint Lucia Odlum, Josie and company joined the St. Lucia Labour Party in parliament to oppose John Compton's bid to clothe himself with an Independence constitution. I was elected to parliament in 1974. Gairy, on the other hand, had met with even more obstacles than Compton had in his bid for Independence. Bishop's New Jewel Movement (NJM) was one such obstacle. 'Uncle' Gairy was determined to eliminate each obstacle as best he could. At the time there were massive demonstrations in the streets of St. George's. The same scenario was played out in St. Lucia a little later. The unfortunate shooting death of Rupert Bishop, father of Maurice

Bishop, during one of these demonstrations in Grenada may have marked the turning point in the politics of that island. It may well have determined the response of Bishop the younger, to the shooting death of his father. The politics of the southern Caribbean had therefore continued its lurch towards peoples' power and deadly force. No one could predict with any accuracy where the pendulum of the peoples' wrath would finally settle.

The protests over political independence in Saint Lucia were often heated and caustic but never violent. To be certain, the threat was never far from the surface but it never escalated into a national uprising, because unlike Grenada no one had shed his or her blood; so none grew because none was sown. Perhaps the Government of Saint Lucia had learnt well its lessons from the mistakes of Gairy. Besides, Compton was far less of a show man and debonair politician than Gairy, his counterpart in Grenada. In the final analysis both men got their prized political independence because the British government pretended to be fed up and washed its hands as Pilate might have done when the innocent Christ was presented to him by his fellow Jews. The truth of the matter was that both Gairy and Compton were judged to be preferable to the radicals who had emerged from Rat Island in Saint Lucia, and who had kept secret their internal discussions, more than people of colour were credited with at the time.

Before the achievement of political Independence, it had become acceptable that London was always willing to play along with leaders who were legitimately elected by the people provided such leaders were pliable, smart and knew when to speak and what to say. In such matters the British were always straight forward - never complicated. But they never admitted any of this of course. One had to learn such things on one's own. Unfortunately, some people never learnt anything from England or Europe.

Those who followed the developments in the Caribbean at the time may have concluded that the cold war had migrated from Cuba to its southern neighbours. It seemed obvious therefore that the United States government would continue to keep an eye on Cuba and Russia and make certain they did not extend their influences further south into these newly emerging independent territories of the East and South Caribbean.

Matters had taken such a grave turn in Grenada that on the night of Independence Gairy and his friends went ahead anyway, and raised the new Grenada flag at Fort George, in near darkness. The night the island severed its final official ties with Britain, was a night many people would prefer to forget. At the time, only a small minority of the population still supported Gairy and his government. But that did not matter to 'Uncle' and his friends. Nor did it seem to matter to the British government either. Those who supported the Independence adventure that night were reported to be the direct beneficiaries of his largesse; including those who got lands after the acquiring and dividing up of large sugar estates in the early fifties. Notwithstanding what anyone thought or said of the matter, Grenada became an independent country on the night of 7 February, 1974 - less than one month after Rupert Bishop was shot and killed by people loyal to Gairy.

The elections following Independence saw Bishop and Whiteman win parliamentary seats along with Blaize, who was also returned to parliament. They were still in opposition as Gairy again won the general elections and formed the government. However, the opposition to Gairy did not end there. It continued to build up with the apparent mobilization of the entire island's population, on the streets of St. George's. Matters came to a head on the 13 February 1979 whilst Prime Minister Gairy was out of the country on official government business. Early that morning, it was reported by Radio Grenada that armed men had overpowered police guards at police headquarters and at the Prime Minister's official residence. They then proceeded to take over the lone radio station on the island. At first, the whole nation appeared to be in a state of shock. As the day progressed and it became clearer that the NJM was consolidating its grip on power, their supporters began to relax and some took to the streets in jubilation. Many supported the 'Revo' as Grenadians came to call the armed take over of Gairy's government. Those who supported Bishop and the boys thought that since they had contested and won general elections, they would now reform the entire elections system, including the voters' list and perhaps even design a new constitution for the island, and then return to the polls as soon as practicable.

That was not to be. As the Peoples' Revolutionary Government (PRG) - as they called themselves - consolidated their hold on power, it became clear that what Grenada had on its hands was a full fledged Communist/ Socialist PRG. Rallies were held by the PRG and the people were being constantly mobilized by Bishop and company. Neither at these rallies nor anywhere else did the PRG ever give any indication it intended to hold democratic elections. As time passed it appeared that the people of Grenada had decided to hold their peace on the question of free and fair elections. The news reaching the rest of the Caribbean was that more Grenadians were also becoming uneasy about the unity within the Bishop-led government. The rest of the Caribbean looked on and waited. London too, appeared to be playing a wait and see game. Washington was uneasy about a possible connection between Grenada and Cuba, and they voiced their concerns, quietly at first to friends, and later much louder to anyone who would listen. As if to follow Washington's lead, some governments in the Caribbean also made public their displeasure with the PRG.

But Bishop and the PRG continued to consolidate and confirm their hold on power. As they did, trained technocrats from the Caribbean and elsewhere volunteered help in the country's many new development initiatives. Rallies were often held in the open spaces all over the island in order to mobilize the people and to keep the country sensitized, informed and ready for anything the 'enemy' might throw at it. Little did they know that the enemy would come from within. Had they studied the history of revolutions more closely they might have been better informed, how revolutions often turned on themselves.

It was also reported to the wider Caribbean about the excesses of the PRG, including the detention and arbitrary arrests of persons who had voiced opposition to the manner of its operations. Those who were close to the government believed there was division over both the arrests and the calling of elections. As it turned out, the people of Grenada were also divided on these issues. Such differences may well have opened up the Augean stables and allowed the ill winds which finally blew the whole experiment apart. Whatever the exact truthfulness of the stories told by those who were present as well as by those who may have received it second hand, there were divisions which were not mended and which led to the fall of the PRG. Exactly the same summary may also be made in the case of the Labour government in Saint Lucia around the same time.

The following account is one told by persons who lived in Grenada at the time and who were in a position to receive authentic, first hand information on the workings of the PRG. Bishop was the 'de facto' and 'de jure' leader of the PRG. His position was challenged because he was accused of not carrying out the decisions of the central committee of the army and party. Unlike other governments with similar constitutions in the Caribbean in which the Prime Minister is the boss, in the case of the PRG, the central committee was the supreme ruling body. That body decided that Bernard Coard would share power with Maurice Bishop and that the two would run the government jointly. But Coard remained chair of the all powerful central committee. Although the Grenada constitution was set aside when Gairy was overthrown by Bishop - a lawyer by training - Bishop apparently still carried the duties of Prime Minister, as if the abandoned constitution was still in place - an understandable assumption since the Governor General was still in office. This was a mistake which probably cost him his life and which led to the downfall of the PRG and PRA.

The Central Committee was made up of top ranks of the army and national security personnel as well as the top persons from the core of the party and government. It was therefore the most powerful organ of governance on the island and had certainly replaced the old Cabinet which the Independence constitution had enshrined, as its modern day ten commandments. The all powerful central committee dictated both policy and the day to day operations of the government. Bishop was therefore reduced to a single small voice which could not call fresh elections in Grenada (even though he may have wanted to do so) nor could he do any other thing which normal Prime Ministers in the Caribbean were able to do. Henceforth anything the people wanted in terms of national development would have to come from the central committee. It alone could take life and perhaps even give life had they remained in office long enough to prove it.

The end results of internal changes within the now ruling elite were that the leadership of both government and party was shared between Bishop and Coard. From the point of view of outsiders (and perhaps as a result of western propaganda) the latter (Coard) seemed the hard line Marxist/Leninist, while Bishop was seen as more open to suggestions on the way forward. But this may have been a wrong impression. What was certain was that Maurice Bishop was a peoples' person and probably enjoyed much greater loyalty and love from the Grenada masses. Bishop was projected to the Caribbean as more conciliatory and as having more feeling for his peoples' need for free expression and open debate. The people of Grenada soon became aware of a serious rift within the PRG. As word spread, people started gathering in St. George's to satisfy their curiosity and be part of the goings-on. Others had heard that Bishop had been under house arrest and they wished to see for themselves in order to confirm or deny the story.

In response to the peoples' gathering impatience on news about Bishop, the so-called hardliners, under Coard, shut down the only telephone company on the island. The situation on the ground at the time was described by many as not too dissimilar from that of 1974 when Rupert Bishop was killed. Soon it was learnt that Maurice Bishop was released from house arrest (by a crowd of persons who had invaded his home) and taken by those who had freed him to Fort George (renamed Fort Rupert after the shooting death there of Rupert Bishop in January of 1974).

It is reported that the Central Committee then sent two armoured vehicles and a detachment of soldiers from the Peoples Revolutionary Army (PRA) to Fort Rupert where Bishop and some of his Ministers including Unison Whiteman had gone with the crowd after he was set free, by the people. It is also alleged that the advancing armoured vehicles were fired on by one person, using one round of ammunition and this is what may have led to the bloodshed and mayhem which followed. But how do we know for certain this is not the version put out by those who wanted to save the necks of those who had ordered the army to shoot to kill? No one can tell for certain who fired that fateful shot - if indeed there was such a shot fired. In response therefore, the armoured vehicles opened fire, as soldiers are trained to do, and a number of people were injured and killed. Some hurt themselves jumping over the walls of the Fort to relative 'safety', on the outside boulders below, at the sea's edge. When all was said and done, Bishop, Unison Whiteman and several others lay dead at Fort George.

In the aftermath, it became clear that both the army and Coard were in the thick of things as far as the control of Grenada was concerned. No one can recall who shared power with Coard after Bishop was killed. No one has answered the question: why should Bishop have had to share power with him and with no one else. But by then such questions and perhaps their answers too, were moot.

Soon afterwards, the American and the British governments decided that they had had enough of the Grenada experiment. What was becoming increasingly clear was that the people of Grenada had themselves had enough of the PRG and PRA. So too had some of the governments of the Caribbean. Some Caribbean brethren had long suspected that the plan to rid the Caribbean (and Grenada) of the PRG and PRA had been well laid by the Americans and the British long before the death of Bishop and Whiteman. The events in Grenada under the eccentric Gairy were now beginning to look like child's play, in comparison to what the PRG had done. Still, some on the Caribbean left at the time were opposed to any outside interference in the internal affairs of Grenada and of the region. I can't recall whether those who said that, had first tested the views of the people of Grenada. In any event it is one of the favourite pastimes of some Caribbean personalities from all sides of the political divide to presume to know what is best for 'the people' and then from such untested presumptions proceed to implement change, however undesirable.

Caribbean leaders were aware that America and England were in possession of the fire power to remove the remnants of the PRG in Grenada from office. In a strange way, history was to repeat itself in Grenada. This time the de facto leader of the country after the slaying of Prime Minister Maurice Bishop and company was Bernard Coard, his former deputy. Whereas it was the British who had taken Minister Gairy away to their waiting war ships, after they had arrested him on squandermania charges in the early sixties, this time it was the turn of the Americans to arrest those leaders from Grenada who had committed perhaps an even greater evil than Gairy. The only difference between the British Government's approach to such matters and that of their American allies was that the former preferred the diplomatic options rather than force, to resolve the Grenada situation. America did not agree, and she would do whatever she pleased because she understood that power came from the barrel of a gun. The British also understood this but they were less inclined to spend money on bullets than were their American friends. The important point here is that the two kept their differences to themselves.

Using the pretext of saving the lives of American students studying at the offshore medical school in Grenada known as St. George's University, the American war machine moved into operation and put down the remnants of the PRG. The Central Committee headed by Coard had given orders to resist and the Cuban construction workers who lived and worked in Grenada at the time did their best to assist. But it was all in vain. Within forty hours of the American invasion the PRG was no more.

To ensure their ventures proved a constitutional success as well, the Americans had taken the precaution of removing the Governor General - Paul Scoon – from his official residence in St. George's and taking him for safe keeping on one of their battle ships. This move ensured that Sir Paul who represented Her Majesty the Queen of England as Head of the Government of Grenada had no way of communicating with Her Majesty in London - or with anyone else for that matter - without the knowledge of the American army and navy.

To show where the real power (and money) lay in the Caribbean basin south of Cuba, the Barbados international airport was commandeered the night before the invasion of Grenada by the Americans. The only airport on the island was closed to all commercial traffic for two consecutive nights, 21st. and 22nd. October 1983. This was to allow America's military full use of the facility as the staging points for the mission code named 'Amber and the Amberines' – the attack on Grenada and the PRG. The mission was to take down the PRG, now headed by Coard. In the Caribbean only Prime Minister Tom Adams of Barbados and Eugenia Charles of Dominica may have known of the invasion before it took place.

It had been reported by a close friend and confidant of Prime Minister Charles, that she was whisked away from Dominica on an unmarked aircraft to the French Department of Guadeloupe. Once in Guadeloupe she boarded an American army plane which deposited her in Virginia just outside Washington D.C. at three o'clock in the morning. Later she was booked as Ms. Anderson at a hotel nearby. A little later that same morning at around 10.30 she attended a scheduled meeting with President Reagan at which the President's press corps was invited. Ms. Charles was celebrated as the Iron Lady of the Caribbean perhaps in answer to England, which had announced to the world that their Prime Minister Margaret Thatcher, was no man; but an iron lady. The Caribbean, right in keeping with its weak and demeaning propensity to copy all things foreign and European, named their first female Prime Minister the iron lady of the Caribbean. Perhaps Mrs. Thatcher and Ms. Charles had more in common than I thought at the time. They both must have shared an equal abhorrence for the very names of communism and totalitarianism. That much they must also have shared with the bible toting, nigger-hating, far-right of American politics.

After the press briefing in Washington with President Reagan, Ms. Charles was flown directly to Barbados where other Caribbean Prime Ministers were gathered, for a briefing. Her mission was obviously to act as messenger for the United States and President Reagan and to brief Caribbean leaders that an invasion of Grenada was taking place as they met in Barbados. That was the first time many Caribbean leaders may have had first hand information on what was going on in their own backyard. For the first time, it appeared Washington had taken over the leadership role of these islands from England. Margaret Thatcher, then Prime Minister of England remained stoic, distant and quiet. She appeared not to have been briefed by her good friend President Reagan on what he was doing in the Caribbean which for centuries had been the preserve of Europe, particularly Britain, France and Spain. It was for these reasons and more the Monroe doctrine was established by America, to finally let Europe know that her infant had now grown to manhood, and did not want her to visit without America's say so. Europe may not have bothered if by that time that infant had not raised a sufficiently large army to back her words with action.

The American invasion of Grenada did not find the PRG or its supporters totally unprepared. To its credit the PRG military did not all pack up and run. When American helicopters began to descend on the island from warships to 'rescue' students at Grand Anse beach, they were fired upon and at least one came down with the loss of American lives.

However, the American military persevered. Military personnel and hardware were dropped on the beach at Grand Anse and American students were picked up and returned to waiting war ships. Within days the tension in Grenada began to dissipate. The invading Americans themselves had set up several road blocks around the island in order to secure their position. The Governor General resumed his duties and an interim government was set up to administer the affairs of the island and to prepare it for national elections. There were between seven hundred to one thousand students at St. George's University when the Americans invaded. All were evacuated successfully. Many had left earlier to other islands nearby, for safety. A point of interest which ought not to be missed by persons interested in such matters was that Sir. Paul Scoon, Governor General, was at the time directing the affairs of State from the safety of the American war ship. From there he delivered frequent addresses to the people of Grenada. The question was: Did he inform Her Majesty the Queen of England whom he represented as head of the government of Grenada of the goings on at the time he was held by the Americans?

We must now return to the invitation issued to the Louisy government of Saint Lucia to be the guest of Prime Minister Bishop and his PRG at the second anniversary celebrations of the 'revo'. There were other Caribbean leaders in Grenada at the time and as far as I could tell we were all treated graciously. It appeared, however, that the Saint Lucia delegation, particularly Foreign Minister George Odlum had a little more than congratulations on his mind when he arrived in Grenada.

The day before he left Grenada he informed me he had had a private discussion with Prime Minister Bishop and asked for a few young men from Saint Lucia to be trained as security agents in Grenada and suitable small arms for these persons after they had learnt to use such arms. Odlum assured me he had mentioned the matter to Prime Minister Louisy who did not object to the scheme. He had also arranged for me to remain in Grenada for an additional day, so that I may accompany the arms to Saint Lucia. I did not object when Odlum informed me that I was to be flown directly to Saint Lucia by personnel of the Grenada government and on their private aircraft.

At the time the idea of a specially trained group of young party loyalists to serve as personal bodyguards to the Ministers did not surprise me. I learnt later from Mr. Louisy that he had agreed to the training of two or three young men from Saint Lucia who were to become a part of the Saint Lucia service upon completion of their training. That is not the way Foreign Minister Odlum seemed to have understood it as far as he told me.

Odlum and myself had previously attempted to discover from the Commissioner of Police in Saint Lucia and his Secret Service officers the files they had kept on the two of us, during the time we were in opposition. We met with a blank wall. In fact it would be true to say that some senior police officers treated us with contempt, even though we were now Ministers of the Government. We were surprised that the top brass of the Force had communicated with the Prime Minister our request for those secret files and received his support, or so we were told, in denying us, access to them.

We were by then aware that in the matter of national security each Caribbean country - including the so called more developed ones - was kept informed of important security issues within and outside their borders by Britain and the USA who it appeared had given themselves 'carte blanche' to do this. This act of assisting in national security by the USA and Britain is seen as a friendly one even though no government in the region knew what exactly the British or the American Governments were after. The arms of most Caribbean governments were also twisted on matters of foreign affairs, especially within the region. Indeed it is widely believed that the arms of Caribbean governments are twisted ever so often and so firmly that many wonder how so many persist in office even though to do so seemed to risk fractured arms.

The long and short of our sojourn into the old police station at the top of Bridge Street in Castries was that neither Odlum nor myself ever got to read any security reports about ourselves or any one else for that matter. It became obvious to us that those in the local police force, who had been trained as spies and secret agents, were the property of Washington and London. It did not matter that the government of Saint Lucia paid their salaries. There are Ministers of the governments of these Caribbean islands who will never know the truth about the security of the region or indeed of their own personal security.

We left office without the benefit of reading any secret reports which the police may have had and which concerned us. We were convinced that neither Saint Lucia nor the other islands in the Caribbean, small or large, are entirely responsible for their own security and defense. We concluded that political Independence was (is) therefore a sham and would remain such until there is one West Indies nation, sharing resources, and contributing to a joint regional defense.

Whereas in the time of Maurice Bishop, George Odlum and company the concern was communist expansion into the south and east Caribbean, today the fear is international terrorism and the laundering of drug money. These two are now linked by those who express such concerns and it is believed that money from illegal drugs goes to fund terrorist activities. There is also evidence to suggest that those who make the connection know of what they speak.

There are still many people who persist in the notion that some communist conspiracy had been hatched at Rat Island in Saint Lucia in the early seventies. Those who had gathered there were certainly not the run of the mill conservative 'nice-guys' who would pity the plumage and forget the dying bird. No, it was not that at all; but there was also no conspiracy to enslave the Caribbean masses all over again. Those who had gathered at Rat Island that day were well looked after by their Saint Lucian hosts and the many pretty ladies who were invited for drinks after the talks were over.

It is a most welcome and sophisticated aspect of that particular gathering at Rat Island, that those who attended were all from the Caribbean - from Jamaica in the North West to Guyana in South America. We parted that important meeting with the understanding that what we found praiseworthy in other countries we were to carefully imitate and what in them may have appeared defective we should in our own countries - and laws - amend. We also understood the value of secrets, even though those locals who were attracted to the cause of the struggle at home may have missed the point of knowing when to say nothing. In fact, it could be postulated that loose talk from idle tongues and jealous minds were the root causes that set George Odlum and me apart. I had outgrown the worn-out mode of dress of the Forum period and the lifestyle which was threatening to confine me to domino tables and rum shops around my constituency. I needed a fresh breath of air and without the same politicians always at my ears trying to direct my every move and even my thinking on political issues. I took a hard long look at myself - an inventory of exactly where I was in life at that time, so to speak - and then decided that it was time to take a short holiday and read some new books.

We were heading inexorably to that place where the best of friends - and family too - must part because the road has forked and each new direction beckons a different and unique personality, who is at the time prepared to explore new paths, new ideas and new friends.

The Political Twins, Adrift
Post Hurricane Allen (1980)

Refrain from seeing and speaking the vices of mankind
which you know is in yourself.
Allam Sir Abdullah: The wisdom of Muhammad.

I had been warned by friends who swore they were in no way 'political' that the time would come to walk away from the seemingly close bond George Odlum and I shared. They observed that in the continuing political in-fighting within the Labour government of 1979 to 1982, Brother George was not listening to anyone or caring about the concerns of his allies and party supporters. Many such persons, I was repeatedly reminded, had expected the Labour Government - including the likes of Louisy and Odlum - to settle down quickly; to correct the things it had criticized in the former government which needed amending; and to bring new prosperity to the people of Saint Lucia. At the time, even the government's sworn opponents had conceded that the Labour government was endowed with the talent to get its manifesto proposals off the ground, and to begin a new path to comprehensive education and national development.

There was therefore widespread disappointment and disillusionment when, instead of doing what was expected of it - working as a united team for the good of the country - the ugly leadership struggle continued to dampen the enthusiasm of many Labour supporters and eventually threw the government into a disastrous tailspin. It was at this point that I began to realize that I had allowed my support for Brother George to override the principles for which I stood. The shared political ideology that had guided our actions thus far had been trampled upon and then lay shattered around me. The struggle had been hijacked into a one-man effort before I had quite realized that I was sucked into a side show and national conspiracy which I did not initially bargain for. I had supported and respected George Odlum my entire life, first as a master (teacher) at St. Mary's College, then as a brilliant goal keeper for the island, and later as one who had made the island proud through his achievements at Universities in England. But above all this, I was also growing in independence, in the belief of my own talents and ability and above all in the knowledge that only God would direct my final destiny and what, if anything, I was to achieve for Saint Lucia.

By then too, I had also discovered that both Odlum and I were strong 'A'-personalities even though I may have often deferred to him due to his seniority (he was at least seven years my senior) and for the reasons I have just stated. The protracted leadership struggle would, however, take us to a point where I had to finally decide for myself which was the correct political path for my constituents and my country. I had to come to such a decision regardless of the direction and agenda of George Odlum or anyone else. This was a very difficult bridge to cross and I knew that once it was crossed there would be no turning back. The relatively long road we had travelled together was now at its end. I could not convince him to stop the quarrel with Louisy and I had come into the world with many blessings which would not allow me to be led or follow anyone down a precipice. I therefore had little option than to separate, when our differences over the leadership issue became untenable. It was at that point which the political road on the island took a decisive turn, so to speak. Saint Lucia did not easily recover from that drifting apart of Odlum and myself and many who are alive at the time of this writing, believed that the dream of a more perfect, self-assured and self-reliant people, disciplined to military precision even as it espoused the causes of true liberty and freedom, had been lost forever, at that point when the 'political twins' were separated.

Towards the end, it became generally accepted that the leadership struggle had more to do with the power relations of the cold war, and its impact in the region, than the mere pandering for position by obese, middle aged men seeking to massage their individual egos. A clear and perhaps unkind conclusion is that people ought to be careful the role they allow (or tolerate) from aging politicians who have passed their useful lives. This obviously points to the constitution and how we shape the future. It would do no harm to bear in mind that in politics, it is the people, and they alone who determine the final outcome and shape of the future, by which (or what) they shall be governed. From a distance, it now appears that the people of Saint Lucia were mere spectators in the political struggles between Prime Minister Louisy and his deputy George Odlum, and the Machiavellian twists and turns that returned them to the past which they had so firmly renounced in the elections of 1979.

I think it is fair to say that by mid-1970 the Saint Lucian electorate had become more passionate about politics than before and that they were fully alert to the pros and cons of the leadership struggle when it erupted. Still, it was largely left to the media with its known biases and human imperfections to analyze and present the power play and in-fighting as these journalists may have genuinely understood and interpreted the quarrel. At the time, I recalled journalists shied clear of interviewing me because it was assumed that I may have been too biased to offer a correct analysis of the situation. Even though I supported the 'progressive' radical, leftist politics at the time, I also saw the in-fighting as larger than either of its two main antagonists. But how could I explain this to persons who either did not want to know the truth or who had their own means of getting to their version of what was considered gospel, at the time? Of course many journalists would swear on oath that theirs was balanced and objective reporting; and there would be few bold enough to question them. I knew that cutting my own path would be seen as a test of merit, especially by those journalists who had been fed the weekly diet of Odlum's Crusader offerings. I was also aware that few, if any, who swallowed up these weekend offerings ever bothered to question the authenticity of what they had been fed. It took only one negative headline and a message of condemnation in that paper, and soon that thing or person became an enemy of every Odlum disciple. No one knew whether those who read that paper ever tried to match the writer's actions with his words. Those who were smart enough merely read and smiled and went on with their lives, knowing that the more things changed the more they remained the same on the other hand many who read the Crusader at the weekend simply did not care. The negative fixes were their opium and gospel all at once and they needed the word for their personal comfort and perhaps for their salvation too. Knowing all this, I still decided to step up and do the right thing and in so doing prayed that time would be my greatest ally and witness. I hope that it will some day be said that I did the right thing when it was most needed to be done, and when my country called upon me to stand alone - as a man and a patriot.

At the time, agriculture and the banana industry in particular, was recovering very rapidly from the ravages of Hurricane Allen. My reputation as a Minister of the government responsible for agriculture was growing as fast as the recovery within the sector after the hurricane. That was a feather in my cap which may have brought jealousies even from those I thought were my friends and supporters. I was merely doing my work and I thought in the end that it was what had made John Compton such a force on the island in his time. So why were other politicians who had campaigned for an opportunity to outshine Compton now quarrelling instead of working as hard as they could to outshine even the workaholic, whom we had replaced? Besides, I had grown up in the town of Vieux-Fort where the American work ethic said that the most difficult job did not tire the body; only when the mind became tired did a man need rest. So the Americans in the town in which I grew up paid a better wage and demanded more and better work. The infrastructure they left behind and what they have made of their own country speak for themselves.

After much soul searching, and a careful review of the political road which we had travelled thus far, I decided to confront Brother Odlum at his office about my misgivings and growing opposition to the toll which the leadership struggle was taking on me personally, and also on the nation, at large. When I arrived at his office that day, I saw several persons seated there, some of whom are still around, at time of writing. They include the garrulous Rick Wayne of Mr. World fame and publisher of the local Star newspaper and television talk show host, Mervin Johnson a taxi operator with vast experience and Titus Francis, a former prominent Trade Unionist on the island, together with Vic Fadlien. I reminded Odlum that he knew as well as I did that in politics one was expected to stretch the fabric of any given challenge (including one's adversaries) as tightly as possible. And that one should also be aware how far to pull (or push) without bringing damning retaliation, chaos and destruction to the very thing that one had set out to protect, preserve or build. Of course one can always argue that it was better to destroy what was inferior and build anew, but it would be a correct decision only if those making such a choice were in the firing line of the process .

I did not then, or at any other time suggest to Brother George that he should resign from the government or to give up his dreams of leading the island one day. But I assured him that whatever his positive dreams were or may have been for the country, the leadership quarrel was sure to frustrate every one of them. Indeed, if anything, that struggle was likely to ruin even his most patriotic objectives. I was aware there were a handful of people around Brother George at the time who would buckle at telling him the truth. But I had earned the right to speak to him candidly, or so I thought at the time, without offending him or hurting his feelings in any way. The gap between student and teacher had by then sufficiently narrowed to allow for a frank and truthful dialogue, including a parting of the ways on an issue that we both considered non-negotiable.

By then I had also observed that many Labour Party supporters whom I had spoken to were hoping that the passage of Hurricane Allen would be used to good effect and treated as a sort of blessing to stop the quarrel and make a new start in the governance of the country. Even the rank and file, including the lower income and the poor, who did not support us at the time, were hoping for a fresh start in the Labour government. Our friends in the region reasoned that we would surely use the lull after the hurricane to restore some personal pride and dignity to ourselves. But these two - pride and dignity - were very scarce commodities at the time. It was not the first time the people on the island were ahead of their political leaders. Neither would it be the last time that leaders would encounter such great difficulty in refusing to listen to the voice of the people. Yet these were the same persons who, when it was convenient, liked to remind their listeners that the voice of the people was (is) the voice of God!

Admittedly, the situation was a bit confusing at the time because Odlum and the Labour Party still enjoyed a reasonable following of diehards. But such following as they enjoyed was being eroded even as we spoke at Odlum's office that day. Many genuine Labour supporters were already saying openly that the quarrel was dragging the government back into opposition and at the same time clearing the way for the return of the man whom the Crusader newspaper had taught its readers to call 'papa diable' - 'father devil'. Brother George did not need anyone to remind him that last time the St. Lucia Labour Party had tasted political office was in 1963. It was then approaching the end of 1980, when we met at his Brazil Street office, in Castries.

After I had made my feelings known to Brother George and our close political associates who had gathered that morning, the place became very quiet for a moment. I was aware neither they nor Odlum had expected what they had just heard me say. I did not make a fuss nor did I speak loudly. Most people knew I had supported our joint political efforts over many years and some may have found it strange that I had finally made up my mind to take a more independent stand on issues facing the government (and country). Even those who, like the rest of the population were fed up and disenchanted with the protracted leadership struggle would smile and bear it, whenever George Odlum put on his personal charm. He was very disarming in a one-on-one situation, especially with the opposite sex. But noticeable cracks were by then appearing elsewhere in the ranks of the progressives. They came in the form of whispers and coded messages sometimes directly to Odlum himself. It also appeared, however, that some persons who had Odlum's ears were also working to destabilize the Labour government and to neutralize persons such as myself who they could not get close to and were less likely to influence. Besides, some of Odlum's confidants frankly feared my politics and perhaps my cast of an independent mind as well.

Odlum's friends and allies were by then suggesting the formation of a third political party, to be headed by him. Remarkably, no one could tell with any clarity whether that new political party would remain in office as a coalition government with the St. Lucia Labour Party or whether it would prefer to join with the opposition party of John Compton (the UWP), in a bid to form some sort of unity government without the need for fresh general elections.

As the hurricane recovery effort continued it was Odlum who began to pull the pieces of reckless speech and conduct together again. About weeks after I had spoken to him at his office he called one morning to inform me he planned a public meeting on the Castries market steps to disclose corruption he had uncovered in the Ministry of Communications and Works. Specifically, that public meeting was to discuss the manner the Government Ministry in question was handling the procurement and distribution of lumber and other building materials in the post-hurricane reconstruction effort. Frankly, I could not believe what I was hearing. It was as if the man had not understood a word of what I had said at his office. I reminded him of our conversation and then told him in clear language that he should not expect to see me on the Market Steps that night. This was exactly the political situation that I had hoped to avoid. I wanted Odlum to stop his abuse of confidentiality and I also wanted the wayward Ministers to mend their ways. But what does one do when neither is listening, and one is powerless to do anything about it. It was at such times, I asked myself how I ended up in such a mess. Why didn't I start my own political party or perhaps join another as political leader as happened often over here. I should have been in a position to fire these bastards who would not listen to the voices of the people!

I bristled at the audacity and boldness of the suggestion that I should appear at a public meeting on the Market Steps in order to provide more fodder for our opponents. I had made up my mind that that game was over and that perhaps people were being paid to keep the fight alive. Peter Josie would no longer be a part of this charade. At the time I also asked myself whether the voice at the other end of the telephone line (Odlum's) was capable of hearing or listening to any voice except the one which was in his own head. Of course I did not attend that public meeting or any other, from that time onwards. That telephone call had convinced me that this was a person who was disconnected from reality and who may have been too far gone to reason with. I was therefore more determined than ever that I would not be destroyed by his recklessness and obvious selfishness. The thought crossed my mind several times that the goodly

Brother George may have been in the employ of the secret service of either London or Washington - or both. Even then there were few others in politics who spoke more frequently or more convincingly about the need to listen to what the ground was saying, than Saint Lucia's number one political animal - George Odlum. He seemed then on a special mission to let everyone know that he (and perhaps he alone) was aware of what the grass roots were thinking - and saying and even feeling. But he never admitted in private or public what his brain (and mind) would select out from his sources, only that which suited his particular purpose.

I did my best to restrain any undignified outburst to which my gut feelings were then prompting me, knowing well that any such display whether in private or public, would let out more than I wished to, at the time. Instead, I suggested as politely as I could in that earlier telephone conversation that, perhaps he, George Odlum, should confront Prime Minister Louisy, and the entire cabinet if needs be, with the information he had received. I also reminded him to take along any available evidence, remembering how certain persons in the government loved to enquire after evidence, even when they were often sitting on it. I even suggested that he should demand the firing of the said Minister once his evidence was overwhelming and fool proof and promised he would have my support, then. Furthermore, I suggested that the government could ill afford another scandal, so going public with any kind of negative information would be too much to expect the people and opposition to continue to bear without exploding into righteous indignation; perhaps revolt. At the same time that I made my views known to Brother George I continued to distance myself from what he was about to do on the Castries Market Steps. I knew his public exposure of the Minister of Works was bound to point a finger at him for remaining a Minister in a Government which he was describing in such unflattering terms in public and as often as he had done. But Odlum must have studied political propaganda and psychology and knew better than most people that all he had to do was stay on the message - no matter how untrue - and be in the public's face as often as possible. This little Christian community of righteous Roman Catholics and others had not been used to such barefaced boldness. It was instead a very secretive community which abhorred naked exposure, especially in public. Now here was a man, understandably protestant in religious orientation and upbringing, who had experienced his own run-in with the mighty Catholic authorities on the island. A case in point was the appointment of Education Officer in the Ministry of Education which he had been denied and which many persons thought was still fresh in his mind. It may well have entered the minds of political observers that Odlum still bore a grudge and that he seemed prepared to use his position as a Minister of Government to confront those whom he perceived to be against him. In his public speeches Odlum had often made the historical link between the church, colonialism and racism and cast aspersions that these three were issues which still needed to be confronted.

Besides, if he confronted the Prime Minister and Cabinet on what he was alleged to have discovered in the Ministry of Communications, Works and Transport, then why not make it an issue of personal integrity, an offer to resign on the matter if the Prime Minister took no action? Only then, I said, were people likely to respect you as a stalwart and champion, who stood by the things he said and wrote. It did not matter what his detractors and opponents thought of him at the time, I still thought the man was salvageable but I did not think I had the ability or the energy with which to do it at that late stage of the leadership struggle. Having communicated my opinion by telephone on his allegations of the discovery of corruption in the government, I considered my part in the new threat which was sure to lead to the demise of the Labour government as well as to the peace and tranquility of the country. I did not bother to let everyone within my constituency group or other close political associates or even family know about that conversation, or the decision I had made to keep away from Brother George. That may have been a huge mistake. I continued my work as Minister of Agriculture, Fisheries and Lands with the farmers and fishermen of the country and I paid little attention to anything Brother George or anyone else who was close to him did, or said, from that time onwards. My strong belief at the time was that my work would speak for me; perhaps better than words could ever do.

The decision to follow my own mind and counsel may have been a wise one, but on the other hand the strategy to withdraw into myself may have been a big mistake, on my part. Clearly, it did not work. I was surprised at the degree of venom with which I was attacked by Brother George and his acolytes. It reminded me of the actions of persons who lived in abusive situations and in which one partner decides that he or she has had enough and decides to leave. At which point, of course, we discover to our horror that the other party would rather have the one who decides to leave dead, than to live alone or, in peace, with a new lover. Yet such a relationship never entered the formulations of our politics or that of our personal lives.

To my surprise therefore, Brother George's venom then became directed at me. For some time I did not recognize myself either in his weekly Crusader newspaper or in his many vitriolic speeches on the market steps. Had this been a more educated and sophisticated society at the time, Brother George would surely have been finished politically. But this was

Saint Lucia which he knew well enough to have described it as a salt-fish and green figs society. At the time, no one seemed kind enough to say or write to the Brother, that he whom the Gods wish to destroy, they first make mad. There came a point, I decided, that if no one would tell him or reply on my behalf, then I would do so myself. I therefore decided to bare my fangs, retrieve my Magnum .375 from its hiding place and put on my fighting boots again, in order to defend myself and my family. The days following my decision to tell Brother George where to fall off were not the best days of my life. He had fully energized the half-crazed political neophytes who were then clinging to his coat tails and they seemed at the time to be falling over themselves to out trash-talk each other as far as Louisy and myself were concerned. I discovered that I had been placed in the Louisy camp long before I knew it. In Brother George's books, it seemed there was no room for independent thinking. One had to be either on Louisy's side or on Odlum's side. We seemed to have been thrown back on classical Christian ethics by persons who had long abandoned religion. But I reminded these new acolytes around Brother George as best I could, that I would not be intimidated by their rhetoric. I made it known that I was born and raised in a place at a time when war and conflict were the order of the day and many family members were determined to serve in the Second World War. In fact when I was growing up we were constantly reminded by our elders that people had to stand up and fight for freedom and democracy. That spirit of 'standing-up' had not left me even though in my youth I did not quite understand why freedom and democracy were so important to those who advocated it.

I had made up my mind that it was better to be seen as taking a clear and inde-pendent stand for party and country rather than to be seen either as a vacil-lator or worse, somebody's else's tool. I reminded myself that in the early days of the St. Lucia Forum, George Odlum would never address a public meeting in my absence or without my assistance. I was to start the meeting if the crowd seemed uncooperative and to calm them down so the others who if they wished to speak would then have an easier time doing so without much heckling. At other times when the crowd was receptive, I would leave the platform and walk amongst the people in order to get a better feel of their mood and the issues that were uppermost on their minds. I often arrived early at the venues at which we intended to speak and helped set up the loud speaker system. I had an easy relationship with the rural folk and I was fluent in Creole which Brother George had not yet mastered, having left for England before his Castries background had properly allowed him to assimilate the language. So Brother George knew and understood better than most, my true value to a political party or to the process of change which we had both been advocating. By 1979, after the elections, he had surrounded himself with certain novices who were themselves in search of attention and their fifteen minutes of fame in Saint Lucia.

At one point Brother George even let it be known from his public pulpit speaking with the aid of a powerful public address system, that it was I who had introduced him to the rural communities on the island and I who had helped him develop his Creole. The unspoken part of that back handed compliment was his implied communication to his listeners that, he on the other hand had helped with my English. That may well have turned out to be true had he not slept so much at the front of the English Literature classes at the time he was a paid teacher at St. Mary's College and poor me, a student who may have seen more than was intended. Thankfully, I never gave anyone reason as far as I am aware, either publicly or privately, to interpret Brother George's words in ways he may have deliberately left open to their fertile imaginations.

By then the stain of division had been set. Brother George was in a very ugly mood and probably for the first time, may have taken a moment to look at his situation objectively. He lashed out at me in print and voice at every opportunity. In turn I demonstrated, perhaps to the surprise of a few impartial observers, some scathing attacks of my own. It was then that I also singlehandedly started the publication of a weekly newspaper for the Labour Party which I called Etoile - Star, and which was published fortnightly by the Voice Publishing Company. I soldiered on bravely as I told myself that I would meet any challenge, overcome any adversary and conquer every obstacle - and finally confront Brother George one-on-one, when the time was right. He knew me well enough and had tested me in the use of firearms on more than one occasion to appreciate what he was up against. I also reminded myself that I had the political legitimacy among the genuine rank and file all over the island which I had earned through hard, honest toil.

Soon after the hurricane of 1980 and as if by an act of divine intervention, the United States Ambassador to Barbados and the East Caribbean - Sally Shelton - paid a visit to Saint Lucia. We met at her invitation and she asked me to consider accepting an offer from her Government under the country's 'International Visitor's Programme', to visit and familiarize myself with her country. The Ambassador explained that the programme was developed in order to give persons, who were potential decision makers (and opinion shapers) from foreign countries, some opportunity to get to know and understand the United States of America better. That familiarization tour was for a period of four or six weeks and the recipient of the invitation had to decide on an option before he or she left home. I chose the four weeks option.

At the time I had hoped I did not seem too enthusiastic at the prospect of getting away from St. Lucia when the offer was made. Frankly, I had actually toyed with taking a break from the pressure and strain of politics, but decided against it when my wife informed me that George Odlum had met her and suggested to her that I should leave the island. To this day, I find the gall it took any political person to stoop so low, very disturbing, indeed. Of course I refused to go anywhere, because to have done so would be to relieve him of the type of criticism he had not hitherto experienced and which I knew he did not like. In my public life I had met many people who seemed very adept at throwing punches but who were very sensitive and touchy to criticisms of any kind. What did I make of such persons? First, I stayed as far away as possible from such persons and then looked at the mirror as often as I could to remind the man in the mirror that Saint Lucia (and the world) could ill-afford such megalomaniacs. It would be wise advice to anyone to desist from dishing-out what they can't handle themselves.

Ambassador Shelton's invitation was a matter of public knowledge and other Saint Lucians including Gus Compton, one of George Odlum's close friends and colleagues had earlier accepted one such invitation from the International Visitors' Programme. The controversy in the Louisy government had by then become such a huge waste of my time that I think it must have taken many prayers from my mother and father, to earn me such an invitation. However, no sooner had I accepted it than all sorts of vicious little whispers began to be spread about me. I was accused of selling out the struggle and abandoning my constituents at a time when they both needed me, although the last part was muted so no one would think me indispensable. The problem with my critics and opponents was that any of them who had been offered the same invitation would have accepted it and disappeared into the dark of night without the least trace. I was by then fully convinced that those who pointed the accusing finger at others were most often the very same persons who carried the darkest secrets and the most dastardly ways of thinking and of seeing. Such whispered rumours were not new to me so I was not surprised by any of it. What was worrying to many people was that the tense situation on the ground seemed ready to explode into violence at any moment. The perfect recipe for more shattered dreams only needed the correct ingredient to set it aglow. Of course the real worry and hurt was that I would not be around to direct traffic or perhaps to be used and then sacrificed as some lamb as Maurice Bishop would soon become in Grenada. I am no born again anything; but I know that I am a very special person and that this was true long before I knew myself.

I had noticed very early in our political relationship that Brother George had almost a macabre sense of the use to which the dead politician ought to be put. For him there were few tasks more deserving of fulfillment than to prepare and deliver a Eulogy at the passing of one who the public loved or who had done some form of national service in his passing. Whether it was at the funeral of Victor Fadlien in Castries, or of Tim Hector in Antigua, George Odlum lived for making speeches. Let him have a large audience to address and then give him a large jug of lemonade to quench his insatiable thirst. Then place a powerful microphone in his hands and that Brother would speak the clothes off any unsuspecting listener, if they stayed long enough to hear him out. Heaven would not permit that he spoke over my dead body - and for that I thank the God to which my father and mother prayed. I have said before that God had known me and loved me long before I ever knew who I was. I believed at the time of Ms. Shelton's invitation He was fully in charge and as He had always promised, if I would take the first step, he would finish the job. I had told Brother George to please get off my back and God had now taken over and was getting me out of Saint Lucia, at least for a short period. He was in charge now and I knew His strong hands had guided me and would continue to do so, no matter what the mission.

When all was said and done it became obvious to even his most ardent supporters that Bother Gorge was not a happy camper. He may have been even unhappy when I left the island for the US on that Visitors programme. I travelled from Saint Lucia via Barbados to Washington, D.C where my briefing and official visit to the USA was to commence.

One would have to be forgiven for thinking that Brother George shared a bond which many believed went far beyond simple politics. His behaviour at the time may even have caused some persons to think that Brother George had some sort of blackmail hanging over my head. Two weeks into my visitor's programme in the U.S. I received a call from Saint Lucia's Ambassador to the United Nations Dr. Barry Auguste, who was in New York, at the time. Dr. Auguste explained that he was calling on behalf of the Minister for Foreign Affairs of Saint Lucia - his immediate boss - who requested that I return home urgently. I could not believe this man would not leave me alone. I took time to explain to Ambassador Auguste the whole situation I faced at home, the reason I accepted the U.S. Government invitation and that he ought never to contact me again regardless of the situation on the island; unless it was from my immediate family. I couldn't believe the lengths which Odlum would go to in order to have his way. Unluckily for him, I was my parents' first child and I was

332

raised to be very independent, believing that once God was with me then I needed no other. I have tried others but I find this the most comforting thought of all, and it's all in my mind, which is the most empowering thought I experience each day.

For all his attempts to woo me back into the leadership struggle, I should have lost all respect for the man. But George Odlum was definitely in a class by himself. Perhaps the reason we made such good synergy was that we both knew that I too was in a league of my own. He also knew that I would have done everything to be rid of the poverty, the ignorance and the backwardness I saw around me on the island. Sadly, the template was torn when the dream became shattered by the parting of the political twins. The reason this island continues to wander without a steady compass is because no one has dared to build a new template and take it at great personal sacrifice to the people at large, cutting across political parties. This glaring lack of sacrifice and commitment is what is lacking in those who set themselves to lead Saint Lucia. It was the Forum that had first taught us to be fishers of men long before the treachery of party politics conspired to dim her focus. There would be no turning back for me until the hands of the great 'I Am' were to bring us back for one final swing before he called Brother George home.

By then of course it was very difficult, if not impossible to reflect on Jane Austen's incisive and probing words that 'there is in every disposition a tendency to some particular evil, a natural defect, which not even the best education, can overcome'. Fortunately or unfortunately politics allows us an opportunity to examine such dispositions (characters) up close and personal if we are so inclined to do. And we ought never to be afraid to use the God given power of our intellect to make judgments about people and situations. It is strongly held by many that God has given us an even greater gift than reason or intellect - I refer to instinct - that little voice within each of us. It is the voice (and gift) of serendipity - the faculty of making happy and unexpected discoveries by accident guided only by our instincts. This, when properly taken into account with the instincts which He has also blessed us with, we can count ourselves ready to go into most, if not all situations. I would therefore not exchange the political experience which George Odlum and I shared for anything in the world. It meant that much to me! Such characters only pass this way but once.

CenacThrows in the Towel

There is, I believe, in every disposition a tendency to some
particular evil, a natural defect, which not
even the best education, can overcome.
Jane Austen: PRIDE and PREJUDICE.

I have often wondered why so many political leaders set themselves up as sacrificial lambs to be soon cast aside, no matter how graciously, often before the end of their tenure. Is it because they share that common natural propensity to some particular evil or defect which their superior education had not overcome? Why do so many people readily accept the accolade of political leadership when they are obviously so unsuited for the task? Is there a hidden, particular evil in each of our dispositions which drives us, even when education warns against it, to accept a role for which we may have been rendered unsuited by nature?

The pressures of the leadership quarrel exerted such forces that soon, even the long and strong bond between Brother George and myself would be rent in twain and cast an emotional darkness over the Labour Party and Government. Soon after the Louisy budget of April 1981 was rejected by the House of Assembly, Prime Minister Louisy resigned. Winston Cenac then emerged as Prime Minister. George Odlum who had long claimed a special friendship with the new Prime Minister also left the Government (and party). Michael Pilgrim and Jon Odlum - the latter, George's younger brother - also resigned from the government but maintained their seats in parliament.

The year 1981 would therefore prove a very crucial and eventful one for the Labour Government and for Saint Lucia. Louisy, who had managed to hold on to office in the face of the seemingly un-ending barrage of attacks and ridicule, had finally gone. The island then seemed free of its national political malaise as the leadership struggle seemed over. By then however, the sharks in the political opposition had smelt blood; their killer instincts were now fully aroused and they began to circle nearer and nearer in ever tightening rings around the prey. The victim had been so weakened from its internal injuries that the practised masters in the art of politics plotted to deliver it the final blow, of death. The words 'Et tu Brute' would now become relevant in this small public space, especially for the likes of the island's Foreign Affairs Minister who just adored English Literature, and understood the circumstances of these words. George Odlum, who had spent so much of his time reading these old English classics, would also be pushed aside to make room for other political actors. These were a strange cocktail of the moneyed few, mixed with the religious right and a sprinkling of ambitious trade unionists - the new guard dogs in the mix. The ruling clique which was used to wielding political power was also closing in and poised to regain power.

On balance, the year 1981 had opened on a positive note for the Labour government. The National Commercial Bank of St. Lucia was officially opened on Saturday, 3rd. January, 1981. At the end of its first official working day, general manager, Mr. Mc. Donald Dixon, expressed satisfaction with the manner which St. Lucians had turned out to support the bank on its first day of business. Dixon predicted that the bank had a great future, if business should continue in the same spirit. Thirty years later, the NCB has been renamed and re-branded: 'The Bank of Saint Lucia' and many Saint Lucians are today proud owners of its ordinary shares. By some estimates, it is now the largest bank on the island. Such an achievement was one of the many visions of the progressives within the St. Lucia Government of 1979 -1982. That group had also attempted to revive the well known 'Sou-Sou', and also encouraged the growth of Credit Unions on the island.

To consolidate the steady gains which the island had achieved, 1981 was declared 'Agriculture Year'. The aim was to bolster fruit and root crop production, and to re-establish the growing and rearing of a wider variety of crops and animals, and to modernize the banana industry. By that declaration the government hoped to increase and spread farm income; to lessen the strangle-hold the banana industry had on the psyche of the farming community and to re-examine proposals for local 'value added' to its primary agriculture product. It was important to take another long hard look at the vital banana industry, which had contributed significantly to economic growth but was also responsible for large scale deforestation of the island. In many instances the felling of perennials impacted negatively on the island's water catchments, thereby decreasing sources of clean water for human consumption. The reckless use of chemicals by some farmers was also polluting steams and rivers, killing off useful species of fish and prawns. The latter were a source of additional protein to some rural folk. It was hoped that the declaration and focus on agriculture throughout 1981, would begin to halt and then reverse the senseless rush to plant bananas on every square inch of available land, as was done in the sixties and early seventies.

By the middle of January of 1981, the St. Lucia Labour Party, as if not satisfied with the problems facing it, met in the town of Soufriere, in an executive committee conclave, for the purpose of querying a visit to Cuba by Senator Frances Michel. She and the government Public Relations Officer, Victor Fadlien had travelled to Havana, Cuba to attend the second congress of the Cuban Communist Party. To some members of the Labour Party it was much ado about nothing. To others it was made to look a very serious crime indeed. The childish, imbecilic comments from certain persons within the executive of the Labour Party had unfortunately set the tone for more internal wrangling and dissention. It was believed that the commotion was meant to divert attention from the political storm which was gathering and threatening to wipe the government away.

Senator Michel had explained herself 'ad nauseam' to the executive committee, but her savage persecution would not stop. Certain persons refused to accept that she had been invited to Cuba as the President of the Farmers and Farm Workers Trade Union of Saint Lucia, to attend a meeting of organized Cuban workers – 'Central Trabajadores de Cuba'. They therefore persisted with their bogus charges, which was to result in her dismissal from the party. What was most despicable to many observers was the sinister manner the mischief makers, plotters and affiliated party hacks were able to silence the only woman who dared to speak out on the ills affecting the society, particularly that which impacted women, at the time. It had not gone unnoticed that certain persons who would not raise a finger to help the poor and distressed, had somehow found themselves in the bosom of the Labour Party – the so-called party of the 'malheureux' - the poor. The hard work of raising a people from poverty to prosperity was never properly explained as persons such as Frances Michel was doing. At the time the idea to let all voices contend, was anathema to the local political culture of the island. Democracy meant little to such persons and they would sooner kill free speech and debate, than be deprived of the opportunity to siphon St. Lucia's scarce resources into private bank accounts overseas. I can speak this way because I am not from Mars and I know well those of whom I speak. Unfortunately, in the matter of her visit to Cuba the party executive found her guilty of a crime meriting her expulsion from the S.L.P. At this, I wondered aloud, what George Charles, the first leader and a founding father of the party, would have thought of those who had done this to Sister Frances.

Senator Michel had built a sizeable following for herself and the Labour Party by her determined and strident campaign for better wages and conditions for farm workers. She was a formidable platform speaker and did not mince words when she felt passionate about a subject. In fact, by her candour and incisive political commentaries she put many more experienced men from both political parties to shame. That may have been her real problem in this largely male-oriented salt fish society. If the Senator's side show of a party trial was meant to distract the party and public from the ever growing crisis of confidence in the government, it did not succeed. After the Senator had appealed to the High Court to quash the decision of the party's executive, passions became even more inflamed. There was now no stopping the storm which would destroy the Labour Governments of both Allan Louisy and Winston Cenac.

The matter finally reached the High Court, with Justice Eardley Glasgow, presiding. Senator Michel was represented by solicitors Vernon Cooper and Victor 'Pic' Lewis. The re-igniting of the leadership quarrel and the flaring up of the Frances Michel affair was too much for the young Senator Kenny Anthony to take. He, who had first resigned as Senator and Minister of Education, had been recalled by Prime Minister Louisy (and Odlum) and he was assured by both men that there would be no more in-fighting and division. It was on the basis of such an understanding and the anticipated calm political waters which were to follow, that Anthony felt compelled to rekindle his Ministerial duties in the Louisy government. Alas, when both Louisy and Odlum broke their promise and the quarrel flared up again, Anthony was again forced to tender his resignation from the Senate and government. His young heart must have palpitated in mournful distress. So he resigned a second time from the Labour government, and later disappeared completely from the island. He was not heard of again for a very long time.

After his second resignation Senator Anthony was replaced in the Senate by Hilary Peter Modeste, who soon took up the duties of Minister of Education and Culture. Modeste had previously served on the Executive Committee of the St. Lucia Teachers Union with Anthony and had also taught for a time at the A Level College, in Saint Lucia. He was an Economist by profession and at one time served the UWP, as Secretary.

In the meantime, more pressure began to mount on Odlum to resign from the government. That pressure came from the rank and file of the party who thought Anthony's second departure was on account of Odlum's stubbornness. Some persons used the print and electronic media to express their concerns on the rekindled leadership struggle. Still others used paint and graffiti to mark their displeasure on public buildings and on the streets in towns and villages. The campaign to remove the government from office seemed more organized and determined.

In a piece to the Voice newspaper, one writer described Odlum's tactics as 'a tired conundrum' and wondered whether the politician was 'losing his intellectual vitality'. In the midst of the side show of charges and counter charges, of resignations and appointments, the hands of the clock were moving inexorably toward 'D-day' - 'Destruction Day' - for Louisy and his government.

The 1981- 82 budget was down for presentation on Monday 6th. April, 1981. The rumour mills were working overtime in anticipation of the political turmoil that was bound to ensue from the budget debate. One rumour was circulated that none of the five official UWP opposition members of parliament would support the budget. Neither would the Odlum brothers and Michael Pilgrim, it was claimed. By then, I had made it abundantly clear that I had no wish to bring down the government, and to that end had long dissociated myself from the constant bickering and attacks on it. Yet I was on the horns of a dilemma because I also thought it was time for Louisy to pass the baton to some other, more dynamic person within the government.

In a private conversation with Prime Minister Louisy, who needed my vote in order to pass his budget, I found him too dodgy, cagy and reluctant to openly level with me on the plans, if any, which he had for reshuffling the Cabinet, assuming his budget succeeded. That did it for me. I made no commitments to anyone and on budget day no one knew for certain where my vote would be cast. Some persons apparently did not pay close attention to my independent spirit. Others continued to see only what they wanted to in the situation the country faced at the time.

Word got out that Odlum was holding secret talks with the official opposition - meaning John Compton. As if to signal their intentions, George Odlum, Jon Odlum and Michael Pilgrim, stayed away from parliament during Louisy's budget presentation. However, there was a full House when the time came for the question to be put and for the votes to be counted for its passage or rejection. Before the fateful vote was taken, certain government parliamentarians were interviewed by the private media. The following is a sample of three comments from government members, at the time. Gregor Mason, Member for Gros-Islet: 'If there is any member of the House who is thinking of not supporting the budget, he should be out'. Michael Pilgrim, Member for Castries North/East: 'The budget is a good one; but does the government of Allan Louisy have the will to implement it'. Evans Calderon, Member for Choiseul: 'The U.W.P. came to power in 1964 by the treachery of two Labour M. P's. It will not happen again'.

When I was asked what I thought of the budget proposals, the sentiments I expressed then, were not dissimilar to those of Michael Pilgrim. Allan Louisy's budget of 23rd. April 1981was not passed by the House. Louisy announced that same day that he was stepping down from the office of Prime Minister. He understood that convention dictated he had to go after his failed budget, and his departing was a relief to many. It relieved the tension which had dogged the island for some time. But the island still had a long way to go to recover. It should also be noted here that Louisy could have advised the Governor General to dissolve Parliament and call fresh elections, but he did not exercise that constitutional option. The man therefore played hard ball with his political opponents until the very end. The opposition no doubt continued to sense a weakness in the government and was determined to settle for nothing less than the dissolution of parliament and the holding of new elections. They threatened to table a no-confidence motion in Parliament. As strange as it may seem, Odlum and his new party (the PLP) were all over the electronic media claiming they did not wish to bring down the government - just Prime Minister Louisy. But for many Labour stalwarts it was then too little, too late.

After the resignation of Prime Minister Louisy another rumour took wings that I, Peter Josie, was tipped to become Prime Minister. The Voice newspaper of April 19, 1981 headlined in bold caption: 'Government faces new crisis'; 'Josie rumoured to be next PM'. After Louisy, names of various Labour Parliamentarians, from the remaining nine, floated about as possible replacement. Winston Cenac who had earlier resigned as Attorney General was one of those. At one point I had the support of eight labour M.P's, including Cenac himself. Remy Lesmond the ninth member needed for a majority, was wavering. During a closed-door meeting at the Prime Minister's official residence, Lesmond left ostensibly to make a telephone call in a room next door. When he rejoined the group, the discussion was reopened and Cenac got the nod to replace Louisy. Winston Cenac therefore became the third Prime Minister of an independent Saint Lucia. That telephone call by Lesmond and the directive he must have received to support Cenac I later learnt came from a certain financer who had supported his campaign.

While Cenac and the Labour Party were trying to constitute themselves into a new Executive (Cabinet of Ministers) the official opposition along with their friends in the Chamber of Commerce and the Trade Union

Movement were planning political moves of their own. It was however, to the Christian Church Council which the Leader of the Opposition – John Compton - had officially turned, in order to seek help in bringing about fresh general elections. Compton had written to the Churches, seeking their intervention and soliciting their aid to have the Governor General dissolve Parliament and call fresh elections.

The acting Governor General at the time was none other than Boswell Williams, from the well known and respected Williams family of Vieux-Fort who were all staunch Labourites. The opposition had never supported the appointment of Boswell Williams as Governor General. The reasons were historical and may have had to do more with personal differences over Williams's alleged purchase of Crown lands at the time he was employed as a senior civil servant, in Saint Lucia.

The Christian churches for their part, perhaps remembering the early radical Compton and the absurd things which he had once written about certain sisters of the Church, using the pen-name 'Jack Spaniard' were disinclined to support his prayer and petition. Their reply to his letter could not have been impeached on any ground. Furthermore, they pointedly warned the opposition that any change of government and the calling of elections must only be done in the manner provided for by the St. Lucia Constitution. Perhaps this was a veiled warning that events in Grenada which led to the forceful overthrow of the government would not be tolerated in fair 'Helen of the West' - Saint Lucia. To counter the moves against the Labour government, I decided to keep our supporters' spirits up, by regular updates via the electronic media, using the government public relations office. One such media reported that; 'Josie announces that the dark political cloud which had engulfed St. Lucia for over a year was about to be lifted, and that a new government would soon be formed'. At the time there was still a determined contest of wills to break the government and to call elections, as opposed to keeping hope alive. Completing the five-year-term in office and aiming to contest the next elections on an equal footing with the opposition, seemed a desirable political goal for the Labour government.

The Leader of the Opposition could not have been too distraught over the 'safe' diplomatic response he received to his letter, from the Christian Council. The Chamber of Commerce was by then quietly working behind the scenes with certain trade unions to force the government out of office. Soon, the Civil Service Association (CSA) which had no dispute with government, called its members out on strike. The C.S.A. threatened it would remain on strike until the Parliament was dissolved. To rub salt into the wound, the association also announced that it was seeking support for its stand from other trade unions on the island. At the same time, the Chamber of Commerce also announced a one-day-shut-down (strike) of its business houses in Castries. The atmosphere was becoming heated and tense once again.

All this of course was political theatre - the stuff of real politics. One should note here that George Odlum was at that point no longer in the picture. He had then been pushed off centre stage by the conservative right. John Compton and his associates were now showing their true colours after Odlum's preliminary weakening of the government. Feeling cornered, and in search of a path to blast a way out, I hit back at the Chamber in a fit of fury threatening to burn down the whole bloody stinking town with all the cynical and sexually depraved political perverts in it. I was aware of my stridency and I wished at that point to make those whose only selfish focus was personal profits, pay. Even Odlum, the man whom many believed could not have been outdone in the art of 'trash-talking' and the issuing of veiled threats, took me to task for the threat against Castries. Of course that was a laughing matter coming from the man many believed had been responsible for the 'Plywood city' situation nearly two years earlier. Alas, good sense prevailed. There was no bloodshed, no riots, and no violence as some naysayers had predicted. After all was said and done Castries continued on its dysfunctional, hypocritical and rodent-infested ways, perhaps needing stronger medicine to clean and beautify it each passing day.

As tension grew and loose words were bandied aimlessly about, a new cabinet was formed under the luckless and irresolute Winston Cenac. A 'new' Labour government continued to limp along in office, with the blind appearing to lead those who would not see. The Cenac government lazed around in office until its leader was finally manoeuvered to the edge of the proverbial precipice where he was then persuaded to jump, taking his government and supporters with him. These had been the hands and voices of those who Cenac thought were friends and gentlemen. It was their way of having him throw in the towel in order to clear the way for fresh general elections.

It was therefore by such deceit and Machiavellian sleight of hand, that Prime Minister Cenac's resignation, some six months after he was sworn into the office, reached the desk of the Governor General. The political sharks, who better understood the art of politics, cunning and deceit, had prevailed once more.

Before continuing, it would be useful to quickly review the formation of the Cenac Cabinet and the election of a new Speaker, for the House. Speaker Clarence Rambally, apparently growing fed-up with the continuing uproar and disunity in the House, resigned in disgust. The record of Parliamentary Debate of the Second House, Third Session (1981-1982) dated 11 January 1982, reveals the following make-up of the House of Assembly:

Prime Minister	-	*Winston Cenac*
Minister of Trade, Tourism and Foreign Affairs	-	*Peter Josie*
Minister of Agriculture, Lands, Fisheries	-	*Gregor Mason*
Minister for Communications and Works	-	*Remy Lesmond*
Minister of Health	-	*Bruce Williams*
Minister for Legal Affairs and Attorney General	-	*Kenneth Foster*
Minister without portfolio	-	*Allan Louisy*
Minister without portfolio	-	*Cecil H. Lay*
Member for Choiseul & Fond-St. Jacques	-	*Evans Calderon*
Member for Castries South	-	*Jon Odlum*
Member for Castries South-East	-	*George Odlum*
Member for Castries North-East	-	*Michael Pilgrim*
Leader of the Opposition	-	*John G.M. Compton*
Member for Central Castries	-	*William G. Mallet*
Member for Castries North-West (Babonneau)	-	*Allan Bousquet*
Member for Micoud North	-	*Rodney Jn. Baptiste*
Member for Dennery North	-	*Ferdinand Henry*

When the listed Honourable gentlemen met to elect a Speaker of the House, Prime Minister Cenac nominated Donald Clarence Alcee, an Electrical Engineer. The opposition United Workers Party nominated former Speaker Wilfred St. Clair Daniel. Not to be outdone, George Odlum, the putative leader of the PLP, rose to nominate Donald Blanchard (alias, 'Dockie') – described by a newspaper as 'a noted destitute and drunk, who roams the streets of Castries' – as their choice for Speaker. It was noted that the move by the PLP was designed to ridicule Donald Alcee, who shared the first given name with 'Dockie'. Compton, the consummate political animal, sensing the ridiculous debasement of the process of selection of a Speaker immediately withdrew his nominee, after hearing Odlum's. Alcee was duly elected Speaker. Later, the UWP boycotted his taking of the Oath of Allegiance in protest over his appointment. It was believed that the opposition had engineered the resignation of Speaker Rambally as a time wasting device and also to prove that Rambally had by then switched allegiances from Labour to UWP. In the following elections of 1982 the former Speaker was a candidate of the United Workers Party, in the Castries South/East constituency. He won that seat too, soundly defeating George Odlum of the PLP and Kenneth Foster of the SLP.

The rearranging of the government and the election of Speaker Alcee, may have finally settled the quarrel in the government to remove it from office. But then there was even more political drama unfolding as Compton and Odlum now found themselves in an unholy alliance - a sort of marriage of convenience - to unseat the government even as they jostled amongst themselves for supremacy. As the opposition persevered in its destructive path to glory, the Cenac Cabinet sought to pursue perhaps a little tentatively, in the view of some, with the business of government.

By August that year, (1981) plans were well in train for the hosting of the Organization of American States General Assembly in Saint Lucia. Critics of the government did their best to derail this hugely important morale booster for the country and the government. The OAS conference was to be chaired by none other than your humble servant, who had been sworn in as the Minister for Foreign Affairs in the reconstituted Labour government, under Prime Minister Cenac.

Throughout my very active political life and up to the hosting of that OAS conference, I had played along – not always happily - with friends who wished to label and place me neatly into somebody's handy political tool kit. After the formation of the Cenac government, I made up my mind to demonstrate that I was a free thinker; a free spirit which was nurtured on self-confidence and love from my family, my school and my church leaders. My earlier display of humility may have been seen as weakness by those who wished to see in me only the images which their own pitiful little lives were reflecting.

The OAS meeting presented me with an opportunity to demonstrate once and for all, both my independent spirit and my professionalism in chairing such a huge conference. It was also an opportunity to highlight both my competence and political bearing within an international setting. I wanted to prove to the naysayers that I was unafraid and not intimidated by such high company or by the barbs of the jealous mendicants that were little more than an embarrassment to the country, at that time. Several regional and world leaders were expected to gather on the island for that auspicious OAS conference. It was perhaps to deny me the opportunity to show a high profile leadership quality, and the fear that my performance as chair of that meeting may help to turn the fortunes of government around that the opposition tried so hard to derail that conference. But I would have none of it. Thankfully, I got the full support of Prime Minister Cenac and other Ministers of his government - including that of Allan Louisy and Cecil Lay, who no longer sat in cabinet.

As I went through my paces in the new Ministry of Foreign Affairs, I continued to do all I could for my country, my party and the constituents who had elected me to Parliament. I kept reminding myself that this was a gathering of men who were all sinners and who at some point had fallen short of what their people (and God) expected of them. Armed with such knowledge, I was to be careful that none of the pomp and ceremony, including the respect which mighty presidents paid to the chair, should ever enter my head and lead me into the immodesty of arrogance. I had always acknowledged to myself that the struggle was never about me, personally. I was merely the vehicle which was available at the time through which the peoples' struggles for justice, education and progress could be driven forward. Neither was the work about building a political party, although that would have been a welcome off shoot of my involvement in party politics, at the time. The whole effort therefore in one's public and political life was about building and developing one's country and its citizens.

As the island prepared to host the OAS conference towards the end of 1981, the media, chose to focus on the attempts by the opposition to discredit Prime Minister Cenac. It was obvious that the media did more than report the news; quite often it also invented it. It appeared bent on assisting the opposition to probe for some personal weakness in Prime Minister Cenac. It took a macabre sort of pleasure in reporting an apparent miscalculation by Prime Minister Cenac, in calling for a lunch break during the debate in the House of a money bill. At the time both Evans Calderon and Allan Louisy were out of the Chamber. Prime Minister Cenac did not have the requisite number of votes to pass a resolution, in their absence. His motion for a short adjournment was rudely denied when the opposition of eight voted against it. Such childish conduct would have received the treatment it deserved from a more mature and intelligent press. But no one bothered to report that voting on a motion to adjourn a sitting of the House was never answered with a no vote. That was not how the parliamentary system was designed to function. But don't tell this to an unhappy and rebellious pen in search of a cause, to avenge its psychological battles. Of course Louisy and Calderon soon returned to the chamber and the House was adjourned, but by then the neophytes with pen and paper in hand already had their fun, reporting on the incident. Soon after that incident (August 1981), the opposition was at it again. Two months later, October, to be precise, it tabled a motion of 'no confidence' in the government. It prepared a 'shopping list' of some sixteen charges, three or four of which reached back to the time when Michael Pilgrim and the Odlum brothers were a part of the Labour government. That motion when presented, debated and voted on, was defeated by nine votes to eight.

The outcome must have frustrated the opposition out of its wits. It had once again been denied a small toe-hold within the nine elected members who formed the cabinet - and government. At least three of the opposition charges in that motion are note-worthy. First, the charge of 'ineffectual leadership' was that which Odlum had at first criticized Allan Louisy of, in an earlier address to the Chamber of Commerce. The second was 'the consideration involved in a preliminary acceptance of a proposal for the establishment of a Casino', on the island. That idea had first been raised by Premier Compton, in his search to diversify the tourism economy. The third charge concerned 'the loss of private sector confidence'. In a moment of inspired incisiveness, (and bravery) Prime Minister Cenac accused the private sector of inefficiency and indifference. He said they were obsessed with distribution (buying low and selling high) while opportunities for production of needed goods and services went a-begging. Such an accusation was bound to anger his local fifteen-per-centers, as George Odlum had labelled them.

Before the 'confidence' debate the corruption charges and other similar indictments by the opposition were struck off the list of resolutions to be tabled before the House. The Speaker had used his power under section 23 and 36 of the Standing Orders of the House, to do so. One final point of note was that the 'confidence motion' was brought, not by John Compton, the Leader of the Opposition, but by George Mallet, the representative for Central Castries and deputy leader of Compton's party - UWP.

Towards the end of 1981, civil servants were becoming more restive and militant. They began issuing threats against the government and stipulating unilateral deadlines by which their demands were to be met. They made threatening demands for retroactive pay, and actively baited the government for a fight. They 'directed' that the government should not under any conditions agree to the International Monetary Fund (IMF) draconian structural adjustment schemes. 'Stridency' and 'revolutionary militancy' were too soft to describe those who led the CSA at the time. One insider likened them to paid servants of the opposition and Chamber, bent only on removing the Labour government from office.

Trade union agitation was timed to escalate as the OAS Conference drew nearer. Notwithstanding the loud talk from our friends in the unions, the OAS conference was shaping up to be a huge success. However, more agitation was to follow from the unions and the opposition. Some among them still wanted to see the conference fail. Those who opposed the government seemed to do all they could to see that important conference fail. The government for its part, had to work very hard to ensure the opposition did not have its way and that the government was not merely clinging to power, but working. Of course those who were bent on frustrating me personally were also setting themselves up for failure and disappointment which then seemed the lot of so many otherwise useful politicians. In summary one could say that the OAS conference turned out to be a huge success and a sort of personal triumph for me, and Prime Minister Winston Cenac. We had refused to bend to any opposition demands and we had emerged triumphant on that occasion.

By then no one could get me to cower or play along with their little outdated, conservative agendas. Their most virulent political attacks fell off me like water off a duck's back. I remain convinced that my political opponents would have supported anyone else apart from a progressive and radical, for the post of Prime Minister of St. Lucia. I have often wondered whether that had been the paid purpose of those who ingratiated themselves within the inner circle of the Cenac Government. Perhaps I was also ruled out as being too frequently unsmiling and serious.

Not satisfied with their failed attempts in the House of Assembly, the opposition began to target and attack individual Ministers. Their nefarious plans first chose Prime Minister Cenac, believing him the most vulnerable of the nine. He was then accused of fraternizing with a pretty young maiden in the civil service establishment. They sweetened their rumour by quoting an alleged donation of several thousand East Caribbean dollars from him to her. Some even volunteered that the ten thousand dollars he had allegedly given to her was for a cup of coffee and a croissant. Of course such charges were never proved and in any event few people had taken the charges seriously. All it did was to prove to what low level the earlier high standard of public debate (especially at the time of the St. Lucia Forum) had fallen.

Not surprisingly, the atmosphere remained charged with accusations of infidelity and immorality. Soon after the money accusation, a friend of the government observed to Prime Minister Cenac in my presence, that he ought to be wary of certain friends because they were so wicked they made Satan cringe and run when he saw them approaching. Even Satan feared losing his throne to such superlative evil. So disgusting and vicious were the personal attacks against the Prime Minister at the time that they seemed to have affected his family. I recall seeing his dear spouse sprinkling what I assumed to be 'blessed' (Holy-water of the Roman Catholic faith) and other suitable concoctions, in each corner of the Prime Minister's official residence, when I visited him there. This action I assumed was in keeping with the island's cultural practice of warding off evil spirits which then threatened to overwhelm even the peace and quiet of the Prime Minister's official residence.

Not satisfied with their unproven charges against the leader of the country, they came to my home one evening and set fire to a small Korean-made car, belonging to the Ministry of Agriculture which, at the time was parked there. The resulting fire damaged my house, burning off the wooden frames of windows, breaking glass from both door and windows and costing in excess of sixteen thousand dollars in repairs. No one has ever apologized to me or taken responsibility for setting that fire. I have therefore never been compensated for the material loss which I suffered at the time, or the waste of valuable time which that political fire cost me. Neither have I winced or cried aloud. No one was ever arrested and charged for the offence. I pray that my two young children who were both asleep at the time have by now overcome the psychological trauma of that incident.

There is a saying on this island: 'Man proposes but God disposes' and although some have made politics their religion, I continue to pray that they will see the evil of their ways before too long. There are to my mind few things which are more painful than to be removed from one's accustomed comforts, and into something new. The inculcation of new ideas for persons stubbornly holding onto the past is equally difficult and painful. Yet, there are few things more rewarding, more healing and more transforming than letting go of the old and letting God guide us to a new place. That applies equally to a person as it does a nation. Yet it is very difficult for people who have learnt dependency to let go and to become independent. In my books, it is often far better to be a dishwasher in a highly trained and well motivated army that is well paid and looked after, than to be a general in some indisciplined killing gang which some leaders prefer to call an army.

Christmas 1981 was almost stolen from the church-loving people on the island by certain of their friends in opposition. However, the goodwill and 'Christian' charity of the St. Lucia people prevailed. The nation enjoyed a happy and peaceful Christmas even though the malcontents in the society grumbled between food and drink, as they went from house to house. Christmas had passed and it was now 1982. Not surprisingly, the year opened with even more political drama, than that which marked the end of 1981. No matter how hard the Cenac government tried, the opposition would not let up its protests. Their constant agitation, protests, street drama and excesses were now threatening to overwhelm law and order on the island. Public political meetings, street demonstrations and other forms of protests were constantly being planned, or were in progress, in the capital or elsewhere. Thankfully, there was always more drama, suspense, and even a little occasionally stolen comedy, than tragedy and destruction.

When the House met on Monday 11 January, 1982 prayers were said by Reverend Patrick Anthony, of the Castries Roman Catholic Parish church. Parliamentarians prayed and seemed committed to invoking divine intervention for a better, more peaceful year. However, the second prayers had ended chaos broke out again in the House of Assembly. Soon after the Speaker had wished everyone a 'Happy New Year', the Leader of the Opposition stood to enquire whether a Bill entitled 'Legislative Council (Contracts with Government) (Disqualification) (Amendment) Ordinance was down for all three stages of debate, at that meeting. The Speaker indicated that the matter would be dealt with at its appropriate place on the Order Paper. The opposition was not satisfied with that reply. Prime Minister Cenac then stood to explain that the resolution would be presented by the Attorney General, because it dealt with a legal matter. That explanation did not appease the opposition, either. If anything, it made matters worse. Compton was now supported by George Odlum, member for Castries South/East, and leader of the new political party. Odlum's PLP seemed at the time an unwelcome appendage to Compton's opposition, UWP.

Observing that Odlum was electronically wired and carried a hidden microphone on his person intended for outside transmission, Evans Calderon, the Member for Choiseul/Fond-St. Jacques, immediately sprang to his feet, to inform the Speaker what Odlum was up to. More confusion followed after that discovery. At the time, I could also have informed Calderon and the house that this was not Odlum's first time at such childish recklessness. He once attended cabinet wired with a similar tape recording device hoping to catch his Ministerial colleagues, in a compromising dialogue regarding the Hess Oil deal. There is at least one senior journalist on the island who can verify this.

Upon Calderon's discovery, a heated discussion followed. The calculated mischief intended for the House of Assembly that day, soon became public knowledge. By then, it appeared the Odlum side-show was stealing the spot-light from Compton. But the old fox was too cunning by half, and would not allow Odlum to steal the show. At the time these two seemed engaged in a sort of Indian war dance for turf, even as they supported each other against the government. As soon as the little hidden microphone episode was over, the opposition refocused on the point raised by Leader of the Opposition. A heated 'legal' argument ensued.

Several other heated exchanges then followed between Attorney General Kenneth Foster, on the one hand and Leader of the Opposition John Compton, on the other. Compton, who had initially refused to give way to Foster on a point of order, soon did so. No one knew for certain the reason Compton gave way. However, before Foster could explain the point of order, the Member for Castries North/East, (Michael Pilgrim) also stood up, on another point of order, to challenge the very presence of Foster, in the House of Assembly. Pilgrim accused Foster - the former Minister for Communications and Works - of not returning advances to the Treasury on overseas trips which he had earlier taken as a Minister of the Government. Such prompt returns-on-advances, Pilgrim argued, were an important requirement under the financial rules and regulations of the country. Such rules, when disobeyed, should disqualify a Member from sitting in Parliament, Pilgrim insisted. In the meantime, yet another side issue was threatening to subsume the procedural matter which the Leader of the Opposition had first raised. On sensing a third threat to derail his personal (and official show, and responsibility) the Leader of the Opposition rose and called for an adjournment to the proceedings. He also proposed that the Speaker inform His Excellency the Governor General, of the gravity of the situation. He said he was certain that the advice which the A.G. would in turn give to His Excellency would be 'dissolution of this House, and a calling of new elections'. The master craftsman was in his element, and his show would not be taken over by pretenders, even ones claiming political sagacity. Soon thereafter, more confusion followed.

After a long and heated exchange between the Speaker and the Member for Castries South/East, (George Odlum) the Speaker finally moved that the House be adjourned. The time was 11.30am – an hour or so after the House had opened with prayers. Not to be outdone, the Leader of the Opposition again stood up, this time to challenge the moving of the motion for adjournment by the Speaker. The Opposition Leader advised the chair of the difference between 'adjourning' a sitting of the House, and 'suspending' it. He then observed that the Speaker was authorized to do the latter; not the former.

Finally, Prime Minister Cenac stood and proposed the adjournment, saving further bickering and avoiding embarrassment to Speaker Donald Alcee. More excitement was to follow Cenac's proposal for an adjournment. The following is a verbatim copy of how 'Hansard' - the word-by-word recording of the business of Parliament, described the moments which followed after the question was put for adjourning the House. "At this point in time there is great disorder and general chaos with plenty blowing of whistles in the House of Assembly. The Mace is snatched from the Sergeant-at-Arms and thrown about the Chamber". As this is an account of events which I witnessed as a sitting Member of Parliament, I should add for the sake of clarity and precision that, when the Mace – the symbol of Imperial Majesty and Power in Parliament - as described by 'Hansard' was being 'thrown about', it changed hands only among the PLP - the breakaway faction of the Labour government and certain of its well placed supporters, within the chamber. These PLP supporters had been seated in the visitors' gallery, mere ten or eleven metres from the action.

'Hansard's' report of the incident with the throwing about of the Mace in Parliament ended this way: "The Sergeant-at-Arms tries to retrieve the Mace. During this display of disrespect, the Prime Minister and Members of the Government benches leave the Chamber. After a great degree of difficulty the Mace is retrieved and the Speaker leaves the Chamber, preceded by the Sergeant-at-Arms, bearing the Mace. The House is adjourned in this chaotic fashion at 10.58 am to 11.30a.m. At 11.25 a.m. the Clerk re-enters the Chamber and announces on instructions from the Prime Minister that the House is adjourned 'sine die'.

Throughout that episode with the 'Mace' I remained glued to my seat, transfixed and detached and thanking God quietly, that I had not been chosen to lead the government when Louisy left. What earlier had seemed a curse, I now counted a blessing. I think I learnt that day that it is possible to remain quiet and detached from events in which one is also deeply and emotionally involved. A local journal reporting on the incident in the House of Assembly was headlined 'Much Heat in the House'. It reported that the government of Prime Minister Winston Cenac had suffered a near humiliating defeat at the hands of the opposition that day. It also observed that the newly elected Speaker seemed to have had no control over the sharp exchanges between the government and the opposition, during that sitting.

For those who may have questioned where Peter Josie was during all of this, let me repeat: I was there, in Parliament and I saw and heard everything that happened that day. I also understood and believed what took place that day, had little to do with the progress of the people of Saint Lucia. I chose to remain in my seat and be quiet because I interpreted the shenanigans in the House as the work of paid agents whose duty it was to keep the long suffering masses of people ignorant, backward, and powerless. At the moment I interpreted the display in the House of Assembly as the work of desperate men using the relative safety of the chamber to show they were bit actors who could play the part of rogue, ruffian and unmannerly bare-footed scum. It may also have been a planned side show to demonstrate to the gathered crowd how cunning and 'politically astute' each of the mimic actors in that said parliament had become. Unfortunately, other than Willie James and one or two other journalists, few people expressed any revulsion at the uncouth display, then or afterward.

Before its final fall from grace, there was a time soon after Cenac was sworn in as Prime Minister that it appeared that his government would survive another year or two in office. But that was not to be. Many observers believed that Prime Minister Cenac was treated even more harshly than his predecessor in office - Allan Louisy. Cenac's former friend and confidant, George Odlum, - a man with whom he had spent many happy hours in Britain, eating, drinking and reminiscing about life back home – was now his harshest critic. It was perhaps Odlum's persistent and vociferous criticism, not to mention the ten thousand dollars which his Crusader newspaper claimed the Prime Minister had given to the young civil servant to purchase coffee and a croissant which may have finally got the better of poor Cenac. The Odlum and Compton double barrelled blows seemed to have unhinged his flagging confidence, breaking his spirit and finally felling his government. If we add to this the persistent corruption charges levelled at Ministers of the government - carrying out private 'notaries' work in public office - then clearly, we had a poisoned cocktail which was bound to render a weakened Prime Minister useless - perhaps a relic of history, even before he finally threw in the towel.

Earlier, I did not bother detailing which politicians in that chaotic sitting of the House had actually disturbed the Mace, threatening to throw it completely out the chamber. I have since been reminded that a factual, blow by blow description of that particular drama has been written by Willie James, a freelance journalist working on the island at the time. I have read James' description in 'St. Lucia's Turmoil', a small booklet which he produced soon after the incident and which I fully concur is an accurate account of the 'Mace-throwing' event.

Later when I reviewed the unkind attacks on Prime Minister Cenac, especially in the Crusader newspaper, with its cartoon caricature of him as 'Count Snacula' I fondly recalled the morning many years before he became Prime Minister, when I was awoken at four o'clock by George Odlum at my Black Mallet Gap home, to say that the police were seeking to have us arrested. He suggested that I get dressed and come with him to a hiding place which he had arranged and where the police would not easily find us. I did not recall committing any offence for which I had to dodge the police, or which might merit an arrest. But, I judged that in the political climate which existed at the time (Compton was then Premier of Saint Lucia) anything was possible. I therefore took Odlum at his word, and hurriedly dressed, leaving the comfort of my bed, for an unknown destination. It was only after we had driven for ten minutes or so, on the Bocage to Babonneau road, that I was told we were headed to Bois d'Orange via Union and Corinth, to the house of a close friend. It turned out we were headed for the residence of Winston Cenac, Attorney-at-Law. Cenac was a St. Lucian by birth, a former Attorney General of Dominica and Grenada, who had on at least one occasion, acted as Governor there, by appointment of Her Majesty in Council. From all accounts, he had a fairly lucrative law practice in St. Lucia at the time he took us into hiding at his house and long before he entered party politics. We stayed there the entire day, and left very late that night. We showered and had meals there. We were well looked after during the day, after Cenac had left home for work. That night we were happily transported by armed policemen in unmarked police vehicles and driven to our respective homes. To this day, I have not been given a satisfactory explanation of the events which had prompted 'Brother' George to believe we were to invade Winston Cenac's private domain, seeking refuge from the police at that ungodly hour of the morning. Why should one run for political cover at an hour when most decent law abiding citizens were fast asleep, unless one was involved in much more than simple electoral politics? At the time, only the SSU patrolled in their armed 'cage' seeking known and dangerous felons. I think it is true to say that even our bitterest opponents did not consider us clients of that deadly Para-military group within the local police force. From my recollections, neither Cenac nor Odlum ever raised the incident of that early morning's refuge at Cenac's place at Bois d'Orange.

Other events it appeared had conspired to erode confidence in the Cenac government. For example, by the end of January 1982, over 1000 telephone subscribers in the Castries area had signed a petition protesting against payments for new telephone rates which they alleged were unilaterally imposed by Cable & Wireless, the lone telephone company on the island, at the time. It was also reported that certain cows, which were not strays, were set loose at Choc public cemetery, near Vigie airport in Castries, wreaking havoc, destroying graves of loved ones. Sensing the ugly mood which was building up in the country, the Voice editorial at the end of January 1982, cautioned "No Return to 1979". But the paper need not have worried. Neither Michael Pilgrim nor Jon Odlum could, or would fill the large gaping hole left next to 'the Big Brother'- George Odlum, by my departure. There would therefore be no 'Labour' victory, following the party's split, no matter how the hypocritical PLP tried, for a reunion.

Many were of the view that Prime Minister Winston Cenac faced more severe opposition pressure than Louisy ever did. It is fair to say too that he was literally hounded out of office and tricked out of the game in a manner which may not have worked against the cunning and astute Louisy. It seemed strange to many people that Cenac should have caved in so readily after the fight Louisy had put up against his parliamentary opponents.

The final moments in office of the Labour government are instructive. The party's central executive committee had arranged an indoor meeting at Kimatrai Hotel, in Vieux-Fort, for Sunday, 17 January, 1982. The purpose of the meeting was to fashion a united response to the growing call by the Chamber of Commerce, the Opposition, and the Trade Unions (and Odlum's PLP) for the Labour government to go. The Kimatrai meeting also aimed to bolster the courage of Prime Minister Cenac and declare a tough stance against his political opponents. The meeting planned to ask the Prime Minister to hold the fort, and not give in to opposition's demands for his resignation.

Before the fall of the Cenac Government, the campaign by the unions and the Chamber of Commerce for Compton to return to office had begun. Local and respected journals on the island apparently thought nothing of printing lies and complete fabrication, believing such would help their cause. At one point a local newspaper reported that Guyanese military personnel were in St. Lucia - presumably to help the Cenac government stay in power, by force of arms – a charge which was completely fabricated, and false. Not a shred of evidence was ever offered to support these wild allegations. The paper also said that the government was gradually setting the stage for civil war; another damning and slanderous lie.

As if taking his cue from the paper's editorial outburst, one Steve Charles, writing in the same newspaper shouted: 'Go now, Mr. Cenac' and Steve did not even bother to say please – a common courtesy amongst well-mannered Saint Lucians at the time. To add insult to injury, no one seemed to be asking kindly anymore, or addressing the government with any respect or decorum. Each call for Cenac to demit office now had an edge to it. Gentle persuasion was a thing of the past. Political activists were now treating the Prime Minister as if he was some moron, lacking understanding, even when it became clear that he would throw in the towel.

I have often wondered what might have happened if at an unguarded moment of such overwhelming political pressure on the Prime Minister, a sudden rush of adrenalin had created a temporary insanity, infusing the gentle Cenac with a bull's reckless urge, to attack and fight. Even now, many years later, his few remaining friends still think he would have earned the admiration and respect of party stalwarts, seeking vengeance, had he done something - anything - to cause his opponents to think a second time before disrespecting him. Had he done 'the-bull-in-a-China-shop act', of which so many lesser mortals have been accused in one country or the other, he may have been remembered as a hero for some daring political act.

But rather than attend the planned indoor meeting at Vieux-Fort, Cenac was inveigled to attend talks in Castries with the same persons who were plotting to get him and his government out of office. Compton, Odlum, the

Churches, the Chamber of Commerce and the Trade Unions had made no bones about their intention. The political jackals had timed their meeting to perfection. They emerged from every dark hidden closet in Castries and after threatening and terrorizing Prime Minister Cenac in sham negotiations they drove him to Government House to seal the deal, forcing him to tender his resignation (and that of his government) to the acting Governor General. Prime Minister Cenac agreed to have his government replaced by an interim one to which it was agreed four of his Ministers would be appointed. He did this without any sort of consultation with his colleagues in Cabinet, except perhaps Remy Lesmond who at the time seemed assigned by his handlers to stick to Cenac like a wet T-shirt. While all this was taking place at Government House in Castries, the central executive committee of the SLP waited patiently for Cenac to arrive for the scheduled meeting, in Vieux-Fort. Only after he had resigned and his government was no more did I receive a telephone call from Remy Lesmond - he seemed in love with the telephone - to say that Cenac had just thrown in the towel. It did not take long for this bit of expected bad news to sink into the collective consciousness of those who had gathered for the executive meeting. For a moment I was at a loss for the reason that telephone call came to me, and not to the Secretary or Chairman of the party. I quickly realized however, that someone must have asked Lesmond to make that call. He was the same person who had altered the balance of voting in Cenac's favour, after Louisy had resigned. I was never able to detect what, if anything, Lesmond derived from those crucial telephone calls. I contented myself with the thought that whosoever was directing Lesmond's telephone fingers may have had good reason to suppose that I would be around to pick up the pieces when the party and government lay shattered and broken in early 1982. The words of Ms Austen in 'Pride and Prejudice' come to mind again, at this point. 'There is, I believe, in every disposition a tendency to some particular evil, a natural defect, which not even the best education, can overcome'. To which I can only add: 'Better an enemy you know than a friend who is jealous of you'.

It was noteworthy that the executive, which was waiting that Sunday at Kimatrai, when the news came, all agreed that Cenac's absence had spelt bad news for the party. I listened with interest and growing cynicism as I wondered what I had done to find myself among such cluelessness, such conservative, fear filled people, and such emptiness. My heart went out to poor Winston Cenac when I heard that he had thrown in the towel. Yet my mind was also thinking: 'easy come, easy go'. He had always seemed so clueless and out-of-touch in the arena of politics unlike the law, into which he seemed to have fitted as though it had been cut for him. Having been battered and abused by the political animals he once considered friends and colleagues, his hasty resignation probably lifted a great burden off his sagging shoulders. It must also have been a relief to those who were near and dear to him. His leaving was nevertheless quite anti-climactic and was embraced even by pseudo-revolutionaries within the hypocritical Trades Union movement that once advocated a more cathartic change.

The fall of Labour also gave comfort to those who had been drained emotionally by the constant political bickering and in-fighting. It also gave comfort to those within and outside the Caribbean who feared the St. Lucia Labour Party (and government) had been too close to Maurice Bishop and the PRG of Grenada. The unkindest cut of all for true Labour stalwarts must have been to witness the manner in which 'Brother' George (Odlum), having divided the government (and party), was later to join John Compton and Henry Giraudy (political leader and chairman of the UWP respectively) on a public platform in Central Castries, to celebrate the completion of their joint and destructive enterprise.

No useful purpose can be served by repeating some of the verbal exchanges between Odlum and myself at the time. In any event, some of it is unprintable. Besides, all has been forgiven under the very large banner we all called politics. It is now all water under the bridge, as they say. I however, remain buoyant both by the accuracy of Willie James' little booklet and by the positive role which I finally played in salvaging the St. Lucia Labour Party at a time when I was the only one left to lead it. The others had either deserted or were too fearful to show their heads in public. Labour Party supporters seeking revenge and retribution were to be sorely disappointed. There was little time for conjecture at that stage of the game. It would have been too uncharacteristic of Prime Minister Cenac, to do anything that might have changed the dynamics of St. Lucia politics back then. He had not only been pressured to resign his office that day; he was also persuaded to support Michael Pilgrim as 'Interim Prime Minister' - an oxymoron the plotters and their 'legal' advisers had invented. The Saint Lucia Constitution Order, (1978) made no provision for such fancy footwork and legal fiction as the plotters were then fashioning.

When the final hour came, it did so in the form of a series of letters, well planned and worded in keeping with the fiction which had been invented and cloned to the Saint Lucia constitution. The final settlement ushering the fall of the Labour government came in the following sequence of events: (1). A letter of resignation from Prime Minister Cenac. (2). A letter from Cenac (now, simply a member of parliament for Soufriere) indicating his personal support for Michael Pilgrim, as interim Prime Minister. (3). A third letter, this time from five elected members of the United Workers Party, signifying their support for Michael Pilgrim as interim Prime Minister. (4). A fourth Letter, from the three elected members of the PLP – Jon Odlum, George Odlum and Michael Pilgrim - supporting Pilgrim as interim Prime Minister. These letters were to be delivered to the acting Governor General at the same time by the various parties, meeting at Government House, in Castries. It was reported that the delegation had to wait several hours due to the absence of His Excellency from the premises at the time.

If ever proof was needed that the pen is mightier than the sword, this was it. It is noteworthy that the plotters had so little trust amongst themselves that they opted to travel to Government House all at the same time taking the disrobed Cenac along. Also, for the record and perhaps too, for future debate among students of politics is this observation: 'If it was considered unethical and immoral for Winston Cenac to govern with a one-man majority, why was it acceptable for that same Cenac with his single, one-man-vote, to now make Michael Pilgrim Prime Minister'? The simple answer is that majority rules. If so, then why was Cenac's one man majority not good enough to keep him in office? OK, I get it, his AG had messed up. I trust that everyone who reads this keeps that in mind. So we understand the reason that a single vote was not good enough for Cenac, but that it was fine for another. In any event, why didn't the Jackals demand that Prime Minister Cenac call fresh elections right away instead of supporting an 'interim' government? Was it to put the election machine into the hands of the opposition?

Was there another reason Cenac was not allowed to dissolve parliament and call general elections himself? Why then, the charade of an interim government? Was it to symbolically force Pilgrim and Odlum to accept the same Allan Louisy once so vilified and ridiculed, as Prime Minister and now together again in their new oxymoron? Or was there another reason Cenac had to go? Or was there a planned betrayal of the Labour government long before the elections of 1979? The Governor General, it was later reported, was at the Vigie beach with his family when the plotters came visiting that Sunday, had to hurry back to Government House, where he was then pressed into service by those gathered there seemingly unable to await the next working day to crucify the innocent Cenac and to take the government from him.

I wondered at the time what would have happened in the period of colonial rule – with a white 'British' Governor stationed at Government House – and with these same plotters needing his aid on a Sunday morning, to bring down a duly elected government. Would Odlum, Compton and company have disturbed the British Colonial Governor on a Sunday, his day of Anglican worship? Better still, would a British born Governor have condescended to meet with that band of desperate political opportunists on such a day? There seemed at the time no precedent for such Sunday politicking involving the representative of the Crown on this island. One therefore feels certain that in times past, Her Majesty's armed guards stationed at Government House, would have told these uninvited Sunday-demons in clear language, where to get off.

The full details of the trickery which ensnared Prime Minister Cenac that Sunday could be gleaned from the public address to the nation which he gave the following evening, Monday January 18, 1982. In it, he said he had reached an agreement to resign and to help reconstitute a new government for the island, headed by Pilgrim and including four (4) Ministers from the Labour Party, three (3) from the United Workers Party and Pilgrim from the PLP, as Interim Prime Minister.

Within hours of Cenac's broadcast to the nation, both Pilgrim (PLP) and Compton (UWP) had renounced the formula publicized by Cenac, and which both men (and their parties) had agreed to abide by. First, Compton claimed his party had second thoughts on the agreement. Shortly thereafter everyone was blaming Henry Giraudy, the UWP chairman, for Compton's somersault. Pilgrim and Odlum, sensing the difficulty in explaining to PLP followers their opportunistic involvement with former Prime Minister Louisy who, they had so abused and vilified, and with the official opposition, had little room to manoeuvre. As usual they decided that the best form of defense was to attack - so they went berserk with their public address systems not allowing anyone within hearing distance suitable rest. Winston Cenac, who had apparently trusted Compton and Odlum, (and others) to uphold the agreement they had ironed out, was now all alone. The PLP and the UWP had now dropped the innocent Cenac as they would a very hot potato. Had someone else been Prime Minister, would that have happened?

Soon after Cenac resigned and the Labour government fell, 'Brother George Odlum, and Michael Pilgrim of the PLP joined Compton and Giraudy of the UWP for a once in a life-time public display of the possibilities of politics. These cunning political animals appeared together on the William Peter Boulevard in Castries – the regular meeting place of the United Workers Party. The majority who had gathered there looked on and marvelled at what party politics had come to. Political pundits saw the shameless posturing by the holier-than-thou 'progressives' as yet another sign of the duplicity and conniving which had crept into local politics. Yet for students of politics, that moment may have been the finest hour for both George Odlum and John Compton, because the two had managed to change political reality on the island. They had done this by first creating monsters of each other and later, in their moment of 'victory' they had each succeeded in re-branding the other, thereby offering a more personable and civil side to each other's character. Those who wondered whether they were Saint or Saviour, would not have long to wait before they got their answers.

Having achieved their primary objective of bringing down the Labour government, Compton and Odlum were to later turn upon each other inflicting heavy political body blows and broadsides. It still seemed to some observers, however, that Odlum and his PLP were more obsessed with harassing and tormenting the Peter Josie-led St. Lucia Labour Party, than the Compton-led UWP. Sure, Odlum still criticized Compton who hit back suitably. Many believed however that this cat and mouse game was all there was to their 1982 election campaign. Their earlier marriage of convenience was now over, and the divorce seemed acrimonious and ugly. But not everyone was fooled.

The news that Cenac had finally thrown in the towel reached the people of St. Lucia with both joy and sadness. Joy because it offered them a fresh opportunity to make a choice of new government - and hopefully a new start as well. There was also sadness at the thought of intelligent men, in whom the electorate had placed so much trust and confidence, displaying such immaturity, selfishness, envy, greed and deceit, so shamelessly. The people were therefore thankful that the embarrassing and childish leadership quarrel was now behind them. Still, the question may be asked, even today: 'Have the people learnt the lessons of those years or can history repeat itself in this fair Helen of the West'? The safe and perhaps correct answer to this question is this: Only time will tell!

What seemed most certain at the time is that the country ended up with Michael Pilgrim as Interim Prime Minister and was back at the polls after only two and a half years of the SLP's five-year term. Perhaps we may suggest here that the people of Saint Lucia had wanted only a coffee but those whom they had elected at the time, laced the coffee with personal greed, envy and deceit that the people were forced to forget how depressing it was under a former regime, and almost revolted. In their rejection of the Labour government, they ended up with an interim one which was created by the hands which were by then accustomed to manipulating the politics of the country from behind locked doors. After Cenac had thrown in the towel, it was therefore time for an interim period during which the people were to gather their senses and learn to put the past behind them. It was also expected that they would return to the stone which they had at first rejected in the construction of a new and better country.

Pilgrim's Interim Cabinet

I only wanted a coffee, but as a former waitress, remembered
how depressing it was when people only ordered a beverage
Emily Griffin: Love the one you're with.

How does one put into words the twists and turns of political life which finally deposited Saint Lucia into the hands of an interim government in early 1982 from a popular mandate which was to last until 1984? If anyone had seen this coming, and could answer this question, then it remained a closely guarded secret. It appeared at one time that those who had shouted the loudest for a 'whole meal; rather than a 'snack' (Cenac), in criticism of Winston Cenac as Prime Minister, were now stuck in limbo and with no sign of any sort of meal or snack. Perhaps we may be charitable and say that Pilgrim's interim government was more of an 'interim appetizer' rather than the full meal some smart Aleck had at first demanded. Interestingly, it was plain to see that no one even bothered to ask by what constitutional sleight of hand the country arrived at the oxymoron it called an 'interim Prime minister? The usually correct, and often courageous Voice newspaper, never bothered to explain the constitutional conundrum into which the island had been plunged. In any event it appeared that those who wanted change and who also understood how fraught with difficulty that road then was were to settle for the mess of Pilgrim's pottage - though not of his own doing - until the promised general elections. At the time, only a handful of its citizens seemed to realize that there were moves by the PLP elements within the interim government, to extend the interim period. The idea was to complete the two and a half years which were left from the mandate given to the SLP by the electorate.

For many ordinary supporters as well as for the party's executive, the unkindest cut of all was that of Cenac agreeing to support Pilgrim as interim Prime Minister. No one (including this writer) seemed to fully appreciate the reason Cenac had chosen to support Pilgrim, rather than call fresh elections, which he had the constitutional authority to do, if he wished. It is common knowledge that one of the most cherished and guarded privileges of the office of Prime Minister is that of dating and calling general elections. It is a duty jealously guarded and cautiously preserved by every leader of government who has emerged since Britain began to quicken the pace of offering independence to her former colonies in the late fifties. That privilege was handed down to emerging Prime Ministers in the tradition of British parliamentary democracy. Saint Lucia was no different, even though its opposition parliamentarians had argued for a different constitutional model for the island, at the constitutional conference. Now that the constitutional authority to call elections was passed to new hands, the electorate had no option but to wait and see what date would be set for the new poll. At the time, many SLP stalwarts believed that the election campaign called for a few good and fearless men to stand up to the likes of Odlum and Compton and their newly re-energized supporters. Indeed Labour Party stalwarts shouted loud enough for everyone within ear shot to hear that had either Louisy or Cenac called upon the party's foot 'soldiers', and then threw in the towel, and called elections, things may have turned out differently. But all this speculation was a little late in coming and frankly, served no useful purpose. Indeed on sober reflection resigning from office may have seemed the honourable thing to do for Winston Cenac. It would have been preferable to call a meeting of those who had put him there in the first place, before he made his final decision. Even with the obvious pressure which had been exerted by both the Chamber of Commerce and the major Christian churches on the island, the more appropriate and manly thing to do might have been to call his Ministers together before he did what was forced upon him. At the time a little moral suasion and pressure from both family and friends might have completely bamboozled the gentleman politician - Winston Cenac. The Prime Ministership was simply too great a burden to bear by poor Cenac or anyone else of his constitution and stamina. His parting may have left many people in the lurch.

Cenac was heavily criticized within the party, not so much for resigning as he did but for accommodating the demands of the political hyenas, which were bent on using the young Pilgrim as interim Prime Minister. In addition, the support for Pilgrim may have been forced upon him by former friends, who had assured him that a genuine National Government was in the making - even though it may have been a temporary one. The seething verbal attacks levelled by Labour against the Cabal that had brought down their government were parried, often without success and even denied at times. But no one in the SLP took these denials seriously. There were wild speculations that certain Ministers were paid to bring down the Labour government. Other arm-chair pundits claimed the reason Cenac supported Pilgrim as interim Prime Minister was the fear of violence which was being threatened nightly, from political platforms of the opposition, and which threatened to destabilize the country. It was claimed by the sweet voice of reason that any God-fearing man would have called it quits, as Cenac had done. Before we leave Cenac for Pilgrim, some persons had suggested that, without the church and the prayers of the faithful, there would have been an ugly ending to the political turmoil of the day. Such intense political pressure as existed aided by the persuasive powers of religion would have broken far stronger men than the timorous Winston Cenac - or so it was claimed.

A certain young man, who was also a plain spoken trade unionist at the time, was among those who were quite vocal in the opinion that 'Brother' George Odlum was a plant in the Labour Party, serving British and American intelligence interests. Their only 'proof' however, seemed to be, to use their own words that 'no one had ever left Oxford University in England and afterward, to ground with the grass roots of their impoverished societies, such as was demonstrated by Walter Rodney, the Guyanese-born lecturer, then working at the Mona campus of the University of the West Indies.' So in the eyes of certain young radicals at the time, 'Brother George' was too smart by half to have committed to the struggles of the underdogs, having passed through Oxford University and gained entry into the good life. The fall backwards from Oxford to Cul-de-Sac was too much for some such as our young trade unionists, to fully appreciate.

Unfortunately for this young trade unionist, Odlum and his PLP were just beginning to exercise political authority, as Michael Pilgrim was soon to be sworn in as Prime Minister, following Cenac's resignation. In an address to the nation soon after being sworn in, Pilgrim said in part: "Corruption had been discovered in the previous administration which could have serious implications for the security of the State". Pilgrim may have been referring to a newspaper report at the time which said that, in addition to the platform rhetoric and the savaging of each other at every opportunity, "there were other issues potentially damaging to certain politicians. This involved the issuance of Saint Lucian passports overseas", it said. Apart from the straight forward illegality of the process, the paper said the discovery had an additional, more damaging dimension to it. It added that the passport issue went to a possible cover for the recruitment of mercenaries overseas for activity in Saint Lucia. It is worth noting here that around that time, a certain Labour politician in neighbouring Dominica was charged with the offence of importing arms and mercenaries into Dominica - using illegally obtained passports - for a violent overthrow of the Eugenia Charles government. It was a charge for which that same accused politician served a lengthy prison term, in that island.

In a rebuttal statement on behalf of the St. Lucia Labour Party, the media reported that Peter Josie - then SLP leader - said that he had written to the Director of Public Prosecutions (DPP) asking 'to investigate the issue and to determine whether there was a case to answer'. It said that the letter had been copied to Prime Minister Pilgrim. It was further reported that 'Josie had informed the media that he had been reliably informed that another letter had been received by Mr. Pilgrim from 'official sources' in London regarding a case of fraud, involving a senior politician and a high ranking Police officer, both from Saint Lucia'. Josie challenged Prime Minister Pilgrim to make these available to the public. At that time, however, it appeared that neither the British government officials in London nor the political parties presently forming the government of the island were interested in pursuing such scandals. The reason seemed clear enough at the time. Why should those who had connived to bring down the Cenac government and now held the reins of office care about the scandals which they may have invented in order to embarrass the Labour government of which they were a part. Indeed, for a time it appeared that the interim Prime Minister had begun to take his duties seriously, preferring to focus on arrangements for the holding of general elections on the island, and ensuring the continuity of government administrative functions as he did so.

The passport scandal and all the other misdeeds, of which former Ministers of the Labour Government were accused, were now treated by an increasingly cynical electorate (and the political opposition) as the accustomed shenanigans of deceitful politicians. The electorate was witnessing a standard of deceit, double-speak and outright lies in a manner they had never seen before. Such conduct from grown, respected men whom many people looked up to was bound to have a negative effect on the island and on the psyche of its population in coming years. This was unfortunate, because some of the key players had started off being held in such high esteem by the people of the island, back in the day.

The cynicism and distrust of politics and politicians at the time seemed to have been confirmed by the appointment of former Prime Minister

Louisy as Attorney General in the interim government. The appointment of Honourable Allan Bousquet as Minister for Health was also seen as further proof to many that, the more things changed, the more they remained the same. Some questioned whether it was by accident or design that the two most senior gentlemen in parliament were chosen to head these two important portfolios in the interim administration. Or did someone deliberately foist the two on a youthful Pilgrim as a bad joke in retribution for his past platform rhetoric? The obvious question on everyone's lips at the time was: "What transformation had overcome the man that neither Pilgrim nor Odlum wanted as their Prime Minister in the first Labour government, to have merited him a position in Pilgrim's interim government? Besides, 'wasn't the other most senior serving member, Allan Bousquet constantly held up to ridicule in Odlum's Crusader newspaper as the epitome of grammatical butchering, within parliament'? On the other hand, one may also ask what could have motivated Louisy, a pensioned High Court Judge, to accept service in a government headed by those who had so bitterly vilified and stigmatized him, as slow and incompetent? Yet, Louisy was the linchpin of Pilgrim's interim government, as all Attorneys General are wont to be, dominating the political system where procedural doubts and difficulties arise during governance.

On reflection, political researchers and other pundits will most likely see many of the charges against former Prime Ministers Louisy and Cenac as 'politically inspired' and aiming to sow confusion and doubt in the minds of the electorate, and undermine confidence in their respective governments. Such tactics are not new in politics, and are common fare in the Caribbean. What many found regrettable was that these charges and accusations should have come from within their governments and they seemed powerless to dismiss the offending Ministers. On the other hand, it ought to be a concern in the region that political parties anoint themselves watchdogs of the people while holding little or no consultations with those whom they are supposed to be representing. Too often the opposition thinks it has a duty to fabricate and twist the truth, often using clever language in which words are thrown about as baited lines to catch unsuspecting fish. By casting doubt and using clever innuendoes and aspersions, the opposition which often has more time on its hands than it knows what to do with, can raise the political mischief level, whenever it chooses, to the discomfort of governments and its other perceived opponents, alike.

It is also fair criticism that certain governments attract deserved hostility by reacting too hastily and heavy handedly, in response to vague and dubious charges against them. It is not uncommon in the Caribbean for the opposition to spread malicious and reckless rumours which it cannot prove. Such rumours can damage the image and reputation of both the government and the country, in the eyes of the outside world. It may even affect the willingness of entrepreneurs to invest. But who cares? Certainly not the opposition! Those who indulge in such behaviour tell us that all is fair in war and politics. What they always omit to say, however, is that people whose conduct is informed by negative aspects of politics, find it more difficult to settle down into positive work rhythm when they form the government. Unfortunately, in less well educated societies in which people lack the ability to read and critically analyze news reports, government and opposition propaganda can often become biblical truths, taking on a life of their own. This constant conflict and warring may be sending the wrong message to the youth and may even prepare the ground for conflict and disunity within the population. In time, such conflict and disunity can also lead to increased criminal activity.

Many aspiring Caribbean politicians have been destroyed by such rumour mongering and gossip. In certain instances, even decent law-abiding citizens, who are not involved in the cut and thrust of party politics, can become caught up in the web of deceit and gossip. Such abusive schemes against law-abiding, upright citizens are unfortunately becoming more frequent with each passing year in the Caribbean.

When it was learnt that the UWP (and its chairman) had rejected the deal Compton had made with Cenac and Odlum, it is said that he was so distraught by the harsh rebuttal which he received from his friend and party chairman, Henry Giraudy, that he immediately tendered his resignation, as party leader. No one knew for certain what Chairman Giraudy might have said to Compton afterwards in private, but many assumed that after the severest of tongue-lashings, they met behind closed doors, hugged and made up, supposedly in the interest of party and country. The public was later informed that Compton's resignation letter was not accepted by the party executive (including Chairman Giraudy) and that instead, he was asked to lead the party in the 1982 general elections. It will be recalled that Compton had also led the UWP to electoral victories in 1987, 1992, and then demitted office in 1996, only to return ten years later to head the party once more and lead it to an improbable seventh electoral victory - counting those of 1964, 1969 and 1974 - a record which will be very hard to equal, far less to surpass.

The clear message from Chairman Giraudy was that his United Workers Party did not need quick fixes as that offered by Odlum and his ilk. In order to achieve its goals of electoral victory, and social and economic progress for the people of Saint Lucia, the UWP knew what needed to be done, and it did not need Odlum to advise it. Besides, Odlum had for many years previously, taunted both party leader and chairman, inventing creative and derisive Creole sobriquets for each. Odlum also saw to it that his followers practiced using his invented creations. Giraudy may have also determined to jettison Odlum's politics by virtue of the latter's faked portrayal of the revolutionary Fidel Castro, whose political style was alien to the debonair, exuberant and incisive Giraudy. The latter confided to close friends and colleagues that 'Brother George' was just a mean-spirited 'Castries-boy', who had been denied entry into the inner sanctum of the local bourgeoisie and the moneyed enclaves in Saint Lucia, hence his deep unhappiness and chagrin. Giraudy and others of his age believed that Odlum's major problem and the source of all his political energy was the rejection he suffered earlier. Brother George probably never got over the fact that 'Barber' was rejected as a profession for his dad, after he had written it on his application for Oxford. In its place was substituted the words 'Hair Stylist'.

It would therefore be true to say that chairman Giraudy had absolutely no use for the 'excess baggage' (of the PLP) which longed to cling to the coat-tails of the UWP, just when the 'flambeau' party was striding confidently to victory, in mid-1982. Public rejection may have been the bitter pill which the newly formed PLP was to swallow at the time. Such rejection may have aroused many deep emotions in the man who would be leader but never volunteered the reason he needed it so badly. Indeed, he was often to deny that he wished to become Prime Minister. Of course every Saint Lucian who was following the events of the period has an opinion on Brother George Odlum's views on the post of Prime Minister. At the time, the word on the ground was there were secret meetings between the UWP and certain trade union leaders along with the Chamber of Commerce aimed at crafting a new formula (following rejection of Cenac's proposal) for inviting persons into Pilgrim's interim government. That new formula agreed to a team of technocrats, along with a token Minister from each of the three parties including Pilgrim (PLP) as Prime Minister, Louisy (SLP) as Attorney General and Allan Bousquet (UWP) as Minister of Health, to keep the semblance of elective democracy in the public's eyes. From such a formula, there emerged a new and largely unknown group of young and supposedly bright and academically qualified individuals, who were to be charged with keeping the machinery of government functioning, as the country prepared for general elections. No one to this day – except of course those who had appointed themselves arbiters, general overseers and God – knew how these persons (including senior parliamentarians

Bousquet and Louisy) came to be chosen members of the so-called interim government of Saint Lucia.

The argument was made at the time that the island needed 'technocrats' rather than 'unschooled' politicians to run its affairs. No one seemed to know for certain whether any thought had been given to compulsory inclusion of such trained personnel (technocrats) in a party's team of candidates for elections. Apart from their technical competence, few persons seemed to have bothered to raise the issue of character, integrity or moral and ethical considerations of such declared technocrats, or potential Ministers of the government. With the passage of time and with more Saint Lucians exposed to technical qualifications, other important ingredients such as integrity and moral and ethical standing will, it is hoped increasingly loom larger in choosing political representation and other public officials. Some persons observed at the time that a system ought to be devised for selecting more rounded and trustworthy individuals to elective politics. Furthermore it was argued that integrity, morality and honesty should always play an equal or larger role than mere academic qualifications whenever the public is offered a choice of parliamentary representative.

Some persons have been quick to remind the rest of the population that local technocrats are from the same stock as those of the unlettered in the population. In addition, they claim, such technocrats are as likely to inherit the same dastardly character flaws as others in the society. Those who have fallen by the wayside, seemingly without hope of recovery were also a part of the same society. The undeniable benefits of a sound education, in the view of many should always be accompanied by a basket of values as the society canvasses, and discusses and forges ahead to a better way of ensuring it selects its best and brightest people to lead it.

Soon after Pilgrim was sworn into office, the UWP, which had recently been the official opposition voice in Parliament, sensing its ascendancy within the electorate again, demanded loudly and publicly that fresh general elections should be held within 90 days. Some political analysts interpreted that call as a signal that the UWP did not trust the Pilgrim/ Odlum political juggernaut. The 'UWPees' believed that the two may have hatched a scheme to extend the life of the 'interim' government, 'ad infintum' or for at least ten more years. The UWP therefore took it upon itself to be ever wary and vigilant - and alert. Compton and Giraudy kept a very close eye on Pilgrim and company, and everyone in the UWP, along with the Chamber of Commerce and the churches, was asked to keep an even closer watch on Brother George Odlum. The word on the ground was that 'Odlum was the real power behind Pilgrim' but many electors also believed that Compton and the UWP were keeping such close watch that neither Pilgrim nor Odlum were able to indulge in any games while the interim government remained in office.

It also appeared that Compton and Giraudy were determined to leave no room for any tricks and games by either Odlum or the junior wide-eyed novices in Pilgrim's interim government. Political pundits observed that the new technocrats were relishing their new status. An uncharitable character compared them to kids at Christmas who had received from Santa, the toys which they had written to him for. But that may have been a little naughty and off target. The interim Ministers were chosen to do a job and the general feeling at the time was that they did the best they could in the circumstances.

Odlum was breathing down his neck at every turn, and seeming to mime each word which fell from poor Pilgrim's mouth as if he had prior knowledge of them; Compton and his party were also keeping a very close watch on the goings-on within the Pilgrim administration. The interim Prime Minister therefore seemed straight jacketed and restricted. To be candid, everyone expected Pilgrim's role in the interim government would have been limited by those who had placed him there, in the first place. At the time, he then appeared to have both hands and feet shackled. Any keen observer was bound to notice that Saint Lucia was then truly in a state of tranquil immobility. The electorate appeared to be in a trance-like phase and oblivious to their surroundings yet somehow closely marking each minute, as the day to cast their ballot for a new government approached. As if to ease the anxiety and suspicions which the UWP and its supporters were experiencing at the time, Prime Minister Pilgrim in a 'Thank-You' statement to the nation, broadcast simultaneously on radio and television, said he had selected the three political leaders Compton, Louisy and Odlum to form a three-man committee of advisers. Odlum seemed then quite content to serve with the same persons he had hounded out of office - Compton and Louisy.

In the meantime, and as if to confirm Compton's suspicions of Odlum and his perceived dexterity at political manipulation, the latter floated the idea that the interim government may remain in office for a longer period than the allotted three months allowed it. Of course Odlum was careful to add 'if that was the wish of the broad cross section of the people' recalling the British Government attitude on political Independence for the island, when the idea was first proposed. But Compton and party chairman Giraudy would have none of it. They immediately rebutted, restating the country's clear expectation of early general elections, possibly before three months after their installation.

Meanwhile Odlum and his new mates had tried very hard to sell their PLP message to the electorate, and at times they even masqueraded as if they were the real (and true) Labour Party. That approach by the PLP seemed to have caught the SLP off guard for a while, but it soon found its campaigning voice again and began to expose the blatant duplicity of the masqueraders. This new development between the two factions of 'Labour' was to prove more icing on the cake for Compton and his UWP. The United Workers Party was now smiling all the way to the next general elections. The intense politicking among the three political parties of the day was extended to the 'Letters' columns of the island's leading newspapers. No one knew for certain the origins of such letters although a few brave and apparently frustrated souls, did attach recognizable names, to their missives. Many 'Nom-de-plume' letters, however, seemed to have been planted in there by party political activists and other sympathizers seeking to promote their own interests and those of their party and its leader.

To add to the intrigue of the many published 'pen names' a new document purporting to be a copy of a letter which it alleged had earlier been written by George Odlum, to one Wolfgang Bartsch was now making the rounds. That letter was dated May 1, 1982, (a public holiday on the island celebrating 'Labour Day') and using the letter-heads of the Ministry of Foreign Affairs, with the signature of George Odlum - Foreign Minister. In it the passport scandal was again discussed and this time, with both the purported writer and recipient apparently making fun of the desperate state of politics in the country. The letter to Dr. Bartsch, from the office of Foreign Affairs, also claimed that Michael Pilgrim was Prime Minister in name only. It claimed that it was he, Odlum, who made all the useful decisions for the interim government. Many people believed that that sentiment may well have had a germ of truth to it.

Such dirty political tricks of forged letters and signatures and other printed matter bearing cut and paste photographs of targeted politicians' alleging shady deals, were all new to the island at the time. However, the general view was that very few persons, if any, had been fooled by such forgeries. The average citizen felt then that such political tricks were more reminiscent of Latin American politics, where new and expensive consultants were hired by those who organized and financed political campaigns, in order to put a more palatable spin on deception. How these perpetrators were able to get an exact copy of Odlum's signature and a letter-head from his Ministry of Foreign Affairs is still a matter of conjecture. More importantly, how such political dirty tricks would affect the future of Saint Lucian and Caribbean politics, no one could tell. Some persons at the time understood that foreign hands were involved in such dirty tricks even though many locals could not quite fathom the reason for such foreign interest. The question of why certain persons would go to any length to 'win' elections remains relevant. The stakes had been sharply raised in the 1982 elections which seemed to have been manipulated and controlled by foreign public relations firms, charging large sums of money for their services. But few party officials were openly admitting this, and if and when they did, it was in the safety of private homes and offices.

As I watched and studied the unfolding events, I could not help recalling the words of V.I. Lenin, (leader of the Bolshevik revolution) for his insightful observation that may be summarized in six words: 'there is no politics without education'. That view, when read together with the thesis of a Saint Lucia born Nobel Laureate, Sir Arthur Lewis that 'education, not money, is the real cure for poverty'; seems to point to a convincing link between politics, education and poverty. Poverty, however, persists in the Caribbean amidst much politics and seemingly a concerted attack on the eradication of illiteracy and the education of citizens, particularly the youth. However, it ought to be observed here that few English-speaking Caribbean countries have had the guts – some would say the testicular fortitude – to attack the scourge of illiteracy and poverty in the same manner as did the revolutionary and visionary Fidel Castro of Cuba. One must concede, however, that the efforts in the post colonial era of attacking illiteracy and poverty, has had measurable success in most Caribbean countries. Still, there are too many remaining pockets of poverty and ignorance. These two continue to stalk the Caribbean as the twin pillars of evil, retarding economic growth and progress.

To be fair, many Caribbean governments including those of Saint Lucia have made a commendable effort in attacking post-colonial education, particularly since political Independence. Clearly much more needs to be done. Perhaps the focus now needs to shift from the three 'R's' to technical training, sex and family-life education and broad survival skills aimed at creating self-employed entrepreneurs (job creators), rather than job seekers. The most difficult hurdle one suspects will be that of replacing man-made religious indoctrination and exploitation. Perhaps a search for something deeper and grander than the rush to riches and the increasing greed is needed now more than ever. Furthermore, a culture of tolerance of other peoples' views ought to be encouraged even as these Caribbean societies guard against fly-by-night schemers and preachers who claim to come in the name of God and leave with the peoples' hard earned savings.

Unfortunately, many years after the passing of Lenin, and then much later of Sir Arthur Lewis, one still witnesses a general and growing disrespect for education especially among young males in the Caribbean and elsewhere. The situation seems exacerbated in places where drug trafficking and other 'easy' money beckon the 'fatherless' and misguided youth. The apparent new culture of uncaring and reckless living, leads to an early death. In addition, many Caribbean youth experience abuse from adult perverts, who set out to deceive the innocent. Schools are unable to cope with such kids who are so damaged psychologically they become a menace to both teachers and other children. To further aggravate these societal ills such children as well as many other 'normal' ones are often caught in a single minded pursuit of early gratification of consumer goods and other trinkets targeted at young people by television and radio Executives. Sex-for-pay has become an attractive option where the craving for 'goodies' exists and money is in short supply, within the family. The setting of long term goals and the discipline and hard work necessary to achieve these goals, are anathema to such misguided minds.

In addition, the lack of a concerted drive for educational achievement amongst some youth comes with a very high price tag. Society suffers as a result of anti-social behaviour, crime and violence which many experts have connected to a lack of skills and job opportunities. Exacting revenge by one-on-one killings over drug turf and gang differences is an increasing nightmare, which the State is seemingly powerless to stop. In a few former European colonies the death penalty seemed at a point of extinction or at least approaching that point. Many Governments (and Judiciaries) are reluctant to implement the death penalty for fear of offending Europe - the same Europe which everyone knows has mastered the art of killing, and stands ever ready to kill again, if it cannot have its way in the world. Sadly, amidst the carnage and early death one also detects a certain reticence on the part of the leaders in the society to change. There is an inexplicable reluctance to initiate and set examples of a more cautious, reflective, and prudent life-style. Instead, new politicians seemed anxious to flaunt their acquired wealth and to imitate the 'nouveau riche', flashing shiny cars and jewellery and generally making fools of themselves.

It is a great pity that the above list does not exclude local and Caribbean parliamentarians and other highly placed government officials. Such persons rising from humble beginnings and now advertising their riches are proving poor examples for the youth of the Caribbean to emulate. As if to add insult to injury each succeeding generation seems more negatively impacted by the get-rich-quick-pandemic of the previous generation. Regrettably, the 'new' political players have not yet learnt the art of living peaceful, happy and quiet lives. They too often project an image akin to that of local (and foreign) drug-lords. This is anathema to the ideal standards of the society which the progressive left had once envisaged. Besides, such apparent flaunting of materialism can easily be misinterpreted by the youth as an ideal for which to strive. Pandering to the negative values which are threatening to destroy civil society (and the youth in particular) is an expression of weak leadership. In a God-fearing society there ought to be no room for such leaders or for such display of ostentatious living.

There is now a vicious tide of haste on the part of those who feel undone by history to grab and accumulate as fast as they can. This tide seemed determined to sweep everyone along before it. Even church leaders and others who advocate a moral and ethical high ground seem caught up in this global rush for money and riches as the poorly educated mendicants and lost causes in society. Too many Caribbean politicians and otherwise decent citizens are falling victim to the mad rush for 'the better life' grabbing where they would otherwise be better advised to give, in charity and love.

On the plus side, a few newer politicians are increasingly becoming aware of the need for a new and revised education syllabus. These few wise leaders see the need to mobilize their countries towards the achievement of higher all round standards in education, in order to achieve desired social and economic progress. Even so, very few politicians seem prepared to step forward and grab the ethical and moral high ground. Too many leaders seem reluctant to set targets of social behaviour for the country and for the youth to copy. This attitude has led some to ponder whether we must have a bloody revolution before Saint Lucia can be mobilized for a new and different and inclusive political, social and economic agenda. The laid back attitude on the part of the political leadership therefore begs the question: 'Is there a vision for educational achievement which this or any other country within the Caribbean proposes for its citizens in the next twenty-five years or so? How would such education guarantee growth, jobs and economic prosperity?

An objective review of the social and economic status of Saint Lucia since adult suffrage will reveal that many devoted persons, including teachers and Ministry of Education officials, have tried hard to provide better education and training opportunities for its citizens. In this regard perhaps we have not documented in sufficient detail and with scientific precision the many persons, both local and foreign, who have toiled long and hard in the field of education on the island. Many of the former educators worked under very trying conditions and in circumstances which only the most dedicated could have survived. We ought therefore to hold up before Caribbean youth, (and people) such examples of sacrifice and dedication, as these pioneers in the field of education displayed. Perhaps one day a suitable list of the biographies of these early pioneers will be compiled and published and made available to schools, public libraries and bookshops in the Caribbean.

The time has come for the Caribbean African Diaspora to see itself as one and the same origin as their black brothers everywhere. Henceforth, the celebration of Nobel Laureate week in Saint Lucia for example as well as that of other Laureates in the Caribbean should be broadened to include the work of Martin Luther King Jr. and Frederick Douglas among others. It has not been lost on the more observant enthusiast in the Caribbean that the public holiday in the USA to mark Martin Luther King's birthday falls two or three days before the start of Nobel Laureate week in Saint Lucia, to honour its two international sons - and Laureates. All this is merely to re-emphasize that those who occupy political office have a special and unique opportunity to make a difference in their societies through an unwavering and single minded assault on education. Perhaps we need to also keep in the forefront of our minds that the real cure for poverty is education and not money.

After a public address to explain what the persons who had taken the government from Winston Cenac were doing, the time soon came for Prime Minister Pilgrim to name his team of Ministers – his Cabinet. It was widely known that the new Cabinet was selected by the opposition parties, meaning Compton and Odlum, as well as by the Chamber of Commerce with possible input from the Trade Unions. Pilgrim did not disclose, nor did anyone volunteer what the criteria for selection were. In any case no one seemed to care. Instead, most people seemed interested only in the date when the next general elections would be called.

At the time of their selection, many believed the interim cabinet revealed more of the thinking of Compton and Odlum, than that of Pilgrim himself. The youthful Pilgrim seemed then, merely a front-man, taking orders from his principals. The latter was somewhat confirmed when in his first address to the nation on radio and television much of what he said had already been revealed by both Compton or Odlum on their respective political platforms. Pointedly, in Pilgrim's first address as Prime Minister he promised to dissolve parliament as soon as possible, and seemed anxious to ring that election bell. It is a privilege very few persons will ever experience in their life time. Only after his opening remarks, as if on second thought, did he mention the selection of a new interim cabinet. But these were minor lapses (with no infelicities) as expected, from a young and excitable Accountant who had been chosen to measure the priorities of a nation rather than to estimate the profit and loss of a private business.

Compton and his party were obviously ecstatic to have been given a second chance at general elections half way through their five-year term in opposition. Since its victory of 1979 the Labour government had tried very hard to shoot itself down and Compton and company were happy, to assist. So when the Labour government finally succeeded in destroying itself, Compton and his UWP 'flambeaus' were there to pick up the pieces. The latter therefore willingly agreed to continue where they had left off prior to their rude awakening in 1979. Some have suggested that John Compton had only reluctantly accepted such an early return to government. His opponents had accused him of impatience, haste, and undue eagerness for political power. The first observation was contrary to the prevailing view at the time that Compton was impatient in opposition and could not wait to resume office. But being the sensitive soul he was, knowledgeable observers believed that he had not fully recovered from the serious political body blows and humiliation he suffered in the elections of 1979. It was for this reason, some assumed, he may not have been quite ready to resume office. Some said he was still licking his wounds. But those who say this know too little of the political animals who lived at the time.

Before the process of selection got under way however, it was rumoured all over Castries that Pilgrim had been handed a list of persons whom he was to contact for the available six Ministerial portfolios. This was subsequent to his original naming of Allan Louisy and Allan Bousquet to his new cabinet.

In that first address, the interim Prime Minister also rambled some mishmash on the triumph of democracy and people power. This statement was not accompanied by a clear analysis in the view of many, of what had led to the leadership struggle and the role of his present advisers in the crisis which had brought so much disgrace and shame to the nation. Pilgrim said: 'Persons abroad have ridiculed us and cast unsympathetic and derisive remarks about our government' Interestingly, Pilgrim did not say 'our country'; instead, he said 'our government'. He then added: 'Some of this castigation we richly deserved' as if accepting blame on behalf of an entire party and people. Was it the same party and people who were begging that the leadership struggle be stopped, and that the country be allowed to progress peacefully? He did not elaborate. He should have explained these important issues. Perhaps his speech writer was in no mood to retrace the steps which had taken them thus far.

Many who by then had become tired of Odlum's often repeated (and written) 'ideas' described Pilgrim's speech insultingly as 'Odlum's mouthpiece'. Following that address everyone anticipated the announcement of Pilgrim's new Cabinet. They did not have long to wait. It appeared that whilst decent citizens slept, others were planning and canvassing the next bunch of people who would help Prime Minister Pilgrim lead this country to the next general elections.

It appeared that such a list had been prepared by the same joint committee of business, Trade Unions, the United Workers Party and Christian Churches which had been quietly plotting a future course for the island. No one had accused these groups of imposing their wills on the country and to do so without the least semblance of a mandate, from the people. Political insiders had observed that these may well have been the same set of sinners, who were pulling on puppet strings behind the scenes. Many believed that these people lacked legitimacy and were too scared and corrupt to face the public in free and fair elections. Yet they seemed to be forever manipulating influence from a place where they could not be seen or heard.

Everyone knew Pilgrim was powerless to act on his own initiative as a normal Prime Minister would. In fact, it would be true to say that during the three months of Pilgrim's government, Saint Lucia was ruled by an oligarchic-dictatorship - a sort of ingenious oxymoron, created by the plotters and Jackals mentioned earlier. One therefore felt a certain pity for Prime Minister Pilgrim who could do very little of his own volition. His 'nice guy' image served him well at that time as some people still clung to his words perchance to salvage hope. However, others feared that Pilgrim was not allowed to adlib a statement, especially when addressing the media. Every word he spoke, had to be vetted by his handlers - or so it seemed. His was a closely choreographed act, tightly scripted, and even more tightly delivered. He simply served those who had installed him as Prime Minister!

At first glance, many political observers believed that Pilgrim's new Cabinet looked more like a bunch of neophytes, plucked from the comfort of their family homes with many perhaps still wet behind the ears. On a more positive note, nobody claimed that these young persons were in search of public approbation or were otherwise seeking personal fame. Equally, no one had suggested that any of those who were to be named interim Ministers of Pilgrim's Government were prepared to sacrifice their lives for the sake of the churches, the unions or the political parties. In any event towards the end of the long period of instability on the island, the people appeared ready for any change which seemed reasonable and superior to that which they were to replace. In fact, it seemed then that any reasonable group which was ready to work to restore the country to a state of normalcy would be welcome.

It is to their credit that the Ministers agreed to serve with the interim Government when they did. No one knew for certain how many others had turned down the call to assist Pilgrim's interim government and it appeared no one bothered to ask. That is therefore even more reason to commend those who took up the challenge when they did, even knowing it was for a temporary period. Notwithstanding the shortness of time and the possible ingratitude of many, one feels certain that the interim Ministers did the best they could in the circumstances. No form of specific training in governance or in matters of civil protocol and procedure was available at the time, as far as one could tell. Those wishing for a career in politics were in many instances left to their own devices.

Such new entrants to politics therefore took that crucial step at their own risks, and that of their families. The friends and families of these young technocrats who had agreed to serve in Pilgrim's government were doing so with the best of intentions. After the destructive hurricane of 3 August 1980, and the damaging leadership struggle, the country was enjoying a bit of calm. It seemed a politically neutral period for non-political persons who wished to serve. After their swearing, in the calm and peace - serenity even - that had descended on the island, continued for sometime thereafter. In that peaceful atmosphere, the new Ministers went about their business with calm and composure. They were not harassed by the fallen and weakened politicians, or any of their supporters. The people seemed to have decided to bide their time until the moment when they would exercise their political franchise - the legal right to vote. They were also aware that this new interim government must have had the full support of the Christian churches, the Chamber of Commerce, the trade unions, and at least two of the political parties.

The St. Lucia Labour Party was completely demoralized and it no longer posed a threat to anyone. It was attempting to recover its voice and prestige. The serious damage it had suffered in government at the hands of those who called themselves 'Labour' was sure to condemn the party to many years in the wilderness of opposition. It was a very sad time indeed for the supporters of St. Lucia Labour Party. They were in the main largely innocent on--lookers in the drama which had played itself out before their eyes. The rank and file of the party was powerless. They were also leaderless. The promising young prospects who offered any hope for the rebuilding of a strong political organization were too timid to leave the safety of their homes. For many others their battered and tired minds could find no creative way out of their morass. These could only gaze blankly at the shattered dreams which lay about them.

Finally, the patience of the people of Saint Lucia was rewarded with the naming of the island's 'interim' government by Prime Minister Pilgrim. Looking back at the photographs of these young technocrats, it was impossible to detect any trace of malice or ill-will on their innocent-looking faces. If a picture is worth a thousand words, one felt certain that theirs would be worth much more than that, at today's inflationary prices. They seemed so innocent, almost angelic; leaving one to wonder what had enticed them to do what they did, when they did it.

That is not to say that innocent-looking faces are not without ambitions or that they may never have faltered before. Whatever their shortcomings, they were fully covered at the time, and no one was in the mood to search or to start a new fight. The people were in no mood for any negativity or confusion. Enough was enough. Each new Minister must have fancied his or her self playing an important role in the future development of the country and using politics as the means of service. Notwithstanding these observations, one cannot help feeling even now that these young persons had agreed to serve in Pilgrim's government, only after the expressed permission of relatives, friends and other supporting networks. It was difficult to dismiss the feeling at the time that they were pressed into service by invisible and powerful hands. Each had taken the oath of office to serve Queen and country, and to do so by God's grace. Soon after the swearing ceremony the composition of the 'interim' team was made available to the general public.

It is with some unease that one must now reveal that after several searches in the official gazette of the government of Saint Lucia, no recording can be found of the appointment by the Governor General, of Ministers to serve in an interim government. Why did the official government gazette carry the appointments of Allan Louisy and Allan Bousquet, and not that of the others? Is this observation worthy of research and explanation? The Saint Lucia gazette of January 30, 1982 records the following at pages 50 and 51: (1) by his Excellency Mr. Boswell Williams, Governor General of Saint Lucia. To: The honourable Allan Fitzgerald Louisy. Greetings; Pursuant to section 60(4) of the Constitution of Saint Lucia, and acting in accordance with the advice of the Prime Minister, I hereby appoint you the said Allan Fitzgerald Louisy to be a Minister of the government, to hold such office in accordance with the provisions of the said constitution. (2) And all Her Majesty's loving subjects in Saint Lucia and all others whom it may concern are hereby required to take notice hereof and to govern themselves accordingly. Given under my hand and the public seal of Saint Lucia at Government House, this 21st day of January 1982 in the thirtieth year of the reign of Her Majesty Queen Elizabeth the second... By His Excellency's command. The identical information was recorded at page 51 of the same gazette for Minister Allan Bouquet.

The information published by the government Public Relations Officer and released to the various newspapers on the island, revealed the names listed below as Ministers to serve in Pilgrim's interim government.

1. *Michael Pilgrim (Elected)* - *Prime Minister*
2. *Allan Louisy (Elected)* - *Attorney General*
3. *Allan Bousquet (Elected)* - *Min. of Health*
4. *Senator, Merlyn Combie* - *Min. of Social Affairs*
5. *Mr. Leo Clarke* - *Min. of Education*
6. *Mr.Cromwell Goodridge* - *Min. of Communications & Works*
7. *Mr. Alfred Jn. Baptiste* - *Min. of Youth and Sports*
8. *Mr. George Louis* - *Min. of Agriculture*

Since rendering service in Pilgrim's interim administration, many of the above persons have disappeared from view; perhaps preferring a quiet life away from the hustle and bustle of partisan politics. Only one seemed to have been bitten by the political bug and the public image that has been shaped to date. But that singular ambition has not, unfortunately, always marked his conduct by a display worthy of emulation. Of the others, there have been one or two sightings per year recorded by casual observers. Another two have reportedly stuck to their chosen professions, making money and living well. Many locals have been led to believe that such persons were deemed to be too smart to have opted for a life of partisan politics, after their stint in Pilgrim's interim Government.

Certain persons have suggested the compilation of a dossier on those 'interim' worthies, perchance to determine where else they have exercised their God-given talents, and to encourage them to share their experiences with the rest of their countrymen. Perhaps Saint Lucia needs such persons today as much as it did in the past. The experiences gathered since 1982 would serve the country far more effectively at this time, than they might have done then.

Prime Minister Pilgrim himself has been content to remain completely out of politics, surfacing once every six months or so, from his busy private avocations to attend a funeral or other important public function. Since his departure from politics, his most remarkable public service was heading the team which made funeral arrangements for the late Sir. John Compton, Prime Minister, in September 2007. There, he again distinguished himself, making everyone, including those of his home town of Vieux-Fort, proud of him. His true mission however, was to hold the fort; ensure that the voters list and other preparations were ready for elections in three months time, and then to happily hand over the country to the new government, after general elections. Those who had placed him as interim Prime Minister hoped that it would not enter his head as it did 'the cock who thought the sun had risen to hear him crow', - quoting George Eliot.

Elections at Last…May 3rd.1982

He was like a cock who thought the sun had risen to hear him crow.

George Eliot

Whatever may have brought the country to its second general elections in two and a half years following the SLP's popular mandate, did not seem a good omen for the country, at the time. A return to office of Compton and the UWP so soon after their ignoble defeat was the last thing the country expected. Equally, no one expected such disunity and confusion within the government of the Labour Party which was elected in 1979. By that time it was common knowledge that politicians would only listen to whatever it is they wished to hear. Most of them made friends very quickly but soon after elections were just as quickly to disengage themselves. That was true of every politician, regardless of the party they had condescended to associate with for the purpose of elections. It did not matter how filled with accusations the scroll of a previous government or parliamentarian, but politicians often re-invented themselves and presented the newly reborn persona to the electorate, for further favours. An angry and disappointed electorate would judge as harshly as it thought it was treated.

The laws which govern the holding of elections on the island are quite clear. They stipulate who may or may not contest and specifically mention poor mental health and insanity as reasons for disqualification of a candidate for elections. But as far as I recall these laws do not require a candidate to show proof of sound mental health.

Following its experiences between 1979 and 1982, it was suggested that a mental health certificate from a competent doctor ought to be made a requirement for each candidate seeking political office. It was also contended that the island should henceforth be spared the lunacy of public figures whose minds were observed to take flights-of-fancy which were contrary to the best interests of the people, or the country. It was hoped that such revised laws and procedures would provide an opportunity for persons resident in a particular constituency to challenge a candidate desirous of representing that constituency. At the time, some observers claimed that there were too many political hopefuls (some persons said scoundrels) who were nursing psychological wounds and other infirmities of the mind who needed to be dissuaded rather than encouraged into politics, or any other form of public service for that matter.

By early 1982, election fever had gripped the island, due in part to persistent agitation by the combined opposition of PLP and UWP. The entire country had become impatient of the constant bickering and the leadership quarrels, which had shamed and embarrassed the nation. Shortly after the swearing in of the interim Government and the announcement of a date for elections by interim Prime Minister Pilgrim, the country seemed to have breathed a collective sigh of relief.

Those who had been impatient for elections did not then seem to appreciate the necessity for a cooling off interlude, not only to allow the country to calm down, but also to offer the island's electoral commission the time it needed to properly prepare for the holding of another election. That interlude, some believe, may have saved the island's fragile democracy from violence and abuse following the turbulence and uncertainty of the previous two years. That interim period was therefore proclaimed a 'blessing-in-disguise' by many thoughtful persons who seemed to understand politics. It was believed that had the country proceeded to elections in the heated confusion of the leadership struggle, the outcome may have been even more regretted, due to the perceived likelihood of an armed revolution, or severe civil disturbance.

Thankfully, although that 1982 election campaign was full of heckling and acrimony, it never descended to the level of that of 1979. On occasions, the noise and acrimonious exchanges threatened to turn ugly, but the police and UWP supporters were up to the challenges, and would have none of it. There would therefore be no repeat of 1979 - period! Still, for those criminal elements within the society who were itching for it, the election campaign of 1982 was not without its share of excitement. Certain public meetings were known to have been disrupted by persons throwing stones and rotten eggs into the crowd at the front of those meetings. That campaign was not for the faint hearted. I recalled arriving at a public meeting at upper Waterworks road, where I found Leroy Butcher standing all by himself addressing a sparse crowd at which one or two rotten eggs had been fired. I was impressed at the way candidate Butcher (for the Castries North/East constituency) stood his ground that night. If I were to be asked to select a bunch of the most dedicated, loyal and nationalist fighters to defend Saint Lucia, my first choice would be those candidates who stood and contested elections with (and for) the St. Lucia Labour Party, when there was nothing to be gained and only integrity was at stake. As was to be expected, persons who had persisted in their opposition to the Labour government grew in strength with each passing day, and the police, to their credit, were now in full force and appearing to be impartial perhaps seeing the writing on the wall, as it were. It became evident very early in the campaign that things would not be permitted to get out of hand as they had done in 1979. From my own observations, no one was allowed to disturb the public meetings of the United Workers Party, as had been done in the previous campaign of 1979. The unspoken policy of the law enforcement authority in 1982 seemed to have been to allow the PLP and the SLP to fight each other, leaving the field free for Compton and his party to sail peacefully home to victory.

There was at the time a sort of whispered conclave of understanding among persons who had assumed the role of preserving St. Lucia for God and not allowing it to slip into the hands of wicked men - by which was meant, radicals, communists and other assorted nondescript fly-by-night politicians. Such an attitude ought to be seen (and examined) against the early consolidation of Maurice Bishop and his Peoples' Revolution Government (PRG) in Grenada, and the call for more radical political, social and economic change elsewhere in the Caribbean.

Meanwhile, the PLP was doing all it could to pass as 'the real' Labour Party. Its critics had likened the PLP's to a 'soldier crab' which would not (or could not) build a home for itself, but instead, entered and used another's exoskeleton, as home - and camouflage. The tactic of using its opponents recognized venues for the holding of its public political meetings may have fooled some novices to the game, but the trick was generally unsuccessful. Those who did not support the UWP could tell the difference between SLP and the PLP no matter how hard the latter tried to pretend that the 'L' in the middle of the name was to stand for L-O-V-E as well as Labour.

The PLP had also signalled its desire for some sort of arrangement (accommodation) with the SLP for the elections. But the latter would have none of it. At that time Odlum and his PLP were so despised within the ranks of Labour that the mere mention of his PLP would send certain SLP stalwarts into a fit of raving madness. The SLP therefore continued to regroup and as it did so it began to show glimpses of its old fighting spirit. As the campaign intensified, even the well advertised (and managed) image of Michael Pilgrim as 'Ti-Jezie' (Little Jesus), no longer held any terrors for his opponents. Pilgrim was by then being attacked mercilessly, as yet another of Odlum's creations that had backfired. By that time even his dear friends were whispering questions about the man's psychological wellness.

When it became clear that the SLP would not budge from its refusal to reunite with PLP, the latter was then forced to dig deeper into its bag of tricks. They came up with the idea of a 'national-unity-government' in which the PLP also tried to interest Compton and his UWP. At the time the proposal seemed to political observers as the last grasp at the straw by a drowning man and his ill-fated political canoe. Of course it was completely rejected by Giraudy and the UWP claiming that the olive branch offered by Odlum and his PLP was insincere, unworkable and too opportunistic. Odlum seemed to have played his last card but those who knew him well thought he may have had one more trick, which he might have picked up from his many years in England. Sadly, this was not to be. He would now be left to dry in the cruel political no-party-land and there perish or survive on his own. He had nowhere else to turn and the minions around him had no clue or solutions to offer. His bags of tricks had truly dried up and even his public charm had deserted him, as many supposed could have been judged by his writings in his weekly Crusader newspaper.

As though to prove the new depth to which he had fallen at the time, a joke began to circulate around Castries which was told to me by a senior police officer. The incident probably captured the Brother's failing luck even amongst those who remained supportive to his cause. The officer was on hand when one of the several PLP public marches and demonstrations was on its way through the streets of Castries. The march soon reached the vicinity of the building which housed the office of the Prime Minister, in those days. He said that as the marchers closed in on that office building, a few of the more robust ruffians who had formed some sort of shield around Odlum, took a firm hold of his ample girth, and then lifted him clear off the side walk, next to a large window, south of the Treasury office, and attempted to deposit their leader, inside the building. Their declared purpose was to sit 'brada George' (Brother George) in the Prime Minister's chair, which at the time could have been accessed from the Treasury. That move had apparently taken our Brother (Odlum) by complete surprise, but he played along with the antics of his 'captors' perhaps displaying once more his love for street theatre, and his flair for the impromptu. But in their anxiety to execute the lift, their awkward grab had Odlum momentarily off-balanced which resulted in his trousers coming apart, at the front and back seams. Unfortunately, the rupture of his clothing exposed his underwear and backside for all to see. In that unguarded moment of heightened excitement a woman was heard to shout in her native Creole: 'Gardez bonda brada George' (look at Brother George's backside)

Of course that ridicule brought a hearty round of laughter from those near the action, according to our police rapporteur. At that, Odlum was reported to have been so embarrassed; he disappeared for the rest of the day, leaving the protest march to others. That incident proved that in public theatre and street comedy it is difficult, if not impossible, to control the reaction of one's audience. One has therefore to be on the alert and be prepared for any eventuality or have sufficiently sensible people around to help deal with unforeseen developments. That incident may have also served to highlight the fact that no matter how well planned, such large street demonstrations and protests marches can easily get out of hand.

Another incident which may have served to dull the edge of Odlum's appeal in that campaign took place in the Castries South/East constituency which he contested against UWP candidate Clarence Rambally, former Speaker of the House of Assembly, and Kenneth Foster (SLP). At a particular public meeting of the UWP in that constituency, Odlum arrived there with an entourage of hecklers determined to make life difficult for candidate Rambally and his party colleagues. It appeared, however, that Rambally and his family had plans of their own. It was reported that as soon as the heckling began certain security personnel hired by some undisclosed persons in the UWP began firing live ammunition in the direction of Odlum and his mates, thereby forcing them to retreat and take cover. They fled down a steep muddy embankment of a nearby ravine, in a reckless almost vulgar disregard for each other, and created fast tracks across fully grown banana fields. This cowardly flight by Odlum and his gang was executed at such a hurried pace and with so little caring for the indignity and cowardliness it portrayed, soon became another fascinating political banter for those who could still appreciate such comedy. His political opponents on hearing of the hasty cowardly retreat by 'de hardest hard' - as he then liked to be called - right away began a new campaign slogan, saying: 'forward ever, backward river' in mock simulation of the PLP political anthem of 'forward ever, backward never'. After that incident, Brother George appeared to have completely lost his mystique and it is believed that he never completely recovered from that cowardly display at Bexon that evening.

There remains one last juicy tidbit which ought to help shine more light on the Jekyll and Hyde personalities of the period under review. The following information was circulated in whispers by certain close associates of Brother George. One moonless night after a hectic evening of public meetings and few celebratory drinks afterwards, Brother George was rudely awakened by an arsonist, who at the time doubled also as a foot soldier, of his party. This particular individual had done 'work' for which he expected to be paid. Our short-tempered criminal soon got tired of being given the run-around by Brother George, and his mates. He therefore decided to take matters into his own hands. One night, he crept into Brother George's bedroom in dead silence as the 'Big Brother' lay fast asleep. Suddenly, as if some hidden hand had shaken him out of his slumber, Bro. George sprung up with a start. It may have been the invader who had deliberately touched him, or some other secret angel from within that woke him. Who knows? As he came to his senses, his hand instinctively reached beneath his pillow, in search of his short-nose .38 calibre revolver. The uninvited invader, on seeing this, calmly pointed the pistol at the huge mass of humanity which lay before him and asked in his fractured English: 'Is dat you lookin for'? Before a reply had formulated itself into sound, the man added that he had come for the money owed to him and he would not leave without it. Perhaps it was the dead-panned face and the cold, life-less eyes of the intruder staring at him which brought him to his senses. It may have been the sight of his own silver brand-named pistol pointed at him, which finally got his attention. Whatever it was he seemed to have sensed the danger which faced him. The terror-stricken Odlum then hastily dived beneath his bed with his right hand and promptly pulled out a cardboard box, from which he proceeded to fish out, a handful of hundred dollar bills – all US currency - which he then hastily handed to the intruder. No other words were exchanged. Our arsonist is reported to have then left the Brother's bedroom, as quietly as he had entered. As a final parting insult the intruder is reported to have turned around and promised to deposit the firearm on the large SUV parked outside the Big Brother's House. Friends from his inner circle opined that had such a performance been scripted, it may not have turned out as authentic as it did. The details were said to have been described by the Big Brother himself making certain that those who heard of his ordeal would not repeat a word of it until time with him was no more. This experience was hardly the unique little episode some people made it out to be in the political life of the Big Brother. Indeed it were better that certain stories of which I had first hand information remained buried with that political actor whose constant mantra was that politics was the art of the possible. Besides, George Odlum believed - and to a large extent he also proved it - that in politics, as in life, use is everything. His was to constantly test the fabric of life by pushing politics to the outer edges of its potential - for good or evil.

At the time when this particular incident was reported to have taken place there were several other reported break-ins at 'Valhalla', George Odlum's Marigot Bay residence. The media was never informed what exactly was stolen or removed in these break-ins and the police have never recovered anything of value, as far as I am aware.

While all this was taking place, Compton and his UWP merely sat back and enjoyed the contretemps between their political rivals. As they watched their once feared political opponents fight among them selves for the crumbs of political support, Compton and his UWP seemed to be smiling all the way to the next opening of the new parliament, following general elections. Some people believed that the quick turnaround in the politics of the island was nothing short of a miracle. Others, perhaps less emotional and more objective, saw the greed and impatience of certain Labour Members of Parliament and called it what it was. Notwithstanding the veracity of those who understood the political realities which the country faced at the time, many persons were still saddened that it should have reached such an impasse. Others were merely content to put the fall of the SLP government down to the power of prayers and the intervention of foreign forces and others from on high.

In the period leading up to the general elections of 1982, the heated exchanges between the parties continued at full throttle. At the time I was accused of having such a cozy relationship with Comrade Forbes Burnham of Guyana, it was believed that I had arranged with him for a shipment of arms into Saint Lucia in order to assist the SLP fight its wars. Of course none of this was true. At the time I denied every charge, right there and then, but no one cared to listen. There was nothing sinister about the relationship between Burnham and myself. In fact, it would be more correct to say that President Burnham was the one who befriended me. He had good reasons then for so doing. He had gratefully acknowledged my stance in his country's dispute with Venezuela over the Essequibo region, in north/east Guyana. The latter had threatened to annex Essequibo making it a part of the Republic of Venezuela.

During that period I was Minister for Foreign Affairs of Saint Lucia. In that capacity I had taken a very strong pro-Guyana stance on the threat by Venezuela which claimed that a former settlement between European colonial powers had entitled it to Guyana's Essequibo region. That region comprised about one third of the 86,000 sq. miles which made up the country known as Guyana - formerly British Guiana. That region is large enough to hold the entire population and land masses of the rest of the English-speaking Caribbean.

I was contacted by Guyana's Foreign Affairs Minister Jackson whom I had not previously met. He thanked me on behalf of President Burnham and the Guyanese people for my stance on the land issue. Jackson also informed me that Burnham wished to meet with me in order to thank me personally. After our first meeting we developed a comradeship and a political bond. We met several times afterwards; sometimes in Europe and at other times in the Caribbean and Guyana. Burnham continued to invite me to his country even after I ceased to be a Minister in the Government of Saint Lucia. On one of my visits the President asked whether there was anything I wished him to do for me. I said there was none but that if anything should come up, I would let him know.

Later, I asked that he host two of my children at the youth skills training programme which his government had instituted on the declaration of Guyana as a Co-operative Republic. President Burnham readily agreed to my request and I duly arranged to have my daughter Petra and my son Lance travel there with me, in order to execute the plan. However, upon our arrival the officials who were administering the programme deemed my children too young (and too small) for the rigours of their training scheme. But rather than sending them back home to Saint Lucia, the Guyana government arranged for the two to stay in Georgetown at the house of the Manager of the Bank of Nova Scotia in that city. That person was none other than Saint Lucia born Chester Hinkson. From all reports the kids had a very fine time frolicking in Chester's private swimming pool and also enjoying the most delicious meals which were on offer in Guyana at the time. They were also shown lots of motherly love by Chester's wife, Delicia.

I returned to Georgetown to pick up my children some six weeks later, to fly them back home to Saint Lucia - and school. When Burnham found out that I was in his country he arranged for a small twin-engined Guyana army plane to fly us back to Saint Lucia. I had no prior knowledge of the arrangements. That aircraft was piloted by two Guyanese in army uniform. We made a safe landing at Hewanorra airport, some two hours after we departed Timerhi International airport in Guyana. There were no arms and no ammunition on that aircraft as far as I could tell, and therefore none were landed in Saint Lucia from that aircraft, at that time or at any other time of which I was aware. The aircraft which dropped us then made a swift turn around and headed back to Georgetown. There were no other persons on board except the two pilots, my two children and myself.

Upon our arrival in Saint Lucia we were met by my driver and special assistant, Mr. Harold Poyotte, a Saint Lucian who had spent many years working as a lorry driver in England. Poyotte had returned to his native country after forty years in England. He approached me soon after the elections of 1979 and offered himself as the best personal driver any Minister of the government had ever employed. He also assured me that his services would be available with guaranteed punctuality, twenty-four-seven. All he needed, he said, was at least two hours notice before an official engagement. I liked the offer of 'guaranteed-punctuality' and decided to give him a try. At the time it had become a bad national habit, especially amongst farm workers, to absent themselves from work the day following a public holiday. Mondays, after a hectic weekend of feting, were also set aside for rest and recuperation. That habit seemed to have also crept into the monthly paid staff of the government. In those days it appeared that even the private sector was not spared such poor work ethic.

My need for a competent and punctual driver, led me to recommend Poyotte to the office of the Minister of Finance for an appointment as driver in the Ministry of Agriculture. Prime Minister Louisy made the necessary arrangements and in quick time, Poyotte was appointed driver and personal assistant to the Minister for Agriculture. He was not very well known on the island at the time, because of the many years he had spent off it. When it was discovered that the bald-headed-cigar-smoking Poyotte was employed full time as my driver and personal assistant, the opposition parties and their newspapers threw a tantrum. They began attacking him as though the man was some newly discovered assassin from a foreign land, hired to do my bidding. The real fear may have been that Poyotte had been employed as some sort of talisman to help me relegate my opponents to the 'waste basket' of local politics. I was aware that the politicians who kept the most noise were often the very ones who carried on the most underhand and nefarious acts, when they thought no one was looking. These were the same persons who were prepared to sleep with the devil one night and the next morning, be the first to attend church service - or Holy Mass. Such politicians were never without a stash of US currency hidden where they could retrieve it with the least difficulty. They kept the country in a state of constant agitation and by so doing diverted attention from their shady dealings, as they pointed fingers at others.

Poyotte soon became a target of such politicians and their party operatives. The poor man was relentlessly harassed by these hooligans, particularly in the city. It was as if the laws of libel and slander had taken a hiking holiday. Those who fancied themselves foot soldiers and thinking Poyotte may have been armed and dangerous, were often to abuse and insult the man for no reason whatsoever. It was a mark of the peoples' ignorance at the time that many did not need any form of provocation before they launched an attack on their perceived opponents. Thankfully, Harold Poyotte was a jovial sort of fellow who paid little attention to his detractors and hecklers. I, however, warned him that some idiot may chance an attack on him, if they became carried away by emotion and recklessness, especially after drinks. Of course there was no truth of him being armed and dangerous. He certainly knew how to defend himself, as he was also an amateur boxer in England. But he never carried a firearm.

The truth is Poyotte was embarrassed by all the attention he was getting. On several occasions he offered to resign from the job. I explained as best I could, the reasons he should 'let the dogs bark' as they say. If they in fact attempted to hurt him, then he was free to use maximum force to defend himself, I advised him. I also reminded him that the words of his tormentors often spoke more about them, than they did of him and his friends. I took time to point out to him the many persons of goodwill who often stopped to chat, and offered a kind word of support, as we went about the business of the State.

In the meantime the PLP was still trying to prove that it was one and the same thing as the St. Lucia Labour Party. By then the SLP leadership had had enough. Perhaps the last straw in its on-going deception to pass off as the St. Lucia Labour Party was its attempt to hold a public meeting at the Mauricettes' residence in Marchand, Castries. Whitney Mauricette was at the time a stalwart and former executive member of the SLP. He had won Castries Town Board elections in the sixties on an SLP ticket and his house was a known SLP meeting place. In addition: 'The Mauricettes' were my in-laws and I was the political leader of the SLP'. Of course the PLP's advances were firmly rejected by Mauricette, who also had some choice but friendly words for the PLP leader. Those who became aware of George Odlum's tricks were forced to ask, what sort of mind would try such a stunt anyway?

The message which such conduct suggested to the SLP was that its 'friends' in the PLP were desperate to find a way out of the hole they had dug themselves. Their frustration seemed then to show at every turn. Each time they opened their mouths to speak, more venom spewed out of it, yet behind their bold public utterances some were busy quietly trying to woo the more gentle spirits within the SLP to some sort of negotiated accommodation or settlement by which to contest elections and help them save face. It seemed they were finally waking up and smelling the coffee but, they did not like what they saw coming once they became aware they were no longer dreaming. Those whose heads were not buried in the sand had seen the hopes and dreams of 1979 lying shattered before them. But these SLP supporters also knew that the failure was due to the problems within their party and no one else was to be blamed. Experience teaches us that there are costs to be borne from each mistake one makes along life's journey.

The PLP-inspired heckling against the UWP and the SLP was particularly noticeable when new candidates of those two parties were called upon to address a public meeting for the first time. The hecklers knew of the sure nervousness of a new candidate's first public address. The public was also aware that if a nervous candidate were to mispronounce a word or two or commit some other sort of gaffe, such a blunder would send the hecklers' into a state of frenzy. They would then turn around and use the poor candidate's mistake to label that candidate with a suitable sobriquet that may last for the duration of the campaign, and at times for the balance of his life, if he was unable to make fun of his gaffe. Towards the end of that election campaign some of the harsh tactics of the PLP began to backfire on them. Their scare tactics no longer intimidated their opponents as they had done earlier. But the PLP, never stopped trying to find a road back from the precipice. Creativity had by then appeared to have deserted them. The PLP became increasingly nervous and frustrated as it became more evident with each passing day that they were staring into the jaws of defeat.

To pave the way for the anticipated elections, the sittings of the Senate and the House of Assembly first had to be officially dissolved. To that end, the Saint Lucia government gazette dated Saturday 30th. January 1982, number 5, read as follows: 'Pursuant to section 27(2) (c) of the Constitution of Saint Lucia, His Excellency Acting on the advice of the Prime Minister declared the seats of the following Senators vacant'.

Senator	-	*Charles Augustine*
Senator	-	*Thomas Walcott*
Senator	-	*Clarence Rambally*
Senator	-	*Peter Hilary Modeste*
Senator	-	*Edward Harry Joseph (Chef Harry)*

In addition to the notice informing of the vacant seats in the Senate, other gazette notices were to follow. That proclaiming the dissolution of Parliament, read as follows: 'Whereas by subsection (1) & (4) of section 55 of the Constitution of Saint Lucia, and whereas it is expedient that the existing Parliament of Saint Lucia be dissolved on 6th of February one thousand nine hundred and eighty two; Given under my hand and the public Seal at Government House this 27th. Day of January, 1982'. It was therefore now officially confirmed that the long awaited elections would finally be held.

In early April and following the January gazette notices, another government release announced that by virtue of section 29 (1) of the House of Assembly (Elections) Act, 1979, (No.8 of 1979) an Electoral Commission was appointed comprising: Chairman, Mr. Maurice Salles-Miquelle, Mr. Gerald Guard and Mr. Edward W. Rock. The Commission then set about its work, first appointing Mr. J. Mc. Clair Daniel, Chief Elections Officer. By the middle of April (1982), Daniel had issued yet another notice in the gazette, (of No. 16 of 1982, page 321) advising the general public that the election writ had been issued by the Governor General on April 6, 1982 and that the date fixed for the nomination of candidates for the general elections of May 3, 1982 was April 20, 1982, within the hours of 9 a.m. and 12 noon.

In addition to the above releases, the Chief Elections Office also caused to be published in the official gazette of the 14 of April 1982, (pages 380 to 393) a full list of Presiding Officers and Poll Clerks for each of the 17 constituencies and the polling divisions within these constituencies, covering the entire island.

Many of the candidates of the three parties who agreed to contest the 1982 elections were new to politics. Little or nothing was known of them either by the party which was proposing them for these elections or by the people who were asked to vote for them. It seemed the only persons who were familiar with certain of the candidates at any depth were those from their homes and communities. Some candidates appeared unfamiliar with the electoral process and the steps that were to be taken by a candidate vying for political office, in order to secure nomination and select agents and poll clerks. Amidst the excitement and information overload - sometimes even contradictory ones - which often characterize such elections, the three political parties finally announced their list of candidates. Each party announced one candidate for each of the seventeen constituencies. There were also two 'independent candidates' whose presence went largely unnoticed.

The following is the list of candidates of the St. Lucia Labour Party showing their respective constituencies and the candidates' trades and/or profession at the time:

St. Lucia Labour Party (S.L.P)

1. Austin Jude - *Castries N/W Babonneau (Farmer)*
2. Henry Marquis - *Micoud South (Farmer)*
3. Cecil Lay - *Vieux-Fort North (Farmer)*
4. Daphney Murray - *Castries South (Home maker)*
5. Kenneth Foster - *Castries South East (Barrister)*
6. Winston Cenac - *Soufriere (Barrister)*
7. Carlisle Jn.Baptiste - *Anse-La-Raye/Canaries (Technician)*
8. LeRoy Butcher - *Castries North/East (Economist Lecturer)*
9. Peter Josie - *Vieux-Fort South (Agronomist)*
10. Hilary Modest - *Castries Central (Economist)*
11. Remy Lesmond - *Dennery South (Builder)*
12. Thomas Walcott - *Gros-Islet (Civil Engineer)*
13. Patrick Fell - *Castries East (Businessman)*
14. Gregor Mason - *Choiseul (Agriculturist)*

15. Neville Cenac	-	*Laborie/Saltibus (Law Clerk)*
16. Peter Wilfred	-	*Dennery North (Salesman)*
17. Reynold Charles	-	*Micoud North (Farmer)*

As the campaign progressed, frequent power-cuts in electricity across the island continued unabated. These outages became a source of grave concern to everyone. Some believed that they were an attempt to embarrass Prime Minister Pilgrim and his government. Others were inclined to think the outages were due to human error in construction and maintenance of these huge machines. Others merely interpreted them as a reminder that Pilgrim and his PLP were to avoid playing any games with the date of elections, as it was widely rumoured they were planning to do.

As the date for elections drew closer, a new group calling itself the 'International Committee of Concerned Saint Lucians', was formed in New York. It appeared that the reason for its formation was to float certain names in the public domain in Saint Lucia for future elections. It also said that 'it was concerned about the difficulties being experienced by the island at the time, and over the last two years'. Strangely, after the first press releases, nothing more was heard from that New York group. It apparently did not succeed in its bid to have a look-in at the candidate selection process of the party which it thought was destined to win the coming elections – the UWP. The opportunistic behaviour of certain Saint Lucians, then resident in New York, has been a side show of every election since this island's Independence, and probably long before that, as well. It seems certain to continue, according to certain sources of credible information. Some of these New York based 'Lucians' are also great talkers and writers. Indeed many may even be well meaning in their desire to see their island progress and are determined to assist in this regard. But others have argued that if they love their country, as they say they do, then why don't they work hard, save, study and return home to invest in business, politics and whatever else they may choose to do.

Around the time the Saint Lucia group in New York announced itself, the SLP also disclosed there were several persons receiving two or more identification cards by making false representations to the electoral office. The information released by the SLP of apparent fraud in the voter registration process spread quickly. At the time, some feeble response came from the electoral office; but the SLP, now beginning to feel its strength again, started to issue veiled threats and promised to take matters into its own hands. It did not bother to elaborate what its words meant and many within the party quickly warned against such bravado, fearing the tone of such messages would do the party more harm than good.

In my capacity as political leader, I was approached by certain senior executive members of the party and persuaded by these gentler souls, to issue a statement to the media restating the party's position on free and fair elections and emphasizing that it was those who attempted to corrupt the democratic electoral process who were spreading the seeds of violence and rebellion. The SLP also claimed that it was determined to fight such abuses of the process. I was also warned by party insiders to be as tactful as possible in my public utterances as my advisers did not want it to appear that the party was deliberately stirring unrest and mischief. Clearly, the SLP was bent on distancing itself from the turmoil of its immediate past. Strategically, we were to project the impression that we had learnt from our mistakes. But the judgement and punishment which was to occur on 3 May 1982 would be lesson enough for everyone desirous of learning.

Although the statement which I issued at the time warned against corruption of the electoral process, our friends at the 'Voice newspaper' chose to stick me in their newspaper headline of Saturday 3 April, 1982, with the banner: Josie to SLP: "STAY IN LINE". Perhaps a more appropriate headline would have read: 'SLP WARNS AGAINST ELECTORAL FRAUD'. But the Voice couldn't seem to care less and no one except the rich and connected (or famous), told it what to do.

In the meantime, the UWP team of candidates for the 1982 general elections was announced. It was touted as the most balanced and experienced of the three parties and invited the electorate to think unity and leadership. The following is the list of UWP candidates for the 1982 general elections.

U.W.P Candidates (1982)

1. *Leonnard Riviere* - *Soufriere (Barrister)*
2. *Brendan Hippolyte* - *Laborie/Saltibus (Security)*
3. *Eldridge Stephen* - *Vieux-Fort South/(Businessman)*
4. *John Bristol* - *Castries/North East (Insurance Executive)*
5. *Murray Thomas* - *Vieux-Fort North (Sales Rep)*
6. *Brian Charles* - *Choiseul (Sales Clerk)*
7. *Peter Philip* - *Gros-Islet (Businessman)*
8. *Louis George* - *Micoud North .(Teacher/Farmer)*
9. *John Compton* - *Micoud South (Barrister/Farmer)*
10. *Desmond Brathwaite* - *Castries South (Printing)*
11. *Clarence Rambally* - *Castries/SouthEast (Barrister)*
12. *Romanus Lansiquot* - *Castries East (Public Relations)*
13. *Ira D'Auvergne* - *Anse-La-Raye/Canaries (Barrister)*
14. *Allan Bousquet* - *Cast.N/W Babonneau (Seaman)*
15. *Clendon Mason* - *Dennery South (Barrister)*

| 16. George Mallet | - Castries Central (Insurance Broker) |
| 17. Ferdinand Henry | - Dennery North (Businessman) |

In the meantime the Electoral office in Castries had issued all the necessary notices for general elections. These included the writs to candidates, publishing the names of returning officers and poll clerks; publishing the supplementary list of electors; notices of location of polling stations, times of opening and closing of voting, among others. These notices along with other bits of information were also published in the official government Gazette. They covered each of the seventeen constituencies and also included 'nomination day' and 'polling day'. The Government Gazette also published the resignation from office of Michael Pilgrim, interim Prime Minister, in an extraordinary issue, recorded as volume 151, no. 21 and dated Tuesday 4, May 1982 – the day after general elections. That notice cleared the way for the Governor General to appoint a new Prime Minister.

By then all talk of 'national unity' had been thrown off the election train. Opponents of the idea did not anticipate its early resurrection, unless they had use for someone such as Brother George Odlum in future. Not a word had been heard from the so called 'Committee for National Unity' ever since it had taken a full page advertisement, announcing its presence and swearing sincere and abiding nationalism. Some observers suggested the committee had gone into hibernation having accomplished what it had set out to do – creating the conditions for the peaceful return of Compton and his UWP to the seat of government.

For these elections I had switched constituencies from Castries East to Vieux-Fort South. In that contest certain persons sent letters to the press questioning my change of constituency. Of course these missives took the opportunity to advocate support for Eldridge Stephens, the United Workers Party candidate, for Vieux-Fort South. I tried not to pay attention to such feather-weight attacks especially in places the electorate never bothered to look. I had always preferred a campaign where I could meet and speak with the common folk especially in a closed town-hall type situation where I could assess and see and feel for myself such persons who wished to ask questions, no matter how difficult these may be, and to give a candid reply.

After many anxious weeks of delay (and perhaps waiting) the PLP finally released its slate of candidates. That list in the view of many was made up of persons who were less likely to excel in serving their country at the national political level, than had been promised. But the leadership of that party did not seem to care. It had earlier criticized Compton as running a government with a group of incompetents. It now seemed determined to do the same. The following is a list of candidates which the PLP eventually announced and published as their choice to contest the general elections of 3 May, 1982.

PLP candidates (1982)

1. Philip Jules   -   Gros Islet (Businessman)
2. Vance Pilgrim   -   Castries East (Pharmacist)
3. Antonius Gibson   -   Castries Central (Elec.Technician)
4. Anthony Bellas   -   Vieux-Fort North (Agriculturalist)
5. Stephen Mathurin   -   Micoud South (Welder)
6. Lennard Leonce   -   Babonneau (Agric. Engineer)
7. Sam Augier   -   Soufriere (Sales Rep.)
8. George Goddard   -   Choiseul/Saltibus (Trade Unionist)
9. George Odlum   -   Castries South/East (Economist)
10. Richard Edwin   -   Dennery North (Trade Unionist)
11. Modest Downes   -   Vieux-Fort South. (Teacher)
12. Jon Odlum   -   Castries South (Community Organizer)
13. Frances Michel   -   Anse-La-Raye/Can (Realtor)
14. Michael Pilgrim   -   Castries/North/East (Developer)
15. Gilroy Satney   -   Choiseul (Teacher)
16. Clive Alexander   -   Laborie/Saltibus (Salesman)
17. Victor Fadlien   -   Micoud North (Disc Jockey/Announcer.)

A reporting on general elections as contested in Saint Lucia and the rest of the Caribbean would not be complete without some elaboration on the important matter of financing of election campaigns. In the mid-seventies it became apparent to many persons here that money was playing an increasing role in the build up to general elections. It was observed that campaigning for elections was moving further and further away from the grass roots and community town halls, of the fifties and sixties. Increasingly large week-end rallies that more resembled huge music festivals and which cost large sums of money were taking over the style of campaigning. The accent seemed increasingly on entertainment rather than on education, and the sharing of manifesto proposals, and other ideas for national development. The personal one-on-one touch was slowly giving way to the more impersonal 'music festivals' which employ foreign guest artistes in order to draw larger, and ever larger, crowds. This change had driven up the cost of election campaigns exponentially and nobody knew for certain who (or what) is funding such campaign rallies. Many people, however, now worry aloud that the source of such funds are either foreign government or drug lords - or both.

When I first contested general elections in May 1974, I chose to run in the geographically small but densely populated constituency of Castries East. Even so, supporters were demanding that they be accommodated as camp followers wherever my campaign team travelled. I soon discovered that transportation costs were the most burdensome liability of my election campaigns. Other items of expenditure such as posters, pamphlets, banners, and paid radio and television advertisements paled vis-à-vis transporting supporters about. Printed T-shirts with party slogans also took a large chunk of change. Back then candidates were supported financially by friends and well wishers. Today, the large weekend rallies seem to conspire to make the campaign expenditures of the seventies and even those of the eighties seem like pocket change to a minor.

Some political observers have claimed that political expenditure got out of hand in the seventies when the conservatives and their western allies pulled out all the stops in order to block the ascendency of the left in the region. The status quo at the time had no answers for the arguments and incisive criticisms of the rising vanguard of young graduates returning to the Caribbean to carry on the struggle where Garvey, Marryshow, Butler and others of that ilk had left it in the thirties and forties. The search for adult suffrage and improved constitutions had taken the struggle one step forward. Now the demand (and the new struggle) was to return to the masses the respect, the pride and most of all the wealth which had been stolen from them.

The establishment and their friends fought back by providing political parties with large weekend rallies and buses loaded with persons anxious for entertainment to attend as many of them as possible. The end result was to diminish serious political discussion and debate and to relegate political campaigning to the politics of cricket, rum, music and sex in a way never seen before. Politics was therefore gradually reduced to mere show and entertainment, not to be taken seriously. Even as these rallies were organized, however, the conscientious candidate, especially those who are financially able to do so, still kept his or her constituency warm with regular outings, and walk abouts. But in reality, it was the weekend rally which both the youth and middle aged were most interested in attending - to see and hear foreign artistes perform. Well organized and properly advertised Sunday afternoon political rallies attracted many thousands of persons from all walks of life. Such large numbers of persons were never seen before at 'political' events. By 1982 a political party which was serious about putting on a good showing at the polls was forced to follow the pattern, and organize its own weekend rallies of entertainment and show, engaging local and foreign artistes. The St. Lucia Labour Party barely managed to do so in 1982. After the party had been forced out of office in disgrace, few but the staunchest of loyal supporters would invest any cash in the party's campaign. By then such financial support had become a sort of business investment, and business was always reluctant to invest where there were no prospects of returns on their investments.

It was whilst contemplating the predicament in which the St. Lucia Labour Party had found itself that I received a telephone call out of the clear blue sky, from an old friend in Barbados. That call was supposedly to wish me well in the coming elections and also to offer a small financial contribution to assist in my campaign efforts. There was, however, one minor problem in meeting the wishes of that particular caller. He was to leave Barbados for Canada in a couple days and I was to come and collect his offer, before he left for his travels. I therefore immediately contacted LIAT (Leeward Islands Air Transport) to fly me to Barbados and back. To my utter disappointment there were no available seats either to or from that island on that day or, for the following two days. It was suggested that my only chance of getting to and from Barbados in the time frame that I desired was by chartered flight. But how could I reasonably be expected to invest in a chartered flight, I thought, without a clue exactly what was on offer.

Then a miracle happened. Someone at LIAT informed me that the company had just chartered Mr. Ewart 'Yerti' Hinkson, a St. Lucia born pilot with many years experience, to fly to Grenada (from Saint Lucia) to pick up a patient who was bound for the Queen Elizabeth hospital in Barbados. I was also informed that pilot Hinkson was due to return to St. Lucia immediately afterwards. After some brief negotiations I paid LIAT the full fare to Barbados and back, and I was soon on that chartered flight to Barbados via Grenada, with pilot Hinkson. We took off in a small eight–seater aircraft with me as 'co-pilot' and with full confidence that the gods still had use for me.

We landed safely at the new Point Salines Airport (now renamed Maurice Bishop International) about fifty-five minutes or so after take off. The patient was promptly wheeled onto the aircraft on a stretcher which was made to fit on the floor of the aircraft, in which the seats had been removed. The patient's son and daughter (both appearing to me to be in the mid-to late thirties) sat at the back of the cockpit in the only other available seating on that aircraft at the time. I remained seated in the cockpit next to Pilot Hinkson. We soon left Grenada and waltzed our way through the scattered clouds from there to Barbados. We reached our destination safely in about the same time as it took from Saint Lucia to Grenada. While the business of the sick was being looked after, I made a bee-line to immigration and then to the exit lounge and did what I had set out to do in Barbados. My contact (and friend) was at the airport waiting.

After a brief exchange of pleasantries, I hurriedly returned to the departure lounge and soon boarded that same aircraft back to Saint Lucia. Before departure however, I discovered that the business-minded LIAT authorities in Saint Lucia and Barbados had promptly arranged to replace the six seats which had been removed from the little aircraft. That was done in order to accommodate six Saint Lucians who were patiently waiting at the airport in Barbados to get back to Saint Lucia. By the time we left Barbados the sun had passed its mid-point so we were flying straight into its brilliant face. It was uncomfortable in that narrow front seat, but I would take the sun any day before rain and clouds when I am seated in one of these 'iron birds'. We had an uneventful flight back home and upon arrival I was met at Vigie airport (renamed George F. L. Charles airport) by one party stalwart, to whom I had disclosed my brief absence from the island.

After we had alighted from the small aircraft and were inside the terminal building at Vigie, a young vibrant Saint Lucian male who had made the trip with us from Barbados approached me and said 'Mr. Josie, I would never have travelled on that little plane if I did not see you getting on it'. I may have told him I did not quite follow his line of reasoning, but that we each had a role we are to play on our earthly journey and that nothing can happen to change that mission until that role has been fulfilled, to the satisfaction of the true and living God, Most High. I think he got the point by his broad smile and hearty handshake after my little speech.

It is commonly accepted that financing election campaigns is going to continue to pose a bigger challenge in future if we do nothing about affording newcomers to politics an opportunity to make their case free of charge on national radio and television. The media, which has been making increasingly loud noises of late about its role as watch dogs of and for the people, should play some part in helping facilitate regular political discourse without its own biased involvement in the debate. But that would be an extremely difficult task in small societies such as ours where jealousies are often rife and crooked, and dishonest men lurk at every corner waiting to influence the way the media does its work.

At the time of writing there seems to be only two options for financing election campaigns and for allowing different ideas to contend. One is to open up the public media (at taxpayers' expense) to those who think they have a contribution to make in politics. The other is to monitor and limit contributions to individuals and political parties. In addition, new election laws should ban T-shirt advertising political personalities or political parties. Watchdog national democracy groups should be set up in each community to monitor and report on any extravagant expenditures or gifts offered by candidates to constituents. There must be established in law a ceiling of expenditure for each candidate and political party. Each candidate must by law be in a position to explain his or her sources of financing. No candidate ought to be allowed to spend in an election more funds than that prescribed in law.

Unless something is done very quickly about election campaign financing, the Caribbean may wake up one day and find that the entire region is under the direct control of a foreign country in the way it once was. Perhaps it may also discover then, that the region is also shared with the largest international drug cartels that by then would have controlled sufficient government interests in and around the region to make them indistinguishable from an independent foreign power.

This present generation ought, therefore, not to shelve the serious matter of election campaign financing, leaving it for others to solve. If we have learnt anything, it is that history is past politics and politics present history; both are constantly on the move and neither will be held back.

UWP Wins: Landslide Victory

History is past politics, and politics present history.

Sir John Robert

On the night of May 3, 1982 when it seemed that his party was heading for victory - and long before the official results - the leader of the UWP, John Compton, took to radio and television and announced that his party had won the elections. The time was around 8.55 p.m. barely two and a half hours after the polls had closed. Although many on the island had predicted such an outcome they were nevertheless taken off guard by Compton's early claim to victory. Persons who loved to record the details of the balloting in each constituency and enjoy the suspense of anticipating election results were known to be disappointed with Compton's early claim. In this country the counting of votes cast for each candidate usually begins immediately after the official closing of the polls soon after the last voter has cast his or her ballot. The time lapse between the shutting of the doors of the polling stations and the commencement of counting of the ballots is that which is allowed to last-minute voters who may have been standing in line to vote after the doors to the polling station were closed.

The early trend which the counting of the ballots revealed was that which most people had predicted and therefore came as no surprise to them. Even so, hardly anyone expected such an early announcement by the leader of the UWP. Persons who were paid to monitor and relay the elections results to the general public that evening, were also reported to have been caught off guard by Compton's early announcement. Compton seemed like a man in a great hurry to reclaim the government which many people said had been virtually handed to him by the quarrelsome Labour Party.

After Compton announced his party's victory the PLP and the SLP were reported to have been dazed by the knockout punch the voters had delivered at the polls. They were apparently caught in a Machiavellian web of deceit and denial which they had themselves spun. The former immediately set about denouncing the results as fraudulent and rigged. They claimed that 'foreign elements' were involved in the fraud and accused such 'elements' of dirty tricks, and of aiding the winning party. The PLP also claimed that their supporters saw 'red-hearts' on their ballot papers, instead of black images of their party symbol - a heart-shaped figure. They may have forgotten to inform the skeptical public that only their party (PLP) was so negatively impacted by the 'fraud' which they were supposed to have detected. How that party came by all this information was never disclosed – not even to their staunchest supporters. Thankfully, very few persons took the PLP claim seriously. Only the most reckless and naive may have been impressed by the 'red hearts' accusation.

It was observed that during their long and spirited election campaign the PLP seemed to have posted images of hearts all over the island. These were to be found on private and public buildings, on school fences and gates, on telephone and electricity poles, on shop windows and public facilities such as bathrooms and of course on the insides of dwelling homes - even in bedrooms. Unfortunately, in this national exercise of massive indoctrination and political propaganda, no one had taken the time to inform supporters of the PLP that their party symbol would not be printed with red ink on the ballot paper. Instead it was to appear in black ink as was everything else printed on the ballot papers. During its campaign the 'red heart' had become the captured prisoner of a party aiming to use that colour to deceive those who associated 'red' with the St. Lucia Labour Party. It may also have used that colour to extract financial support from foreign governments which hold that colour very dearly.

By their constant displaying and advertising of their 'red heart' symbol on every available lamp post, public buildings, supporters' homes, and other hastily constructed bill boards, the PLP's attempt at mass psychological indoctrination may have worked to their downfall. Its leaders may not have been aware of the effect which the 'red' heart symbol was having on the psyche of their supporters. But the political leader, who was familiar with Hitler's methods at the time he was preparing German youth for an assault on the rest of the world, may well have known exactly what he was doing.

Soon after the polls were closed at Vieux-Fort South in which constituency I contested the 1982 general elections, I met a certain medical doctor who was employed as a consultant at St. Jude hospital, in Vieux-Fort. That doctor, who is alive and well at the time of this writing, confided that when he was handed the ballot paper on the morning of May 3, in order to cast his vote, he was certain he saw a red symbol on that ballot paper. He repeated that it was at the very first glance he had seen the red symbol next to which he intended to cast his vote. He then added that he was also aware the ink used for printing the ballot paper was black. "So why was he seeing red, I asked myself." Of course, our goodly doctor quickly admitted that a second glance at the ballot paper which he held in his hand Voila! The symbol was black. In that quick fraction of a second, the mass indoctrination of the red hearts almost had a medical doctor fooled. He had at first seen a red heart which he believed then, the majority of other PLP supporters must have seen on their ballot paper, on that day. This medical doctor at least had the good sense and presence of mind to re-examine the ballot paper which was handed to him, the morning of election. He assured me (and his friends) that there was no red heart on his ballot paper. However he seemed certain he had at first seen one. The question therefore is: Why (or how) did this highly trained and qualified medical doctor see 'red' instead of 'black' which was on that ballot paper? Secondly, if this could have happened to a smart doctor what should one expect of the poor fellow who had followed his party blindly and whose waking moments are filled with the obeah (and voodoo) of every description?

When the dust had finally settled on the elections of 1982 and the votes had all been counted, the full extent of the people's wrath against the two Labour parties became crystal clear. Those who would not listen and who thought they could have hoodwinked an entire nation with sweet-sounding phrases and lofty promises, were to be sorely disappointed. Their machinations and falsehoods had come home to roost. The election results were a great embarrassment to them and their ill-informed advisers. The people seemed so determined to vote out the Labour 'boys' that not a joyful sound was heard until they had done what they had set out to do. They had lined up near polling stations from five thirty that morning and waited patiently in line to cast their ballots. They had turned out to vote in even larger numbers than they had done in 1979.

Interestingly, once Compton and his UWP had been declared victorious, those passive, distant and unsmiling faces which were observed on the voting lines at polling stations around the island, soon burst into jubilation and hearty laughter. There was much hooting and tooting of car horns and other forms of noise-making and general rejoicing. The electorate appeared to have achieved their heart's desire at that particular election. After Compton had first made it clear that his team had won the vote and had later received confirmation from official sources, he immediately contacted the office of the Governor General and made arrangements to be sworn in as Prime Minister, the next morning.

The election results revealed that only in the towns of Vieux-Fort and Soufriere in which myself (political leader) and former Prime Minister Cenac respectively, contested, did the SLP salvage some pride and emerge with its dreams, instead of the nightmare which many had predicted. It was evident that the SLP might have won more seats had there not been a third party contesting. Indeed, the PLP may well make the same claim, but the former party was more firmly established on the island and the latter was merely a splinter from it. The remarkable power of Odlum's persistency and his determined efforts may have been most evident in the many votes which he and his PLP were able to garner, especially from the unsuspecting young urban 'cowboys' of the day. When the votes were all counted and the results analyzed, it showed more candidates had lost their deposits ($250.00) than at any other previous elections in the history of adult suffrage on the island. Many PLP candidates appeared to have performed more creditably than expected, although that party won only the Castries South constituency which Jon Odlum contested.

In the Castries South/East seat where PLP leader George Odlum was up against former House Speaker Clarence Rambally (UWP) and Kenneth Foster (SLP), Rambally won handsomely. Many interpreted the PLP leader's loss as the end of the road for both himself and the PLP. There were some whispered suggestions from certain Odlum fanatics that Jon Odlum should be asked to resign from his hard-won seat in order to allow big brother George, to contest and hopefully win that seat in a by-election. Of course those who had suggested that never bothered to offer another parliamentary seat to Jon Odlum. On hearing this, I would not have been the least surprised had Jon Odlum told the bearers of such vicious and infantile thoughts, which cliff they should jump off.

As the full import of these elections began to be more fully appreciated some diehard anti-Compton people were still asking aloud: 'what would have happened had there been a strategic alliance between the two opposition parties, the SLP and PLP'? There is little doubt in certain minds that the electorate would not have been fooled by such a convenient alliance. There was no love lost between these two political parties at the time, and everyone knew it. The plain truth was that very few supporters of the SLP any longer trusted the leadership of the PLP. The SLP party stalwarts believed then that too many politicians had disrespected the common-sense-savvy of the average citizen, and that people had to pay for their mistakes. At the time, it was also suggested that those politicians who believed that they alone knew what was best for Joe Public, ought not to be allowed to contest elections. How to achieve this was, of course, the million dollar question. Of equal interest may be the fact that many (some say most) politicians are yet to discover what actually motivates the average citizen to vote the way he or she does at elections. .

After the routing his party suffered in 1979, no one had predicted that a mere two-and-a-half years later, Compton would have been back as Prime Minister. However, once the door to new elections was opened, everyone, it seemed, both in Saint Lucia and in the Caribbean region correctly predicted the return of the former government to office. The UWP were of course jubilant and perhaps more so because they had wisely not accepted Compton's earlier letter of resignation as political leader and instead asked him to lead the party in the 1982 election race. The man, who never said die, had been given an early opportunity to reclaim the government he so loved to head, and he did it using his opponents to do the dirty work for him.

After the election results became public property there was a huge sigh of relief throughout the island. The festivities which ran well into mid-morning of May 4 were typical of the celebrations with which supporters of winning political parties greet such favourable election results. As was to be expected, there were some gloomy faces in the midst of all the rejoicing and drinking and fêting. It was also distressing to see so many people who had believed many of the lies they had been fed from certain politicians, go about stone-faced and dazed as though they were sleep-walking and unable to come to terms with the reality that had hit them. Among the staunch supporters of the victorious side there were many who contented themselves with a prayer of thanksgiving. Others simply went about their daily lives as if their voting and their party's victory were every day occurrences, which they took in stride. These people may well have been the backbone of what is widely known, but little spoken of on the island as the core prayer warriors of the nation. Even as the celebrations continued, the newly returned Prime Minister was already on the airwaves letting everyone know what the priorities of his new government would be, once they had settled in office: job creation, law enforcement and foreign investments among others.

Crime was not a major concern at the time, but there were signs of increasing lawlessness especially on the roads where too many people continued to drive without due care and attention. Bad driving, poor road manners and impatience and indiscipline were already showing their ugly heads on the island. Some persons seemed to have believed at the time that, by returning Compton to office, the anticipated job creation and the improvement in the governance of the country would have helped ameliorate the increasing incidence of lawlessness. Others were however quick to observe that John Compton was never a strict disciplinarian. Some claim that under his watch too many people got away with murder - literally.

Prime Minister Compton had often referred to that period 1979 to 1982 as 'years of hard labour', and urged Saint Lucians never to forget that, and to avoid a repetition at all cost. No matter what the future may hold, Compton told Saint Lucians, they were never to drop their guard again. In short, the people of the country were advised to do everything within their power to avoid a return to the ugly and embarrassing years of the country's trial by political opportunists and sweet-talking con-men and other assorted fly-by-night political entities.

The official and final elections results were published in the government Gazette and the newspapers on the island. The following are the results that appeared in the official government Gazette.

1.	John G. M. Compton	-	Member for Micoud/South.
2.	William G. Mallet	-	Member for Castries/Central.
3.	Joseph R. A. Bousquet	-	Member for Castries North/West Babonneau.
4.	Clendon H. Mason	-	Member for Dennery/South.
5.	Leonard J. Riviere	-	Member for Soufriere
6.	Ferdinand Henry	-	Member for Dennery/North
7.	Romanus Lansiquot	-	Member for Castries/East
8.	Clarence Rambally	-	Member for Castries South/East
9.	Ira d'Auvergne	-	Member for Anse-La-Raye/Canaries.
10.	John L. Bristol	-	Member for Castries North/East
11.	Peter P. Phillip	-	Member for Gros-Islet.
12.	Brian Charles	-	Member for Chois./Fond St.J'cks.
13.	Louis George	-	Member for Micoud North
14.	Eldridge Stephens	-	Member for Vieux-Fort/South
15.	Neville Cenac	-	Member for Laborie
16.	Cecil Lay	-	Member for Vieux-Fort North
17.	Jon Odlum	-	Member for Castries/ South.

The Gazette of May 7 th. 1982 (vol.151, No. 22) said in an extraordinary edition, that John Compton had been appointed Prime Minister by the Governor General after taking the Oath of office at Government House, earlier. One week later, the government Gazette of Friday 14th. May in volume 151 No. 24 announced the appointment of Mr. Neville Cenac as Leader of the Opposition in Parliament.

The House of Assembly met at 9.15 a.m. on 8 th. June 1982. The Clerk read the Proclamation given under the hand of His Excellency the Governor General, Mr. Boswell Williams, and the public Seal of the State, at Government House, Castries Saint Lucia on the 28 th. day of May 1982.

The first order of business was the election of Speaker. Mr. Wilfred St. Clair Daniel was elected Speaker. He was nominated by Prime Minister Compton and seconded by the Leader of the Opposition Neville Cenac – aka 'Chandelle molle' (soft candle) younger brother of former Prime Minister Winston Cenac. In seconding the Prime Minister's nomination, the Opposition Leader said: "In keeping with the past tradition known to me, I will second the nomination of Mr. St. Clair Daniel." The lone PLP Member of parliament in the House, Jon Odlum, had other ideas. The member for Castries South promptly got to his feet and nominated Mr. Cyril Landers, a Barrister by training, as Speaker. Interestingly, Odlum's motion was seconded by none other than Cecil Lay, the member for Vieux-Fort North and the only other member of the SLP in parliament. Yet Lay had chosen to vote with Jon Odlum against the nominee of the Leader of the Opposition, a member of his own party. What Jon Odlum's nomination and Lay's support said quite clearly to everyone was that, even in defeat, the St. Lucia Labour Party was still divided and not at peace with itself.

Perhaps tempers had not yet sufficiently cooled since the earlier quarrels within that party. It appeared the divided Labour parties were condemned to fight amongst themselves, even after the most ignoble defeat at the polls.

When the votes were tallied for the position of Speaker, there were 15 in favour of St. Clair Daniel and two against. Daniel therefore took the Oath of Office and the Oath of Allegiance as Speaker of the 'House' for that parliamentary term. Prayers were read by Reverend Halley Marville of the Methodist Church. The third session of the first House had therefore officially begun, with Speaker St. Clair Daniel in the Chair. Soon afterwards, the other unelected parliamentarians (Senators) took the Oath of office. Eldridge Stephens Member of Parliament for Vieux-Fort South was elected Deputy Speaker of the House. He was nominated by Prime Minister Compton and seconded by his deputy, George Mallet. The House then recessed at 9.47 a.m. and resumed at 10.50 a.m. in joint session with the Senate to await the arrival of His Excellency the Governor General who was to deliver the Throne Speech. Following the speech, there was a brief adjournment to allow His Excellency to take his leave. He was followed by the Senators present in the joint session, just concluded. The House resumed at 11.10 a.m.

The Prime Minister and Minister of Finance laid the Estimates of Expenditure for the financial year 1982/3 and also the estimates of Revenue for the same period. The House then stood adjourned until 3.30 p.m. that afternoon when Prime Minister Compton proposed to introduce the motion that: "this House approves the Estimates of Revenue and Expenditure for 1982/3".

Hansard reported that in the afternoon session, all members were present except the Member for Vieux-Fort North (Cecil Lay) and the Member for Castries South/East (Clarence Rambally). At 3.45 p.m. the Prime Minister delivered his budget address. It ended at 5.04 pm. The House then adjourned to Friday June 11, for the debate.

As the House of Assembly resumed its sitting to await the presentation of the annual budget, newly appointed Senators were introduced into the chamber. They then took the oath of office which was administered by the President of the Senate, Henry Giraudy, a Barrister and Chairman of the United Workers Party.

The two Senators chosen by His Excellency as his representatives as the island's Independence constitution allowed were: Mr. Ornan Monplaisir, a businessman and Land Surveyor, and Dr. Joseph Edsel Edmunds, an Agricultural Scientist. Other Senators sworn in on that day were: Dunstan Fontenelle, Steve Annius, Austin Glasgow, and Mrs. Veronique Mathurin all nominated by the Government, and Kenneth Foster and Remy Lesmond nominated by the opposition Labour Party. I, Peter Josie, was also nominated a Senator by the Leader of the Opposition in the House. My name was submitted to His Excellency along with those of Foster and Lesmond. The name - Peter Josie - was also published in the Saint Lucia Gazette of Friday May 14, 1982 (vol.151 No. 24) and before I had given my consent to the nomination. I therefore, declined the appointment on that ground and also for the fact that the other opposition nominees to the Senate were not those proposed by the central executive of the St. Lucia Labour Party, which had met at the home of Gregor Mason at Sans Soucis, Castries days earlier for the specific purpose of guiding the parliamentary group on how to conduct itself when the new session of parliament opened.

Bearing in mind that which had contributed to the party's downfall from government, the executive committee was determined to follow the guidelines set down in its constitution. It therefore advised the Leader of the Opposition accordingly. It had arrived at its choice of Senators after a rather lengthy discussion the previous evening at the home of Gregor Mason. Although at the time, I did not wish to appear insensitive to the criticisms of division which continued to be levelled at the SLP, I nonetheless believed there was an important point of principle to be upheld. I therefore declined to take up the offer of a seat in the Senate. It was a little awkward to refuse it when I did because the recommendation had reached the desk of the Governor General and had in fact already been published in the official government gazette. I confess that at the time, I still had a very strong desire to serve my country at the highest political level, but such ambition I thought also had to be tempered by my own judgment of how I would best serve. Besides, if I had learnt anything from the politics of the leadership struggle, it was that henceforth I would be more circumspect with the company I kept. After the fall of the Louisy government I made up my mind I would no longer tolerate an organization which involved some of the same unprincipled personalities. It means that if I was to remain in politics I would either join to the UWP or form my own party. Declining the appointment as Senator in 1982 was therefore an easy decision to make. I regretted that the SLP no longer represented the ideals and principles of its founding fathers which had drawn me and other members of the St. Lucia Forum to it.

Also, at the time, I was still political leader of the St. Lucia Labour Party and had just led that organization into elections in which so many had deserted the party for 'safer' grounds. I was also aware that some, who had chosen to remain with the SLP after the split, had done so at a great personal sacrifice, knowing the long road ahead in opposition would be tough. At the time many others had left the party, some fleeing the country.

Evans Calderon, a barrister by training and the former member for Choiseul/Fond St. Jacques was chosen to replace me, as Senator. I am still of the opinion that a citizen, when called to serve his/her country should have very good reason for refusing to do so. Such refusal ought to be carefully weighed and well thought out. In addition, one should always give due weight to the thinking of one's family on such important matters. In the final analysis, however, persons who volunteer to serve must first aim to be at peace with themselves and with their God, whatever they perceive him to be. When all is said and done, if one discovers that national service were to militate against such peace of mind, then perhaps one ought to decline and pass such service to other more capable hands. My guiding philosophy in this is to work in such a way that I leave the country a better place than that which I found.

At the time, Prime Minister Compton had also set about naming a new Cabinet. Mr. Compton gave some early indication of breaking with the past 'politics-as-usual' by his appointment of Ms. Margherita Alexander of Vieux-Fort, a bright and qualified young teacher at St. Joseph's Convent - the premier girls' Secondary School on the island at the time – as Minister of Education. Ms. Alexander's appointment as Senator and Minister was seen as a brilliant move which had fascinated and excited the country and set it talking. Compton then appointed George Mallet as Minister of Trade Industry and Tourism, and Peter Phillip, Minister of State in that Ministry. Allan Bousquet was appointed Minister of Health and Clarence Rambally (a former Speaker in the Louisy government), became Minister of State in that Ministry. Clendon Mason was appointed Minister for Communications and Works and Brian Charles, Minister of State in that Ministry. Romanus

Lansiquot was appointed Minister for Community Development and Social Affairs and Lennard Riviere was appointed Attorney General and Minister for Legal Affairs. Compton, Prime Minister, also retained the portfolio of Finance for himself. He reappointed John Bristol Parliamentary Secretary in the Office of the Prime Minister.

There were many raised eyebrows when the important Ministry of Agriculture was not filled, at the same time as others. More than a few persons found it curious that the well liked Ira d'Auvergne who was also considered a very close friend and confidant of Prime Minister Compton, was not immediately appointed Minister of Agriculture. Compton obviously had other ideas - and perhaps bigger fish to catch. Speculation soon became rife and rumour mongers had a field day as they stoked the fire of gossip, over who Mr. Compton would appoint to the important portfolio of Agriculture, Lands, Fisheries and Forestry. All sorts of wild speculation ensued with the media becoming involved in the national past time of name-dropping. Poorly informed discussions broke out like the common cold all over the island. Names of prospective Ministers of Agriculture were thrown carelessly about by the rumour mills, now seemingly operating at full throttle. The rumour mongers who had refined gossiping to a fine art had quickly hi-jacked all sensible discussions on the matter. These were seen to gather at street corners in the towns and villages on the island, where they threw up in gay abandon, the names of their preferred candidates for the post which only the Prime Minister had the authority to fill.

It was in such an atmosphere of speculation and excitement that I received a visit from Reginald "Moppers" Mitchell, of Lafayette and Company on Bridge Street, in Castries. Mr. Mitchell was a close friend and relative of Compton, with whom I had often exchanged pleasantries. During the rumours the two of us met at my mother's house at Reduit, Gros-Islet. Mitchell asked me in a rather conspiratorial but direct tone, what my reaction would be if I were to be told that Compton was considering me for the position of Minister of Agriculture. Although the question did not take me completely by surprise, based on the rumours which were flying about at the time, I replied that the man would have to tell me this himself. On reflection I should have replied differently, perhaps even asking for time to think about a more thoughtful reply. My judgement may have been clouded at the time by the feeling that I should probably take a break from politics. I fooled myself that mental fatigue was responsible for the manner I replied to poor 'Moppers' that day. Instead, it may have been that I had not yet reached my personal Damascus moment, wherein I would be lifted from one state to a better and superior other. In the Caribbean, we say; 'you are never ready, until you are ready' and this is truly loaded with all sorts of meanings and innuendoes.

In a later discussion with someone whose opinions I respected, and who I had known for many years through school and sports, I confided that I had regretted not having been better prepared to offer a more reasoned and suitable reply to Compton's messenger. I revealed my error because that particular individual was one of those who had earlier hinted that there may be something on the cards for me, in the Compton government of 1982. My only consolation is that it was always better to make 'mistakes' when one was young and strong, rather that later in one's declining years. In the former there is a chance of a full recovery, whereas errors made in one's senior years are often more difficult to recover from. Besides, there are fewer things in life that are worse than seeing a grown man cry, tears of regret.

At the time, I also comforted myself with the thought that nothing happens before its time - a popular saying on the island. On reflection I cannot truthfully say that I have regretted that particular episode of my early political life. As fate would have it, in late 1996 after Prime Minister Compton had demitted office he chose Dr. Vaughan Lewis as his successor. I was invited by Dr. Lewis to serve as Minister in the Ministry of Agriculture (1996-1997), in his government. Compton at the time worked with Dr. Lewis as Senior Minister - a Lee Kwan Yew, Singapore moment - in the Caribbean.

The talk at the time among the UWP faithful was that Compton needed an energetic person in the Ministry of Agriculture and so there were those who believed that Lewis' invitation to me was engineered by none other than Compton. I was later informed that there was a concerted lobby by Compton's personal supporters to create a place for me in his Government, even after he had appointed Ira d'Auvergne as Minister and Ferdinand Henry, his deputy in the Ministry of Agriculture. It warmed my heart somewhat to witness the many former political opponents within the UWP who were willing to let bygones be bygones. It is perhaps a credit to Compton that Saint Lucians will openly reveal to anyone who cares to listen that in politics one has opponents; not enemies.

Having said all that, one ought also to add that in the immediate post-1982 general elections, I felt I did not need the UWP or Compton to mark my political report card. I reasoned that no one could judge me if they had never been where I had, or felt what I did or saw whatever I had seen. This matter of rejecting the judgement of others remains one of my core principles. I ask for and I may only be willing to accept advice from people who are knowledgeable (and experienced) on the subject matter of my interest, and I feel certain I can trust. It makes no sense seeking enlightenment from a fool - even the book of Proverbs in Holy Writ, advises its readers on where and from whom one ought to seek advice.

It was difficult to predict at the time how Prime Minister Compton and I would have worked in his government in order to transform agriculture on the island. Some folks had suggested that I may have fitted nicely into the seemingly tightly run UWP ship of State, piloted by 'Daddy' Compton. But I was filled with doubts at the time. I may not have been willing as some were, to ask how high, when 'Daddy' said to, jump! At the time, it was generally accepted that everyone in the Compton ship of State pulled in the same direction as their captain. On the other hand, his detractors accused him of leaving no room for individual initiative or creative thinking within his government. However, Compton's approach seemed to have served the island well when it did and particularly after the Labour fiasco of 1979 to 1982.

Since the early nineties, there has been general agreement that each Minister of the government ought to be allowed full control of his or her particular Ministry and that the Prime Minister ought to be consulted in cases of doubt or difficulty. One can therefore say that there is little to be gained by speculating on what could have been. Had Compton not taken the task of almost every Minister of his government, who else was there to help? Besides, it makes little sense to look back and engage in purely speculative 'what ifs' as some people are prone to do. It is even worse to look back with regret. History is replete with examples in which one wrong (or correct move) has changed the fate of countries and that of the world forever. Perhaps the best recourse is for one to record as accurately as possible such human frailties (and mistakes) as one perceives them, in the hope that the same shall not be repeated by future generations.

The clear lesson here is that one who may be contemplating a career in politics should first seek to understand the personal sacrifice it entails and the uncaring and ungrateful attitude of the many who benefit from one's national service. It is a tough life; not one for the faint hearted, but for those who dare to be different. One ought to always be aware that political parties come and go and that people change, as the world changes. One must therefore be prepared to change and adapt if one is to avoid the pitfalls and the inviting embrace of the scrap heap of history, wherein the bones of failed politicians are interred. When therefore one feels that the principles for which one's political organization once stood have been bastardized and trampled upon by megalomaniacs who call themselves leaders, one ought to do the right and proper thing - and leave. One cannot keep blaming youthful exuberance for selfishness and for the failures one experiences - one must either change or perish.

After Prime Minister Compton had finally appointed the Ministers to serve in his 1982 Cabinet, the opposition party also named certain persons to act as 'shadow' spokespersons for the various Ministries. In an apparent effort to promote democracy and good governance, the Voice newspaper at the time, thought it useful to publish a list of names of those persons who had been selected by the opposition SLP, for the role of shadow cabinet. The list of shadow Ministers was as follows: 1. Peter Josie: Agriculture, Foreign Affairs & Home Affairs. 2. Remy Lesmond: Communications, Works and Transport; 3. Paul Hippolyte: Planning and Development; 4. Hilary Peter Modeste: Education and Culture; 5. Leroy Butcher: Trade, Industry & Tourism; and Neville Cenac: Community Development, Youth and Women's Affairs. A release from the party also promised to announce its shadow Minister for Health, at a later date.

No sooner had Compton's new cabinet been sworn in than a number of deft political moves were made by the government all seemingly aimed at restoring confidence in government and politics generally. In this they were assisted by US Ambassador Milan Bish who wasted no time in visiting the island from his Barbados office, to confer with Compton. Talks were held between these two on the immediate priorities for Saint Lucia's development agenda. Messages of congratulations were received from friendly governments who seemed happy to have John Compton back at the helm in Saint Lucia.

As part of the continuing political gestures aimed at early demonstration that things were already improving on the island, the newly sworn Minister of Trade announced a reduction in the price of sugar from $1.25 per pound to $1.00 per pound - a significant saving, it was claimed by a spokesman for that Ministry. Persons who were to benefit from such a reduction in the price of sugar were not informed at the time of its announcement whether a similar reduction would be realized in the price of goods in which sugar was an essential ingredient.

There was also, an announcement to the effect that a women's desk would be established at the Ministry of Social Affairs. A 'clean-up' campaign by the same Ministry was also announced and was to commence shortly, it assured. There appeared some urgency in cleaning up the city of Castries, perhaps by the same persons who saw to it that the city remained dirty and untidy during the rule of the Labour government. The citizens of the city were reminded by those new converts that 'cleanliness was next to Godliness' – and after the earlier disunity within the SLP no one was in a mood to disagree with the government.

Perhaps the most important announcement at the time came from the Amerada Hess Oil Company – remember them? The 'Voice' newspaper carried a picture of Prime Minister Compton turning a switch to start the flow of crude oil from an Amerada Hess oil tanker which had arrived loaded with crude oil from the Arabian Peninsula. It was the first time storage tanks at Cul-de-Sac built by Hess Oil were being put to use. The newspaper reported that some two hundred and one million gallons of crude oil were to be discharged from a super tanker named 'Saint Lucia' plus one million gallons of gasolene and another eight hundred thousand gallons of diesel for the island. Happy Days were here again!

But all was not peace and love and hunky-dory in the new UWP government. By early August 1982, the government had recalled envoy Barry Auguste who was originally chosen by Compton's pre-independence government, to assist it in setting up the island's United Nations offices in New York. No one seemed certain at the time why the services of Ambassador Auguste were dispensed with. Word around was that he had grown too close to George Odlum and company and that he had also acquired a new taste for fine wines and foods - a too expensive taste for the island's fledgling economy to bear.

There were also disturbing reports that Louis George, the Micoud North representative, who had won his seat by a fairly wide margin over both his political opponents was unhappy not to have been named Minister of Education. He was therefore becoming a little restive, to put it mildly. Word soon got to Prime Minister Compton who must have felt that George's popularity in Micoud was too delicate a political issue, to allow him to sulk and fester with dissatisfaction. Word on the ground in Micoud was that the people of that village - many of whom were among Compton's staunchest supporters - felt alienated by what they considered the harsh treatment of a son-of-the-soil, in Compton's selection of Government Ministers. They made their displeasure known to 'Daddy' Compton, who, as any good father (and political leader would), accommodated their demands and appointed Louis George, Minister for Education. Margherita Alexander was disposed of without noise or fanfare. It was noticeable that the top educators on the island at the time offered neither prayers nor questions, on Ms. Alexander's departure. She therefore left her Ministerial post as quietly as she had entered it and not a sound was heard in anger or in fury, at her departure. How her presence would have changed the contours of education on the island is anyone's guess. It is said that one never regrets what one does; rather it is what one did not do that is often regretted. There is no measure, no yardstick, by which to judge what Ms. Alexander might have accomplished, as Minister of Education of Saint Lucia. For the record, it ought to be said that Louis George did distinguish himself in that Ministry, and that more schools were built and more teachers trained and recruited during his time there.

Another notable development soon after the new UWP Government was sworn into office was the early announcement of Castries City Council elections to elect a Mayor and Councillors for the City. The Voice newspaper of June 26, 1982 carried the following headline: 'City votes in December'. But no sooner had that announcement been made by the office of the Minister of Social Affairs, than it was recanted. Decades would pass, and at least two more changes of government would follow before any further talk of municipal elections was resuscitated. Sadly, there has still not been any election for the position of Mayor or that of Councillors for the City of Castries or indeed in any other town or village on the island since 1982.

Around the same time as the announcement of City Council elections, it was also reported that Prime Minister Compton had returned to the island from a visit to the United States of America. There were also reports, in the newspapers, towards the end of June 1982 of a new industrial thrust for the island. As usual, such an initiative was never followed up by those who were privileged to make such announcements. Nothing new was subsequently disclosed to the press or to anyone else. The announcement of a positive outcome of Compton's trip to the USA was probably meant to revive hope in the island's manufacturing sector. At the time President Ronald Reagan's Caribbean Basin Initiative was still a pipe dream that some thought was worth pursuing. Apparently Compton was one of those Reagan acolytes who was determined to keep hope alive. He simply refused to bury the dead initiative, preferring instead to flog a dead horse. Everyone except the new UWP knew that the American President and his chief advisers had long given up the ghost of a prosperous Caribbean built on supplying cheap clothing and other low valued goods and trinkets to their wealthy neighbours up north.

In the opinion of many, the immediate post elections period belonged squarely to Prime Minister Compton and his United Workers Party. At the time the opposition went completely silent except for the occasional cry of despair coming from the PLP who were still trying to keep the invented story of their 'red hearts' fraud alive in the public domain. When all was said and done, it was the Voice newspaper that the island had turned to for factual information as the paper summarized the year, 1982.

The following is a brief summary of its observations. In its edition of Thursday 30 December 1982, the paper said: 'the end of three years of intense political upheaval, the election of a new government and an economy in jeopardy were the principal highlights of life in Saint Lucia in 1982'. It pointed to the tensions and heated debates of the first half of 1982 and observed the calm which had descended on the island after the elections of May that year. It said: 'the country's once buoyant economy with all three of the main foreign exchange earners - Tourism, Agriculture and Industry - all showed marked decline; a balance of payments situation at a record high of E.C. $264 million and unemployment at 27 per cent'.

The newspaper also noted that 'the attempt by the Cenac government to amend the 1960 Contracts with Government (Disqualification) Ordinance, which was intended to be retroactive, and viewed by the opposition parties as an attempt to exonerate government back bencher Evans Calderon for allegedly participating in a government contract, thus contravening the country's laws - was the last straw for the people. They erupted in street protests which finally brought down the Cenac government'.

The paper also disclosed that according to the constitution, a Minister who took part in a government contract automatically loses his seat in Parliament. Calderon, who was Attorney General (A.G.) and Legal Affairs Minister at the time he allegedly drew up the deed of sale for the government purchase of the building in the city, was serving as a backbencher. He had declined a Ministerial position when Cenac replaced Louisy as Prime Minister. The paper noted that 'the SLP's problems had not ceased as Neville Cenac, younger brother of Winston Cenac became Leader of the Opposition and did not see eye-to-eye with Josie, the party leader, on the way forward for the SLP'.

In its summary, the newspaper also reported that 'legal' death (hanging) by the State of criminals found guilty of murder had resumed in September of 1982 when two men were executed for the murder of two young pregnant women. It was the first execution in almost a decade, reported the newspaper. It also mentioned a loan of $122 million East Caribbean dollars given to the new government by the Caribbean Development Bank (C.D.B.) perhaps emphasizing once again, the confidence such institutions had demonstrated in the return of Compton to office. The paper repeated the story it had first carried, (in August, '82) of the official opening of the Hess Oil facility.

One could therefore say with candour that the Voice correctly and accurately captured the major social, political and economic concerns which impacted the island and its people in 1982. It was a year of many troughs and peaks and a year in which good seemed to have triumphed over evil. The paper praised the steps which were being taken by the newly elected government of Prime Minister Compton in order to set the island on a new course to economic recovery, political stability, social development and peace. This was a lot easier to say than to be observed by politicians who were out seeking their own aggrandizement rather than educating and empowering their own people. Having been at the centre of these events between 1974 and 1997, I can say with certainty that the lack of knowledge and education have been the main impediments in the country's drive for social, political and economic progress.

From Canouan to Castries to London:- A *Journey to Remember.*

Life is real! Life is earnest! And the grave is not its goal.
Longfellow, a Psalm of Life.

In an essay competition for senior secondary schools in the Caribbean, on the life and times of Abraham Lincoln, I recall the winning essay was written by a student from the island of St Kitts, (St. Christopher). I recalled the winning essay was read before the entire student body at St. Mary's College, St. Lucia, one afternoon after the day's afternoon prayers were over. This was around 1958. I still recall a quotation from that essay which went something like this: 'what is the formula for the fiery jet of flame that burns more vigorously on the bitter cries of his adversaries and sheds light over millions making the paradoxical fog of his life a little clearer'. I can't tell for certain why that particular arrangement of words made such a lasting impression on my mind. Neither do I know for certain, why they have refused to go away so many years later nor after millions of other words have themselves reached out seemingly from every quarter to demand attention. I, however, recalled the words of that essay, (I have not read the original text) but I recall the essence of it here, in order to ponder the original query and to examine it more closely as it may apply to the life and times of a lesser known leader – John George Melville Compton. Compton was from the shores of a little known island in the Caribbean, St. Vincent Grenadines and became one of the most successful politicians and Prime Ministers in the entire region and possibly the British Commonwealth of Nations. Prime Minister Sir John Compton did not set any slaves free in his time neither did he command any army or lead an all conquering navy, to victory over his foes. But the story of this

Canouan youth seemed to those who cared to look more closely, perhaps as inspiring as the great American President, Abraham Lincoln.

The turning point in the life of the young Compton came early. It seemed to have been guided by the simple words of an unknown widow who saw the lad fishing, and carrying his fishing rod on his back, on the rocky shores of Canouan, a short distance from where she lived. That widow's voice asked in a tone half pleading and half admonishing, perhaps even angelic: 'John, why are you out fishing when you should be at school'? The youth had no ready and reliable answer to such a profound query. That woman, his unlikely Guardian Angel, may have done more that day, than pose a simple question. She afterwards reported to those who mattered in that little boy's life, what she had seen, and may even had explained what she then advised the lad to do.

That was the way in which people cared about each other in the Caribbean back in those days. And if for any reason that child who had been spoken to was rude to the perfect stranger who had corrected him, he would most likely be punished appropriately, by the stranger, and afterwards by his own parents or guardian. So speaking to the youth that morning on that Canouan beach and seeing the wisdom of her concerns, was enough to get his guardian thinking. Indeed, soon thereafter that little boy was removed from his enticing fishing holes on the rocky shores of his little Canouan and sent to Micoud, Saint Lucia, to live with his mother's family and other relatives. He had now taken the journey, at age thirteen or fourteen which would transform him from a little fisher boy into a fisher of men. That encounter on a beach in Canouan was to remain a family secret until the passing of Sir John.

Since his passing, St. Lucia and the Caribbean have heard more of his life's work than at any time when he walked the unbeaten path that few had dared to tread. In his lifetime very few persons got to know him well. It appears to those who observed him closely that as a condition of his friendship one had to first prove one's dexterity on a sailing vessel, similar to those his family built in Canouan and Saint Lucia. Growing up in Saint Lucia with its strange sounding Creole language must have posed a challenge to the young Compton, as it did for many others. He must also have had a tough time among the children he encountered at school. I have met many persons who are convinced that boys are the handiwork of the Devil himself. So energetic and troublesome are they, that there are those who say that even Satan rejects the company of boys, finding them too troublesome, energetic and playful to be of much use to him in the pursuit of his greater objectives.

On the passing of Prime Minister Compton in 2007 many discovered for the first time, a person they wished they had known better. The widespread grief that covered the entire island was testimony enough to the high esteem in which he was held by so many –including many of his previous political opponents. Since that time there have been renewed calls from all quarters, by citizens of every stripe, to tell the story of those who have passed this way and whose lives were examples of service to country and to humanity. Such persons went far beyond the call of duty as it were, in order to serve the social, economic and political advancement of St. Lucia and the wider Caribbean. It is no surprise therefore that since his passing suggestions have been pouring in from all quarters on how best to honour the memory of one who gave his life in service to the people of his adopted land.

The declaration of a National Hero, the erection of a suitable monument, the naming of a day to pay homage, the renaming of Hewanorra airport are just a few of the suggestions to date. To be sure, it would not be easy to arrive at a suitable tribute which pleases everyone. Of this we are certain. We are assured of this because this island has made an art of being contrary and different.

Notwithstanding the meritorious gestures to which many St. Lucians will readily agree, I nonetheless add my own voice for the simple purpose of broadening the list of ideas which have been offered so far. In so doing I have been reminded of Sir John's love for children and his deeply held conviction that to educate a child is to save him or her from poverty, ignorance and disease. It is also to prepare such a child for service to the nation and to the Caribbean and the world. To prove his deep passion for education, his family has opened a scholarship account for the children of St. Lucia at the local branch of the Bank of Nova Scotia. Those who offered wreaths were advised to deposit the value of these wreaths into the Scotia Bank Education Account.

In 1967 the Compton Government initiated a school banking and savings programme on the island to mark its constitutional advancement into Statehood. I suggested at another place that this savings programme for the nation's children which was unfortunately discontinued for reasons that have never been explained, ought to be restarted as a way to mark the memory of former Prime Minister Compton. That programme should be restarted with each school child being encouraged to save at least one dollar each week for the first five years of schooling. Thereafter the savings should be increased to five dollars per week and afterwards to ten dollars per week until that student attains the age of eighteen. A plan should be devised whereby each child's total contribution at the end of his or her secondary school days should be matched by the government at the age of seventeen or eighteen. It would be useful for those who wish to reject such an idea, to consider how much the country spends on feeding and caring for young incarcerated persons at the Boys' Industrial Centre at Gros-Islet, or at the Bordelais Correctional Facility, in Dennery.

I have long believed that it should be the stated policy of every political party (and government) to afford each child the benefit of a basic education up to age eighteen at least, before he or she is encouraged to choose a career path. One can only imagine what it would feel like to a young person, being taught the value of saving and then later leaving school with start-up money to invest in his or her private enterprise under supervised guidance from banking and business experts. (This is one more reason why we established our own indigenous National Commercial Bank). It is not that difficult to imagine the type of society St. Lucia would become had our public schools been encouraged to instill the discipline of savings amongst its students, especially if this was reinforced at home, by parents and guardians. Had the schools on the island continued the savings programme which was started forty years or so ago, who can tell how such funds may have been used today in order to provide social mobility and economic development for the country.

It has been repeated ad nauseam that Sir. John often paid from his own pocket for the education of many children in his Micoud constituency and elsewhere on the island. He purchased primary and secondary school books, bought school uniforms and even paid for their University fees and travels, when they were old enough and still could not meet the full costs of their education. Of course some he also trusted with loans for fertilizing their banana fields and much more. He was fond of repeating that tomorrow's votes will take care of themselves; our job is to educate today's children. No one who studied his methods was surprised at the number of young people who manned and carried his last campaign in 2006, at age 82, when his energies were so clearly being tested. He probably gave more to the youth of Saint Lucia from his personal resources than anyone will ever know. This has led many persons on the island to observe that such personal burdens on a politician's pocket ought to be taken over by the State, in order to save future politicians from exploitation by certain ruthless citizens. Even though the State was to play a larger role in educating its citizens, many believe that politicians such as John Compton would still find ways to help deserving cases from their personal resources. Perhaps this is the reason some have been moved to pose the question publicly about finding more (and better ways) to finance the education of the most needy in the population. Perhaps at Sir John's passing it may be the correct time to start helping our children to learn how to save (thrift) and also to learn the difference between the value of things and their cost, or selling price. Surely, no Saint Lucian (or Caribbean child) must ever be allowed to forget that it was the Caribbean's own Professor Arthur Lewis, Economist and Nobel Laureate who first posited the thesis that, the cure for poverty was education; not money!

The implementation of a school banking and savings programme does not have to be instituted at the expense of, or as replacement for, any other idea which the nation may decide to honour Sir John's memory. We must teach the youth to appreciate the value of things as opposed to the cost price and price tags. They must learn to recognize quality and how to measure it. In the names of all our past political leaders we must establish a public education programme aimed at teaching the youth to become less inclined to mimic foreign styles, values and tastes and instead create local cuisine, fashion and music that the world would be anxious to purchase from this region. It is well known that when people are engaged in positive, rewarding and safe enterprises, they are less inclined to indiscipline and being disrespectful to themselves and to other human beings - even animals.

St. Lucians have suffered a very long history of neglect, abuse and incompetence at the hands of politicians in whom they have placed their trust. There are still too many people on the island without a savings account, and who have very little prospects of ever starting one. A compulsory savings programme started at early school age for every child can help change that around while at the same time help to introduce a new culture of thrift on the island. It has been a commonly accepted view that our future development will increasingly be dependent on our own savings and man-power skills as world resources continue to diminish and more people in richer (and stronger) countries continue to compete for the same things as ourselves.

Everyone, it seemed agreed that a suitably designed stone monument has its place and value, in the many ways in which the country can honour its first Prime Minister. But no matter how well crafted or otherwise built and designed such a stone memorial may be, it can easily become a mocked memory if its raising is not accompanied by full and adequate education, explaining its origin and its purpose, and that icon's place in the country's history. Any stone monument must therefore cut across constituency boundaries and party political divisions. We ought therefore to be careful how we honour those who have served this country and breathed new spirit into it in its darkest hour when it appeared that hope had deserted her people. In time, we ought to agree before the erection of any stone monument to anyone whom the nation chooses, that each monument we put up is a reflection of ourselves, as a people. When a nation erects a monument it does so to honour the hearts and minds (and soul) of its own citizens, both past and present. The stone therefore comes to represent the nation as a strong and united force whose symbolism urges everyone who passes by, to equal and greater deeds for country and humanity. This ought to be the core message in each stone monument, whether erected on this island, or elsewhere. When we are agreed on the necessity to honour our icons in stone, then we are guaranteed that other icons and heroes lurk within the population, waiting the call of history to serve his or her people with dignity, grace and determined rectitude. Then we will be guaranteed that such a stone will never be vandalized or defamed or torn down, by future generations.

Another public holiday in honour of Sir John can easily be turned into an occasion for more feting, drunkenness and disorderly conduct. That Saint Lucian Knight would certainly not have wanted that. Even an airport can fail, if one is not careful to raise it to a worthy international standard comparable to any in the developed world. We may be frank with each other and admit any suitable airport and terminal building will be mainly for the use of international travellers, or locals who have experienced the best the rest of the world has to offer. So why should we sell ourselves short, especially if we wish to honour an icon? Didn't he make it all possible when Hewanorra airport was officially handed back to the island in 1970? Besides, an airport is also a constant reminder of continuous motion and interfacing with the outside world, and the one who led the charge to finally set the island free, understood the great economic boon that Hewanorra International Airport could become for this island and its Caribbean neighbours as well.

Sir John is known to have managed the scarce resources of this country for so long and so carefully that the island seemed poised and ready at his departure for more rapid growth and economic development than ever. The man may be gone but his vision for the complete eradication of the scourges of poverty, ignorance and disease from this island must be continued regardless of those who hold the reins of power. Indeed every political party on the island should be committed to continue at full throttle, regardless of the harsh economic realities the outside world sometimes throws at it.

If I were to be asked what qualities stood out most in the personality of the late Prime Minister, Sir John Compton, it would have to be that he was the consummate outsider. Looking at him and studying him without political blinkers as I often tried to do, I sometimes got the impression that

Sir John was always looking ahead and seeing things which others, viewing from the same vantage point, seemed unable to appreciate. It was as if he possessed the gifted third eye of every true artist. Yet he was not perfect by a long way and often incurred the wrath of his political opponents. Others who were more charitable believed that the people who were around him then, saw as well what he did but, such people were either too timid or too laid back or lacking in energy to pursue their political goals and to achieve as Sir John has done, for his people. Still others were perhaps too polite to openly compete with him for national political honours as they seemed at the time to have been satisfied with his efforts at social and economic development of Saint Lucia.

To see beyond the obvious often means in a practical sense to have acquired some knowledge or insight, wisdom even, by which to comprehend the finer points of any given situation. In the St. Lucia of the fifties (and before) the average citizen in the countryside went about his private business, some staring blankly while others presented a bland, dreamy and often drunken countenance or a gay abandoned laughter that did not seem to fit the poverty around them. A youngster fresh from another land and foreign to the language was bound to be struck by what he came to find. It was perhaps a ready-made environment for one who wished to excel in mass mobilization, politics and revolt. It was a character trait which was very early observed in that youth from the small island of Canouan who was open and inquisitive and brash, to a fault. He seldom allowed matters to pass unchallenged, even when he was relaxing with his friends sailing the Caribbean Sea between Saint Lucia and the Grenadines. In his early political life he seemed to have stepped on many toes; annoying those who thought him crude and even at times, unmannerly.

There is sufficient evidence to prove that he was touched by the social and economic problems staring at him when he first arrived on the island. Unlike others who saw and turned their heads, he was determined to do something about the poverty, ignorance and disease he found here. Having correctly identified the problem he very early determined that one had to be first empowered politically in order to successfully tackle this three-headed scourge plaguing the island at the time. He seemed determined to take the people from where he had found them and to a better place than they had hitherto known. On such a journey the people were also to learn that they were not created, or made, to be merely hewers of wood and carriers of contaminated river water. He therefore refused to allow his followers to behave as the proverbial jackass which labours under its load, and is contented. His mission was to cause his followers to see his point of view and conduct themselves accordingly, for their joint journey of political transformation and progress. But he first had to get them to put down the heavy yoke of colonialism and neo-colonialism, before they were free to move forward. He was the first barrister on the island to take the legal profession from its desk bound home in the capital, Castries, and into the sugar cane valleys and distant villages, particularly the area from Dennery valley to Micoud village, wherein the illiterate masses were purposely huddled in those days for use in sugar cane cultivation.

It is not surprising therefore that those who followed his political career and supported him from its inception were willing to sacrifice their very lives to defend him. At the start of his political career he had identified so completely with the cause of the sugar workers on the island that in the end, he became indistinguishable from their cause. When that sugar industry came to its inauspicious end, it was the same John Compton who was there to guide the workers and the island to the more profitable banana industry. The deep respect and love which many farmers held for him could be seen in the way they were always so quick to defend him, at the same time pointing to all the good which he had brought to them. For this reason his adversaries were always skeptical when pointing out his mistakes and his observed biases. On balance therefore, one may refer to him as an expert politician. Of course he carried the usual scars and blemishes of battles won and lost but, above all, he was a man. He was to say on many occasions to those who would listen that once he had made up his mind to pursue a particular course of action, he followed it through regardless. Perhaps he deliberately did not add that the reason he stayed the course so manfully was that, he always carried out broad consultations amongst his constituency, his family and his trusted friends before he gave public wing to his ideas. Such ideas were therefore always well tested before he took them to the parliament and the nation for execution. Such a procedure may well recommend itself to present and future politicians seeking to copy what was best in Sir John. He fully understood that once he was assured of the support of those near and dear to him, he could rely on them as a trusted cushion, if his ventures were to go awry. One may therefore conclude that there was method (and planning) to his apparent daring and boldness of political action.

The difference between the early John Compton and his later political adversaries such as those of the seventies, eighties and nineties was that that his breed had arrived at a time when the world was waking up and reviewing its stance on human rights, third world development needs, identity and peaceful co-existence, among different peoples and races. By the late seventies the Black Power movement in the Caribbean which at first threatened to overhaul the politics of the African Diaspora in the region had been dissipated and replaced by creeping greed and mounting selfishness and insularity. To be sure Sir John may have tried to accommodate the new politics of African Identity, but he had no stomach for the apparent division among the races the dialogue appeared to be promoting at the time.

His critics observed that he had by that time so fully embraced the example and precepts of the old colonial plantocracy that it became impossible to disengage from it when the time for national identity of the African Diaspora demanded recognition.

His early political battles against the large sugar estates were fought under the banner of the St. Lucia Labour Party. When the hierarchy and government of that party descended into excessive drinking and the progress of the island seemed to suffer, the young Compton left it, along with some trusted friends, to form his own political party which he called the National Labour Movement, - NLM. When it appeared to him that a third party would not succeed at the polls in the culture of a two-horse town, he promptly engaged in what his detractors called a marriage of convenience with the Peoples' Progressive Party, PPP, to form the United Workers Party, UWP.

Prior to that marriage, the NLM was seen as a breakaway faction of the St. Lucia Labour Party. To such persons the NLM was neither national in scope nor labour in character. It did not become a national party until it joined with the PPP which was seen at the time as the remnants of a dying plantocracy. However, by the time the marriage between the PPP and NLM, had taken place, the PPP had begun to garner fair political support island-wide. There was therefore much synergy to be achieved in the new political marriage. It was a divided (and determined) working class coming together with management and property owners, determined to wrest political power from the labourers, peasants, budding trade unionists as well as shop clerks and house maids along with their leaders.

Many who were to comment after his passing, referred to Compton as a simple and humble man. Such phrases and compliments were more common than at any time in the recent period before his passing. There were those of course who did not agree with that assessment. Some persons thought him stubborn, arrogant and cocky. Others thought him pompous and loved white (and foreign) more than he allowed. To many persons who were acquainted with him, Sir John also seemed a very complex individual. Yet, he was at his core a trustworthy leader who conducted the business of State in a simple, uncluttered, open and straight forward manner. Some have gone so far as to question the reason a man who knew how to put fear in the hearts of his opponents and cause them to melt like soft candle one minute, would at the next, cry so readily if a new issue such as an unfortunate death of a friend or his child, were to touch his fragile heart.

His opponents as well as his supporters observed that he seemed to know the correct moment to play the role of a fox and that in which to be transformed into a roaring lion. Few were as incisive in observation or as destructive in criticism of an opponent as Sir John Compton was at his prime. He has described certain political opponents by names which often followed such persons to their final resting places. He was brutal and unwavering in a political campaign. Yet the very moment the campaign was over, or a particular public meeting had come to an end, that same man was all jollity and good humour. Whilst the dust was settling on one meeting or political event, his mind was off to something else needing his attention. He was always very generous even to persons he knew did not support him. He often said he had no political enemies, only political opponents.

Perhaps Sir John Compton understood better than most the injunction: 'To love your enemies and to do good to those who hurt you'. There are to be sure hundreds, if not thousands, of his faithful followers and supporters who will live to a ripe old age and never fully appreciate the full significance of the changes John Compton, the politician, brought to the island. He may never have reached the celestial heights of the flamboyant Eric Gary of Grenada or sterling, almost God-like worship, of the early Eric Williams of Trinidad and Tobago, but he was steady and reliable, and in the stormiest weather his guiding hands were as secure as those of the best political leaders. He was no intellectual in the mould of an Eric Williams of Trinidad and Tobago. He did not peddle his Trade Union credentials as V.C. Bird of Antigua had done, or expose his socialist leanings as readily as Michael Manley of Jamaica did. But he was all that, and more.

By general consensus he appeared to lack the charm and eloquence of Forbes Burnham of Guyana but like President Burnham he was also a consummate pragmatist. He was known to help build consensus in his several dealings with other Caribbean leaders during the many years he served his country. He was never loud and rumbunctious neither did he cackle like a yard fowl, whenever he achieved a development milestone, or some other objective. It is for these reasons that when he spoke his words often reverberated in the capitals of the Caribbean and in certain parts of the developed world as well. He often spoke simply when he was among other leaders or with the simple country folk of Saint Lucia. Many seemed more attentive to his words than those of several of his Caribbean colleagues, whenever he spoke at their heads of government meetings. His uprooting from the island of his birth and final transplant into the fertile soils of Saint Lucia afforded him an environment in which he was to grow and expand. This phenomenon of excelling in a place other than of one's origin – a transplant, as it were - is well documented in the plant kingdom. For example, some major crops in world trade today are produced in places other than where they originated. Coffee (Coffea arabica) is originally from Ethiopia, (Africa) and now its major centre of production is in South America, (Brazil). Corn (Zia maize) originated in Central America, (Mexico) and the centre of world production today is North America, (U.S.A.); sugarcane; (Saccharin officinarum) was first found in New Guinea and today is largely produced in Cuba. Finally, cocoa (Theobroma cacao): was first found is Central America and its largest production in the world today, is in Brazil (South America) and Ghana, West Africa.

If we switch for a moment from plants to humans and we use St. Lucia as an example, we will soon discover that although the island's Nobel Laureates were both born here at least one parent of each of those two worthies was a transplant from elsewhere. It would be interesting to research the family backgrounds of other outstanding Caribbean personalities, especially within Caricom, perchance to discover the original genetic make up of their brilliance. These Caribbean countries have all been blessed with nurturing persons from elsewhere who have been gifted with energy and brain power. That may well be a point to consider in our treatment of those whom we think, wrongly, may have suffered the minor misfortune of birth by being born outside our shores - whatever our place of birth may be.

It would also be a grave error to end this short tribute to former Prime Minister Compton, without a word from the little hand book of power politics he must have used as a guide and mentor for at least some part of his life. That handy advice to a Prince by Nicollo Machiavelli informs us that a Prince is further esteemed when he is a true friend or a true enemy. Such a policy is always more useful than that of remaining neutral. Therein lay a large part of the Compton mystique and secret. He stood by what he believed and what he said and did. He played his politics hard and he also admired those who played hard and fair. In his electioneering campaigns he asked for no quarter and he gave none. As one who loved to sail he understood better than most the ways of the tide. He knew that nature held no malice or grudges and that by studying and observing it one finally learns to master it. He knew as a child that when the tide surges it benefits all who are ready to use it to their advantage. He knew when to chance his ventures, and as an old sea hand, he was seldom wrong about the changing moods of the tides. Sir John used all his cards as wisely as he could up to the very end. He did this to benefit the island he loved and which he called home for seventy of the eighty three years he walked amongst its people and the rest of the Caribbean people as well.

Many would say he was either a true friend or a true enemy, when he was on the campaign trail. Others would call him a true Saint Lucian and Caribbean man. He was distinguished by Caricom with the granting of 'Caribbean Citizenship'. Towards the end many Saint Lucians, called him 'Papa' choosing to drop the second part of the full name which his opponents had derogatively given him. 'Papa'(daddy) John, is gone, long may he live! We may not see the likes of him again, and our country is poorer for it.

Post 1982: A glimpse ahead

The fundamental cure for poverty is not money but knowledge.
Sir. Arthur Lewis: Nobel Laureate;
Economics: Saint Lucia.

The Caribbean has always commanded a higher level of attention in the capitals of politics and commerce than its size and populations would suggest. One reason is Europe, which invested early capital, technology and manpower, in the region. Europe therefore contributed to the region's culture, its education and its religion and its sports. Most importantly, it gave the region its laws and its various legal systems. Opportunities for higher education, although very limited and discriminatory at first, were gladly embraced by Caribbean scholars who excelled in the higher places of learning in Europe, Canada and America. Of these early scholars there was always a small percentage who returned home to serve their own country, and the region. These were often supplemented by professionals sent from Europe to work in Education, Public Health, Administration, Communications and Commerce. Today, the voices of Caribbean diplomats, politicians and scholars are listened to with great interest wherever in the world their skills take them. It is confidently predicted that such voices and skills are more likely to grow than be diminished in the future, especially as globalization opens up the world to better skilled and academically qualified people, than had hitherto been the case - or at least that is what has been touted by the proponents of free trade and opened international borders.

It is therefore not beyond the bonds of possibility that a new breed of Caribbean leaders will also emerge to play a more positive role in shaping the development strategies of their countries and the region, as a whole. Within the framework of globalization, one is therefore more likely to encounter national figures both within the public sector as well as in private enterprise who articulate a more open and robust policy of greater regional co-operation - and unity. Given its historical head-start, coupled with its proximity to North America and the fast-developing South, and Central American markets, the Caribbean region, from Belize, in Central America down to Guyana on the north/east shoulder of South America, is therefore poised to be developed into the skills bank of the entire Western Hemisphere, if it puts its mind to it. In particular, the English speaking brethren in the region have a unique opportunity, if they are able to pull together in the pursuit of such a worthy goal and lofty intellectual idea. It is therefore predicted that the region will continue to be a place of interest well after the drug cartels of South America have transferred their businesses elsewhere, copying large US fruit corporations or have totally transferred their researches to other useful plant and animal species.

Looking back at the events which impacted Saint Lucia (and to a large extent the wider Caribbean) it should be observed that these events had a long gestation period, going back several generations. Unfortunately, at the discovery of the early symptoms of social diseases and distress of the marginalized, the problems were either papered over or those responsible merely pretended that they did not exist and that perhaps time would heal all things. Such an approach has been seen not to work anywhere. Those responsible have discovered that, if the root causes of social problems are not treated, they fester and grow as any malignant cancer would. Their solution therefore takes deliberate policy and focussed attention and action. It has been observed that if social problems are not confronted early and dealt with directly, they often grow very rapidly and their solutions become exponentially more complex and expensive to solve. Once the problem enlarges the whole society becomes threatened, especially in small countries as in the Caribbean. As a result many skilled and otherwise useful citizens choose to run away for their own safety, rather than stay and help find solutions to those social problems at home.

By the sixties and seventies the people of Saint Lucia were developing two distinct and different personalities. One was confident and progressive and upwardly mobile whilst the other was fearful, conservative and held back by religious and cultural mores. One personality was therefore stuck to the images of past master/servant relationship of the colonial era while the other was brash, loud and pretending - at least externally - to have broken away from the colonial straight jacket. The more backward and less developed territories were reputed to hold a larger percentage of citizens who secretly nursed low self esteem and in certain cases, even self-loathing and hatred of their culture and things Caribbean, or of African origin. It had been observed that when there were opportunities for education and travel, a new, more confident and wholesome personality emerged and expressed itself with more confidence and style. Among the latter group there were to be found many Caribbean scholars who were breaching the strict colour barriers of the middle twentieth century. Formerly, with the strict class and colour coded social strata the previous generation of local folks had been rendered distant strangers to any form of social mobility. Armed with such basic knowledge, it was easy to see why certain persons came into politics preaching fire and brimstone, and demanding a better and brighter day for those who had suffered the most from history. But we have also learnt that in the matter of party politics, with its unwritten manifesto of emphasizing differences rather than similarities, one ought not to enter, still bearing scars of hatred, jealousies, and hunger after the creature comforts of life. To do so was similar to adding an explosive agent to an already potent mix of social malaise, including poverty, ignorance, disease and a desire for revenge.

Political parties (and politicians) heightened and exploited the sense of difference which then led some people to turn on each other at the slightest disagreement - or provocation. The advent of black power politics in the Caribbean further exacerbated these differences which existed between peoples and their political parties. Perhaps such differences - perceived or otherwise - provided new cover for persons who secretly harboured unresolved personal issues. The public venting of political differences soon became a means by which to insult one's opponent and to use 'black power' as excuse for additional mischief. The advent of the international Black Power movement in the Caribbean was therefore a cause for condemnation rather than a reason for celebration by many blacks, poor and middle class, educated as well as uneducated. It unfortunately provided yet another layer of difference for deviants seeking to make capital of differences in race, and to attempt to punish the offspring of those who had been the main merchants and beneficiaries of colonialism and even slavery. In the circumstances, even the bravest (and boldest) patriotic voices never bothered to enter the debate or tried in any serious way to explain that out of the introduction of Africans to the Caribbean had arisen a new people; those infused with the bloodline of native Carib, the European (England, France and Portugal) and the far East - India and China.

This lack of informal education coupled with the dearth of formal schooling was the corner stone for illiteracy, ignorance, poverty and disease which afflicted the early citizens and retarded social and economic progress. It has been claimed by some scholars that to this lack, one may also add a liberal (and unhealthy) overlay of religious indoctrination. This latter evil, it has been widely claimed, had also served to divert attention from the physical needs of the masses and to focus instead on the spiritual hereafter, to which only faith was to bear witness. Such were the realities of this island's foundation which had its unique additional shell of French influences and which gave to it its Creole heritage and language. It seemed at times, a deliberately planned and painstakingly wrought foundation which will take many years of fresh enlightenment and hard work to amend, and to refine the final Saint Lucian product for the new global environment.

It is from such a historical mixture of studied indifference and at times deliberate mis-education, through faith-based organizations that the culture of both its leaders as well as top civil servants and teachers had unfortunately emerged to continue undermining the independent (and progressive) thinking people, throughout the Caribbean. It is also that which has assisted in keeping Saint Lucia and its neighbours in a state of mental bondage, some thirty-two years and more (at time of writing) after political Independence. Unfortunately, in the case of Saint Lucia political Independence got off on the wrong footing, and therefore it could not have announced itself as purely Saint Lucian, or Caribbean or even revolutionary. It appeared to me that many political aspirants were either too timid or too afraid to express an opinion on how they saw Saint Lucia's role in the changing Caribbean political landscape and in the African Diaspora.

The negative political experiences of Saint Lucia and the rest of the Caribbean between 1970 and 1990 ought to give every patriot cause for study and analysis rather than a mere shrugging of the shoulders or a dismissive attitude which many are apt to assume. It is not sufficient to treat such experiences as simply a fact of Caribbean life because the natives are too stupid and backward for their own good. Indeed, such negative attitudes are certain to guarantee that the mistakes of the past are more likely to be repeated than not. In the context of the political turmoil this island experienced between 1979 and 1982, the correct questions need to be asked and the answers rigorously analyzed and debated without the intrusion of personalities either foreign or local, to blemish, diminish or frustrate such debate.

For example, what was the reason that John Compton and his UWP were returned to office so soon after their severe loss to the St. Lucia Labour Party in the 1979 general elections? Some have suggested that the reason may have been the excessive and ill-directed energy - and restlessness - of the team of politicians who were swept into office in 1979. Others say it was the deliberate imposing of a senior citizen upon the body politic of the Labour Party, which was the precursor to its later problems, in office. Whatever the reasons for the leadership quarrels in the SLP government, one thing is certain; they did not happen by accident or by mere co-incidence. Indeed, some persons have suggested that the leadership issues were caused by the same forces which have dogged man all his life - greed and envy. Many were to insist that the issue had nothing to do with colonialism or neo-colonialism or of the last three hundred years of Caribbean history. Take your pick and make of it what you will. But as everyone knows the present and future are always being shaped by the past and the present. In the end the more powerful force is always expected to triumph. The reason is simple enough; power never gives unless a greater power demands.

At the time that John Compton and his party were returned to power in Saint Lucia in 1982 the left-leaning Maurice Bishop and his PRG still held sway in Grenada. After the demise of the Labour Government in Saint Lucia, Prime Minister Bishop lost a reliable and trusted friend. It was no accident that after John Compton's return to office, his first overseas visitor was the United States Ambassador for Saint Lucia and the East Caribbean, based in Barbados - Milan Bish. What did that Ambassador discuss besides aid to Saint Lucia? Only the most unrepentant buffoon will think anything else but, Grenada! The disquiet over Grenada among the Western allies grew steadily as President Ronald Reagan fingered Russia for building an international air base on the island, in order to facilitate its trans-shipment of arms to Africa. The White House then assured the world that such arms were to assist anti-democratic rebel groups on the African continent, destabilize burgeoning democratic institutions and legitimate governments. These statements clearly placed Grenada in the crosshairs of America's anti-communist expansion in Africa. It also placed that island at the centre of cold war politics between America and Russia - the West versus the East, as it was dubbed at the time.

The postponement of free and fair democratic elections, as had been predicted by some Grenada watchers, soon became a fait-accompli. This development was (inadvertently or otherwise) accompanied by the harassment and detention of opponents of the revolution. Together, they seemed to have had the effect of eroding the popularity of the Bishop Government, both at home and in the wider Caribbean - including of course Saint Lucia. The news reaching the rest of the Caribbean from the western press was that Grenada had swung further left than its former supporters had been led to expect or had been promised by the leaders of the revolution.

Word soon got around that there were bitter rivalries among the persons who were at the leadership of the PRG. It was alleged that the chairperson behind the moves to remove Bishop from the chair of the powerful central committee was his deputy, Bernard Coard. The committee is alleged to have appointed Coard to share the job of Prime Minister, and party leader, with Bishop. Such rivalries within the PRG were alleged to have been far deeper than mere ideology. They may also have been the results of petty jealousies and rivalries that existed between the guys who attended the Grenada Boys Secondary School (GBSS) - Coard and company - and those of Presentation College old boys - Bishop, Whiteman and friends. Some Grenadians had observed that although Coard had worked his way up within the NJM it was clear to many that Unison Whiteman, a past student of Presentation College in Grenada was in fact Maurice Bishop's closest friend and confidant. Bishop and Whiteman seemed to enjoy each other's company both before and after they entered politics and government. They had obviously developed a strong bond which dated back to their early school days.

To add to the chagrin of Bishop and his PRG in Grenada, the very conservative Mary Eugenia Charles, led her Dominica Freedom Party (DFP) to victory in mid-1980. This development along with the return of John Compton in Saint Lucia would prove deadly to Bishop and the Grenada experiment. Eugenia and Compton were known to be birds of the same feather - both were very conservative and pro-western - in their outlook on politics and their way of life. These two would later be joined by Prime Minister Son Mitchell of St. Vincent and the Grenadines and the trio was to prove a powerful triumvirate which appeared to set the pace in all things political, within the Windward and Leeward islands grouping, for many years. The three were anathema to every radical voice in the region and sub-region in their heyday. The days of the PRG (and PRA) and the hardliners who would soon extinguish Bishop and his trusted friends and supporters were therefore numbered.

Ms. Charles had replaced former leader Oliver J. Seraphin who in turn had replaced Patrick John, the island's first Prime Minister, and former leader of the Dominica Labour Party (DLP). Seraphin and John had both served in government; and Patrick John was Prime Minister. Major disagreements within the John government led to his downfall and the emergence of Oliver Seraphin, who replaced him, as Prime Minister. The latter had earlier (1980) represented his government in Dominica at the first anniversary of Bishop's PRG. That move may also have made him a marked man. Both Oliver Seraphin and Patrick John lost their seats in Parliament at the 1980 polls which swept Ms. Charles into office.

Also in office at the time was Prime Minister Milton Cato of St. Vincent and the Grenadines. From all external appearances Prime Minister

Cato seemed to have taken a rather lukewarm approach to the political shenanigans within the politics of the Caribbean at that time. He therefore left the leading roles within the OECS, as far as Grenada was concerned, to Charles of Dominica and Compton of Saint Lucia. The other leaders were either overwhelmed by their own internal affairs or were silenced by external powers seeking to overthrow the PRG. Word on the ground was that Grenada had to be returned to the fold of democratic law and order as practiced and accepted by the rest of the OECS and by CARICOM. In other words, Grenada had to be returned to the West. It was time to end its flirtation with Cuba and the Soviet Union. Although it appeared at the time that Maurice Bishop, a British trained lawyer, was bending towards some , sort of compromise (and compliance), as far as the West was concerned, it was too little, too late. By then it appeared that the hardliners in the army and central committee in Grenada, had carried out a palace coup, and seemed to have rejected any compromise on the freeing of prisoners who had not been charged with any crime or on holding general elections.

It was assumed by those who study politics that Washington and London may have been working furiously behind the scenes, using their diplomatic machinery within the region, to rid Grenada - and the south Caribbean - of what they saw as a growing threat and nuisance. Word on the ground in the Caribbean was that certain OECS leaders had been carefully handpicked by Washington for focussed diplomatic attention, and readied for diplomatic action. Interestingly, some of these same Caribbean leaders were at loggerheads with Washington over its support for Chiquita, Dole and Del Monte in its banana wars over the lucrative European banana market. These three US multi-nationals already controlled the entire North American market including Mexico and Canada, and they seemed bent on depriving the Caribbean of their less than ten percent share of the European banana market.

The political pendulum in the East Caribbean had swung full circle and the conservative right-leaning leaders were in the ascendancy. In Dominica, Saint Lucia and Saint Vincent, the banana industry was still doing relatively well. It had by then become the main revenue earner of all three islands. Grenada was a bit different. It still had its cocoa, nutmeg and other spices along with an eye on Tourism. It appeared that the economies of all four Windward Islands were set to get off the ground. All four islands were relatively stable since adult suffrage. But by the late seventies, change had arrived, and events were moving quickly. By late 1983, these changes were being reversed and at that point many people in the Caribbean were said to be concerned that events in Grenada had taken an unhappy turn with the killing of Bishop, Whiteman and several other people. The Caribbean public as far as one was aware, then seemed prepared to support an American intervention in Grenada and to return that island to normalcy and back within the OECS family - following the reported incident (and killings) at Fort George, in Grenada.

The Organization of East Caribbean States (OECS) in the meantime, was moving full speed ahead. Its new charter was soon ready to be signed in St. Kitts (also called St. Christopher), in the Leeward Islands. Ms. Charles of Dominica also attended the signing ceremony along with Maurice Bishop of Grenada. Prime Minister Louisy had stepped down from office, so Prime Minister Cenac signed on behalf of Saint Lucia. He was accompanied on that trip by his Minister for Foreign Affairs - Peter Josie. It was therefore Cenac and Josie and not Compton or Louisy (or any others) who signed the Treaty of Basseterre on behalf of Saint Lucia, thereby bringing OECS unity one step closer. If there had been secret meetings between Bishop and Ms. Charles during their stay in St. Kitts, these were not made public. What I recall seeing was the large outpouring and warm embrace with which the rank and file on the island of St. Kitts had welcomed Maurice Bishop. It was clear to me that the broad masses of the Caribbean carried within their hearts the wrongs of the past, and a special admiration for anyone who would set these demons of our history to right.

The rift between Bishop and Coard had by then widened beyond repair. In October 1983 the Caribbean and the world learnt that Bishop had been placed under house arrest. Later, it was reported that Maurice Bishop, Unison Whiteman, Jacqueline Creft and several others were shot and killed at Fort George by elements of the PRA. Their bodies were taken away and have not been recovered up to the time of writing, almost thirty years later. To this day no one has identified the mass grave into which the dead bodies were reportedly dumped. Perhaps it was that brutality and the apparent hardening of the ideology of the PRG, now under the control of a Central Committee which finally got America and the rest of the Caribbean to act. No one knows for certain what may have actually triggered the American invasion of Grenada. The downfall of the PRG and PRA may have been plotted and planned long before the events at Fort George.

At the time of Bishop's murder, Eugenia Charles was Chairperson of the newly formed OECS council of Prime Ministers. By then the entire Caribbean seemed to be in sympathy with Charles and company on the anti-PRG stance. Even persons who were known to have supported the Grenada revolution now turned against the killers of Bishop. However, notwithstanding the general inclination of the Caribbean peoples against Coard and his PRA, Guyana and Trinidad two of the largest, resource rich, and hence more influential members of Caricom, made no secret of their objections to external interference in the Caribbean at the time. These two and perhaps one or two others saw the events in Grenada as a purely internal matter, and if anything ought to be resolved by the Caribbean, possibly Caricom. Perhaps the leaders of Guyana and Trinidad were not aware that certain other key leaders from the region, notably Dominica, Saint Lucia and Barbados, had already agreed with Washington that Barbados was to be the staging post for an armed invasion of Grenada. To spice up the operation, the Regional Security System headquartered in Barbados had also agreed to provide ground support to the American troops scheduled to land in Grenada. The code name 'Amber and the Amberines' was chosen by the American forces which would soon make its fury felt in little Grenada.

The American invasion of Grenada and the removal of the PRG and PRA from office was said to have brought immediate relief to many in the region, especially Grenadians who had fled home and were hiding all over the Caribbean and as far north as Canada. A clear lesson from this entire episode in the region is that might is always right. For the first time within CARICOM, it appeared that the OECS and Barbados had won the day. They had might on their side even though they may have lacked the force of moral authority. There was clearly division within the Caribbean community on the invasion of Grenada by American forces. Such gunboat diplomacy Caribbean thinkers had thought was a thing of the past.

What of the future? Before we attempt to speculate on a reply, an even more urgent question needs to be addressed. Had these East Caribbean islands (the OECS) been united under one central government would any part of such a union have dared to remove the government from office? Apart from the important political considerations, who is there so bold as to argue that these small specks of land in this broad Caribbean Sea can survive on their own in this increasingly globalized world? If we have learnt anything from the events of the seventies to the nineties it is that these small Caribbean countries (including Trinidad and Jamaica) can no longer live at arms length from each other and pretend that what happens in one island is not the business of any of the others. The Caribbean, especially Caricom, must be guided to greater unity or it should be dissolved and the entire project restarted with those countries that are most likely to form a political union.

It is heartening to see that some progress is being achieved in building a stronger bond among the East Caribbean (OECS) islands and countries. Freedom of movement of capital and skills is a sine qua non if these islands are to survive in this competitive global environment. However, it has to be acknowledged that even a united OECS is still a very small entity in terms of the global village. But truth be told, it is a much more significant speck than any of its constituent parts standing alone.

Even as these small islands pursue a closer union amongst themselves they ought to always keep in mind the bigger picture - of Caribbean unity, and CARICOM. Within this broader picture is to be found a larger pool of talented and quality Caribbean nationals who are dedicated to the private sector and to the development of the affairs of the entire region. The exposure to secondary and tertiary education within the Caribbean, particularly over the last forty years has helped to unleash the passions of Caribbean youth and has set the region ablaze in a way their parents and grand parents may not have imagined. Better education has also raised the political bar in the Caribbean region. It has instilled in the hearts and minds of citizens a common history and legacy, while at the same time affording them the ability to pursue separate and independent paths to economic empowerment.

Those who resent the intrusion of foreign cultures into the region would be well advised to channel such negative energy for the promotion and creation of the best within themselves and the rich heritage of the Caribbean peoples. The young political tigers of the Caribbean must redouble their efforts to redeem the extreme exploitation and abuse of the past. They must also ensure that these scattered Caribbean jewels which they call home, can once again become the common patrimony of all who live and work there. In the past, only the boldest visionaries had said to the Caribbean peoples that they and they alone were to be the subject and object of their social, political and economic development. Equally, only a few sons and daughters had told them that the Caribbean was their home and that in unity, there was strength. Many had to learn such lessons on their own, as the policy of the colonial era was aimed to divide and rule the region for the benefit of others.

The rise of Bishop and Coard in Grenada had propelled the struggle of the Caribbean working class, as well as the illiterate and dispossessed people of the region, to a high standard of international recognition in the same way Marcus Moriah Garvey had done in the thirties. They had therefore opened the eyes of the people to the social and economic problems which had beset them and had gone one step further than Garvey and placed the struggle in an ideological global context. By their close association with other like minded brethren in the Caribbean, the whole region had come under close scrutiny by those international forces with interests in the region. It is therefore from that ideological cold war perspective that the long, disturbing and debilitating leadership struggle in Saint Lucia has to be studied and understood.

That struggle occupied centre stage in Saint Lucia and the south Caribbean for over two calendar years. The obvious difficulty which the student of politics will inevitably come up against is the role of Bernard Coard and his friends in Grenada vis-à-vis the role of George Odlum and his friends in Saint Lucia. Why didn't these two lend critical support and strengthen the anti-Gairy and anti-Compton radical left at the time? These two struggles were seen at one point as a fight between the old and the new; - conservative versus liberal, the aged versus the young. But surely, all the evidence at the time said that these and the other struggles of the region were much more than that between personalities or political parties. It was that of crystallizing the entire abuse and exploitation of a race, a class and a people, and placing their struggles within a context which was both global and revolutionary. It was also distilling the best aspects of a people who had overcome adversity, and at the same time copying from them that which best fit our circumstances, in the Caribbean. It was finally standing up and declaring our independence and our refusal to be emasculated as the new mimic men of the region. In time, it was also truly a struggle between the two superpowers of the day for ascendancy in the Caribbean and for each to enhance its global reach and influence.

It would not be an unkind statement to observe that before the seventies, the people of the Caribbean had never placed their struggles for better wages and working conditions in any global ideological context. Their leaders saw colonialism and the exploitation of their labour as a common legacy of all Caribbean peoples who worked long hours for low wages. But these leaders were soon to discover that their people in the region were not unique to the sense of the exploitation of the labour of the working class by capital. Their struggles therefore - at least theoretically - soon became linked to those of workers internationally. It was in such a climate of an increasing awareness of the international nature of all workers' struggles that the new political activists arrived on the scene in the sixties in the Caribbean. Those who arrived a decade later were also to take on board the Caribbean political train, the ideas of black empowerment and the African heritage which had for so long been denied. The seventies were to change all that, and to prove to the Caribbean peoples once and for all that the root causes of their poverty were not to be found in the colour of their skin, but in the fact that they lacked knowledge - education.

Today, the dilemma which every Caribbean island must face – including those initially regarded as more developed – is that although they each desired political independence after the failure of the West Indies Federation, it is now obvious that none can sustain independence alone, over the long run. A time must therefore come when the people, with new leaders will rise to forge a better and stronger union out of the feeble but worthy experiment they called 'Caricom'. Until that is done these islands will continue to be exploited individually by every fly-by-night demon, posing as an investor. Increasingly, these imposters will force the weak and vulnerable island governments, against sustainable efforts aimed at preserving their unique environment and cultural heritage. This rage to make the whole world the playground of the few with no boundaries must be resisted in 'our' Caribbean.

Annex

But you have not answered my question, said Lynch.
What is art?
What is the beauty it expresses?
Art, said Stephen, is the human disposition of sensible or
intelligible matter for a esthetic end.......

James Joyce:
The Portrait of the artist as a young man

The period in Saint Lucia's history which this book attempts to highlight was one of the most difficult and trying times in the life of the island and indeed the wider Caribbean. The seventies was a time of change and upheaval in which many felt a genuine search was being made for self-identity as well as social, economic and political direction by a certain small section of the region's young political activists.

By 1979 these political activists had gained a foothold on political power in Saint Lucia but unfortunately soon ran into a long, protracted leadership struggle which ended in the government's demise after just two and a half years in office. Even their staunchest supporters got fed up with the constant bickering and were soon calling for fresh general elections. The events described earlier in this compilation did not emphasize sufficiently the achievements of the St. Lucia Labour Party government at the time and lest anyone think that nothing was accomplished during those terrible years of the leadership struggle, the list below is published to give the lie to that view. The fact is that even as the local and regional media had a field day reporting and seemingly encouraging the leadership quarrel within the Labour government, no one was bothering to pay attention or to report the achievements the government from 1979-1982 for the people of Saint Lucia. This list is therefore published for information and for those who seek truth.

Notwithstanding the apologists and those who may wish to claim that very little or nothing was achieved during those crucial years of the leadership struggle the record will show quite differently. It will reveal that the leadership struggle was in large measure a 'side show' which was allowed to dominate the airwaves, playing to opposition agenda, and denying the many achievements of the government even as it searched for common ground to move the island's people into a new and better place on the world stage.

It would therefore be a grave omission if such a record or the events of the time in the political evolution of this island, when the 'Leadership struggle' raged on and so much was made of it in both the local and Caribbean media, were not put right. One needs to highlight the many achievements of the Labour governments of both Louisy and Cenac (1979 – 1982). The government at the time did not only indicate a clear intention to right the many wrongs of the past but it also attempted to indicate a new direction for the social, political and economic future of the island.

This summary of their achievements is therefore an attempt to set the record straight for those who seek the complete picture of what was done by the island's government in its bold attempt to sever the psychological shackles that still bound its small population of one hundred and fifty thousand, mainly black Africans and former slaves, to their dreadful and inhuman past.

Ministry of Education and Culture:
- Introduction of co-operative education and practices in 28 schools.
- Introduction of a school feeding programme in most depressed areas.
- Completion of an engineering design for a new R.C. Boys school at Castries. School extensions at Dennery and Millet.
- Construction of new schools at Augier, Ciceron, L'Anse road, Morne Dudon, Richfond and Soufriere.Rapid expansion of school building programme aimed at elimination of the 'shift system' by end of 1982.
- Increased staffing in most schools.
- Free school books for Junior Secondary schools.
- Free Maths books for Infant schools.

Ministry of Health:
- Free hospitalization.
- Increase in primary health care facilities.
- Introduction of dental health care programme.
- Strengthening the environmental health institute at the Morne, Castries.

Ministry of Trade, Industry, Tourism and Foreign Affairs:
- Hosting of a very successful OAS conference.
- Participation in launching of Organization of East Caribbean States.
- Major tourism promotion drive in the USA, U.K. West Germany and Latin America.
- Stabilization of prices for basic commodities such as sugar, rice, flour by the strengthening of the Central Purchasing Unit within the Ministry.
- Central purchasing of cement in order to lower the unit price per bag to local consumers.
- Distribution of profits from trading in cement to small local businessmen.
- Proposal for setting up a small Trade monitoring committee to replace certain important foods and certain other items with locally grown produce.
- Introduction of regular dialogue with local business people.

Ministry of Finance, Planning and Development:
- Complete reorganization of this Ministry for a more efficient functioning of its several branches.
- Introduction of strict financial management.
- Establishment of a National Commercial bank for the citizens of the island.

- Formation of a Development Bank to accelerate the development process.
- Reorganization of the National Development Corporation for more rapid response and efficiency.
- Help in establishing small indigenous hotels.
- Purchase of the failed Halcyon Days Hotel at Vieux-Fort, then in Receivership.
- Paid out over $11 million in back pay to public servants.
- Increased allowances for Income tax assessments.
- Massive duty free concessions on lumber and other building materials for the post Hurricane Allen rebuilding effort.

Ministry of Agriculture:
- Reorganization of the Ministry so that it focuses on delivery mechanisms to satisfy the needs of farmers.
- Expansion of staff of all divisions within the Ministry.
- Increased training opportunities for staff.
- Re-organization of Union Cadet Training Scheme to full Agriculture College status.
- Development of plans for establishing Agriculture College campus at Mabouya Valley, Dennery.
- Establisment of regular Minister/Farmer contact by planned on-farm visits.
- Increase in types and values of subsidies to farmers.
- Increase attention to co-operatives development.
- Establishment of pig farmers co-operatives.
- Establishment of food producers co-operatives.
- Tangible recognition of farmers' efforts by awards of prizes.
- Farmers tours to Banana handling and ripening process in the U.K. and tour of National Agriculture Exhibition in England.
- Special attention to Fishermen's problems and help from Stabex funds after hurricane Allen, in 1980.
- Establishment of and improved cold storage for fishermen at major fish landing sites on the island.
- Initiation of tree crop development and agricultural diversification island-wide.
- Increased production of milk and beef from livestock development programme at Beausejour government farm, Vieux-Fort.
- Increase in national pig breeding herd at Beausejour government farm,
- Vieux-Fort.Comprehensive assistance to the sector post hurricane Allen; for example, $7.6 million went to banana farmers; $1million to Fishermen; $0.25 million to food crop farmers.
- Established a Commission of Enquiry to look into farmers' complaints and malpractices in the Banana industry.
- Introduction of Wild Life protection legislation and established 'Jacquot', (The St. Lucian Parrot as the national bird and the 'Calabash' as the national plant.
- Redesigning of the Model farms project in the Dennery and Roseau valleys.
- Purchase of Dennery Farm Co. with a view to scientific agriculture development

- Establishment of a Land Reform Commission in an attempt to regularize
- Family/Agriculture land ownership and to cure farm fragmentation resulting from the Napoleonic code (Code Noir) imported into Land laws on the island.
- Designing of Land Reform programmes with O.A.S assistance.
- Rapid increase in food production throughout the country especially after Hurricane Allen.
- General involvement of the entire island population in the agriculture production effort by encouraging housewives to save seeds of permanent crops for transmission to agriculture stations for propagation and planting in the crop diversification drive.

Apart from the above listed work programmes a number of inland feeder roads crucial to the success of the agriculture production drive were undertaken by the Labour government. Many of these roads were either commenced or earmarked for construction by the former government and had to be completed or totally rebuilt by the Labour government even as it continued its senseless sideshow leadership struggle.

Work was also done on a number of playing fields throughout the island and specifically at Belle Vue, Grace and La Ressource and Pierrot in the Vieux-Fort area; Marisule, Corinth and Gros-Islet in the north of the island, Vigie playing field in Castries; also in the town of Soufriere and the villages of Micoud and Laborie and the communities of Grande Riviere (Dennery) and Augier (Laborie).

At the Ministry of Communications, Works and Housing there were several projects deserving mention, all crucial to the building of the foundation on which future prosperity was to be built. The telecommunications system was modernized and the work of introducing new telephones started by the former administration continued apace. Repairs to Hewanorra airport in the south of the island to allow it to accommodate wide bodied jet aircraft were undertaken as a matter of some urgency. Major repairs to the East coast road especially at the Barre d'Lisle slip were undertaken. A six million dollar asphalt plant was established at Vieux-Fort to assist in road construction programme.

- Drainage and land fill at Dennery and Vieux-Fort. New water supplies at Dennery Bouton, Belle Vue and Malgretoute.

- Renewed rural electricity drive begun by the former government. Completion of housing units at Reduit Park (Gros-Islat) started by the former government. Over $300,000 made available for on-lending to house builders with a maximum of $15,000 to each borrower.

Ministry of Planning and Development:
Sale of government lands to lower income citizens at peppercorn rates in the following areas: Richfond, (Dennery); Morne Giraud, (Gros-Islet); Ciceron, (Cas tries); and New Dock, (Vieux-Fort). In addition, the government acquired more

lands at Soufriere for the establishment of affordable housing units for the residents there.

Sixty percent increases in wages to its daily paid employees. It also agreed to a 45% increase in wages to port workers at both Castries and Vieux-Fort. It did all of the above and more while the embarrassing leadership struggle raged and undermined it. Of course, in the end that 'internal battle for ascendancy' provided its opponents with the perfect excuse to frustrate the new path to social and economic development and the general direction of the government and country.

THE ST. LUCIA MANUFACTURERS ASSOCIATION

c/o P.O. Box 1080
Castries, St. Lucia

March 24, 1982

The Hon. P. Josie
Leader of The St. Lucia Labour Party.
Castries

Dear Sir,

We are addressing the attached 'open letter' to yourself and
to the leaders of the other two parties contesting the
forthcoming election, as we feel that the issues raised are
extremely pertinent at this time, not only to ourselves
and our employees, but to all members of the electorate.

We trust that your responses to our suggestions and proposals
will be aired during the election campaign, and will assist
in arriving at policies which can be incorporated in your
party's manifesto.

We look forward to receiving your reactions to these proposals.

Yours faithfully,

for ST. LUCIA MANUFACTURERS ASSOCIATION

G. Devaux
PRESIDENT

444

By His Excellency Mr. Boswell Williams, Governor-General of Saint Lucia.

[L.S.]   BOSWELL WILLIAMS,
              Governor-General.

To The Honourable JOHN GEORGE MELVIN COMPTON, Member of the House of Assembly.

GREETING :

Appointment of John George Melvin Compton to be Prime Minister.

I.   Pursuant to section 60 of the Constitution of Saint Lucia and subject to the provisions of the said Constitution I do hereby appoint you the said John George Melvin Compton to be Prime Minister of Saint Lucia with all the powers, rights, privileges and advantages to the said Office belonging or appertaining.

Officers, etc., to take notice.

II.   And all Her Majesty's loving subjects in Saint Lucia and all others whom it may concern are hereby required to take due notice hereof and to govern themselves accordingly.

GIVEN under my hand and the Public Seal of Saint Lucia at Government House this fifth day of May, 1982 in the Thirty-first year of the Reign of HER MAJESTY QUEEN ELIZABETH THE SECOND.

BY HIS EXCELLENCY'S COMMAND.

SAINT LUCIA
PRINTED BY THE GOVERNMENT PRINTER AT THE GOVERNMENT PRINTING OFFICE,
CASTRIES.
1982.   [Price 50 cents

Address to the U.N. General Assembly, September 1981
by Peter Josie, Minister of Foreign Affairs, Saint Lucia

' MR. PRESIDENT,

LET ME FIRST CONGRATULATE YOU ON YOUR ELECTION TO THE PRESIDENCY OF
THE THIRTY SIXTH SESSION OF THE GENERAL ASSEMBLY. NEED I SAY, MR.
PRESIDENT, THAT THE GOOD CHANCE WHICH BROUGHT YOU TO THE GENERAL ASSEMBLY
WILL ATTEND THE WORK OF THIS AUGUST BODY THROUGHOUT THIS SESSION.
PERMIT ME ALSO, ON BEHALF OF THE GOVERNMENT AND PEOPLE OF SAINT LUCIA,
TO EXTEND A SINCERE WELCOME TO THE NEWLY INDEPENDENT STATES OF VANUATU
AND BELIZE AND TO CONGRATULATE THE LATTER AS THE MOST RECENT MEMBER OF
THE UNITED NATIONS.

IT IS IMPORTANT TO RECOGNIZE THAT THE GOVERNMENT OF BELIZE HAS
TAKEN ITS RIGHTFUL PLACE IN THIS FAMILY OF NATIONS AFTER THE LAPSE OF
SIXTEEN YEARS BEFORE THE GRANTING OF INDEPENDENCE. IT IS MORESO FRUSTRATING
WHEN THE DELAY IS ATTRIBUTED TO A TERRITORIAL DISPUTE BETWEEN THE
UNITED KINGDOM AND GUATEMALA. IN THE CHAMPIONING OF DEMOCRACY AND PEACE
IT IS CERTAIN THAT THE FINAL VICTORY OF BELIZE WILL FURTHER ENHANCE THE
WORK OF THE UN.

MR. PRESIDENT, THE POLITICAL SITUATION IN THE WORLD REMAINS IN LESS
THAN SATISFACTORY CONDITION AS WE MARK THE THIRTY FIFTH ANNIVERSARY OF
THE UNITED NATIONS, WHICH, LIKE THE FABLED PHOENIX, ROSE WITH RENEWED
VIGOUR AND DEDICATION, TO BEGIN A NEW AND REJUVENATED LIFE. THERE
WERE THE LESSONS, AND THE EXPERIENCES OF OUR PAST HISTORY: BUT HISTORICISM
HAS LITTLE TO SAY FOR OUR PERFORMANCE TO DATE IN OFFSETTING THE EVIL OF
MAN'S INHUMANITY TO MAN. AS THE BARD STATED "HUMANITY PERFORCE MUST
PREY UPON ITSELF, LIKE MONSTERS IN THE DEEP."

THE UNITED NATIONS, WAS THE HOPE OF ALL OF US. IT CONTINUES TO BE
THAT HOPE, AND IN SEEKING TO TRANSLATE THAT HOPE INTO THE REALITY

TO: Mr T. Scott
          Ag. Superintendent of Civil Aviation

          Mr M. Scholar
          Controller of Customs

          Controller of Immigration Services
          St Lucia Royal Police Force.

cc: Mr. Peter Josie,
          Hon. Minister of Tourism

FROM: Manager, British Airways, St Lucia

27 November 1981

Gentlemen,

On Sunday 20th December, the disembarking passenger load from
BA254 is expected to be 420, more than double our normal
disembarking load.   The flight is scheduled to arrive at
1625 direct from London, at which time an Air Canada and
BWIA flight will also just have landed.   A total of nearly
600 passengers can be expected to arrive in a very short space
of time.

We shall be most grateful if you would arrange for sufficient
immigration and customs personnel to be rostered to cover all
the available positions and thereby minimize the potential
discomfort to this very large group of tourists.

I would further advise that the incoming loads on BA256 of 27 December
and 3rd January (arrival 2010) are also expected to be very large –
over 300 in each case – and we would be grateful for your
co-operation in expediting these arrivals also.

Yours sincerely,

P.P.R. JONES
Manager St Lucia

BEACHCOMBER LTD.
P.O. BOX 934, CASTRIES ST. LUCIA
TELEPHONE: 5241, 2, 3
CABLES: BEACHCOMB ST. LUCIA
TELEX: 6375 BEACOMB LC

December 16, 1981

PRESS RELEASE

BEACHCOMBER ANNOUNCEMENT

On Saturday December 5th 1981 an article appeared in the Crusader entitled "Is Josie Fonder of Honda". In the same issue a letter by one Christine Charles appeared under the heading "Bobol Exposed". This article and letter insinuated that Beachcomber Limited as agents for Honda cars had:-

1. "a deal with the Minister of Trade Mr Peter Josie" whereby the minister "has agreed to allow the import of 30 large executive type Honda cars free of duty for the use of the OAS conference to be returned to Beachcomber after the conference without payment of duty".

2. The letter also implies that the Minister of Trade is in possession of one of the Honda vehicles which were the subject of the alledged deal. Similar insinuations were made by The Leader of the Opposition at a public meeting on Tuesday 15th December on the William Peter Boulevard.

Beachoomber would like to state in no uncertain terms that the above insinuations are malicious and completely untrue.

a. Beachcomber as agents for Honda cars has never entered into any agreement for the duty free importation of cars to be supplied to the OAS conference further Beachcomber does not have, has never had and has never ever considered such an agreement. Beachcomber did not supply a single car for the OAS Conference nor was the company asked to.

b. Beachcomber's only dealings with the Ministry of Trade and Foreign Affairs was the purchase by that ministry of one Honda Quintet in November - said car being paid for in full before delivery as per normal business proceedings.

MANAGEMENT

BEACHCOMBER LTD.

SUPPLIERS TO THE BUILDING TRADE
BUILDERS DIVISION · AUTOMOTIVE DIVISION · MARINE DIVISION · TRAVEL AGENTS   HOTELERS
DISTRIBUTORS FOR: HONDA MOTOR CO.   BERTRAM YACHT WHITTAKER   MARINER INTERNATIONAL

8th December, 1981

His Excellency,
Delegate of Libya,
Georgetown,
Guyana.

Your Excellency,

I am pleased to inform you that my visit to your great country was very successful indeed. I was met by the Foreign Secretary, Comrade Ati, upon my arrival at my hotel in Tripoli.

I was rather surprised to learn that our Commissioner in Great Britain Dr. Claudius Thomas had visited your Embassy. I must inform you that I issued no instructions to Dr. Thomas. In fact, I did not even inform him of my visit to Tripoli. He knew of my arrival in London and nothing else. I am sorry for any embarassment which his visit may have caused.

Any contacts or information which I wish to convey to your Excellency, will be done through Arif Ali or Caribbean Times and West Indian Digest in London or through your office in Georgetown, Guyana.

Please express my sincere gratitude to Foreign Secretary Ati for taking time off his busy schedule to see me. Please inform him that I did not meet his Permanent Representative to the United Nations during my brief stop-over in New York, but all is well. The Ambassador had already contacted Saint Lucia's Ambassador to the United Nations.

As expected, my visit to Libya has created some attention and so I have decided to wait till early 1982 before commencing on some of our major Party projects. I shall keep your Excellency posted on the details of our operation.

We look forward to continued co-operation from your Excellency, the Government and Peoples' Socialist Libya Arab Jamahiriyah.

Yours sincerely,

....
PETER JOSIE
MINISTER

By His Excellency Mr. Boswell Williams, Governor-General of Saint Lucia.

[L.S.]   **BOSWELL WILLIAMS,**
           Governor-General.

To:

Senator Margherita Alexander,

Greeting:

Appointment of Margherita Alexander to be a Minister. **I.   Pursuant** to section 60 (4) of the Constitution of Saint Lucia, and acting in accordance with the advice of the Prime Minister, I hereby appoint you the said Margherita Alexander to be a Minister of the Government, to hold such Office in accordance with the provisions of the said Constitution.

Officers, etc., to take notice. **II.   And** all Her Majesty's loving subjects in Saint Lucia and all others whom it may concern are hereby required to take due notice hereof and to govern themselves accordingly.

Given under my hand and the Public Seal of Saint Lucia at Government House this seventh day of May, 1982 in the Thirty-first year of the Reign of Her Majesty Queen Elizabeth the Second.

BY HIS EXCELLENCY'S COMMAND.

Saint Lucia Gazette

Published by Authority

(Extraordinary.)

| Vol. 151.] | FRIDAY 14 MAY, 1982 | [No. 24. |

GOVERNMENT NOTICES

No. 47.

His Excellency the Governor-General acting in accordance with section 67 of the Constitution of Saint Lucia, has appointed the Honourable Emmanuel Neville Cenac to be Leader of the Opposition with effect from 11th May, 1982.

Government House.
Saint Lucia.

11*th* May, 1982.

No. 48.

Pursuant to section 24 (2) (*a*) of the Constitution of Saint Lucia, His Excellency the Governor-General acting on the advice of the Prime Minister has been pleased to appoint Miss Margherita Alexander to be a Senator.

Government House.
Saint Lucia.

11*th* May, 1982.

Saint Lucia Gazette

𝔓ublished by 𝔄uthority

(𝔈xtraordinary.)

| VOL. 151.] | WEDNESDAY, 14 APRIL, 1982. | [No. 16. |

ELECTORAL NOTICE

The General Public is notified that the Election Writ was issued by the Governor-General on the 6th April, 1982 to the Returning Officers of the Seventeen Electoral Districts of the State of Saint Lucia and that the date fixed for the nomination of Candidates for the General Elections of 3rd May, 1982 is 20th April, 1982 between the hours of 9 a.m. and noon which nomination will take place at the respective offices of the Returning Officers as published in the official *Gazette* of Saturday, 10th April, 1982.

The Election Notice, Form No. 6, as also stated in section 37 of the House of Assembly (Elections) Act 1979 (No. 8 of 1979), has, in respect of each Electoral District, also been published in the official *Gazette* of Saturday, 10th April, 1982 and in addition thereto, has been posted or affixed by the Returning Officers in conspicuous places near the principal door of every Court House, Police Station and Revenue Office and any other place they have deemed necessary in their respective Electoral District.

J. Mc. CLAIR DANIEL,
Chief Elections Officer.

13th April, 1982.

SAINT LUCIA
PRINTED BY THE GOVERNMENT PRINTER AT THE GOVERNMENT PRINTING OFFICE,
CASTRIES,
1982.   [Price 50 cents

Saint Lucia Gazette

𝔓ublisheð by 𝔄uthority

(𝔈xtraorðinary.)

| Vol. 151.] | FRIDAY 7 MAY, 1982 | [No. 22. |

GOVERNMENT NOTICE

No. 46.

His Excellency the Governor-General has been pleased to appoint the Honourable John George Melvin Compton to the office of Prime Minister with effect from Wednesday, 5th May, 1982.

The Instrument of Appointment is published herewith.

Government House,
Saint Lucia.

6th May, 1982.

R. MILLBURN & ASSOCIATES

consulting civil & structural engineers
transportation engineers & planners
traffic engineers

SUITE "C"
TOOMBUL SHOPPING CENTRE
SANDGATE ROAD,
TOOMBUL, 4012, BRISBANE

R. MILLBURN D.L.C.(Hons.), M.I.C.E., F.ASCE., F.I.E.Aust., M.CONS.E.Aust.

H. F. GOLDSTEIN DIPL.ING.(Berl.), F.I.C.E., M.I.E.Aust., M.CONS.E. CONSULTANT

A. F. DANIELL B.Sc., F.I.C.E. CONSULTANT

Tel: 266 6741
Area Code: 07
Cables/Telegrams:
REMCONSULT, BRISBANE.

RM/MMM

29th September 1981

The Hon. Peter Losie,
Delegation of St.Lucia,
Commonwealth Heads of Government Meeting,
Wentworth Hotel,
MELBOURNE.

Your Excellency,

I spent a happy and I hope productive six months in St.Lucia
during 1978 as the engineer member of the United Nations Cul
de Sac Freeport Team.

With your permission I write to send a personal message of
welcome to Australia to you, Sir, and to Mr.Thomas and to say
how much I hope that your memories of Australia will be as
happy as are mine of St.Lucia.

Yours very sincerely,

R.Millburn.
R.Millburn & Associates.

November, 1980

Application for USAID from Ravine Chabot Development Organization

Cement	182 bags @ $13.00 per bag	$2,366.00
Concrete blocks	2,936 @ $1.50 per block	4,404.00
½ inch Metal	40 cu. yds. @ $30.00 per cu. yd.	1,200.00
Sand	26 loads @ $75.00 per load	1,950.00
Nails	40 lb (mixed) @ $4.00 per lb	160.00
Lumber (boards)	12" x 6" x 16' (40 lengths) @ $24.00 per length	960.00
Lumber (posts)	3" x 4" x 12' (15 lengths) @ $25.00 per length	375.00
Quarry Waste	20 cu. yds @ $6.00 per cu. yd.	120.00
Boulders	30 cu. yds. @ $8.50 per cu. yd.	255.00
Hinges	54 pairs @ $20.00 per pair	1,080.00
Truck transportation		3,500.00
Local Youth and skilled labour		4,000.00

TOTAL   EC $20,370.00

US $ 7,497.57